ATTEN

T.C.A. Raghavan is a former Indian High [illegible] er to Singapore and Pakistan. He has a PhD in history from the Jawaharlal Nehru University, New Delhi. This was his first book and was followed by *The People Next Door: The Curious History of India's Relations with Pakistan* (HarperCollins 2017).

Praise for the *Attendant Lords*

'This book consists of the biographies of two Mughal nobles, father and son, who played prominent roles over a period of almost nine decades … Raghavan has provided as detailed and critical a narrative of the careers of the father and son as one could wish for. [He] has presented us with such evidence as exists as conscientiously as possible; and for this, as indeed for his whole work, he deserves our gratitude.

Throughout the book, but especially in his chapter 'Afterlife' and 'Epilogue', the author added much to this reviewer's knowledge … [B]oth the general reader and the specialist can read the book with much profit.'

– Irfan Habib, *The Indian Express.*

'Raghavan … touches on issues other than just Mughal history and literature; he also discusses subjects that have, in recent years, again become sensitive issues – language and its (perceived) ties with religion, politics and religion, religious fundamentalism.

The end product is a book that, while it offers an insight into Mughal history during the reigns of Humayun, Akbar and Jahangir, is also a means of reflecting upon language and literature. Through his discussion of Rahim and his work, Raghavan highlights much that would be food for thought.'

– Madhulika Liddle, The Wire

'The political, military and cultural achievements of the two nobles are narrated by Raghavan with textbook precision, but what makes his work topical is the attempt to document the afterlife and continued relevance of these two men … Raghavan effectively manages to sift through the folds of popular imagination and historical realities in order to shed light on the processes which have resulted in the appropriation of historical figures and events so that they neatly fit the contours of present-day language and identity politics.'

– Sabina Kazmi, Catch News

'[T]he book is worth reading for persons interested in early Mughal history, for those interested in the Hindi–Urdu controversy, and it is specifically good for understanding the contributions of Abdur Rahim to Hindi literature.'

– Hasan Beg, *Dawn*

'This is an important historical publication rendered in an engaging narrative style that will entertain the reader. More importantly, it also brings into focus, true to its title, an aspect of a vital historical period otherwise unattended to in such detail ... The book brings alive a luminous period of the evolution of modern India.'

– Wajahat Habibuullah, *The Book Review*

'This is a well-researched and well-written account of Mughal history from the moment of its foundation under Babur and changing fortunes under Humayun to Akbar and Jahangir.

'Weaving political and literary history with the biographies of father and son is not an easy task but Raghavan effortlessly presents the reader with an engrossing account that has a nuanced analysis of textual politics not just under the Mughals but also under the changing political and ideological contexts of colonialism and nationalism.

'Raghavan does an admirable job of bringing texts and changing contexts into conversation to emphasize issues of literary patronage, convention and aesthetic community over linguistic and religious communities' appropriation of a rich shared past.'

– Razak Khan, *Biblio*

'The importance of *Attendant Lords* is that it places these two historical figures in the larger context of nationalism and nation building.'

– Nandini Nair, *Open* magazine.

'TCA Raghavan's *Attendant Lords* … is a major contribution to our understanding of the history of India in the period from the mid-16th to the mid-17th centuries. This is one of the most refreshing historical studies of the era of the great Mughals in recent years.'

– Amar Farooqui, A selection of the most memorable books of 2017, *Biblio*

'*Attendant Lords* is a vivid narrative of the most important period in Mughal history, when rulers were not only consolidating power but also negotiating religious diversity.'

– Sudhirendar Sharma, *Hindustan Times*

'Raghavan excels … Using the personal stories of individuals to trace the history of a period is a style that has largely been abandoned in modern times … The book … will surely be loved by anyone with an interest in politics and literature as well.'

– Rishi Raj, *The Financial Express*

'Raghavan's exposition on the different ways in which Urdu and Hindi literature, as also the Hindu and the Muslim world, eventually claimed Abdur Rahim, is fantastic. After the unexceptional, although critical, reading of Abdur Rahim's life and literary exploits, the last Chapter, "Afterlife: Rahiman and Abdur Rahim", and the "Epilogue" are electrifying.'

– Chirosree Basu, *The Telegraph*

ATTENDANT LORDS

BAIRAM KHAN AND ABDUR RAHIM
COURTIERS & POETS IN MUGHAL INDIA

T.C.A. RAGHAVAN

HarperCollins *Publishers* India

First published in hardback in India by
HarperCollins *Publishers* in 2017
A-75, Sector 57, Noida, Uttar Pradesh 201301, India
www.harpercollins.co.in

This edition published in paperback in India in 2019 by HarperCollins *Publishers*

2 4 6 8 10 9 7 5 3 1

P-ISBN: 978-93-5302-615-8
E-ISBN: 978-93-5264-306-6

Typeset in 11.5/14.25 Adobe Garamond Pro
By Saanvi Graphics Noida

Printed and bound at
Thomson Press (India) Ltd.

MIX
Paper
FSC FSC® C010615

This book is produced from independently certified FSC® paper to ensure responsible forest management.

To the memory of my parents
T.C.A. Srinivasa Varadan
T.C.A. Nayantara

No! I am not Prince Hamlet, nor was meant to be;
Am an attendant lord, one that will do
To swell a progress, start a scene or two,
Advise the prince …

—T. S. Eliot, 'The Love Song of J. Alfred Prufock'

CONTENTS

INTRODUCTION

THIS BOOK is about the lives of two noblemen in Mughal India: Bairam Khan Khan-i-Khanan (c. 1497–1561) and his son Abdur Rahim Khan-i-Khanan (1556–1626). In any period and in any country, these would have been extraordinary men. Bairam was a Persian Turkmen, scion of a distinguished clan that was influential in Persia and Central Asia in the fifteenth century. He stands out in Mughal history as the regent of the empire for five years after the premature death of Emperor Humayun, when Akbar was still a child and too young to rule. Bairam's son, Abdur Rahim, became one of the great generals of the Mughal empire and a premier noble during the reigns of Akbar and Jahangir. Abdur Rahim's political and military achievements surpass his father's, but he is best remembered for his literary prowess. He was one of the great patrons of Persian literature of his time; in the history of Hindi literature, he has an even greater reputation as an outstanding poet in a century of literary achievement. Between them, the father and son straddled some hundred years of Mughal history in India, living through the reigns of four emperors, and their spectacular and turbulent trajectories reflect both the grand designs and the destructive courtly intrigues of Mughal politics.

In the sixteenth and early seventeenth centuries Bairam Khan and Abdur Rahim stood at the confluence of the faiths of Islam and Hinduism. It was a defining time elsewhere too. In Europe, Protestant–Catholic conflicts were raging; Luther and Calvin were advocating an open defiance of centuries of established Roman Catholic doctrine. In England the great Tudors, Henry VIII and Elizabeth I, were laying the foundations of future English maritime and commercial dominance. Kepler, Copernicus, Galileo and Shakespeare were reshaping ideas of science and literature. In northern India too this was the age of a great literary and spiritual effervescence as under the Mughals, India once again entered the age of a centralized empire. With the poet saints Tulsidas and Surdas, a spiritual community of devotion to the Hindu gods, Rama and Krishna, was consolidated and simultaneously Braj Bhasha and Avadhi were transformed from the status of dialects to the maturity of full-fledged languages. If the devotional verses of these poets catalysed this transformation, secular – largely courtly and sensuous – poetry such as of the great Keshavdas played an equally significant role in the literary revolution in north India in the sixteenth century. Literature plays some part in our story too, for both Bairam Khan and Abdur Rahim regarded literary achievement as a means to political status as well as a vital adjunct in its consolidation.

An account of these two lives, substantial and extraordinary though they undoubtedly were, would nevertheless be incomplete if we stopped with their life stories. The shadows of Bairam Khan and Abdur Rahim touch our times as well: these real-life medieval figures have been transformed into templates; their lives celebrated in numerous ways through association with significant milestones or other icons from history. In these narratives, literary enterprise, history, language and religion are inextricably combined within a broader context of nationalism and nation building, as answers to the dilemmas of the present are sought in the perceived certainties of the past.

Above all, this is a story of life and politics in Mughal India. Bairam Khan and Abdur Rahim Khan-i-Khanan were powerful men at the heart of the Mughal court. Their great military feats, political acumen and their closeness to successive emperors brought them great rewards and enviable positions, yet they were prey to all the jealousies and betrayals, ideological and religious contests and controversies that the acquisition of power and the loss of it inevitably brings, no matter in which century or country. Their personal tragedies still resonate each time an act of miscalculation, or misjudgement, or the outmanoeuvring by a rival, or the simple arbitrariness of power takes its toll.

1

BAIRAM

As DUSK fell on the last day of January 1561, an ageing nobleman was boating in the Sahasralinga Talav, on the outskirts of Patan. His bearing was distinguished; even in a boat, his air of authority was apparent. Yet, the entourage waiting on the bank of the lake was quite small. He had spent some time sitting in the small pavilion at the centre of the lake, but now he was being rowed back to the bank.

As his boat approached, a group of men – Afghans by their appearance – came forward to pay their respects. The noble obviously found this unsurprising and directed the boatman towards them, some fifty yards away. The man at the head of the Afghan group greeted the nobleman courteously as he alighted from the boat. As they embraced, the Afghan unsheathed a dagger and planted it in the nobleman's back with such force that it pierced right through, emerging from the breast. Another Afghan struck with a sword to the head. Death came instantaneously, but one source describes the nobleman, blood gushing from his wounds, reciting the words of the Shahadat as he lay dying: there is no God except Allah and Muhammad is his Prophet.

The life of Bairam Khan, Emperor Humayun's most trusted general and Emperor Akbar's regent, ended that evening on the banks of the Sahasralinga Talav in Patan, Gujarat. A Turkmen by birth, his eminent position during the last decade of Humayun's life and in the early years of Akbar's reign is recorded frequently in the miniatures painted to illustrate contemporary milestones. The most dramatic is, naturally, a representation of the assassination. We see the Afghans outnumbering Bairam Khan's small entourage; his followers fleeing in disarray; his camp, some distance away, attacked and plundered; his body unguarded and untended by the lakeside (see Plate I).[1]

Bairam Khan's tumultuous life and tragic end constitute one of the most dramatic narratives of the Mughal era. He was the faithful friend and counsellor of the second emperor, Humayun, and was guardian to the third, Akbar, after Humayun's premature death in 1556. As regent, he was responsible for the consolidation of the empire after the second battle of Panipat. Bairam's fall from favour and his tragic end in Patan on the shores of the Sahasralinga Talav were in some ways a fitting end to his life, the tragedy and pathos of the concluding drama giving a certain completeness to the story.

If the milestones of Bairam's life are well known, the details of the journey are less so. It is with Bairam's patrimony, therefore, that we begin this story; indeed, his foremost modern biographer begins by saying: 'Bairam Khan was no *novus homo:* he had a great ancestry.'[2] This background remained a determining factor throughout his life; his rise to greatness was, to his contemporaries and biographers alike, a consequence of his patrimony. He belonged to the Baharlu clan of the major tribal confederation of the Qara Qoyunlu, which reached its greatest power and spread – stretching over parts of present-day Iraq, Afghanistan, Persia and Azerbaijan – in the mid-fifteenth century during the reign of Mirza Jahan Shah (1437–67). The great rivals of the Qara Qoyunlu were the Aq Qoyunlu; their conflicts and contests dominated a large part of the fifteenth century in that region. A sectarian edge provided an added dimension to this rivalry: the Aq Qoyunlu were Sunni, the Qara Qoyunlu were Shia. The Aq Qoyunlu fared better in the great rivalry and after Jahan Shah, the Qara Qoyunlu were never in a position to assert control over a large dominion of their own.

One of the most prominent tribal leaders of Jahan Shah's court was Ali Shukur Beg of the Baharlu clan.[3] Successive defeats suffered by the Qara Qoyunlu and the Baharlu forced Ali Shukur Beg's sons and grandsons to seek service in the courts of other princes. Linked by numerous ties of marriage with the family of Jahan Shah, Ali Shukur Beg's children were also married into prominent Timurid noble families and, most notably from our point of view, into the family from which Babur was descended. Ali Shukur Beg's grandson Yar Ali Beg and his son Saif Ali joined Babur's service, beginning a connection that saw their descendants, Bairam Khan and Abdur Rahim, serve Babur's descendants – Humayun, Akbar and Jahangir – for almost a century. Abul Baqi Nihavandi, Abdur Rahim's contemporary and – some would say hagiographer – quotes Emperor Babur saying to Humayun: 'Just as our ancestors were hereditary kings so his [Bairam Khan's] ancestors were also sultans.'[4]

Yar Ali and Saif Ali did well in Babur's court. The former is mentioned by name in Babur's autobiography, and other authorities refer to both having been governors of Ghazni at different points of time, Ghazni being part of Babur's kingdom in Kabul. Saif Ali also married into a prominent family and Bairam Khan was born from this union. He could, therefore, claim a distinguished ancestry from both sets of parents and in later years we shall see that his claims to this ancestry would unite him even more closely with the family of the Timurid or Mughal emperors in India, but would also sow the seeds of his downfall.

Despite the high esteem they were held in, the service of Yar Ali and Saif Ali with the Mughals was a fall in status for them when compared to the position of their forefathers as virtually independent rulers. As a child, Bairam's imagination was fired by his father: 'a man of ambitious nature and he made efforts to restore the dominion and glory of his forefathers'.[5] But Saif Ali Beg's hopes were in vain and he probably died early, in Ghazni, when Bairam was still a young boy. Bairam was raised in the cities of Balkh, Badakhshan and Ghazni. Certainly his education – both martial and literary – was of the highest standards, connected as he was through both parents with the high families of the land.

In accordance with the tradition of the Turkic tribes, Bairam had the benefit of an *ataliq* – a close relation who combined the role of guardian and tutor; Amir Beg, a maternal uncle, played an active role in his upbringing and education. This was a common feature of Timurid royal society: '…a young prince (was) removed from the influence of the intrigue-ridden court and forged political alliances often useful later on. For his education, a Timurid prince was turned over at a young age to a noble, often a relative on the mother's side, who becomes the prince's *athka* or *begathka*, a surrogate father, responsible for overall upbringing and training in the martial arts and in princely conduct.'[6]

The ataliq's role was to achieve a balance between literary skill and military proficiency. And so, the interests that Bairam and – to an even greater extent – his son, Abdur Rahim, were to embrace in adulthood were inculcated early:

> The high culture of the imperial court was paradigmatic for mansabdars, administrators and cavalrymen. Emperors, princes and great amirs displayed their skills at court and on the battlefield, manifesting the ideal of the fully cultured man. This ideal combined the two professional types of the Islamic world: ahl-i-qalam (men of the pen) and ahl-i-saif (men of the sword). By their wit and polish, their eloquence and style, their stamina, courage and strength, and their skills with horses, guns and swords, the great men set standards for both groups of men and, combining them in a graceful and commanding way, embodied the ideal against which they had to measure themselves and toward which they had to aspire.[7]

Horsemanship, swordsmanship, musketry, archery were indispensable skills to be imparted and learned. Norms of protocol and comportment were also essential learning for a noble. This was a highly mannered society. If the imperial ambitions of his forefathers had influenced Bairam's father, their literary heritage would have undoubtedly formed part of Bairam's own instruction and education. The achievements of the Qara Qoyunlu and the Baharlu were known to him through the poems of Jahan Shah, of which some two hundred in Turkish and Persian have survived to this day.[8] They were in themselves testimony that political and military prowess were embellished and cemented by literary merit.

Bairam grew up in an environment in which both Turkish and Persian were important, but it was the latter that was on the ascendant. How seriously he took his literary education is testified to by the large body of verse he wrote, some of which at least has survived. A collection of Bairam's verses in the library of his son, compiled about half a century after Bairam's death, is described as having nearly two thousand verses in Turkish, Persian and, surprisingly, Hindi. This is now lost but what have survived are collections of about six hundred Persian and about three hundred and fifty Turkish verses. Some three decades after his death, we find Bairam's collection of verse described as one 'which is in every hand, as his verses are on every tongue'.[9]

Bairam's distinguished ancestry, both patrilineal and matrilineal, set him apart from the crowd of others seeking a career in Kabul, even though he was only sixteen when he came to Babur's court. This, naturally, also had its disadvantages: 'As [Bairam] was related to the Timurid rulers, he was received with favour and respect. Pasha Begum, the sister of his great-grandfather, was Babur's paternal aunt as well as mother-in-law. Though young in age, Bairam was given precedence in the court of all the nobles. The veteran nobles, with wounded pride and jealous of the rising man, grumbled, but Babur justified the superior position of Bairam on account of his high connections and noble ancestry.'[10]

Being well connected helped, but political acumen, literary skill and martial valour were equally essential for success in court. Bairam's later life showed no shortage of these attributes, so it is possible that even at this stage, stories about his precociousness would have spread. In any event, Babur himself – otherwise a master of detail in the *Baburnama* – does not refer to Bairam's entry into his court, nor does he discuss his connections and ancestry. Young men with martial and literary skills and with family connections were at this time not a rare commodity; what truly set Bairam apart were events still many years in the future, when Babur's son, Humayun, would face adversity, loss of empire and exile.

When Bairam joined Babur's court sometime in AD 1512–13, Humayun was still a child. Bairam was attached to Humayun's retinue immediately after arriving in Kabul, but we know relatively little about his time in court. Though references to him increase after Humayun's accession in AD 1530, the gap is significant. Bairam was over thirty years of age in AD 1530 and we know little of him at this point apart from his lineage. There are no references to his marriage, if any, or to his friendships, relationships or interests; descriptions of Bairam in the standard Mughal chronicles establish his ancestry, then pass rapidly to his role during Humayun's difficulties with the Afghans in northern and eastern India.

At the time Bairam came to his court in 1512, Babur had been in Kabul for some eight years. He was born the Prince of Fergana, a territory that now falls in modern Uzbekistan, Kyrgystan and Tajikistan. On his paternal side he was a fifth-generation descendant of the mighty Amir Timur (1336–1405); the Timurid dynasty had ruled over large parts of Central Asia through most of the fifteenth century. His ancestors on the maternal side were equally distinguished and could be traced back to the great empire builder, Chengiz Khan.

Timur and his descendants followed a policy of parcelling out their empire to their progeny and the Fergana valley had fallen to the share of Babur's father. Babur was twelve when he inherited the throne of Fergana along with ancestral ambitions to regain Amir Timur's premier city of Samarqand from the Uzbek family which had displaced the ruling Timurid clan. The closing years of the fifteenth century saw an Uzbek revival as scion after scion of the Timurids lost ground and the most important cities in Timur's empire – Samarqand and Herat – fell to the Uzbeks. When Herat fell in 1507, Babur was the only remaining Timurid who could claim that he still ruled a kingdom. Squabbles among cousins had led to the Uzbek conquest of Samarqand, and Babur's repeated attempts to regain it failed. Regaining Samarqand was not just a dream but a real ambition for him, one that his descendants – five generations of Mughal rulers in India, down to Aurangzeb in the seventeenth century – shared.

The Uzbek revival finally forced Babur out of the Fergana valley towards the south-east, to carve out a kingdom in Kabul. As successive raids on Samarqand failed, something had to be done to augment his resources. Babur looked eastwards. He felt that he had a hereditary claim on the area, up to the Punjab, as this had formed part of the dominion of his ancestor, Amir Timur.

Timur's incursion into Hindustan had lasted only for a single campaigning season – from September 1398 to March 1399. In this brief period his army overran the Punjab, Delhi, Meerut, and went right up to the Ganga at Haridwar. He returned quickly, troubled by news of disturbances elsewhere in his empire, much to the relief of his army, which was worn out by the resistance it had faced in this blitzkrieg and, used to the pleasanter climes of Central Asia, were unable to face the burning summer of north India.

The vanquished were the Tughlaq sultans ruling a large kingdom from Delhi, already in decline by the time of Timur's attack. His invasion was a blow to the Delhi Sultanate, which fractured into several independent kingdoms – Malwa in central India, Gujarat in the west, the Punjab and Mewar in the north and north-west, and Jaunpur in the east. A larger empire would now come only with the

Lodis – an Afghan dynasty – who rose to power in the aftermath of the instability following Timur's raid.

Sultan Bahlul Lodi ascended the throne in AD 1451 and ruled for almost four decades. This period saw the expansion of the Lodi Sultanate and also the coming into India of Afghan tribes in large numbers. Among these migrants was a family whose descendent would assume the title of Sher Shah and re-establish an Afghan kingdom in India, driving Babur's son, Humayun, into exile.

At the end of the fifteenth century Bahlul Lodi's successor, Sikander Lodi, began an impressive reign of some thirty years. His chosen successor, Ibrahim Lodi, had to contend with issues of succession and fractiousness from his principal nobles and tribal leaders, apart from an ascendant Rajput power in Mewar under the capable Rana Sanga.

Ibrahim Lodi's difficulties were the opportunity Babur sought. Beginning in 1519, he mounted four expeditions, each venturing deeper and deeper into the Punjab. The fifth, in December 1525, was at the head of an army 12,000 strong. Babur crossed the Indus, marched into the Punjab, captured Lahore and, defeating such resistance as he met, continued towards Delhi. At Panipat, a small town some 90 kilometres to the north-west of Delhi, his army engaged that of Ibrahim Lodi on 21 April 1526. Babur was heavily outnumbered, but superior tactics and artillery carried the day for him. Ibrahim Lodi lay dead on the field, the only instance of a ruler of Delhi falling in battle.

Babur moved swiftly to occupy Delhi. But if Afghan rule had been broken, the threat to Mughal ascendancy was far from quelled. The most significant threat came from the kingdom of Mewar whose ruler, Rana Sanga, was the head of a large Rajput confederacy. Rana Sanga had awaited the results of Panipat, 'sanguine about establishing Rajput supremacy after the battle whether the one lost or the other'.[11] The two armies met at Khanwa on 16 March 1527, about 16 kilometres from the site where Babur's grandson, Akbar, would later build his new capital, Fatehpur Sikri. Despite superiority in Rajput numbers, Babur's deployment of artillery and archers on horseback once again led to his victory.

Khanwa and Panipat completed, in a formal sense, the Mughal conquest of Hindustan. But by 1529, Babur was visibly in poor health. His end was to coincide with a serious illness of his eldest son and heir, Humayun. Babur famously, as his sister described it, 'walked around him (Humayun) ... and made intercession ... saying in effect: "O God! If a life may be exchanged for a life, I who am Babur, I give my life and my being for Humayun."'[12]

Humayun recovered but Babur's condition deteriorated and he died in December 1530. The dying emperor told his son: 'Humayun, I commit you and your brothers and my kinsmen and your people to God's keeping and all of them are confined to you ... The cream of my testamentary directions is this: Do naught against your brothers, even though they may deserve it.'[13] These last words were prophetic, foreseeing not only the deadly fratricidal struggles that would hasten Humayun's ouster from Hindustan, but also the wars of succession that were to convulse each generation of his descendants.

As the new emperor, Humayun faced formidable challenges of governance. The army and the nobility with him had been in India barely four years, and had few local roots or influence. Their authority stemmed from the reputation of Babur's victories at Panipat and Khanwa, but a weak leader or a military defeat could swiftly unravel the newly won kingdom. The Afghans, especially in Bihar in eastern India, continued to offer strong resistance and had united under a new leader, Sher Khan, the future Sher Shah, to retake their lost sultanate. In the west was another powerful ruler, Bahadur Shah of Gujarat. The defeat of the Rajput confederacy at Khanwa by Babur was for him an opportunity to expand into Rajputana and even stake his own claim to Hindustan.

Yet Humayun's biggest problem was his brothers: Kamran (b. 1509), Askari (b. 1516) and Hindal (b. 1519), each of whom had a clutch of powerful nobles around him – both to support and to lead. The Timurids had no clear rules of primogeniture and if Humayun was demonstrably the appointed and accepted heir, the other princes got their own portion of Babur's realm. To Kamran went Kabul and Qandahar, provinces he had held for some time; Askari was given the province of Sambhal in the east and Hindal received Mewat, adjoining Delhi. Soon after Babur's death, Kamran collected an army and marched into the Punjab and occupied Lahore. Humayun, mindful of his promise to his father and plagued by the growing threat of Bahadur Shah, was left with no option but to confirm for Kamran the areas he had seized. Kamran, the virtual ruler of Kabul and the Punjab, now dominated Humayun's rear as he braced himself to take on Bahadur Shah in the west and the Afghans in the east. He also controlled the route by which the Timurid army in Delhi could strengthen itself with fresh recruits and mercenaries from Central Asia. Preoccupied with these issues, Humayun's early years as emperor were characterized by decisive military activity but also long periods of indolence or attention to matters that appear inconsequential when compared to the military challenges and political threats he faced.

It is at this point that Bairam enters the historical record, during the siege of Champaner, in a campaign against the ruler of Gujarat in 1536. Bairam's role in Champaner was not in any command capacity of significance. But it was at his suggestion that Humayun employed a tactic that successfully breached the fort's defences. The Mughal forces ascended the fortress by a secret route and when thirty-nine men had ascended, 'Humayun himself wished to climb but Bairam begged him to wait and he himself ascended.'[14] As sieges go, this was by no means an extraordinary one, no matter how important Bairam's intervention may have been. The victory at Champaner did make Humayun master of Gujarat, but the advantage gained was only temporary as Bahadur Shah was to regroup and consolidate his position again.[15]

After Champaner, the story is largely one of Humayun's successive failures. His long absence in Malwa and Gujarat led to growing rebellions in the neighbourhood of Agra, where the Mughal court was located. Even more serious was the situation in the east. Sher

Khan was by now the acknowledged leader of the Afghan restoration and showed every sign of becoming even more formidable unless Mughal armies could stop his continued expansion eastwards into the rich province of Bengal. Inexplicably, however, Humayun spent a largely inactive year at Agra after deciding to return from the Gujarat campaign to attend to the eastern Afghans. He spent six months more on a somewhat futile siege of Chunar in present-day eastern Uttar Pradesh while Sher Shah continued with his conquest of Bengal, adding enormously to his resources and to his prestige. At one stage, around June 1538, Bairam was commanding jointly with a number of others a Mughal force sent to capture a strategic route into Bengal – the pass of Teliyagarhi. The Mughal force arrived to find the pass strongly defended by Sher Khan's own son and were convincingly defeated. The rout was aided by a familiar drawback – disagreements between the joint commanders.

Humayun's army finally came face-to-face with Sher Khan's about 160 kilometres east of Chunar, at Chausa, in April 1539. For over two months skirmishing continued between the two forces. Both Sher Khan and Humayun seemed keen to patch together an agreement. One was, in fact, almost finalized: Sher Khan would recognize Humayun as his overlord; in return, he would get Bengal as well as his old possessions in Bihar and the fort of Chunar. The terms even included a provision of a ploy to safeguard Mughal prestige: Sher Khan would retreat and the Mughal armies would make a pretence of following and giving chase to the 'defeated' army.

In the expectation that the real fighting was over, the Mughal army lowered its guard whereupon the Afghans launched a surprise attack. In the battle that followed on 26 June, Humayun's army was vanquished.[16] The emperor himself barely managed to escape to Agra, providentially aided by a water carrier who helped him swim across the Ganga. But a large section of his army, many important nobles, and even many prominent ladies of the harem could not. Humayun was outmanoeuvred both in battle and in the trickery and stratagems which preceded the battle. The Afghans were now supreme in eastern India and Sher Khan had a base on which to build his larger ambitions of restoring an Afghan Sultanate. He moved quickly and titled himself Emperor Sher Shah. Forces were dispatched to principal fortresses in central India and Humayun's dominion suddenly shrunk to the region of Delhi and Agra.

In Agra, feuding between the brothers added to the confusion. Humayun's preoccupation with the campaign in eastern India had given the princes, Hindal and Kamran, the opportunity to pursue their own ambitions. Hindal marched to Agra and established himself as the emperor in all but name. Meanwhile, Kamran, ruler of the Punjab and Kabul, also gathered a large army and marched on to Delhi. Faced with this large force, Hindal rapidly reordered his priorities and submitted to Kamran. The latter's army was, ostensibly, to aid Humayun in his Afghan campaign, but in reality his expectation was that in the event of an Afghan defeat, his army would engage the exhausted imperial force. In case Humayun was defeated, Kamran's plan was to negotiate for better terms directly with Sher Shah, who, Kamran calculated, would not be prepared for another major battle. Humayun himself continued with his eccentricities, one of which was to honour a promise he had made to the water carrier who had helped him cross the Ganga that he would be made emperor for half a day. If those close to him were often exasperated with Humayun, they had good reason to be.

In the event, news of Humayun's rout sobered all three brothers and the Mughals sought to unite in the face of the very real threat to Babur's conquest of Hindustan. Sher Shah himself was not prepared to let the Mughals consolidate in the Delhi–Agra region. As news came that he was marching north, the Mughals, with Humayun at the head of a new army, marched east to confront them. However, disunity among the brothers asserted itself again, and Kamran, with his large body of troops, returned to Lahore, though Hindal and Askari stood with Humayun. In the battle that followed at Kannauj in May 1540, the Mughals were comprehensively defeated. Humayun, with the Afghans in pursuit, was forced to flee to Kamran's capital at Lahore, not even daring to halt at Delhi or Agra. The Mughal Empire in India had now entered an interregnum of a decade-and-a-half of exile and the Mughal court and army scattered to wherever they could find refuge.

Bairam figures only tangentially in this narrative of Mughal disarray; it is clear that he was not counted among the premier nobles of the Mughal court at this time. He was present at the battle of Kannauj: many years later, his son's panegyrist was to write that Bairam's charges twice broke the enemy's ranks and he made heroic efforts to keep the emperor safe from enemy attack.[17] Even were this true, it is certain that Bairam did not hold an important command. An Afghan history compiled during Akbar's reign refers to him as a keeper of the emperor's seals – a post suggesting proximity to Humayun but one ranked fairly low in the nobility.[18] After the defeat of Humayun and the dispersal of his army, Bairam was separated from the emperor for nearly three years, after which he joined him in Sindh. It is from this point really that he becomes a principal actor in the history of Mughal India, remaining so until his death.

The meagre knowledge that we have of Bairam in the years after the Mughal conquest of Hindustan up to Humayun's successive defeats is frustrating, but this changes after the battle of Kannauj when there is (relatively) a rush of information. Bairam is now in his early forties and has served the Timurids for about twenty-five years. After the Mughal defeat at Kannuaj in May 1540, he escaped to Sambhal, about 140 kilometres east of Delhi. This was an important regional capital of the Lodi dynasty and important for Babur too. The mosque at Sambhal, built in 1526 by one of his nobles, is regarded as possibly the earliest Mughal structure in India still standing.[19]

Humayun had been governor of this territory in the period just before Babur's death, and Bairam had friends and supporters there. One of them was Mian Abdul Wahab, described as 'one of the chief men of the city of Sambhal'.[20] However, the then governor of Sambhal was Nasir Khan, one of Sher Shah's commanders, and Abdul

Wahab, fearing his displeasure, sent Bairam to Raja Mitter Sen of Lakhnur, described as a great landholder of the region. Lakhnor or Lakhnur, the 'ancient native capital of the Katharya Rajputs, a little to the east of Sambhal on the banks of the Ramganga',[21] is quite distinct from Lakhnau or Lucknow, which is farther east of Sambhal. Mitter Sen provided refuge to Bairam for some time, but as news spread of a Mughal noble in hiding, he had to hand him over to Nasir Khan.

What saved Bairam from certain death was Mian Abdul Wahab's timely intervention with Isa Khan, one of Sher Shah's most prominent commanders, who had been sent to Sambhal by Sher Shah. Abdul Wahab's friendship with Isa Khan led to Bairam being provided protection by one of the foremost Afghan nobles of the time. Isa Khan himself, no doubt, saw Bairam as a potential recruit for Sher Shah's court and hosted him in his own house for some time.

From this followed a meeting between Sher Shah and Bairam. Afghan and Mughal sources differ substantially in their accounts Mughal sources depict him as a well-established military commander, whom Sher Shah courted, wanting him on his side. They describe Sher Shah receiving Bairam with great respect. At the meeting, 'Sher Khan rose up and embraced him. He sought to attract him by enticing words and remarked, "Whosoever acts sincerely does not err." Bairam answered, "So it is; whoever acts sincerely shall not go astray." In another account, 'Sher Khan used often to say that "when Bairam said 'whoever is sincere shall not go astray', I perceived that he would not arrange matters with us".'[22]

If Mughal accounts emphasize that Sher Shah admired Bairam's unflinching loyalty to Humayun and recognized his importance, an Afghan source, Abbas Sarwani, portrays the meeting in an entirely different light: '...when Bairam was presented to Sher Shah he angrily asked explanation for the delay in the arrival. Isa Khan, in order to save Bairam, replied that he had been in the house of Sheikh Mulki-i-Qattal, referring to the stay at his house for the Sheikh was his father. As it was an established custom among the Afghans that any criminal who took refuge with the relatives of Sheikh Mulki-i-Qattal should be pardoned, Sher Shah pardoned Bairam. At the prayer of Isa Khan, Sher Shah granted Bairam a horse and a robe also.'[23]

Whether Bairam Khan emerged from the meeting as a great commander whose unswerving devotion to the Mughal cause elicited respect in his foes, or as a supplicant whose very survival was at stake, it seems clear that the victorious Afghans did make some efforts to persuade him to join them. Isa Khan played a key role in this, and he was someone of great importance in Sher Shah's hierarchy. He had served in the Afghan courts of Mandu and Ahmedabad and his contemporary importance is evident from his large and handsome mausoleum in Nizamuddin in Delhi, coincidentally adjoining but not entirely dwarfed by Humayun's tomb. The meeting with Sher Shah, at which Isa Khan was present, is believed to have taken place in Ujjain when the sultan was in the midst of his campaign in Malwa. Shortly thereafter, Bairam made his escape and arrived in Gujarat. Here, another friend, Sheikh Gadai, acted as an intermediary between Bairam and the sultan's court and provided sanctuary for eight months. He would continue to play a major role in Bairam's life hereafter. Around this time, the Gujarat sultan offered Bairam a position in his court, an offer Bairam politely refused, finally joining a beleaguered and desperate Humayun in Sindh in April 1543.

After the debacle at Kannauj, Humayun found that the lack of support from his brothers meant that he lacked the strength to take on Sher Shah. The embattled Mughals had congregated in Lahore, but could not agree on a common strategy of military action. Kamran was already in negotiations with the Afghans and it has been succinctly observed that 'Kamran feared Humayun much more than Sher Shah thinking that, while the Afghan should at least be satisfied with depriving him of the Punjab, his brother might wish to resume all his possessions previously bestowed, including Kabul.'[24] Humayun did not agree to the entreaties of nobles close to him that he deal firmly with his brothers and have Kamran seized and put to death. By now the Afghan armies were already deep in the Punjab and a wholescale evacuation of the Mughals followed.

Kamran moved to Kabul and Humayun, recognizing the risk of staying with Kamran, decided to go to Sindh and create a base of operations against the Afghans. The Mughals had virtually been expelled from Hindustan.

In Sindh, Humayun found that he had his back to the wall. Shah Hussain, the ruler of Sindh, had no reason to help a fleeing Mughal emperor, especially when this carried the attendant risk of an Afghan incursion. Humayun had received some assistance from the Rajputs in Marwar till Afghan pressure led that to dry up as well. However, the Hindu Rana of Umarkot, in Sindh, stood firm and Humayun was able to get a brief reprieve. The final stages of the journey to Umarkot were not easy. The loss of dignity was as hard to bear as the physical difficulties of the march through the desert. The emperor's half-sister, Gulbadan Begum, was to recall: 'It was extremely hot; horses and [other] quadrupeds kept sinking to their knees in the sand … on they went, hungry and thirsty. Many, women and men, were on foot.' [25] So low was the morale that at one stage a senior noble, Tardi Beg Khan, demurred when the emperor asked for a horse to carry his pregnant wife, and he himself had to dismount so that she could ride. On an earlier occasion, Tardi Beg had refused to vacate his place on a boat for the emperor's party.

The royal party, nevertheless, reached Umarkot safely and it was there that Humayun's son, the future emperor Akbar, was born at the Rana's fort in October 1542. Humayun then attempted to regain ground with the Rana's assistance. But this was hardly sufficient as the Mughal situation was now extremely fragile. Important nobles were deserting the cause and Humayun soon found himself without either resources or men. Meanwhile, the ruler of Sindh was preparing for a major assault against him that would have delivered the coup de grace.

It was in these unpropitious circumstances that Bairam made his reappearance to join what was left of Humayun's party. His entry was dramatic and, according to some accounts, in the midst of a skirmish when, suddenly, the hard-pressed Mughals found themselves reinforced. We do not know the size of Bairam's force, but his presence at a time when important nobles – such as Munim Khan and Tardi Beg Khan, both of whom we will encounter again – had only recently left Humayun was a tremendous boost to the morale of the dispirited Mughal camp. Humayun's response to Bairam's arrival sums it up: 'The partner of my sorrow is come'.[26]

Despite the rejoicing at Bairam's return, the situation was grave. From Kabul, Kamran rejected Humayun's request for entry and safe passage to Badakhshan in Afghanistan. This was on the basis, not invalid in itself, that once in Kabul, Humayun would not leave. With the ruler of Sindh hard on his heels, Humayun, desperate and shattered by repeated defeats, considered giving up altogether and going on the Haj. At this point Bairam – and most accounts say so clearly – strongly urged Humayun to go to Persia and seek the assistance of its ruler, the Safavid Shah. Bairam's argument was based on his own hereditary connections with Persia and reinforced by the presence of many Turkmen of his tribe and clan in the Safavid court.

Humayun's passage to the borders of Persia was not without its own travails. His original intention seems to have been to first head for Qandahar. But the Sindh ruler, Shah Hussain, was acting in concert with Humayun's brothers, Kamran and Askari. Kamran's reasons for keeping Humayun out of Kabul held equally for Qandahar, which Askari now controlled on behalf of Kamran. Learning of their hostile intentions, Humayun stopped at Mashtang in what is present-day Baluchistan. At this point: 'While the royal party was encamped at Mashtang, Askari planned to capture Humayun suddenly and sent one Jan Bahadur Uzbeg who had knowledge of the locality to have accurate information about the situation of the royal party. This Jan Bahadur ... had served Humayun in India, and feeling for his old master, he determined to reveal the design of Mirza Askari.'[27] It is interesting to see that Jan Bahadur, on reaching Humayun's camp, goes immediately to Bairam Khan to reveal the plot to capture the emperor. Clearly, no time was to be lost, and Bairam was the person who could persuade Humayun to move quickly.

The departure was unceremonious and swift and marked the lowest ebb of Humayun's fortunes. His party was probably less than fifty strong. One estimate puts the number at twenty-two, but an eyewitness account mentions forty men and two women. Their journey westward was largely through territory controlled by Kamran. From a place called Garmsir, Humayun wrote to Shah Tahmasp on Bairam's advice, informing him of his intention to visit Persia and seeking permission to enter the country. Before a reply could be received, however, came news that Askari had sent a contingent to Garmsir; this forced Humayun to rapidly move into Sistan, an area within the Shah's territory and jurisdiction. So swift was their departure that the child Akbar was left behind to be taken by Askari to Qandahar where he was, remarkably – given the history of his father's relationship with his uncles – well looked after by Askari's wife.

The letter that Humayun sent to Shah Tahmasp was, incidentally, composed by Bairam Khan. Written at a time of grave danger, it has been described as 'remarkable for its simplicity, brevity and directness'.[28] Clearly, Bairam his taking charge of proceedings, confident that he will henceforth be able to steer events in Humayun's, and by implication, his own favour.

Bairam Khan thus emerges on the centre stage of Mughal politics, where he remained for the rest of his life. The reasons for his ascendancy are hard to isolate and equally hard to explain. Perhaps it was the dramatic manner of his reappearance, or its timing, at a point when others were leaving and Humayun's fortunes were at their lowest. Bairam was then about fifty years old; he was probably still unmarried and without any useful connections, nor did he possess a clear base of support in, or near, the Delhi–Agra region from which Humayun had been evicted. He was a soldier-courtier with only his name, his background and his wit and loyalty to offer Humayun. Yet

Humayun appears to have embraced these qualities with gratitude; nor, as events turned out, was this gratitude misplaced.

The three-and-a-half years between the battle of Kannauj and Humayun's entry into Persia witnessed a rapid sequence of events and a bewildering chronology. Some threads are of particular significance for Bairam Khan's story and also for the light they shed on Mughal polity; it is plausible to infer that Bairam would have drawn not dissimilar conclusions. But first, what are the significant strands of history that impacted on Bairam Khan up to the time he rejoined Humayun? The most obvious is Bairam's isolation in a milieu dominated by family, relations and connections. We know his lineage helped during his early years at Babur's and Humayun's court, but of the period immediately after that we know very little. Despite being in his late forties at the time of the battle of Kannauj, there is still no mention of a wife. Similarly, there is no mention of relations or clansmen accompanying Bairam during the months he hid in Sambhal and during his flight to, and time in, Gujarat. Three individuals, however, stand out in the narrative of the post-Kannauj period up to Humayun's arrival in Persia: Sheikh Gadai, for having helped Bairam in Gujarat, and the two nobles, Tardi Beg and Munim Beg, who deserted Humayun. All three would play important parts in the future phases of Bairam's career.

We need to note some other factors that influenced the future course of Bairam's life as well as Mughal history. First, the situation regarding Humayun and his brothers: Sher Shah's victory became a strategic rout of the Mughals largely because Askari and Kamran acted in concert with the Afghans to force Humayun out of north India. The relationship of a king with his brothers was a critical one in Mughal polity and was, in fact, a subset of a more fundamental issue: the relationship between the king and his nobles. It seems probable that Humayun, and certainly Bairam, learnt lessons from their unseemly flight out of India. When Humayun returned to power, he was to apply these lessons, if not with expedition, certainly with greater determination, to forge a new relationship with the nobility. Bairam Khan was also to implement a policy of intolerance of any opposition or dissent though, in the end, this was to be a factor in his own downfall. The policy outlived him, however, and was, in many ways, both his greatest triumph and his lasting legacy to the Mughals.

What explains Bairam's own loyalty to Humayun at a time when crossing over to the winning side was hardly rare? Bairam persisted with Humayun despite overtures from Isa Khan, Sher Shah and, later, from the Gujarat ruler, Bahadur Shah. Nor did he desert to one of Humayun's other brothers – many other Mughal nobles had gone over to Kamran. Perhaps Bairam's own age played some role here. He was too old to begin afresh, or so he may have felt. Joining up with the Afghans was also perhaps a non-option for the son of Saif Ali and descendent of a clan that had its own imperial ambitions.

Altogether Humayun spent about fifteen months in Persia. He came with a ragged entourage; he left at the head of a 12,000-strong Persian army, carrying valuables and treasure gifted by Shah Tahmasp. The Shah's treatment of Humayun was 'a curious compound of courtesy and insult, hostility and hospitality, generosity and meanness'[29] and their relationship was a dangerous cocktail of sectarian sentiment, high politics and personal egos. The resultant pressures were understandably great, not just on the emperor himself, but on his entourage as well.

Humayun's reception sometime in January 1544 by the governor of Herat, under direct instructions of the Shah, was a grand affair. He was received by Governor Mohammad Khan, who 'ordered the people of Herat, young and old, to come out of the city and stand in array on the two sides … and welcome Humayun with music and sport'. A near contemporary description of the banquet hosted in his honour puts it thus: '… the sitting of the Assembly commenced, to describe which speech becomes detached from the pen as on account of the elegance of the audience hall, the stars become concealed … Fair women, amiable and meek, expert in rendering service stood in every corner like virgins of paradise in that assembly of heavenly beauty. On account of their spirit stimulating beauty, the thought of life and the next world vanished.'[30]

This lavish hospitality was clearly to set the stage for what would follow, the idea being, of course, to convey the vastness of the Shah's dominion and power and the great generosity and attention to protocol in his court. The Shah's reply to Humayun's original letter was received, and it promised friendship and support. Bairam's clansmen in the Shah's court were aware of his presence in Humayun's party and we find that he was singled out for special mention by the Shah in instructions regarding protocol to governors en route. Bairam was, in fact, sent in advance of Humayun's arrival to pay his respects to the Shah.

Humayun's reception at the Shah's court in the capital Qazwin was also magnificent. 'The Shah of Persia had been arranging for the reception of Humayun with ceremony and magnificence becoming the Safavid court ... When he reached the stage, one day's journey from the camp of the Shah, he was first welcomed by the nobles and the common people. He was then received by the ... wazir, as well as other big officers. When Humayun arrived within one league of the Shah's camp he was received by the princes of the royal family...'

The Shah's behaviour was similarly impeccable: '... on seeing King Humayun from a distance [the Shah] advanced a few steps to the edge of the carpet to receive him ... Shah Tahmasp embraced Humayun and seated him to his right on the carpet. He made kind enquiries about Humayun's health and journey'. Shortly thereafter, 'the Shah told Humayun that he desired him to put on the Persian cap. Humayun agreed and both to flatter his host and justify his action replied that a Taj (crown) was an emblem of greatness and he would with pleasure wear it. Shah Tahmasp then with his own hands placed the cap on Humayun's head.' A mural of the Shah entertaining Humayun exists in the Safavid imperial palace complex of Chihil Sutan at Isfahan, Persia. The mural is dated to the early eighteenth century but was based on an earlier painting (Plate II).[31]

Descriptions of the meeting mention the lavish arrangements, the pavilions and tents raised and the gifts exchanged. Humayun on his part gifted some precious rubies and a very large diamond – some believe it was the Kohinoor.[32] He had evidently kept these to be used as a last resort after his flight from Agra. But behind the ceremonies and the elaborate protocol, the realities of the situation were clear enough and Tahmasp was not one to be subtle. The very next morning, when Humayun greeted him and paid his respects as the Shah was leaving, he was ignored.

Bairam played an important role in this period. The Shah's attitude to Humayun reflected in part major differences within his court and family on the suitable response to this defeated Mughal ruler who was seeking not just refuge, but also assistance. In part the differences arose from religious factors. The Mughals were Sunnis, while the Shah and his court were committed Shias. The hostility between the two sects was an ever-present factor during Humayun's stay in Persia. There are references to the Shah's brothers urging him to put Humayun to death.

Other factors also played a role. One episode, which illustrates the tensions and jealousies that surrounded Humayun in the Persian court, has Shah Tahmasp asking Humayun how he could have been defeated by an enemy as weak as the Afghans. Humayun replied that it was on account of his brothers' enmity. The Persian monarch then said, 'Your manner of treating brothers is not such as they ought to experience.' This conversation is described as having taken place over dinner and when the meal finished, '… Prince Behram Mirza, brother to Shah Tahmasp, approached the latter with a basin and ewer for him to wash his hands. This ceremony being over, the Shah turned to Humayun and resuming the discourse said, "This is the way you ought to have treated your brothers." Humayun immediately assented, which so much offended Prince Behram Mirza that he never forgave him while he resided at court.'[33]

Then there were the political factors. There was a deep-rooted rivalry between the Safavids and the Mughals over control of

Qandahar, which was strategically important to both empires. Memories of Babur's alleged duplicity in past dealings seemed to play their part too. Babur had availed of Safavid help in 1510–11 in attempts to regain Samarqand from the Uzbeks who had ousted him. Shah Ismail, Tahmasp's father, had insisted on Babur accepting the tenets of the Shia doctrine as a precondition. Babur assented but reneged as soon as the attempt to regain Samarqand failed. He showed also throughout his life a fairly obvious revulsion towards the Shia faith. Undoubtedly, Humayun would have considered all this when he decided to take refuge in Persia and seek the Shah's help. And it appears that, from the very beginning, he received clear indications of the importance of the religious factor. Bairam's experiences when he was sent ahead as Humayun's envoy soon after the Mughals had crossed into Persia were not altogether encouraging. 'Bairam Khan attended by ten horsemen went to Qazwin and paid his respects to the Shah. Soon after his arrival Shah Tahmasp ordered him to cut off his hair and put on a Persian cap. Bairam represented that as he was the servant of another monarch he could only do so with his master's consent. Shah Tahmasp became displeased and told Bairam that he might do as he pleased, but in order to frighten him the Shah ordered some prisoners, sentenced to death, to be executed in his presence ...'[34]

Even if some details of this episode can be discounted, it is evident that the Shia-Sunni divide was of significance and remained so throughout Humayun's time in Persia. Bairam, being Shia, become an ideal intermediary between Humayun and the Shah although, as the incident of the cap suggests, it wasn't always easy. As it happens, it was on the religious issue and on Qandahar that Humayun seemingly showed considerable flexibility, and in this Bairam played, along with some others, a significant role. Certainly Humayun himself was not overly concerned about doctrinal differences. As emperor he was believed to have been sympathetic to the Shias on account of the large number of nobles in his court who belonged to the sect.

Humayun's lack of doctrinal prejudice – and also his mordant sense of humour – comes through in the following conversation between him and Kamran before the Persian exile: 'It is said that Kamran was fond of talking to him on the subject of religion; one day, while they were riding together on their retreat from Hindustan towards Lahore, they observed a dog lift up his leg against a tombstone; Kamran remarked, "I conclude the man who is buried there is a Rafzy (heterodox), [i.e. Shia]." Humayun replied, "Yes, no doubt; the dog is an orthodox brute." They were much in the habit of joking on such subjects; but the truth is that on these occasions he merely wished to annoy Kamran.'[35]

Shah Tahmasp's insistence that Humayun first adopt the tenets of Shia doctrine before any meaningful assistance could be provided was unsurprising but certainly galling. It was not religious conviction or doctrinal factors as much as the realization of powerlessness that troubled Humayun as he confronted the option posed by the Persian monarch. But intermediaries from both sides helped bridge the gap. In contrast to others at the court, Shah Tahmasp's sister, Sultana Begum, and his chief minister, Qazi Jahan, argued for a more generous treatment of Humayun. Among Humayun's followers too there were those – and certainly Bairam was among them – who counselled pragmatism, suggesting it would be wise to try to get the best possible terms from the Persian monarch and thereafter attempt to regain the lost kingdom. Qazi Jahan counselled that refusal would imperil not only Humayun himself, but all those who had followed him: 'You are powerless at this time; you know it well. If God and the Prophet send Kufr (i.e., lack of belief) there is no option but to submit.'[36]

Privately, Humayun complained of the Shah's bigotry to his followers, but he also made visible concessions to indicate a change of heart and a new-found devotion to Shia doctrines. Some sources speak of the Shah insisting that Humayun sign papers accepting the Shia creed. Others have Sultana Begum informing Shah Tahmasp of Humayun's true beliefs and indicating that his brothers and several nobles were hostile to the emperor because 'he was a loyal disciple of the family of the Prophet', that is, a Shia. She even quoted verses written by Humayun in praise of Ali and his family. Sultana Begum also advised the Shah that 'he was already surrounded by enemies … Turks, Uzbegs, Circassians and Europeans … [and that] by injuring Humayun he would create more enemies …'[37]

From these circumstances an agreement was stitched together between the Shah and Humayun. The importance of Bairam's role in the entire exercise is borne out by many factors. His own Shia background, the presence of his kinsmen in the Persian court and the resonance of his ancestry made him invaluable to Humayun and also gave him a certain distinctiveness in Shah Tahmasp's eyes. For instance, the Persian monarch is said to have conferred on Bairam the title of Khan when he brought him gifts from Humayun, though some Mughal chronicles indicate the title was conferred by both the Shah and Humayun before Humayun left Persia. The latter may be a subsequent gloss on an event which was, in a sense, a slight to Humayun as Bairam was, after all, his vassal. Perhaps such a possibility was already anticipated by the Mughal party and Bairam had been instructed in advance to accept the honour. Certainly, unlike the previous occasion when Bairam resisted the Shah's request to wear a Persian cap, no reservations appear to have been expressed.

Apart from the religious factor, Qandahar was a major unresolved issue between Humayun and the Persian monarch. It is described as having been the only 'territorial incentive to conflict between the Mughals and the Safavids'.[38] For the Mughals, overlords of Kabul, Ghazni and parts of Baluchistan, Qandahar's great political and military significance lay in the fact that it was vital for the defence of Kabul and for dominating the routes into Baluchistan and Sindh. Qandahar, therefore, had a vast importance in the mental landscape of the Mughals. For the Persians, issues of prestige were equally important. As rulers of the kingdom of Herat, the Safavids set great store by their inherited claim to Qandahar. Possession of Qandahar was thus critical to the hegemonic claims of both the Mughals and the Persians, even outside of their recognized territories.

The terms of the understanding between Humayun and Shah Tahmasp thus inevitably covered Qandahar: it was agreed that Humayun, at the head of a Persian army, would wrest Qandahar from his brothers, Askari and Kamran, and hand it over to Shah Tahmasp. A Mughal possession being passed on to the Persians was the price Humayun would have to pay for Shah Tahmasp's help. In return, Humayun would be rewarded with a desperately needed victory to restore his prestige. Qandahar would, moreover, provide a base for future campaigns to evict Kamran from Kabul and thereafter regain the Punjab and other parts of Hindustan lost to the Afghans. Bairam was the key intermediary. At the final meeting of the two monarchs, 'Shah Tahmasp gave Bairam the roll of twelve thousand Persians who were to form the auxiliary force under Prince Murad and he instructed his son Sultan Muhammad Mirza to send help from the army of Khurasan ...' In the army that accompanied Humayun to Qandahar was Mohammad Mirza, a grandson of Mirza Jahan Shah and thus also a kinsman of Bairam.[39] He was among the more prominent of the Baharlus in the expedition, but there were no doubt many others as well.

Scattered throughout the literature dealing with Bairam's time in Persia are references to his meetings with his kin in Shah Tahmasp's court. There are also references to the Shah's desire to retain Bairam in his service and the offer of the governorship of Azerbaijan, previously held by his ancestors. There is thus little doubt that Bairam used his stay in Shah Tahmasp's court to renew claims to his heritage and ancestry. Humayun and Bairam also travelled extensively in Persia – to Tabriz, Ardabil, the Caspian, as well as to Mashhad and the tomb of Imam Ali Raza.

Qandahar, held by Humayun's brother, Prince Askari, on behalf of Prince Kamran, was strongly defended. Military activity during the siege of Qandahar was therefore accompanied by diplomatic moves to entice Humayun's other brothers and as many nobles as possible away from Kamran. Bairam remained at the centre of these moves and when the siege had extended into its third month, we find him dispatched as Humayun's envoy to Kabul, to meet Kamran. There is a story here, illustrating Bairam's presence of mind and attention to details of protocol. Humayun had asked him to deliver a letter to Kamran, and Bairam's concern, possibly based on information received, was that it might be received without due courtesies. He carried with him, therefore, a copy of the Quran and first held that out to Kamran. As Kamran rose to receive the holy book, Bairam gave him the letter from Humayun. During this mission Bairam also developed contacts with Mughal nobles and princes in Kabul, Badakhshan and elsewhere, gauging reactions to Kamran and to Humayun's possible restoration in Kabul. We can also discern some traces of Shah Tahmasp's own diplomatic moves in these endeavours as there are references to gifts he sent to a number of prominent Mughal nobles in Afghanistan. Evidently, the Shah was making full use of the strategic opportunity offered by the disarray and disunity among the Mughals; Humayun and Bairam at the head of a Persian army were only chief among the instruments to secure his goal of extending Persian influence to Qandahar.

The siege of Qandahar lasted for almost six months. Askari defended it with greater vigour than the Persian army or Humayun had anticipated. The Persian troops are described as weary by the time the military breakthrough came. The surrender may have been largely the result of eroding morale as news came in both of Kamran's growing isolation and of a steady stream of nobles deserting him and joining Humayun.

The final terms were negotiated through Khanzada Begum, Babur's widow, and the fort was surrendered in September 1545. Askari formally sought pardon from Humayun after 'Bairam Khan hung the sword round [his] neck ...' [the traditional gesture indicating capitulation]. The fact remains, however, that it was the Persian troops who took charge of the fort and Humayun sent its treasures as gifts to the Shah.

Difficulties between Humayun and the Persian army nominally under his command began soon after the control of Qandahar passed from Askari to the Persians. The points of dispute reveal the tensions inherent in the alliance between Humayun and the Safavids. The initial bone of contention appeared to be the Persian demand that Askari be handed over and sent to the Persian court. This was unacceptable to Humayun. The long siege had an adverse impact on Persian morale and we hear of 'many Persians return(ing) home without leave of Humayun'. Similarly, there are references to the population of Qandahar being oppressed by the Persians and their 'imploring justice from Humayun'. Tensions also surfaced over dividing provisions between the troops holding the garrison and the Mughals encamped outside; the Persians 'tried to cut off all provisions to the Mughal camp which lay in the neighbourhood of Qandahar'.[40]

At the core of the dispute lay the fact that Humayun's ambitions were not limited to Qandahar; for him the real prize was Kabul. An assault on Kabul required control over Qandahar, which would safeguard the rear, serve as a garrison, and with winter approaching, be a secure staging post as well as providing accommodation for the harem when the main party moved to Kabul. The Persian army, however, had different instructions. Thus, '... when Humayun asked for accommodation the Persian commander replied that as the fort had been delivered to the Persians, no one could be allowed in without the permission of the Shah.'[41]

Amidst these growing tensions, the Persian prince nominally commanding the force, who had been sent by Shah Tahmasp to assist Humayun, died. Humayun's advisors pressed him to seize the opportunity and take over the garrison. 'The chiefs advised Humayun to capture the fort due to urgent necessity and that, after conquering Kabul and Badakhshan, they would compensate the Persians by giving more territories...' A Mughal historian by the name of Khafi

Khan was the most candid in saying that 'Bairam Khan and the nobles decided to take the fort by any means'. The simple truth was, of course, that Humayun's star was again on the ascendant after the success at Qandahar. Chiefs and troops were rallying to him from all directions: his brother, Prince Hindal, had deserted Kamran and joined Humayun. In the end, the fort was seized by the Mughals and the Persian troops were left with no option but to return to Persia.

What remains of interest for the purpose of our narrative is that the fortress was handed over to Bairam Khan in preference to the claims of princes of royal blood. It is easy to see the stratagem in this and, as Humayun wrote to Shah Tahmasp: '... as [the Persian General] Budagh Khan had behaved himself improperly and as Prince Murad had died and as Bairam Khan was among his faithful servants, he had given Qandahar to Bairam as his jagir and the city would remain a dependency of his kingdom.'

One can, of course, imagine Humayun, now increasingly secure, relishing the irony of the situation. Shah Tahmasp's slights, not least of which was awarding the title of Khan to Bairam, were being avenged. The Shah, on his part, does not appear to have objected and in all probability willingly decided to accept the face-saving arrangement. This may well have been the only response possible to the premature return of Persian troops from Qandahar. Alternative speculations are also possible: the Shah may have genuinely believed that Bairam, by virtue of his ancestry and Shia background, had loyalties to him or was at least potentially in his camp, or at any rate was not hostile to Persian interests. There is also evidence of Bairam writing to the Shah – no doubt with Humayun's knowledge – after his installation as governor of Qandahar.

The Mughal–Safavid contest over Qandahar would continue for the next century or so and, in fact, is a dominant theme in the foreign preoccupations of these two empires up to their twilight and end. The Persians would take control of Qandahar again in 1558, soon after Humayun's death, and the Mughals would be left with no choice but to accept the fait accompli with good grace. In 1594

Humayun's son, Akbar, would have his revenge and take the fortress back. Akbar's son, Jahangir, would lose it in 1622 but his son, Shah Jahan, in turn would repossess it in 1638, but only for a few years, as Qandahar would be in Persian hands again from 1649. Thereafter Shah Jahan would mount three costly military expeditions to regain it, but failed each time.

Bairam's tenure as governor of Qandahar is a phase – lasting almost a decade, from 1545 to 1554 – of his physical separation from Humayun's court. For Humayun, the fall of Qandahar marked the formal end of his exile, which had lasted for nearly two years. During this time Bairam was in close proximity to the king-in-exile and often in situations when he was witness to the monarch's personal dignity being compromised. We can only guess at the strain this would have imposed on the relationship between the two. Nevertheless, with Qandahar in his control, Humayun was on the path to being well and truly in control of the destinies of those around him. During this nine-year period, Bairam remained largely at Qandahar, but it was a time of considerable activity for Humayun. The defeat of Kamran and the conquest of Kabul and Badakhshan consolidated his position. But they were by no means definitive victories, for the territories repeatedly changed hands between Kamran and Humayun with bewildering rapidity.

Bairam re-enters the narrative in 1551 when Kamran is on an offensive, and the desertion of Haji Muhammad Khan, formerly a close confidant of Humayun, has jeopardized the gains so far. Humayun dealt with this with uncharacteristic firmness: after first pardoning Haji Muhammad, he ordered his execution, a course urged by Bairam Khan too. It is also of interest to find Bairam being summoned by Humayun at a time when the threat from Kamran appeared severe. Kamran had acquired by means of a matrimonial alliance with the ruler of Sindh, a base for operations against Humayun. Till his final defeat and blinding in mid-1553, Humayun could not rest easy in Kabul and we find in these years a repetitive catalogue of skirmishes and campaigns.

During the relatively sedentary period of his tenure as governor of Qandahar, Bairam also had to manage – with some adroitness – the duality of his situation. Humayun was de facto the sovereign, but a layer of pretence had to be maintained with regard to Shah Tahmasp and the Persian court. It was also perhaps at this time that Bairam composed at least some parts of his *diwan,* or collection of poetry.[42] Certainly we hear that he was patron to many distinguished literary men who gathered around him, as also well-known religious divines.[43]

There is the following exchange of verse between Humayun and Bairam in Qandahar, for instance. Humayun is said to have written after taking Kabul:

O thou friend of my saddened heart,
How thy sweet nature is well balanced!
I'm never at any time without thought of thee
But what sadness hast thou in thought of me?

Bairam's reply is:

O thou who art incomparable shade,
Greater than any praise I can offer thee,
When thou knowest how it passes without thee
Why ask, 'How feelest thou, when parted from me?'[44]

Bairam's poetry ranges 'from devotional odes and panegyrics to romantic and moral themes'; he was also adept at 'making insertions in the poems of the masters which he called *dakhliya*'.[45] Poetry had many functions and one of these was to flatter – not just the emperor, but also those closest to him.

The following description is illustrative of Bairam's tenure in Qandahar: distanced from the emperor and his court, but having to keep track of the current favourites and also to flatter them:

> Shah Abul Maali, who was of noble Sayyid extraction, and of the country of Kashghar, in the symmetry of his limbs and the excellence of his valour was distinguished above all his compeers. To him the deceased Emperor had shown a special favour and a boundless condescension, so that he had honoured him by calling him his son. This man was a dullard … let it be known concerning him that Bairam Khan has written an acrostic in 24 verses of which the rhyme was *azim* and *qadim*, and the rhyming letter mime in such a way that the initial hemstiches composed the words 'Hazrat Muhammad Humayun Padshah Ghazi' (My Lord Muhammad Humayun Padshah Ghazi), and the initial letters of the second hemstiches 'Shahzadah (prince) Jalaluddin Muhammad Akbar'; and the final letters of the first hemstiches the words 'Mirza Shah Abul Maali'.[46]

Shah Abul Maali was one of Humayun's great favourites and Bairam took pains to be counted amongst his friends. His wit and facility with verse served him well in that direction. Once, during a visit to Qandahar by Humayun, Shah Abul Maali, 'being intoxicated by royal favour', killed a well-known Shia courtier – largely on a sectarian impulse but also perhaps because he was drunk.[47]

> When the heirs of the murdered man came to demand justice and the emperor sent for Shah Abul Maali, he put on the dead man's robe of black velvet lined with red and blue, and putting the hanger (i.e., weapon) burnished bright, the very same with which he had dispatched him, under his skirt, swaggered drunken into the royal assembly and denied the deed. Bairam Khan on the occasion quoted these lines:
>
> His dishevelled locks of hair
> Tonight debauch confess
> Lo, a blazing proof is there
> The lamp beneath his dress
>
> The emperor was exceedingly delighted (i.e., with this apt citation); but the blood of that innocent one was hidden in the dust and his murder was never proved.

We do not know whether Bairam acted spontaneously to avert the emperor's wrath on Abul Maali or in concert with the latter. But we should keep in mind his assiduous courting of Shah Abul Maali, for we will encounter a dramatic contrast only a few years later.

Bairam's ability to compose and recite poetry spontaneously was a quality evidently greatly admired. In August 1554, when he arrived in Kabul after the feasting of Eid at the end of Ramazan, Humayun 'for the sake of giving greater pleasure and out of the affection he bore him had the feast repeated and gave an entertainment more splendid than that of the Eid'. This included an archery match and when the king hit a target missed by many experienced archers, Bairam composed the following ode to mark the event:

> Thine arrow has snatched the fastening of the ball from
> the crook,
> It has made the curve like a meteor grazing the Pleiades.[48]

Bairam's literary skills were adroit enough to encompass flattery in its subtlest (for the times) forms. Consider this poem, ostensibly on the astrolabe:

> What globe is this whose axis rests on the centre of the universe
> This full moon across whose midst the meteors dart?
> Though it vaunts itself the equal of both sun and moon
> It gladly enrols itself among the Emperor's slaves.
> The sun's resplendent orb looms not so largely in our eyes
> As the crescents which surmount the banner of the world
> – famed king of kings –
> Both sky and earth are ever subject to his authority,
> Like the seal of a ring on the hands of a monarch as powerful as Jamshid.
> This globe brings with it a golden tray full of ashrafis
> To scatter before the feet of great kings
> The feet of the emperor of exalted dignity, Humayun
> Before whom in order to obtain honour,
> The sky itself laces the head of humility on the threshold of the court.[49]

Despite the importance that Bairam Khan had now assumed in his own right, his personal life continued to be static, with the puzzling absence of a wife and family. His proximity to Persia and to his original clanspeople, his status at both the Safavid and Mughal courts, the high position he had come to occupy and the length of time he spent in Qandahar made him an ideal figure for a major matrimonial alliance or alliances. Was he, in fact, married in this period or even earlier but contemporary accounts missed mentioning it? Or could it be that Bairam's ambition had vaulted so high that he sought an alliance with royalty and none was immediately forthcoming? Given the fact that he later married into the emperor's own family, this line of speculation is not without basis. Bairam's growing ambitions, and perhaps vanity, are reflected in the caustic comment of a contemporary: 'With regard to the titles of his highness, you will do well to give him ever so many more than to other people.'[50]

Bairam's long sojourn in Qandahar was not without its undercurrents of suspicion and intrigue. In 1554, Humayun marched to Qandahar, having received complaints that Bairam Khan was contemplating rebellion. There were many who complained about his supposed allegiance to the Shah and suspicions were easily fanned given that he was a Shia.[51] One account described the situation as follows: '… the lovers of contumacy, that is to say, the envious and the riotous, so distorted the appearance of the sincere loyalty of Bairam Khan, in the clear mirror of the mind of Humayun, that it was inverted and he was represented by them as hostile. Accordingly, an attack was ordered in the direction of Qandahar.'[52]

Bairam Khan's reception of Humayun, the attendant feasts and the lavish arrangements, however, convinced Humayun of his loyalty. Bairam's position was a delicate one, given the circumstances of his appointment, the strategic importance of Qandahar to both the Mughals and the Safavids, and the background of Humayun's sanctuary in Persia. There is, in any case, no real evidence suggesting a basis to Humayun's suspicions. So what could possibly have triggered these?

There is no doubt that the fact of the physical separation, with Humayun in Kabul and Bairam in Qandahar, and the distance between them, would have encouraged intrigue. It is also possible that this episode reveals a change in Humayun – he is more realistic in evaluating threats and less tolerant of allowing opposition to emerge. Humayun's final treatment of his brother, Kamran, illustrates this, as does the execution of Haji Muhammad Khan. Also, Humayun now had his sights firmly set on the reconquest of his earlier domain in India. He needed to ensure that Kabul would remain secure as his assault on the Punjab and Delhi was mounted, and to reassure himself that Bairam Khan could be counted upon in the campaign.

Regaining his kingdom had been in Humayun's mind since news of the death of Sher Shah's son, Islam Shah, in October 1553. Centrifugal forces had always been strong in the Afghan kingdom and could, in the absence of a capable ruler, become uncontrollable. In the aftermath of Islam Shah's death, as many as five Afghan kingdoms emerged – in the Punjab, Delhi, Bihar, Bengal and Malwa. Islam Shah's successor was his cousin and brother-in-law, who murdered the king's twelve-year-old son and assumed the throne with the title Mohammad Adil. He was, however, largely confined to Bihar, as another cousin of the former king seized Delhi and Agra and proclaimed himself Sultan Ibrahim, while the Punjab passed to another claimant, who set himself up as Sultan Sikander. All these short-lived successor states jostled for supremacy, sometimes at war and sometimes in alliance amongst themselves. This was the opportunity Humayun had been waiting for. His own affairs were now more propitiously placed than perhaps ever before. His brothers were now no longer a threat: Hindal had been killed in battle in 1551, Askari was imprisoned and Kamran had been blinded in mid-1553.

With the beginning of the conquest, we enter the last phase in the narrative of Bairam Khan's life, where we see him catapulted to the highest levels of the Mughal system. It is possible to read this in terms of a vindication of Bairam's loyalty and steadfastness. It is equally plausible to see the factors responsible for Bairam's ascent as incubating the seeds of his subsequent destruction. An appropriate place to begin may be with the duality of Munim Khan and Bairam Khan.

Munim Khan's re-entry into the story is itself of interest. He was among those who had deserted the emperor's party during the desperate days in Sindh. Some sources attribute Munim Khan's desertion to a quarrel with another prominent noble, Tardi Beg, whom we have already encountered. Munim Khan not only deserted Humayun, but also crossed over to the emperor's adversary, the ruler of Sindh, Shah Hussain Khan. The latter, acting in concert with Askari and Kamran, was engaged in rapidly boxing Humayun and his entourage in and delivering the finishing blow.[53] Yet, when Humayun returned to Kabul in 1545, we see Munim Khan emerging as a close companion and confidant. Humayun was obviously eager to make all possible efforts to recall the premier nobles back to his side and isolate his brothers completely. At that point, the outcome against Kamran was by no means certain and, in fact, Kabul was to fall to Kamran once more after Humayun's occupation of it. While many nobles vacillated in this conflict between the brothers, repeatedly switching sides, this time around Munim Khan stayed loyal; he was given increasingly important responsibilities and by the time of the final victory and the defeat and blinding of Kamran in 1553, he was one of the emperor's closest advisors.

This is evident from Munim Khan's role and position in the episode concerning Humayun's suspicions of Bairam Khan and his subsequent visit to Qandahar. Humayun intended to replace Bairam with Munim Khan, who accompanied the army to Qandahar. But Munim Khan himself '... though anxious to have Bairam Khan removed from Qandahar was reluctant to take over the charge of that post. Probably he had an eye upon some more important assignment for himself. He advised Humayun against the open dismissal of Bairam Khan. It was at his suggestion that a subtler device was adopted to bring about the removal of Bairam Khan from Qandahar. Before starting back for Kabul, Humayun gave explicit orders to Bairam Khan to mobilise his contingent and come to Kabul as soon as possible for joining the forthcoming expedition to Hindustan.'[54]

What this establishes, of course, is Munim's own restoration as a close confidant of Humayun. But Humayun himself, more calculating and careful, was addressing two different considerations. He was heeding the advice that it would be risky to leave Bairam in Qandahar as he proceeded to the Punjab. But he also required Bairam at his side, at the head of the army of conquest. Whatever the reasons, Munim Khan was left in Kabul to maintain the garrison and remained there for the next four years. This period saw Humayun's victories in Hindustan, his sudden death and the duration of Bairam Khan's regency. Munim Khan's position as a close confidant of Humayun enabled him to maintain a certain profile, although largely in absentia, even during Bairam Khan's regency, and towards its end he was to emerge as a key figure among the forces plotting Bairam's destruction.

The first major engagement between the Mughals and the Afghans took place in Machhiwara, not far from the present-day city of Ludhiana, in May 1555. The Mughals, although outnumbered, carried the day on account of the effective use of mounted archers. Machhiwara demonstrated to the Mughals that the reconquest of Hindustan was indeed a possibility. Bairam then marched from Machhiwara to Sirhind and the whole of the Punjab came into the possession of the Mughals. When the news of the victory of Machhiwara reached Humayun, Bairam was conferred the titles of

Khan-i-Khanan, Yar Wafadar (Faithful Friend), Hamdam Gham Ghusar (Sympathetic Intimate), Biradar Niku Siyar (Well-disposed Brother) and Farzand Saadatmand (Auspicious Son).

Sirhind was the site of an even larger engagement in June 1555. Bairam was reinforced here by the emperor himself as the Mughals faced Sikander Sur, the Afghan ruler of the Punjab, whose army reportedly consisted of 80,000 cavalry apart from artillery and elephants. The Mughals' mounted archers once again led them to a decisive victory. From Sirhind, Humayun proceeded to Delhi and, on 23 July 1555, he occupied the throne for a second time.

Some sources suggest that Humayun conferred the title of Khan-i-Khanan on Bairam after the victory at Sirhind and not after Machhiwara. In any event, it was after Sirhind that Humayun promised his niece, Salima Sultan Begum, to Bairam in marriage. An alliance with such a close relation of the emperor along with the title of Khan-i-Khanan elevated Bairam's standing enormously within the nobility.

During Bairam Khan's time in Delhi we come across another important milestone in his personal life. Humayun, seeking to establish stronger relations with the chieftains of the neighbourhood, married the elder daughter of Jamal Khan, brother of Hasan Khan of Mewat, described as one of the 'great zamindars' of India. Jamal Khan's younger daughter was married at the same time to Bairam Khan. As matrimonial alliances, these appear to be of no great significance and several contemporary chronicles first mention the Mewati princess only when she gives birth to Bairam Khan's son. No source even mentions her name and following our sources we too will deal with Mewat only when the son is older. Hasan Khan Mewati merits closer attention, though. He had once made common cause with Rana Sanga against Babur, despite the Mughal's best efforts to persuade him otherwise. Babur writes indignantly:

> After my conquest of Hind, following the examples of former Sultans, I also had shown Hasan Khan Mewati distinguished marks of favour. Yet this ungrateful man, whose sympathies lay on the side

> of the pagans, this infidel, regardless of my favours and without any sense of the kindness and distinctions with which he had been treated, was the grand promoter and leader of all the commotions and rebellions that ensued.[55]

Elsewhere Babur, evidently still smarting, describes him as a 'little heretic'.[56] Another account, a few years later, described Hasan Khan Mewati as 'an infidel who used the Kalimah'.[57] Bairam Khan's own assessment of Hasan Khan is far more respectful and even admiring, proclaiming publicly that he was a man 'who commanded a large following', 'of kingly appearance' and, perhaps the highest compliment possible, with a 'poetical temperament', whose 'poems are well known'. Bairam's admiration for the patriarch of his wife's family, certainly boded well for the marriage.

It is worth dwelling briefly here on the military and administrative arrangements Humayun made for those parts of north India that he controlled at the time. Hissar and its neighbourhood were assigned to the name of Akbar; Bairam Khan was given Sirhind, in addition to the nominal charge of Qandahar, Humayun's close friend and confidant Shah Abul Maali was given the governorship of the Punjab and Tardi Beg Khan was similarly appointed to Mewat. The latter was among the prominent nobles who had deserted Humayun during his flight through the Sindh. Rejoining Humayun in Kabul, his ascent was rapid, both in Kabul and during the conquest of Delhi, presumably because Humayun had to focus on consolidation and let bygones be bygones. Tardi Beg's return to Humayun's court after the recovery of Kabul thus follows a similar trajectory to that of Munim Khan.

Through the campaigns in the Punjab and despite the success in Machhiwara and Sirhind, the personal rivalry between Bairam Khan and Tardi Beg had come to the forefront and gradually become more visible and increasingly bitter. In the build up to the battle of Machhiwara, differences between them had already surfaced, ostensibly on account of different tactical preferences. On one occasion, prior to the battle of Machhiwara and following a skirmish near Jullundur,

> Tardi Beg wanted to go forward and catch the fleeing Afghans. Bairam did not think it prudent and refused to give him permission. Tardi Beg sent Baltu Khan to Bairam Khan to obtain permission on his behalf however he could. Baltu Khan delivered his message. Khwaja Muazzam Sultan acted rather coarsely and cursed him. Baltu Khan gave some rough replies. The Khwaja gave a blow with his sword that hit Baltu Khan on the hand.[58]

This incident required Humayun's personal intervention to bring about a reconciliation. Clearly, the jealous rivalry between Bairam Khan and Tardi Beg was out in the open by now and infecting both sets of followers. Another episode, again before Machhiwara, brings out the growing hostility between the two:

> When the Mughal army reached the vicinity of Machhiwara, Tardi Beg Khan considered it advisable not to cross the Sutlej but to halt till the rainy season was over. Bairam Khan who believed that halt and delay would only offer time and opportunity to the enemy could not approve of Tardi Beg's plan and decided on immediate advance … (and) crossed the river and prepared for the battle. Tardi Beg was therefore obliged to follow suit.[59]

In January 1556, a few months shortly after the victory at Sirhind, Humayun died suddenly and unexpectedly in Delhi. He slipped and fell down the steps of a structure he had adopted as his library while hurrying to respond to the call for prayers. He died leaving his empire in a state of flux and a son, Akbar, who was barely thirteen years old. The reconquest of India had begun but was by no means complete and while his successor was both identified and accepted as the heir, he was too young to govern. The forces against Mughal restoration were far from neutralized and were, in fact, rapidly regrouping to such an extent that a military setback at this stage could plausibly have led to a Mughal retreat to the Punjab, if not back to Kabul. The Mughal army recruited from Kabul had been formed for conquest; a military setback would have disastrous consequences for the mercenary element that formed a significant part of it.

The news of Humayun's death reached Akbar and Bairam in the Punjab near Gurdaspur. In November 1556 Bairam had been appointed governor of the Punjab in place of Abul Maali. Simultaneously, he was appointed as ataliq of Akbar. When the sudden death of the emperor threatened to splinter the entire framework of the Mughal restoration, Bairam acted with energy and decisiveness. He concealed the news of Humayun's death until he could ensure that the announcement of the succession and Akbar's coronation could be carried out, simply but in good order, near Gurdaspur at Kalanaur. The simple platform erected for the coronation ceremony still stands.

In this fragile situation, Bairam was appointed 'Vakil-i-Saltanat' and he remained for the next four years the central personage of Mughal India. Maintaining control over the higher nobility on one hand and attending to the military situation on the other were obvious priorities, and Bairam needed to act decisively on both fronts. The first person to encounter this resolve was the close intimate and favourite of Humayun, Shah Abul Maali, whom Bairam had replaced as governor of the Punjab. It was this noble whom Bairam, while in Qandahar, had found it expedient to assiduously court with flattery and verse. But now that Humayun was dead, Abul Maali's air of overweening vanity, born of his intimacy with the emperor, became an irritant.

Bairam invited Abul Maali to attend an assembly of nobles immediately after the coronation, at which the young emperor would be present. Shah Abul Maali first refused to attend and then, 'the self-conceited fool made excuses, which were worse than his offence, and among them were that he had not left off mourning for Humayun and supposing that he came, how would HM the Shahinshah [i.e., Akbar] behave to him, and where would he sit in the assembly and how would the officers come forward to receive him'.[60] Bairam enticed him into attending with various promises and concessions and then, at the assembly, in full public gaze, had him overpowered and seized.

Shah Maali's real culpability was clearly that he did not recognize the status of the boy emperor. His seizure in full court after he had been seated to the emperor's right was evidently designed to send a message to other refractory nobles. The significance of this episode was recorded for posterity, later in Akbar's reign, in a painting that conveys the dramatic force of the event (Plate III).[61] It portrays Bairam dominating the centre of the court as a hapless Shah Maali is surprised from behind and his supporters outnumbered and overwhelmed, to the consternation of the other courtiers.

Shah Abul Maali's arrest removed him as a potential troublemaker in the post-Humayun court. Bairam had favoured execution, but Akbar demurred. These developments clearly show Bairam's inclination to act decisively, even ruthlessly, against any opposition within the nobility. The uncertain military situation and the real fear of potential disarray, his position as vakil and Akbar's minority, created circumstances in which Bairam had to rapidly evaluate the threats to the position of the Mughals in India; from there it was a small step – and one common to all strongmen – to the conviction that any rival of his was, in fact, a threat to the entire process of Mughal restoration. We get a sense of the prominent position that Bairam assumes at this time from a painting depicting the young boy emperor out hunting. Bairam dominates the entire foreground and a servant obsequiously stands behind him, waving a fly whisk, even as the young emperor takes aim at his prey (see the front cover).[62]

For a period of some ten months following the coronation of Akbar in February 1556, the Punjab and the rest of north India witnessed a largely uncertain calm as the former Afghan ruler of the Punjab, Sikander Sur, attempted to put together an army of

Afghans and others, while the Mughals sought to consolidate their military gains. What altered this position was the rapid – and perhaps unexpected – progress of a new politico-military force against the Mughal restoration: Hemu. It is evident that this former trader was a man of formidable organizational ability and political sense. In the vacuum after the death of Islam Shah, he became a key player in the Afghan Sultanate, in the service of Islam Shah's formal successor, Mohammad Adil. At the time of the Mughals' initial victories in the Punjab, he was in eastern India, preoccupied with the challenges of intra-Afghan strife. But the threat of an impending Mughal consolidation in northern India and the possibilities opened up by Humayun's unexpected death motivated him to occupy Agra, driving out the Mughal governor with ease. He turned thereafter to Delhi and, in October 1556, led his army against the Mughals at Tughlaqabad. In the engagement that followed, Tardi Beg, governor of Delhi, was defeated and fled the battlefield, joining up in Sirhind with the main Mughal force marching to Delhi.

It was at this juncture, on 25 October, that one of the most dramatic episodes of Bairam Khan's regency was enacted. Tardi Beg was invited to Bairam's quarters and while Bairam excused himself for a few minutes, he was executed by Bairam's servants. This was a momentous act and its significance was not lost on contemporaries and later commentators alike. The message was obvious to all.

Tardi Beg was one of the most prominent nobles of his time. If Bairam as regent had only recently become first among the nobles, Tardi Beg had been a noble of some importance as far back as in Babur's reign. In the battles of Panipat and Khanwah, he had held an important command in Babur's army. He is said to have been part of a select group summoned by the dying emperor when he nominated Humayun as his successor and he was the one who brought the news of Akbar's birth to Humayun. He was made governor of Champaner, a position of importance to the Mughals, after Humayun's early triumph in Gujarat against Sultan Bahadur Shah. Some blamed Tardi Beg for the subsequent loss of Gujarat, but for our narrative, the point to underscore is Tardi Beg's stature from a time when Bairam Khan was relatively, if not entirely, unknown in the Mughal order of precedence. During Humayun's exile and flight, Tardi Beg's role was less distinguished and his selfishness and disloyalty were well known, including the time when he refused to give up his horse for the pregnant empress.[63] He deserted Humayun for Kamran and Askari and rejoined him only after he had reoccupied Qandahar with his Persian army. But the very fact of his presence at all the major milestones of early Mughal history in India serves to underscore the enormity of his summary execution by Bairam.

Contemporary and later chronicles were to engage repeatedly with this controversy, and clearly recognized it as an event of tremendous significance. Certainly, it provides a sense of the conjunction that Bairam and the Mughals found themselves in. The first set of questions pertains to Akbar's role: Was he consulted or did Bairam act on his own? Was Tardi Beg guilty of incompetence or of actual treachery? Finally, what were Bairam's motives in acting thus? [64]

Two contemporary accounts differ radically. One is provided by Bayazid, then in Kabul, who attributes the execution to Bairam's jealousy: in this view Bairam used the fact of Tardi Beg's defeat in Delhi as a reason to remove him. However, Bayazid was in Kabul at a time when Munim Khan, no great friend of Bairam, was the governor. What gives his view some weight is that Bairam went to great lengths to conceal the news of Tardi Beg's execution from Munim Khan and other nobles in Kabul. The news was, in fact, sent to Munim Khan personally by Bairam, but only after the Mughal victory at Panipat. Munim Khan then gave up the idea of joining the Mughal court, reflecting the fear and insecurity of the nobles in Kabul at Bairam Khan's ascendancy.

The other contemporary, Arif Qandahari, was closer to the scene of action. His view was that Tardi Bag's negligence in the battle of Delhi was discussed and investigated by the nobles and the execution was ordered thereafter. The execution was, according to this account, specifically advised by another prominent noble, Pir

Muhammad Khan Shirwani. Arif Qandahari was, however, one of those close to Bairam and served as his steward. Pir Muhammad Shirwani was, and remained till Bairam's own future darkened, one of the regent's main loyalists in the Mughal court.

Later chronicles, by and large, veer towards absolving Tardi Beg of wilful negligence or treachery and attribute the defeat to the superior force and tactics of the enemy. They point out that Akbar had no prior knowledge of the execution and was not, therefore, part of the group that held Tardi Beg to be a traitor and supported the killing. The balance of the evidence, therefore, indicates that Bairam's actions were probably activated by jealousy and the desire to eliminate a rival. This is given weight by Munim Khan's reaction to news of the execution. He abandoned the 'idea of proceeding to Hindustan presumably because he was apprehensive that he might also meet the same fate of Tardi Khan'.[65]

There are other factors that shed light on the roots of this jealousy: Bairam Khan was a Shia and Tardi Beg a Sunni;[66] the latter was among the more prominent of the Turani or Central Asian nobles. Bairam, on the other hand, would have been at the head of the Persian faction which, while strengthened by the Persian role in the Mughal restoration, was still regarded in some circles as somewhat arriviste.[67] Older rivalries and ill feeling existed too, and in the latest Mughal expedition there had been run-ins between the two nobles prior to the battle of Machhiwara. A contemporary traced the enmity back to a clash of egos and personalities in the early part of Humayun's first tenure. 'During the reign of Humayun, Bairam Khan was merely Bairam Beg and his [Humayun's] muhrdar [seal bearer]. One day he wanted to sit on the same carpet with Tardi Beg Khan, then Governor of Etawah, which the latter disallowed.'[68] Bairam Khan's stature in Humayun's court had grown since the Persian refuge of the emperor and no doubt, in his changed circumstances, his personality too would have changed, and old slights rankled even more. A contemporary opinion about him somewhat tartly said that he was 'touchy on the matter of precedence'.

If in this complex web of political rivalry, personal jealousy and ruthless jostling for advantage we find the motives for Tardi Beg's execution, the fact remains that any concern it generated was behind the scenes and muted. Bairam was able to convince Akbar that the execution was an inescapable necessity by pointing to the embattled position of the Mughals; the Mughal nobility, he argued, needed to be cemented together by force.

The broad chronology of events gives us some indication of the precise circumstances. Tardi Beg was defeated in Tughlaqabad on 7 October 1556. News of this reached the royal camp, then in Jullundhur, almost a week later, on 13 October. Many nobles apparently counselled a retreat to Kabul, a course of action rejected by the regent. Bairam and Akbar marched towards Delhi and, during a halt at Sirhind on 23 October, were joined by Tardi Beg and the remnants of his defeated force. It was here that Tardi Beg was put to death. Thereafter the march continued up to Panipat and the two opposing armies halted in its environs. Three days before the battle commenced, we hear of a magnificent feast being organized by Bairam, in which honours and promises of future royal favour were generously distributed. Bairam made a brief speech to underscore the importance of the coming engagement: 'This is the commencement of His Majesty's reign. This infidel has routed the whole royal army, and is now making preparations against us. If you do your best in this business with one heart and soul, Hindustan is yours. I place my trust in God. If we fail in this, you, whose homes are at a distance of about one thousand miles, will not be able to find an asylum.'[69]

Between the defeat at Tughlaqabad and the battle of Panipat was a period of less than a month and a distance of about 300 km. In the two or three weeks after the court received news of Hemu's victory and the final battle, the fate of the Mughals in India hung in the balance as they marched further and further south, away from the relative safety of Kabul towards a battle whose outcome was at best uncertain.

The armies met on the battlefield on 5 November 1556. Estimates of the strength of the two armies vary widely, but a general consensus is that the Mughals were outnumbered in terms of cavalry and war elephants. A chance arrow in Hemu's eye appears to have decided the outcome. But there were other factors too, including better Mughal generalship. A Mughal advance guard captured Hemu's artillery before the commencement of the battle. The Mughals used their mounted archers to good effect against the flanks of the attacking elephants.[70] A rout followed, and the severely wounded Hemu was captured and produced before Bairam and Akbar. He was executed after both Akbar and Bairam struck him with their swords. Whether this was symbolic or otherwise remains unclear; in the eyes of contemporaries and later chroniclers, the victory was a landmark in Mughal history

The outcome of the battle of Panipat conclusively established the military supremacy of the Mughals, although the consolidation was still to come. The Afghans became a more distant threat and the forces represented by Hemu suffered an equally comprehensive setback. Bairam Khan's contribution to the restoration of Mughal fortunes was also firmly established.

Between Panipat in November 1556 and the end of 1557 we find Bairam engrossed in the affairs of the Punjab, looking to contain the regrouping of Afghan forces under Sikander Sur. In an attempt to recover from the defeat at Sirhind, Sikander moved into the Siwalik Hills and finally entrenched himself within a strong chain of mountain fortresses at Mankot. The Mughal siege of Mankot lasted over six months until Sikander finally surrendered. The surrender represents the final blow to Afghan ambitions in India at the time, yet the court, instead of proceeding in triumph to Delhi, remained in the Punjab for four months more. During this period Bairam and Akbar were in Lahore dealing with, among other issues, an uprising by Baluch tribesmen in Multan. The departure to Delhi did not take place until December 1557 and they arrived in April 1558, well over a year after the battle of Panipat.

If the victory at Panipat was a personal triumph for Bairam Khan, two other significant personal milestones were recorded in this period. The first was the birth of his son, the future Abdur Rahim Khan-i-Khanan, by his wife, the Mewati princess, in December 1556. The second, also personal, but of great political significance, was Bairam Khan's marriage to Babur's granddaughter, Salima Sultan Begum, in December 1557.

Yet Bairam's position was not wholly secure. The period between Panipat and the return to Delhi in April 1558 was one of intense rivalry between him and the sections of the nobility that were opposed to him. The execution of Tardi Beg Khan had enabled Bairam to establish something akin to a chain of command, invaluable in ensuring victory at Panipat; these strong measures were accepted by the other nobles as unavoidable. After Panipat, once the reconquest was more assured, however, Bairam's control over the imperial camp and the person of the emperor may well have been questioned by the other nobles and by the harem, then still in Kabul. Munim Khan's anxieties about his position and his decision to postpone his departure for Hindustan have been referred to earlier, and it was perhaps at this stage that the first confabulations took place in Kabul about the means to undermine the power of the regent. While the details of the strategy may not have been fully decided, the fact that the regent could not be left to expand his powers unhindered was a conclusion reached within the harem while still in Kabul.

One of its first moves was an alliance between Akbar and a granddaughter of Munim Khan. This took place soon after his mother, Hamida Banu Begum, and the rest of the harem joined the imperial camp at Mankot. The marriage was arranged despite Bairam's opposition, but the arrival of the harem marked a new equation. In Akbar's immediate circle were two close advisors and near guardians. The first of these was Maham Anga. She had been Akbar's wet nurse and came from a family that traced itself back to Babur's earliest days in

Kabul, if not earlier. She was a woman of great strength and ambition. Equally important was Shamsuddin Muhammad Khan Atka (also known as Atka Khan), whose wife was also a wet nurse of Akbar. He acted as guardian to Akbar as a child and since then had become his closest advisor. With the arrival of the harem the strain between the regent and the circle surrounding the emperor became inevitable.[71]

A dramatic incident towards the end of the siege of Mankot reveals the intensity of the subterranean conflict within the court. The *Akbarnama* describes the situation graphically:

> During the last days of the siege of Mankot, KhanKhan fell ill. Some boils formed which prevented him from mounting a horse. During that time H. M., the Shahinshah turned his attention, as a means of diversion, to elephant fights. Many times did he apply himself to this sport ... One day there was a prolonged contest between two of the royal elephants ... By chance these two elephants during their fight came nearer to [Bairam's] tent. The crowd of the people and the general uproar caused apprehension and annoyance to Bairam Khan, and he came to suspect that perhaps the thing had occurred at the sublime suggestion [of Akbar]. He was confirmed in this suspicion by some strife mongers. He sent one of his confidential servants to Maham Anga with this message. 'I am not conscious of having committed any offence ... and I have not displayed anything except well-wishing respect. Why then have mischief makers imputed some mischief to me and caused such unkindness as that furious elephants should have been let loose against my tent?' Maham Anga by soothing expressions quieted his disturbed mind.[72]

Abul Fazl, the author of the *Akbarnama*, was clearly of the view that this incident was an accident. The principal chronicle of Akbar's reign, the *Akbarnama* is a detailed record of the emperor, his premier nobles and of the important events of the time. It is, of course, full of hyperbole and accords Akbar a near divine status. *Akbarnama* had the blessing of the emperor often speaks on his behalf, but that does not preclude Abul Fazl's own preferences and dislikes from occasionally making their presence felt. Bairam Khan himself appears to have been convinced that the incident described above was an attempt to assassinate him, believing Maham Anga and Shamsuddin Atka to be responsible. Given subsequent developments in which the two were at the core of the conspiracy to destroy Bairam, these suspicions may not have been unfounded. After this incident Bairam ensured that his own trusted followers had charge of the royal elephants; the transfer of Atka Khan to a distant outpost is also suggestive of the intensity of Bairam's suspicions and fears.

The assassination attempt apart, the most important event of this period was the marriage of Bairam Khan to Salima Sultan Begum, Humayun's half-sister and Babur's granddaughter. The wedding took place sometime around December 1557 and its timing was significant. The Mughal court clearly felt that the immediate threats to their position in Hindustan had been neutralized: Humayun had, while betrothing Salima Sultan to Bairam after the victory at Sirhind, said that the marriage would take place after the conquest of Hindustan and the recovery of his throne was complete. Secondly, the wedding took place in the aftermath of what Bairam believed was a conspiracy to assassinate him, and that the principal conspirators were in Akbar's immediate circle. The *Akbarnama* describes Maham Anga, in particular, as displaying great enthusiasm in promoting the marriage, which was not only a reassertion of Bairam's position with regard to the other nobles, but actually enhanced his position.

It was also the subject of much contemporary comment. Later in Akbar's reign, Abul Fazl in particular made no bones about his disapproval. Humayun is described in the *Akbarnama* as having suggested the marriage because of past matrimonial relations between Bairam and Babur's ancestors. Abul Fazl was clearly annoyed that these century-old relationships were allowed to intrude into the present and give legitimacy to what he felt was a most unsuitable alliance: Bairam marrying a princess from the imperial family itself. Referring to the past kinship connections between Bairam's family and the Timurids, he exclaimed: 'Good God! What an imitative world it is!'[73] Clearly such a comment would not have been made by the emperor's authorized biographer unless it reflected the view of the adult Akbar. At the time of the marriage of Salima Sultan to Bairam, the boy emperor was about fourteen, old enough to have formed a view on the marriage based on the views he heard, but too young to prevent an alliance promised by his father to a powerful noble who was now also regent.

After Bairam's death, Akbar married his widow and Salima Sultan Begum thereby entered the royal circle. Paradoxically, this increased rather than lessened the mysteries surrounding her. According to the *Jahangirnama*, the memoirs of Akbar's son, Salima Sultan Begum died in December 1612 at the age of sixty. If this is correct, at the time of her marriage in December 1557 she would have been five years old. Bairam was then at least in his late fifties. Even given the fact that this was a time when matrimonial alliances were often dictated by political considerations, the age difference is considerable. In the early twentieth century, this matter certainly excited the curiosity of the English historian couple, H. Beveridge and Annette Beveridge. The latter hinted that Jahangir may have deliberately suggested Salima Sultan Begum was younger than she actually was in order to maintain the fiction that his father had married a virgin. This, Annette Beveridge felt, was Jahangir's attempt to bring Salima Sultan Begum 'into the circle of Hindu propriety', because he was, as she observed, 'a Hindu mother's son'. She notes, in particular, the observation of a nineteenth-century popularizer of Mughal history, Muhammad Husain Azad, that Salima Sultan Begum was married to Bairam at five 'and that her memory is thus cleared from the reproach of two marriages'.[74] H. Beveridge was to largely confirm his wife's conclusions that Jahangir had deliberately obscured his stepmother's age by quoting a note in the *Jahangirnama* which stated that Salima Sultan Begum had died at the age of seventy-six, in which case she was about nineteen at the time of her marriage to Bairam Khan.[75]

Bairam's marriage to Salima Sultan marked the close of one phase in his role in the reconquest of Hindustan. If the alliance enhanced Bairam's position by symbolically reiterating his own lineage and connections with the Timurids, its timing was such that it appears to have been a means to placate him when opposition to his pre-eminence was becoming apparent. The marriage to Salima Sultan reflects also the recognition that some workable arrangement had to be found to ensure smooth functioning within and outside the court.[76] Bairam, on his part, reassured the senior nobles that he would consult them before putting forward any proposals to the emperor.

Most narratives of Bairam Khan's regency in the period after Panipat see the principal thread as being the constant jostling between the regent and factions of the nobility opposed to him. There were, of course, many other significant events during this period, though they have less dramatic value. The regent turned his attention to securing the outer environs of Delhi since the Punjab was now secure. Expeditions were mounted against the fortress garrisons of Gwalior and Ranthambore, and Afghan rearguard actions in Jaunpur and Malwa were defeated. Also of note was the repossession of Qandahar by the Persians. A local conflict between Bairam Khan's nominee at Qandahar and the Mughal governor provided the Persians with the opportunity to occupy Qandahar. The Mughals were too preoccupied with the affairs of Hindustan to intervene effectively.

These events appear tangential since the main action was unfolding within the court itself. The young Akbar, surrounded by family and Timurid nobility, and increasingly resentful of an overbearing Turkmen regent, was now growing into a young man. Instances of the young emperor chafing at Bairam's high-handedness multiplied and the court was quick to perceive this. In 1558 a noble, Musahib Beg, himself of distinguished lineage, '... unmindful of the obligations he owed to Bairam Khan, began to treat him with disrespect, till at length he fell a victim to his misconduct and was put to death by order of the Protector.'[77]

This incident caused great offence not only to the nobles, but also to the emperor. It was still fresh in everyone's mind when an even more acrimonious dispute arose between Bairam Khan and Pir Mohammad Shirwani. Pir Mohammad Shirwani had entered Bairam's service in Qandahar and his subsequent rise in the court owed much to Bairam's patronage. He was Bairam's accomplice in the assassination of Tardi Beg and Musahib Beg. Pir Muhammad had gradually emerged, therefore, as Bairam's right-hand man and in that capacity was the regent's principal interlocutor with the harem and the rest of the nobility. Pir Muhammad used this position to ingratiate himself with the emperor and, in the process, became powerful enough for the harem and the nobility to see him as a check to Bairam himself. The regent was not one to accept the emergence of potential rivals easily and Pir Muhammad's arrogance and accumulation of wealth further aggravated the situation.

As elsewhere in Bairam's career, a single episode illustrates the barely contained tension among the parties. In late 1558 'Pir Muhammad Khan was indisposed for some days, and the Regent came to visit. One of the servants, who was in the habit of keeping off people, both great and small, came to stop him and said: "Be pleased to wait until your request has been made known, when you have made application you may come in"; on this the astonishment of the KhanKhanan knew no bounds and he said: "For a wilful fool there is no cure." When this came to the ears of Pir Muhammad Khan, ill as he was, he came running and begged forgiveness, saying, "Forgive me, for my porter did not know you." The KhanKhanan answered: "Nor you either".'[78] Another source describes the Khan-i-Khanan as retorting, 'In what way have you recognized me (i.e., accorded me my due respect) that they would do (so as well)?'[79] Pir Muhammad was dismissed, imprisoned and finally exiled. All this was done, as in the case of Tardi Beg's execution, without the prior approval of the emperor.[80] Akbar was enraged, but Bairam Khan managed, his detractors said, to divert him with a proposed invasion of Gwalior. Nonetheless, the dismissal of Pir Muhammad was a virtual coup by the regent and marked the breakdown of the pragmatic, if sometimes uncertain, working relationship between him and the nobles.[81]

Matters unravelled swiftly. Sheikh Gadai, a close confidant of Bairam who had helped him in Gujarat during the days of Mughal defeat and exile, reappeared and was appointed Sadr or chief judge by the regent. Sheikh Gadai was the son of a highly respected divine, Sheikh Jamali, who had been of considerable importance in the closing years of the Lodi dynasty and during Humayun's first reign in India. He lies buried in a tomb-cum-mosque complex that remains a landmark to this day, in the Delhi suburb of Mehrauli. Sheikh Gadai's appointment caused much concern – he was a Shia and his rapid rise disturbed many equations. The nobility and the harem were further antagonized by a number of other sudden promotions and rewards to Bairam's followers, many of whom were given precedence and privileges which exceeded those of nobles of more established lineage. Instances of friction started increasing.

Around this time, a religious divine greatly revered at the time, Sheikh Muhammad Ghaus, came to Agra from Gujarat, and is believed to have been warmly received by the emperor and the noblewomen in the harem. The regent was asked to make suitable provisions for his establishment but

> Muhammad Ghaus, relying too much on his personal interest with the King, neglected to pay that attention to the minister which he always expected, and Bairam Khan made so many excuses and delays that Muhammad Ghaus found his stay at court disagreeable and quitting it, retired to his old family residence at Gwalior. The King was much vexed with Bairam Khan for his conduct on this occasion; and he, observing a visible alteration in Akbar's manner towards him, proposed an expedition against Baz Bahadur, ruler of Malwa.[82]

The suggested expedition against Malwa was similar to the launch of a campaign against Gwalior just after the Pir Muhammad episode. There are, of course, other rationales for both – Mughal control over Malwa and Gwalior was crucial for the stability of the Delhi–Agra region.

It is possible that Bairam's neglect of Muhammad Ghaus was on account of Sheikh Gadai's advice.[83] The latter is described as having been against Sheikh Ghaus on account of 'jealousy, hypocrisy, and envy' and having looked at the new arrival 'as a case of opening a shop in the storey above his own shop'. Evidently, many were beginning to feel that the regent was having to device military expeditions to keep the emperor occupied. We also find a growing campaign of ridicule and vilification against those close to Bairam Khan. One such instance is a graffiti in the form of a verse written on the walls of Sheikh Gadai's house, which punned on his name (Gada means beggar):

> Mention not Gadai's name, eat not his bread
> Since beggary is bad, Gadai's face is black.[84]

Wali Beg, a relation of Bairam Khan, described as his sister's husband, was similarly given rapid promotions although he was regarded as being a recent arrival.[85] Wali Beg's sons were also promoted. Haji Muhammad Sistani, widely regarded as a Bairam Khan favourite, was appointed vakil after the dismissal of Pir Mohammad and the comment made about him was: 'A dog has assumed the status of a sweet seller'.[86]

One more episode stands out in the final months of Bairam Khan's regency. The story went around that Bairam had purchased a poem from the poet Hashim Qandahari and, reordering its verses, claimed it as his own. While this may have been acceptable to many contemporaries as a form of 'dakhliya', insertion, the charge was a source of great indignation to subsequent admirers of Bairam Khan. Kausar Chandpuri, a biographer writing in the 1930s, absolved Bairam of the charge of wilfully passing off another poet's work as his own but conceded there was some truth to the story. Chandpuri believed there was something in the poem that appealed to Bairam and it may well have been a premonition of things to come.[87] That such a controversy arose about the authorship of a poem reflects also the undercurrents of court politics and suggests that the balance was tilting away from Bairam. His appreciation of these verses would certainly suggest to others at the time that even Bairam knew that things were changing.

> What am I? One who has let go of the rein of his heart.
> Who by the hand of his heart has fallen from his feet upon the road
> of trouble;
> Who is become like a madman in the skirts of the mountains;
> Who has without will of his turned his head to the desert;
> At one time like a candle seized by the fire of his heart,
> At another, like the wick fallen into the heart of the fire.
> I, Bairam, am free from care for little or much
> Never have I uttered a single word less or more.[88]

At about this time, sometime in early 1560, two more incidents involving elephants occurred, which Bairam saw as attacks – the first on his dignity, and the second, perhaps, on his life. The *Akbarnama* describes them vividly:

> Of the improper acts which were done by Bairam Khan in consequence of bad company … was the putting to death of the Shahinshah's own elephant driver. The succinct account of this warning-giving occurrence is as follows: The royal elephant became *mast* (rogue) and beyond the control of the driver and attacked one of Bairam Khan's elephants. It struck the other elephant so severely that the entrails came out. Bairam Khan was so enraged that he put the driver to death …
>
> … then one day, one of the Shahinshah's private elephants got *mast* and rushed into the Jamuna. Bairam Khan was taking the air in a boat and the elephant which had got out of hand proceeded towards the boat. The KhanKhanan was much alarmed; but at last the driver contrived to master the elephant and Bairam was saved

> from the animal's attack. When this incident was reported to HM the Shahinshah he, in order to soothe Bairam Khan had the elephant driver bound and sent to him although he was innocent. The Khan ... put him to death ...[89]

This was clearly an intolerable breach of royal privilege and appeared to have been seen as a personal affront to Akbar, who was very fond of his elephants. The estrangement between the regent and the emperor's inner circle was now complete. What remained was the unfolding of the plot and its final execution that ended the regency of Bairam Khan.

The principal moves that ended Bairam Khan's regency are well documented. Akbar left Agra on 19 March 1560, apparently proceeding on one of his hunting trips. He moved swiftly thereafter to Delhi on the pretext of meeting his mother and entered the city on 27 March. Once in Delhi, other nobles were summoned, notably Munim Khan from Kabul and Shamsuddin Muhammad Atka Khan from Bhera in the Punjab. Bairam realized the gravity of the situation and sent envoys, begging the emperor's pardon and assuring him of loyal service. Akbar had the envoys detained. The news of these developments spread swiftly and a large number of nobles, reading the writing on the wall, started leaving Agra and congregating in Delhi.

Bairam's request that he be permitted to present himself in person to the emperor was turned down. Letters passed between Bairam and the emperor: the former pleading his loyalty, the latter unyielding, evidently determined to end the regency. Bairam reconciled himself to the inevitable. A strong regent had been seen as an inescapable necessity after Humayun's death and just before the battle of Panipat, when the new emperor was still barely out of childhood. But the emperor was now nearly eighteen years old and prepared to assert his authority; moreover, the imminent danger to the Mughals had passed. The balance of influence had permanently turned against the regent in the court.

There is at least one account which gave to the growing differences between regent and emperor a religious and ideological dimension. Aziz Ahmed, in the mid-twentieth century, wrote what is often regarded as a classic study of Islam in South Asia. Written when the reverberations of the partition of the subcontinent were still strong, it described Akbar thus as a young teenager:

> A natural lack of prejudice against the Hindus, even a liking for them seems to have been one of the unusual features of his youth, and one of the earliest records of it is a Turkish *gazal* by Bairam Khan, written obviously before 1560, in which the veteran statesman reproaches Akbar for giving preferences to Hindus over Muslims as if he were a Hindu himself.[90]

This verse is included in the published collection of Bairam Khan's verses.

> Muslims and Hindus, both wait at your door
> Desirous of your jagirs
> But the Muslims grieve and are full of sorrow
> You encourage them to marry Hindu women
> This is not Islamic.[91]

If accurate, this would certainly depict another aspect of Bairam's personality. But was he reproaching Akbar for his excessively liberal behaviour towards Hindus? Or is it that Bairam, recognizing the growing gulf between himself and the emperor and a large section of the nobility, was using every means possible to salvage his position, even invoking the sectarian sympathies of some nobles? It is also possible that the ghazal is not entirely authentic. Aziz Ahmed himself notes that it dates to before 1560 – Bairam was assassinated in January 1561. But this was still sometime before Akbar had embarked on the Rajput alliance or exhibited any signs of religious eclecticism or liberalism, which was to become the hallmark of his age. A more likely explanation is that the ghazal is a later inclusion in the corpus of Bairam's verse. Bairam's diwan was collected in different stages by the efforts of his son, Abdur Rahim. The most comprehensive collection was compiled under the supervision of Abdur Rahim's librarian and panegyrist, Abul Baqi Nihavandi, around 1615. It is possible that in the aftermath of Akbar's reign, as more orthodox currents came to the surface, it was deemed politic to have such a verse in the diwan, if for no other reason than to bolster Bairam's posthumous reputation as an early dissenter from – what was regarded as – Akbar's excessive liberalism.

But to return to our story: Bairam was left with no option but to reconcile himself to the inevitable. He gave leave to his followers to join the emperor and decided to proceed for the Haj. Most of his followers had started leaving his camp without seeking permission. In April 1560 we find him leaving Agra and proceeding to Alwar, apparently on the first stage of the journey to the Haj. By all accounts, he was only accompanied by a small entourage, Sheikh Gadai being one of the most prominent. Some relatives were present too – in particular, Wali Beg and his sons, Hussain Quli Beg and Ismail Quli Beg.

Bairam's departure from Agra was presented to the emperor as a rebellious act and a prelude to his intended conquest of the Punjab. Although rebellion was not his motive, news that Pir Muhammad Khan Shirwani – former follower and turncoat – had been appointed as the head of a force to pursue him annoyed Bairam greatly. His attitude of resignation changed to defiance. If the defiance was not directed against the emperor himself, he was certainly determined to act against his enemies who, he believed, now controlled Akbar. We find him turning towards Firozpur in the Punjab. This may have appeared as further proof of Bairam's rebellious intentions to the emperor's camp, but it is interesting to find correspondence continuing between the emperor and the former regent. A letter from Bairam pleads his loyalty and his intention of going to Mecca, but equally carries a clear hint of admonition, if not, truculence. Akbar was to respond with an instruction to him to halt and send to court those of his followers who were inciting him to rebellion. Bairam disregarded this and continued deeper into the Punjab. The stage for a military confrontation was now set and Akbar appointed Shamsuddin Muhammad Atka Khan, Bairam's old adversary, to the position of commander of the army which would face Bairam Khan.

The outcome of the battle in August 1560 was a foregone conclusion – Bairam's small force was routed, many of his followers taken prisoner, and he himself was forced to flee into the Siwalik Hills, taking refuge with a local Hindu ruler, Raja Ganesh of Talwara. The imperial forces in pursuit were joined by the emperor himself, accompanied by Munim Khan. The latter, on arrival from Kabul, had been appointed vakil and given Bairam's title of Khan-i-Khanan. In one of the skirmishes between local Hindu zamindars and the imperial troops, the son of one of Humayun's old followers in the imperial force was killed. News of this was presented to Bairam as a triumph, but it apparently convinced him of the futility of further resistance. He is recorded as having wept on hearing of the death: 'This life of mine is not worth so much that such a man should be killed for my cause.'[92] He then sent a message to Munim Khan, which was relayed to Akbar.

> I have taken refuge with the infidels urged by necessity. If you come and, seizing my hands take me out of the hills, I shall go with you. When to my misfortune, a man like Sultan Hussain had been killed yesterday, how can I approve such unnecessary strife. If His Majesty and the nobles desire for a spoonful of my blood, I shall give a bucketful.[93]

Bairam also insisted that Munim Khan personally escort him – evidently he feared for his life. This too was agreed to. Bairam was presented in court in October 1560. The poignancy of the occasion is captured in the following description:

> … (in) Muharram (of) 968, he flung a handkerchief round his neck and made the prostration of shame and contrition. He laid his dust strown [sic] head at the sphere traversing feet of His Majesty, the Shahinshah, partly with pain, partly with shame for his crimes, and partly with joy at his pardon and wept aloud. His Majesty accepted his excuses, and with his sacred hand raised Bairam Khan's head from the ground of humiliation and embraced him. He took the cloth from his neck and wiped from his face the tears of penitence and the dust of shame. With his gracious lips he enquired about his health and bade him sit on his right hand, as had been the rule when Bairam Khan was Vakil. He bade Munim Khan to sit down beside him while the other officers took their places according to their rank. With his gracious lips he uttered such words of kindness and favour, that the dust of bashfulness and the mist of shame disappeared from his brow. Yet the word remains: *Though the crime be forgiven, shame abideth.*[94]

Akbar gave permission to Bairam to proceed on the Haj. This was the compromise arranged earlier and was possibly the only graceful way out for all the parties concerned.

Bairam left the Punjab and proceeded towards Gujarat en route to the Haj. In January 1561 he halted at Patan. There, on the last day of the month, he went to the lakeside and spent some time in the pavilion at the centre of the Sahasralinga Talav. Perhaps, as he sat there in the approaching twilight, he reflected on the twists and turns of his extraordinary life. On his return to the shore he was murdered by an Afghan whose father had been killed in the battle of Machhiwara by forces Bairam commanded. There is no evidence at all that the murder had anything to do with the court and none consider that Akbar was in any way responsible. Remains of the lake and the pavilion still stand, as does a structure believed to have been the initial burial place of Bairam Khan. His young son, Abdur Rahim, was in Patan with him and the end of the father's story is the beginning of his.

2

THE YOUNG NOBLE

ABDUR RAHIM was five years old at the time of his father's assassination. We do not know for certain if he was a witness to the murder. A boat ride is a fairly obvious treat for a child and it is not unlikely that he would have accompanied his father. But that he came to no harm means that he was not present. Also, the miniature illustrating Bairam Khan's assassination does not show a child. It is possible that the attack took place not far from Bairam's camp, since some sources speak of his possessions being plundered after the murder. If Abdur Rahim did not go to the lake with his father, he would have been in the camp and a witness to the plunder.

A contemporary chronicle informs us that 'the horror of the murder produced great affliction among the people of the deceased'.[1] Three of Bairam Khan's servants had to fight their way to Ahmedabad as Abdur Rahim, his mother and possibly others in the party were taken there for safety. The intensity of those moments is captured in a painting that shows the party fleeing from Patan to Ahmedabad (Plate IV).[2] They are clearly in desperate haste, the child closely guarded, the backward glances of his protectors betraying the very real fear of pursuit.

They remained in Ahmedabad for some four months, then began the long journey to the court. News of Bairam Khan's assassination had reached Akbar, who immediately ordered that the child be brought to him. The order reached the dispirited little party in Ahmedabad 'at the time of friendlessness and orphanage and was healing for broken hopes'. In court, all sources declare unanimously, Akbar's treatment of the child was exemplary and presaged the strong emotional attachment that was to develop between the two. At the very first meeting, 'HM the Shahinshah, in spite of evil speakers and evil thinkers, received that child of lustrous forehead, in the lines of whose brow there were the notes of nobleness and truth, with inborn kindness, and reared him in the shadow of his own supervision.'[3]

Underlining the contemporary significance of this event and capturing the emotions and sentiments of those present is another painting depicting the presentation of the infant Abdur Rahim to the emperor (Plate V).[4]

Such a public demonstration of affection was equally a clear message to Bairam Khan's enemies – and there would have been many in the court – that their disputes with the late regent were not to be visited on the son. But Akbar's sentiments, and the favour he would continue to show to the boy and later the man, may also suggest a residual guilt at the manner of his regent's dismissal and departure from the court.

We know relatively little about Abdur Rahim's childhood and the decade of his life after his arrival in court. That he was well provided for and well educated is certain and, in the light of his subsequent literary achievements, it seems apparent that he was a boy who took his scholastic work seriously. Mulla Mohammad Andajani, one of the foremost teachers and scholars of the time, was his tutor and he would have ensured that Abdur Rahim received the kind of schooling given to the sons of premier nobles. Riding, wrestling, swordsmanship and military training would have been an integral part of his early education. Abdur Rahim grew up to be a well-regarded scholar of

Persian, Turkish and Arabic and would have owed this at least partly to the instruction he received as a child. Apart from these languages we can speculate that he had a Sanskrit tutor too. Acquiring some degree of expertise in these languages was by no means unusual in Akbar's court.

Even in those early years, the Rajput influence in court was growing. In 1562, when Abdur Rahim was about six, came the formal sealing of the Mughal–Rajput alliance with Akbar's marriage to the daughter of Raja Bihari Mal, the ruler of Amber. Man Singh, Bihari Mal's grandson, accompanied the bride and was to become a virtually permanent member of Akbar's court from this time; he certainly knew Abdur Rahim from the time of his childhood. We can speculate that Abdur Rahim spent some time with his maternal Mewati relations and would have had occasion to sharpen his knowledge of Hindustani in their presence. Exposure to the cultural traditions of Mewat may have had another kind of impact too.

Mewat was, through most of the period of the Delhi Sultanate and certainly up to the time of Babur, in frequent revolt against the rulers of Delhi. Hasan Khan Mewati had made common cause with Rana Sanga against Babur despite the Mughal's best efforts to persuade him otherwise.[5] The region of Mewat occupied a strategic triangle that had Agra, Delhi and Jaipur as its corners. Control over it was essential to guarantee security of the Delhi–Agra axis. It was this factor, more than any other, that led to Humayun and Bairam marrying the daughters of Jamal Khan Mewati, a brother of Hasan Khan. By the time of Akbar's reign, Mewat was well on its way to full submission to the Mughals and integration with their empire.

It is useful, however, to dwell on Babur's description of Hasan Khan Mewati as an infidel and 'one whose affections lay on the side of the pagans'. Such descriptions are frequently encountered in Mughal chronicles and were also used against fellow Muslims if they happened to be military or political opponents. Nevertheless, they also reflect modern ethnographic descriptions of Mewati Muslims who continued to follow, till well into the twentieth century, preconversion cultural practices. One nineteenth-century description says that 'as regards their own religion the Meos are very ignorant. Few know the kalima and fewer still the regular prayers'. [6] Other observers 'found it difficult to say whether they were Hindus or Muslims because their beliefs and practices drew upon both religions'. A nineteenth-century ethnographer wrote: 'the Meos are all now Musalmans in name; but their village deities are the same as those of Hindu Zamindars. They too keep several Hindu festivals.'[7] Even as late as the twentieth century, the Meos were known to celebrate Hindu festivals such as Holi, as well as Teej, Amavas, Sankrant, Janmashtami and Diwali.[8]

The syncretic foundations of this order were, of course, to be rapidly and fundamentally altered by new forces, beginning from the late nineteenth century and continuing to this day. Nevertheless, for our narrative, this background provides obvious points of interest as we contemplate the young Abdur Rahim, son of a Mewati princess, spending some part of his childhood with his maternal family and absorbing a variety of influences from and through them.

In Agra, Abdur Rahim would have been reminded of his patrimony, not only by his father's friends but also, no doubt, by his enemies. If the latter were kept at bay by the fact that the emperor had taken a personal interest in the child, the former would certainly have regaled him with details of Bairam Khan's achievements and his distinguished lineage. Bairam Khan's own family, however, was not one with a large clan following or members; Abdur Rahim had few he could call kin. One of them was Hussain Quli, the son of Wali Beg Zulqadar, who had accompanied Bairam on his final departure from the court. Hussain Quli had risen rapidly during Bairam Khan's regency and a near contemporary referred to him as one 'who had not even fought with a chicken' but was given precedence over established nobles.[9] Although arrested during the crisis surrounding the regency, he was released soon after, further evidence that Akbar was not personally hostile to Bairam's family.[10]

In the interregnum of a decade and a half between Bairam's death and Abdur Rahim's adulthood, Hussain Quli was the only member of Bairam's extended family who emerged as a noble of some prominence. In late 1562 or early 1563, he was appointed governor of Ajmer and in that capacity, he was responsible for attacks against the kingdom of Marwar. In 1567 he was in the army that attacked Chittor and he also fought in the battle against Rana Pratap Singh, the ruler of the Rajput kingdom of Mewar. He was then appointed to the important charge of the Punjab, a further sign of the emperor's lack of animosity to members of Bairam Khan's family. In 1573, Hussain Quli was granted, during a ceremonial visit to the court, the title of Khan-i-Jahan. We can imagine Abdur Rahim, then just seventeen years old, present on the occasion, no doubt an emotionally charged one for him and other members of Bairam Khan's family, friends and followers. The honour may well have been seen as partial compensation for past traumas.

It is probable that Abdur Rahim visited Hussain Quli during his tenure as governor in Ajmer and in the Punjab. Hussain Quli was then moved to Bengal where, according to some sources, he faced considerable difficulty in persuading Mughal officers under his command to join campaigns against the Afghans. The Chagtai or Central Asian nobles resented having a 'Qizlbash' or Persian at their head – a replay of the resentment that Bairam himself had faced.

In 1577, Hussain Quli arranged for the moving of Bairam Khan's remains from Delhi for reburial in Mashad in Persia; this had been Bairam's wish and he had bought land in Mashad in the vicinity of the tomb of the revered Shia divine, Imam Raza, for this purpose.[11] The remains of Bairam Khan had earlier – around 1567 or 1568 – been moved from Patan to Delhi by his old friend Sheikh Gadai, to be buried in Mehrauli in the immediate vicinity of the Jamali Kamali mosque. Sheikh Gadai was the son of Jamali, a well-known Sufi poet, and therefore would have had some claim on the mosque where his own father was buried. Abdur Rahim, then a teenager, would certainly have been present at the reburial of his father's mortal remains at the Jamali Kamali mosque.

Hussain Quli Khan died while still in Bengal in 1578.[12] Abul Fazl, while noting his death, observed that Hussain Quli had contemplated rebellion because of the huge booty he had collected in various campaigns. This, however, appears unlikely and the allegation perhaps had its origins in Abul Fazl's own bias against the family of Wali Beg Zulqadar. A modern historian has extended this logic further and suggested that it follows from Abul Fazl's assertions 'that the family of Bairam Khan was still under some cloud at the Mughal court'.[13] The fact of old enmities continuing and the possibility of treachery arising from such enmity cannot be entirely discounted. By 1578, however, at the time of Hussain Quli's death, Abdur Rahim was well established as a rising star in Akbar's court.

During Abdur Rahim's childhood, the first phase of Mughal expansion under Akbar had been completed: the conquest of Malwa in 1561, the siege of Chittor and the victory over Mewar (although the defeat of its defiant ruling dynasty was complete only some decades later, in the reign of Akbar's son), the conquest of Ranthambore a year later and success in Bengal in 1576. By the time of the latter, Abdur Rahim had himself participated in two important campaigns and was well on his way to a career that was distinguished not only by the emperor's continuing favour, but also by his own considerable military achievements.

The political and military career of Abdur Rahim began with Akbar's Gujarat campaign in 1572. Internecine conflicts within the nobility in Gujarat provided Akbar with the opportunity to annex this rich area known for its ports, prosperous agriculture, crafts and textiles. He embarked on an expedition in July 1572 and the sixteen-year-old Abdur Rahim was part of his entourage. One of the halts en route was the town of Patan, the place of Bairam's assassination and burial – although his grave had been shifted by then to Delhi. A moving account has survived of the emperor questioning Abdur Rahim on the details of Bairam Khan's assassination and promising him the jagir of Patan in memory of his father.[14]

Gujarat was in a state of civil war amongst contending groups of nobles. The head of one of these was Itimad Khan, who invited the Mughals to intervene in his favour. He soon found himself besieged in Ahmedabad by his opponents. Akbar's expedition was to relieve the siege and establish Mughal control over the province. News of the arrival of a large Mughal force headed by the emperor himself was sufficient for the siege to be lifted and Akbar's entry into Ahmedabad was easy, without any need for military engagement. He was to stay in Ahmedabad for some four months and return to Agra in June 1573. His return was as leisurely as his progress there – the entire expedition occupied a period of some eleven months. Abdur Rahim was with the Mughal force throughout this period.

The arrangements made by Akbar for the future governance of Gujarat included the appointment of a Mughal governor for the core of the region and the grant of the outlying regions to Itimad Khan. Mirza Aziz Koka, the emperor's foster-brother and one who will figure frequently in this story, who held the title of Khan-i-Azam, was appointed the subedar or governor of Ahmedabad. Itimad Khan held charge over the bulk of the province. This was a practical arrangement in that it left Ahmedabad in the control of a Mughal noble, while it was left to Itimad Khan to secure southern Gujarat for the Mughals. The arrangement broke down, however, almost as soon as Akbar returned to Agra. In June 1573, he received news of a fresh insurrection in Gujarat: not only had the rebels taken Broach, Cambay and Surat, but the Mughal garrison in Ahmedabad under Mirza Aziz Koka was itself under siege.

This was the background to what is arguably Akbar's most spectacular military feat: a rapid march from Agra to Ahmedabad on camel back with only a small group of followers. Even as Mirza Aziz Koka's dispatches painted a desperate situation, Akbar left Agra on 23 August 1573 and in a matter of just nine days reached the outskirts of Ahmedabad – a distance of some 800 kilometres. Barely a year before, the Mughal force had taken over four months for the same journey. But this time the emperor was travelling light; the purpose was not only to seize the tactical advantage of surprise, but also to evoke a sense of fear at the emperor's ability to strike resolutely and swiftly. In the words of the *Akbarnama*: '... HM knew that the chastisement of the presumptuous and rebellious was at the head of the deeds of sovereignty.'[15]

At some point during this furious race, the small party led by Akbar linked up with a larger Mughal force. Akbar had left Agra with a very small group of nobles. We do not know exactly how many kept pace with the emperor, but Abdur Rahim certainly did. His name is at the very top of the list of twenty-seven nobles who accompanied the emperor and completed the march.[16] In the battle that followed, in which the small Mughal force of some 3,000 horsemen faced an army of about 20,000, the command of the centre of the army was assigned to him. He was just sixteen years old and we can imagine his heady excitement as he kept pace with the small group accompanying the emperor. The experience certainly left a deep impression on the young man. Nearly half a century later, besieged inside the fort of Asir near Burhanpur by the Deccan warlord Malik Amber's cavalry, he repeatedly petitioned Emperor Jahangir to come to his rescue in the same way that his father, Akbar, had raced to relieve Mirza Aziz Koka.

The battle itself was an anticlimax. The rebel generals' incredulity at the emperor's rapid journey from Agra contributed considerably to the Mughals' success. The imperial army inflicted heavy losses; one estimate put the number of casualties at 2,000. It was a remarkably successful medieval version of a blitzkrieg. Akbar was to return equally quickly, completing the return journey in about three weeks.

For Abdur Rahim, this episode marked the beginning of an eminently successful military career. He was a mere adolescent during Akbar's first expedition to Gujarat and was quite possibly taken along so that he could visit the scene of his father's death at Patan, but his participation in the second expedition was as a warrior. Less than two years later, in 1575, when barely nineteen years old, he was appointed by the emperor as governor of Gujarat. Admittedly this was in a largely ceremonial capacity since a number of experienced nobles were also appointed to guide and train him. The prestige conferred by the appointment was, however, enormous and the fact that he was a favourite of the emperor was no longer in doubt to anyone in the court, if it ever was.

In the period between 1570 and 1575 we find Abdur Rahim well set on a trajectory that characterized his political career for the next five decades. Yet, this period, as he moved from adolescence to manhood, was fulfilling and creative for other reasons as well, and we find at this time the earliest examples of his poetry.

Abdur Rahim's verse has an enigmatic quality – and we will have cause to mention this repeatedly – in that it is difficult to situate chronologically or even with broad reference to the major events of his life. Scholars of Hindi literature and of Abdur Rahim's poetry have relied on an analysis of the maturity or otherwise of the language used, combined with a significant amount of guesswork in attempts to date different parts of his work. One such effort locates two of Abdur Rahim's works to his adolescence, when he is seen as experimenting with mixed poetry in Persian, Hindi and Sanskrit, though not quite accomplished in any of these languages.

Dated in this manner to around AD 1569 is the composition of *Kheta Koutukam*.[17] This is a work of astrology and the title literally means the 'Play of Planets'. The aim of the work, which consists of 124 verses, is to explore the influence of planetary movements on human destiny. The translations below provide some flavour of the work:

> If the sun be in the tenth zodiac sign, a person becomes very wealthy, handsome, a good rider, very happy and famous throughout the world. If the sun be in a downward course, the individual cannot enjoy his life as his father did.

> If the planet Mars is in the eighth house, the person in question talks rudely, suffers from venereal diseases and proves wretched from the point of conjugal love. He indulges in worrying for nothing but remains alert all along. Further, he suffers from sores, lacks intelligence and becomes physically weak owing to anaemia, itches or similar diseases.
>
> If Saturn be in the seventh zodiac sign, a person becomes loose in morals, suffers from diseases scarcely talks, he becomes dependent and devoid of intellect.[18]

What do we make of this fourteen-year-old poet? The work indicates, of course, the enormous influence of astrology on different aspects of a Mughal noble's life, and the evidence for this is independently voluminous. The *Akbarnama* has over fifty pages devoted to interpretations of different horoscopes cast at Akbar's birth. With the Rajput alliance growing in strength, many prominent Rajput princes and princesses were now a permanent part of Akbar's court. With them were their own large personal contingents that included Hindu astrologers. Many prominent Mughal nobles and royal family members, too, had their horoscopes cast by these famed practitioners, and it is therefore no surprise to see Abdur Rahim's earliest work showing this influence. His own horoscope – and later of his sons – was to be discovered in the late nineteenth century in different collections and libraries of Rajasthan.[19]

The *Kheta Koutukum* is deliberately composed in a mixture of Sanskrit and Persian and after the opening stanza of salutations to the 'sublime object of worship by obtaining the dust of whose lotus feet even gods gain sway over the whole world', Abdur Rahim confidently and precociously asserts that 'Many of my predecessors composed works in a mixed language – Sanskrit and Persian. Following their footsteps, I have undertaken the composition of the work at hand – the Kheta Koutukam.'

The most prominent of these predecessors was Amir Khusrau. He would have been well known to a young boy educated in the Mughal court; a lavishly illustrated work of his, *Duval Rani Khizr Khan,* for instance, was owned by Bairam Khan's second wife, Salima Sultan Begum.[20] Considering Abdur Rahim's upbringing in a milieu largely dominated by Persian and Turkish, but with a growing exposure to Sanskrit and Hindi, the use of a mixed Persian–Sanskrit language is not surprising. Given the prestige associated with Amir Khusrau, such a style was used occasionally even by established poets who wished to try their hand at it as a lighter pastime. Two prominent Hindi poets associated with Akbar's court – Narhari and Gang – also, for instance, composed such mixed verse.

The work, although composed in Sanskrit, frequently uses Persian words: *sipahi* (soldier), *Dabiulkalka* (Mercury), *tabangar* (rich), *sardaraka* (leader), *dostkhana* (house of a friend), *jahan* (universe), etc. The formulaic verses and a lack of consistency in the proportion of Sanskrit and Persian verses suggest the immaturity of the poet, and therefore the work itself has been dated to fall into that period of Abdur Rahim's literary progress when 'neither in Sanskrit nor in Persian did he have a sufficient command over language'. But he was clearly in an environment in which a number of languages were in use.[21]

Such a conclusion appears logical for other reasons as well. Abdur Rahim's mother would have conversed with him in a dialect of Hindi; his father's old retainers were perhaps most comfortable in Persian and Turkish; in the court Turkish still had some residual influence, though Persian was dominant, and finally Sanskrit – due to the emperor's alliance with the Rajputs – would have had a certain exotic appeal.

Probably of the same vintage are some other verses attributed to Abdur Rahim, entitled *Madanashtak.*[22] This is a collection of eight verses based on the legend of Krishna, Radha and the gopis of Brindavan. The language used this time is a mixture of Hindi and Sanskrit. The opening verse is a description of the gopis leaving their domestic chores, children and love-making to run towards the sound of Krishna's flute. The six verses that follow are a description by Radha of Krishna: his beautiful eyes, his hands and fingers, lips and mouth, the ornaments he wears, etc. The thrust of each verse is the intense physical attraction the gopis feel for Krishna, although at least two of the verses describe the passion as a sudden, unforeseen anguish inflicted upon the women. This comes across strongly in the eighth verse, which is also unusual in that it depicts the pangs of separation felt by a Pathan (or Afghan) woman.

> The Pathani, tormented by loneliness and desire, says to her friend: Will you catch that beautiful Krishna and let me meet him. Why don't you do so and so give me love's real nectar to drink. What calamity is this which is upon me?

In these mixed Hindi and Sanskrit verses, Persian words abound: *jhulfe* (eyes, gaze), *kulfe* (sorrow), *roshni* (light), *mast* (uncontrollable or in a trance), *dil* (heart), etc. The form and content of the *Madanashtak* bear an obvious similarity to the vast corpus of Krishna bhakti verse generated in the sixteenth century. The sensuous veneer to these verses is also not unexpected and is a feature of much of the Krishna bhakti verses of the period.

But the language of the verses in the *Madanashtak* is direct, almost blunt. The Pathan woman is demanding and insistent, Radha describing Krishna is candid and forthright. Some of this directness is because of the mixture of Persian, Hindi and Sanskrit. The Hindi words in the *khadi boli* or *bhasha* dialect do not have the softness of Braj or Avadhi, in which Abdur Rahim composed much of his later work. But some of the lack of subtlety could be attributed to the immaturity of the poet himself. One may be right, therefore, in concluding that this work too is part of Abdur Rahim's juvenilia and was probably composed when he was sixteen or seventeen years old, just before he set out with Akbar on the Gujarat expedition.

The *Madanashtak* has many of the characteristics of the Krishna bhkati verse produced in this period. Highly stylized and following set formats, the work could be seen as a literary foray into a poetic form within well-established conventions and themes. It implies a certain familiarity with the Radha–Krishna legends, but this is not unexpected given Abdur Rahim's background and the growing Rajput influence at the court.

Akbar's marriage to a princess of Amber in 1562 had resulted in Man Singh, a nephew of the princess, entering imperial service and becoming a familiar figure in court for the rest of Akbar's reign. Man Singh was eleven years old when he first came to court and there is evidence of his being 'asked to look after and play with the child who later became the Khan-i-Khanan'.[23] A Mughal biography of premier nobles speaks of Man Singh as being among those in charge of Abdur Rahim's education.[24] In fact, over the next four decades there is a great deal of evidence suggesting a close personal relationship, perhaps even real friendship, between Abdur Rahim and Man Singh and it is plausible that they forged this bond as children. Man Singh may well have been the conduit by which Abdur Rahim learnt his Sanskrit and Hindi and also had access to, and the benefit of, the best teachers of these languages. We can also, without unduly stretching the bounds of speculation, think of his mother, the young Mewati widow in the Persian and Turkish dominated harem, finding some measure of companionship in the Kachhwaha Rajput women from Amber.

Notwithstanding his friendships with Rajput princes, Abdur Rahim did not grow up as an outsider in the Mughal court. He was never outside the circle of its principal families: it could not be said, for instance, that he was more at ease with the Rajputs, or his maternal relatives, or even his father's former followers. The emperor's favour and consideration ensured that he had a place at the very centre of the court. One of the means Akbar employed to achieve this was arranging Abdur Rahim's marriage to Mah Banu, daughter of Shamsuddin Muhammad Khan Atka, who was Bairam's rival during the regency and among those behind his unseating. By this arrangement he integrated Abdur Rahim into one of the principal families of his realm.

The family of Atka Khan was particularly close to the royal family itself, his wife having been a foster mother or wet nurse to Akbar. Atka Khan's son was thereby the emperor's foster- brother. The family, on account of this connection, was well known as the 'Atka Khail' and was one of the most prominent in the court. Shamsuddin had saved Humayun's life when the emperor was fleeing after the disaster of the battle of Kannauj and possibly because of this, his wife was given the honour of nursing the child that Humayun's empress, Hamida Banu, was to bear. Jiji Anga was the name given to her as wet nurse and Shamsuddin was designated as Atka.

Humayun had, while crossing into Persia, come close to being captured by his brother, Askari, then in rebellion against him. The main party with the emperor had managed to escape but the infant Akbar was left behind with his personal attendants, who included Maham Anga – another prominent noblewoman and also a designated foster-mother of Akbar – Jiji Anga and Atka Khan. He faithfully watched over Akbar in Qandahar and Kabul during Humayun's sojourn in Persia until the time he was able to establish control over Kabul. Bairam Khan later held Shamsuddin and Maham Anga principally responsible for poisoning his relationship with the young emperor and seeking to disrupt the regency. Certainly, Shamsuddin along with the family of Maham Anga were the leading protagonists of Bairam's downfall. After Bairam's removal, many of his privileges and honours were bestowed on Shamsuddin.

Before long, however, the alliance between Maham Anga and Shamsuddin Muhammad Khan Atka began to unravel as the end of Bairam Khan's regency removed the reason that had bound the two together. The climax came on 16 May 1562. While Atka Khan, who had been recently appointed vakil, was transacting official business in court in Agra, he was murdered by Adham Khan, Maham Anga's son.

The emperor himself was in the palace at the time and had Adham Khan put to death immediately. This prevented further bloodshed, or even a civil war between the Atka Khail on one hand and Maham Anga's family on the other, a conflict that would have drawn in many other nobles. Maham Anga died of grief soon thereafter. The beautiful monument in the Delhi suburb of Mehrauli that houses the graves of mother and son, was built by Akbar and provides a touching end to their story.

Atka Khan's son, Mirza Aziz Koka ('Koka' means foster-brother), was also a noble of great prominence in the court. His career runs parallel to Abdur Rahim's for the next half-century. It is characterized by his extreme volatility, which caused his relations with Akbar and subsequently with Jahangir, to swing from one extreme to the other. He could be openly critical and even defiant of the emperor and, certainly, any other noble may have been executed for the kind of misdemeanours and liberties Mirza Aziz was permitted. Fortunately for him, Akbar had a great sense of loyalty to his former wet nurses – when confronted with yet another situation created by Mirza Aziz Koka's lack of moderation, Akbar is said to have commented: '... between me and Aziz there is the link of a river of milk which I cannot cross.'[25]

Abdur Rahim's marriage into this family was advantageous in two ways: it underscored his special relationship with the emperor and ensured that the Atka Khail, his father's principal adversaries, did not carry the feud with Bairam Khan into the next generation. It also considerably strengthened Abdur Rahim's position in court since the numerical strength of the Atka Khail made up for the principal weakness of Bairam Khan's family, which was its very small size.

The marriage in 1575 was probably one of the important events on the court's social calendar. It was perhaps around this time too that Abdur Rahim, then eighteen years old, was given the title of 'Mirza', another indication of the special status he enjoyed in the emperor's eyes, as the title was usually reserved for members of the royal family or those especially close to it. Akbar referred to Abdur Rahim as Mirza Khan. From his marriage to Mah Banu, Abdur Rahim had three sons and three daughters. It would appear that the children – certainly the sons – were born much later, when Abdur Rahim was in his thirties.

There is, however, one final influence on our young noble that remains to be taken note of – that of his stepmother, Begum Salima Sultan. After Bairam's death and the return of the family to Agra, Akbar married his young widow. She was by birth his cousin: her mother, Gulrakh Begum, was Humayun's half-sister. The marriage was in the form of a generous gesture by Akbar to provide her a suitable position within the harem. She was, in many ways, a remarkable woman; she possessed a scholarly intelligence and with her unimpeachable pedigree, she became one of the court's prominent figures and moved in the highest circles closest to the emperor.[26] She has been described as being a poet herself, 'a reader, a poet who wrote under the pseudonym of *makhfi*'.[27] An incident comes down to us of how her love of books got the historian Abdul Qadir Badayuni into serious trouble with the emperor. In 1589–90 Badayuni was given leave of absence from court, but he stayed away longer than he should have. The emperor noted his absence when Salima Begum wanted a book that Badayuni had taken from the imperial library:

> On account of the book *Khirad afza*, which had disappeared from the Library, and concerning Salimah Sultan Begum's study of which the Emperor reminded me … an order was issued that my *madad –maash* should be stopped, and that they should demand the book of me *nolens volens*.[28]

Although the sources are silent on the association between Abdur Rahim and his former stepmother, a continued relationship between her and Bairam Khan's son after his assassination is not unlikely. Salima Sultan Begum, childless herself, may well have had a reservoir of maternal goodwill for her stepson and been a benign influence through Abdur Rahim's childhood. Possibly Abdur Rahim owed much to her for the excellence of his education, as also his rapid rise. The sensitivity Akbar consistently displayed towards the young Abdur Rahim may have been partly due to impulses from the harem and it would not be far-fetched to regard Salima Sultan as their source.

The first political milestone in Abdur Rahim's adult life coincided with a development of great significance for the Mughal nobility: the promulgation of an imperial order making mandatory the branding of horses in the muster rolls of cavalry maintained by the nobility and other officers. Nobles were required to maintain horses, camels and elephants as stipulated by their rank in an elaborate hierarchy. *Dagh* or branding was, in essence, a system of inspection to ensure that these obligations were being met in full. Default meant a pay cut, full pay being granted only if the entire contingent was presented for inspection and branding. Over the years, the system grew increasingly elaborate and spread across the empire.

At the same time, the military and administrative structure, or the system of mansabdari, was rationalized and reorganized. This placed all imperial officers in a hierarchy of numerical ranks. This rank, and the number, referred to the number of cavalrymen and horses the officer was expected to maintain, specified the official's position in the hierarchy, his military obligation and his salary. A mansabdari rank of 1,000 meant that the officer had to maintain a military force of 1,000 cavalry and would be entitled to a salary that would enable that force to be maintained. Not all mansabdars were military officers, yet all were placed in this hierarchy. Salaries were fixed by taking into account whether military obligations were being maintained or not.

Theoretically there were sixty-six grades in this structure, beginning from commanders of ten horses to those of 10,000. Through much of Akbar's reign, commands of above 5,000 were reserved for princes of royal blood. Salaries could either be in cash or in the form of a land revenue assignment equivalent to the salary. This assignment was called a jagir. Mansab rank was not hereditary – nor was the jagir. Mughal officers were transferable and their attachment to a particular jagir was therefore temporary. The administration of the jagir and the collection of its revenue was carried out by separate imperial officers who had, in principle at least, complete autonomy from the mansabdar who had been allotted that jagir. The branding of horses and other animals was part of an elaborate procedure of inspections to ensure that the system worked effectively and was not misused. The whole structure was thus premised on a certain level of centralism – although to what extent this was actually achieved remains debatable and possibly varied over time and from region to region within the empire.

The opposition to this extent of centralism and, in particular, to the dagh order came primarily from the Central Asian nobility who resented this and other promulgations that increasingly limited their autonomy. As their dissatisfaction become apparent, many were redeployed at the frontiers of the empire, in Bengal and Bihar, where Mughal authority was far from secure. This put their military capabilities to use but kept them away from the centre of the empire.[29] The most prominent sign of protest came, however, from a quarter too sensitive to be handled by simple relocation. Mirza Aziz Koka, then governor of Gujarat, was summoned to court in October 1575. Whether news of his unhappiness with the dagh promulgation had reached Akbar or because the emperor wished to initiate the new order by first getting the leading nobles, especially those close to him, to fall in line, is not clear. In any event, once in court, Mirza Aziz Koka's opposition to the initiative could not be passed over and Akbar deprived him of his rank and, by confining him to his quarters, effectively placed him in custody.

This was not the first time that Mirza Aziz Koka had defied the emperor's will and it would by no means be the last. Defiance, and at other times sullen truculence, regularly punctuated his long career that spanned most of Akbar's reign and the better part of Jahangir's. The real affection in which Akbar held Koka, and the compulsion that Jahangir felt to honour this legacy, meant that imperial exasperation over any act of defiance was short-lived or, at least, relatively restrained. Soon after the dagh episode, Mirza Aziz Koka again challenged Akbar, this time over the emperor's radically liberal attitudes and experiments in matters concerning the clergy and the quasi-religious cult being built around his person. He kept away from the court and, in opposition to the trend of favourites being clean-shaven, kept a long beard. On being summoned he wrote back with excuses and, in the end, an exasperated Akbar wrote: 'You are making all these delays in coming; evidently the wool of your beard weighs heavily on you.'[30]

Akbar's rebuke was expressed in terms of reproach and exasperation rather than anger. Similarly, during Jahangir's reign, Mirza Aziz Koka's career alternated between positions of importance and prestige and periods of forced inactivity, disgrace and imprisonment. His sense of entitlement, his conviction in his own sense of right and wrong and his doctrinal views, coupled with a fatal outspokenness, made him a constant thorn in both Akbar's and Jahangir's flesh. On one occasion, it took the intercession of the harem in the person of Salima Sultan Begum for Jahangir to pardon yet another transgression. But a short time later, Mirza Aziz was back in prison and released only after an undertaking was received 'in writing from him that he would not speak in the Presence unless he was asked a question for he had no control over his tongue'. The extent of Jahangir's exasperation with Mirza Aziz is revealed also when he asked Jahangir Quli Khan, Mirza Aziz's son, 'Will you stand security for your father?' The son's reply is equally telling: 'I am his security for everything of him, but I cannot be surety for his tongue.'[31]

Mirza Aziz Koka and Abdur Rahim were contemporaries for almost half a century and their careers offer much in terms of contrast. The former sought often to establish his independence of spirit, as though daring Akbar and Jahangir to cross the limits of the loyalties that bound them to him. Abdur Rahim, on the other hand, displayed a consistent, almost eager, striving to demonstrate his loyalty and fidelity to the person of the emperor, at least up to the very last phase of his life. Perhaps, along with the differing personalities of the two men, their parentage was also at work here.

One immediate consequence of Mirza Aziz Koka's opposition to the dagh promulgation was his removal from the post of governor of Gujarat. Akbar decided to appoint Abdur Rahim, then not quite twenty years old, in his stead. The emperor's genuine affection for Abdur Rahim and the latter's obvious capabilities undoubtedly played a part, but other considerations also weighed in. The choice of a young man in place of an established noble (Mirza Aziz was about Akbar's own age at this time, about thirty-two or thirty-three) and one who was, moreover, Mirza Aziz's brother-in-law, may well have been designed to allow him the opportunity to make amends and be reinstated. In fact, notwithstanding the great honour, Abdur Rahim's appointment seems to have been a nominal one. He was instructed to follow the advice of four trusted administrators and within a few months was summoned to join the court in Ajmer. Here he remained for the next two years or so till about 1580, when he took part in the Mewar campaign of the Mughals against Rana Pratap Singh and his son, Amar Singh.

The kingdom of Mewar has left a powerful impress on the idea of nationalism in modern India. The Sisodia Rajput clan that ruled Mewar is credited with a history of determined resistance to foreign conquest from the time of the Delhi Sultanate and particularly from the beginning of Mughal rule in India. Rana Sanga, the ruler of Mewar, had faced Babur soon after the battle of Panipat (1526) and his defeat in the battle of Khanwa in 1527 heralded the Mughal conquest of north India. The expansion and consolidation of the empire in the early years of Akbar's reign had seen in 1567 a Mughal siege of Chittor, the garrison capital of Mewar. The siege was protracted; the ruler of Mewar, Rana Udai Singh, refused to submit. The end result was a military success for the Mughals, but the entire garrison perished in the battle and the wives and families of the defenders immolated themselves in a pyre in the act of *jauhar* to save themselves from captivity or dishonour.

The battle of Chittor was fought by the Mughals with the full symbolism of a religious war. Akbar proclaimed it a victory of Islam over the Rajput infidels. Clearly, the mature Akbar of *Sulh-i-Kul* is some years away.[32] Although most of the other Rajput rulers soon entered the Mughal alliance system, the kingdom of Mewar continued its resistance. Udai Singh was followed by his son, Pratap Singh, whose continued opposition to Mughal expansion – despite military defeats, most notably in the battle of Haldighati in 1576 – is a compelling tale in its own right. From the late nineteenth century, this story entered the mainstream narrative of Indian nationalism and resistance to British rule, and Haldighati became the expression of Hindu resistance to Muslim expansion and domination.[33] The nineteenth-century British civil servant and administrator James Todd, well known as a recorder of Rajput history and bardic chronicles, described the battle of Haldighati as being the Thermopylae of Mewar.[34] While subsequent history may have found it easy to paint the dominant narrative as Mughal or Muslim versus Rajput or Hindu, in point of fact there is a strong presence of other elements including traditional intra-Rajput feuding. Thus, the Rajput clan of the Kachhwahas led by Man Singh were often front-line troops in Mughal expeditions against Rana Pratap Singh.

The time Abdur Rahim spent in Ajmer and his participation in the expeditions against the Rana have left only a minor trace in Mughal historical records. He was, after all, still relatively inexperienced and would not have been given a major independent command. In contrast, the interface between him and Rana Pratap has left an indelible imprint in Hindi literature and there is a body of folklore and poetry that romanticizes the historical record of this period. According to this, Abdur Rahim's mother was a Mewati princess whose family had a long association with Mewar. Her uncle and head of family, Hasan Khan Mewati, had been an ally of Rana Sanga during the time of Mewar's resistance to Mughal encroachment and expansion under Babur. However, there is no historical evidence that Abdur Rahim regarded the Mughal campaign against Mewar any differently from other Mughal commanders. Yet there is a body of literary work that suggests a private sympathy Abdur Rahim felt for the besieged rulers of Mewar as they defended their traditions and way of life against an expanding imperial power. The principal source for this lies in Rajasthani bardic chronicles of the eighteenth and nineteenth centuries, from where it travelled to Hindi poetry and literature in the early twentieth century.

One of the most prominent Hindi poets of the early twentieth century (in Khadi Boli, as opposed to Braj Bhasha or Avadhi), was Jaishankar Prasad. In course of time he came to be regarded as one of the founders of the 'Chhayavad' or romantic movement in Hindi poetry, itself a reaction to what was perceived as the pronounced eroticism and ornamentation of courtly Braj Bhasha verse of the pre-modern period.[35] Amongst Jaishankar Prasad's earliest poetical works is a historical drama entitled *Maharana ka Mahatva* ('The Greatness of the Maharana'). First published in 1914, the poem has Pratap Singh, the Rana of Mewar, as its principal hero and protagonist. The conjuncture it locates itself in is an expedition that Abdur Rahim leads against the Rana of Mewar. Other characters include Rana Pratap Singh's son, Amar Singh, Abdur Rahim's wife, Mah Banu Begum, and Emperor Akbar himself. The story is straightforward:

Abdur Rahim's wife is captured by Kunwar Amar Singh. Rana Pratap is mortified at this action and considers it a blot on Rajput chivalry and honour. Mah Banu is, at his orders, returned with all attendant honours to Abdur Rahim's camp. Mah Banu and Abdur Rahim are deeply affected by this gesture. Abdur Rahim loses all desire to defeat so worthy a foe. He asks to be relieved of his command on grounds of ill health. The emperor is curious about this request. On being cross-questioned Abdur Rahim reveals the full story and pleads with the emperor that a foe so chivalrous needs to be treated differently. His courage, pride, chivalry and patriotism distinguish him as one who should receive the emperor's benevolence and mercy: 'He has not attacked us but only wants to retain his own small kingdom. An anonymous, undeclared truce would serve both interests: it would announce to the world your mercy and benevolence while leaving him free to spend the rest of his life in peace'. Akbar pondered deeply over Abdur Rahim's counsel and the move against Mewar was finally given up.[36]

This brief summary conveys little beyond the bare skeleton of Jaishankar Prasad's work. Composed at a time when nationalism was becoming a major inspiration for literary works, the theme of Rana Pratap's chivalry, his fierce sense of independence and the ability to strive for it against overwhelming odds make up one axis of the verse drama. The second deals with the foes who both appreciate and reciprocate these qualities, principally Abdur Rahim himself, but also the emperor. Both sets of protagonists emerge as winners and equals, suggestive of one of the principal themes of Indian nationalism: Hindu–Muslim unity.

How historically authentic is this episode? That Abdur Rahim returned prematurely from Gujarat to join the emperor in Ajmer is established. It is also well established that Abdur Rahim participated in the expedition against Mewar. That military moves against Rana Pratap Singh were largely given up by 1586 or so is also borne out by a number of contemporary sources. From then, till about the time of his death in 1597, Rana Pratap appears to have been left largely untroubled by imperial forces. Is there then space in this chronology for the episode described by Jaishankar Prasad and if so, did it have some effect on Akbar's Mewar policy?

The earliest references to the episode of Abdur Rahim's wife and harem being captured by Amar Singh are found in two Sanskrit works, *Rajprashisht Mahakavyam* and *Amar Kavyam,* composed by Ranchod Bhatt during the time of Maharana Raj Singh, who reigned in Mewar from AD 1653 to 1680. The works themselves are dated to AD 1676, i.e., almost a century after Abdur Rahim came to

Mewar from Gujarat. They describe the abduction of Abdur Rahim's harem by Amar Singh, who however behaved with the utmost circumspection towards the women, treating them as if they were his own daughters and sisters, and returned them with full honour, a matter of great surprise to Abdur Rahim. Assessing this evidence, modern historians of Rajasthan have concluded that the veracity of the entire event is doubtful and that the reference was subsequently greatly expanded and embellished by later writers and historians of Mewar in the late nineteenth century.[37]

There are, however, many other similar tales in Rajasthani literary traditions that also suggest Abdur Rahim's rapport with the Rajputs and the help he gave them. In one of these we have him coming to the aid of a Rajput prince because of the intercession of a bard. Rana Udai Singh, the story goes, had appointed his younger son, Jagmal, as his heir apparent, but after the Rana's death, the choice was not endorsed by other chiefs of the clan and his eldest son, Pratap Singh, was enthroned. Jagmal's bard, Jada, thereupon composed and sent the following four verses praising the Khan-i-Khanan:

> What surprises me is the KhanKhanan's vast – like the Meru mountain – mind
> Is carried by a three-and-a-half span body.
> The KhanKhanan's sword rains fire,
> Burning the brave warriors but sparing those seeking refuge
> Blessed is the KhanKhanan's nature
> Even the vast peaks of the Meru are no more than a speck to him.
> The KhanKhanan's arms are joined to Brahma, Delhi rests on his back,
> Under the blade of his sword are vast new spaces.[38]

When Abdur Rahim wished to reward the poet with a lakh of rupees for each verse, the loyal Jada refused, asking instead for the Khan-i-Khanan's intercession with the emperor on behalf of his master. Abdur Rahim agreed and eventually the tehsil of Jahazpur, formerly a part of Mewar, was given to Jagmal. Abdur Rahim also composed the following verse for Jada:

The Earth is large, the Sky is large
And this Mahdu bard [i.e., Jada] is large.
And the name of Allah is large.
Apart from these no one is.[39]

The British civil servant and administrator James Todd also associated Abdur Rahim with Rana Pratap's struggle against the Mughals. He quoted a folk tale of Mewar which 'preserved some stanzas addressed by the Khan-i-Khanan, the first of the Satraps of Delhi to the noble Rajput in his native tongue applauding his valour and stimulating his perseverance.'

All is unstable in this world
Land and wealth will disappear
But the virtue of a great name
Lives for ever
Putto abandoned wealth and land
But never bowed his head
Alone, of all the princes of Hind
He preserved the honour of his race.[40]
[Putto refers to Rana Pratap Singh, the ruler of Mewar.]

The Mewar interregnum is significant as it gave credence to the belief that Abdur Rahim had a certain empathy for a foe who was attempting to preserve ancient traditions under threat from Mughal expansion. While Abdur Rahim's sympathy for the Rajputs is represented in many chronicles, it is his association with Kunwar Man Singh of Amber and Rana Pratap Singh (and later, his son Amar Singh) of Mewar that has left the greater imprint on Hindi literature. The image of Abdur Rahim that emerged in the late nineteenth and early twentieth centuries was derived to a very great extent from these literary and historical sources from Rajasthan and explain the transformation of the sixteenth-century Mughal noble into a twentieth-century nationalist icon. He is represented as a prominent noble, a successful military commander and a power centre at the heart of the Mughal establishment, who is at the same time sympathetically disposed to Hindu rulers and a Hindu way of life and tradition; in brief, the Abdur Rahim that emerges from the Rajasthani sources epitomizes a synthesis and fusion between the Mughal and Hindu worlds. How this view grows and how it measures up with the other parts of Abdur Rahim's life and career are a theme to which we will periodically revert.

After some two years in Ajmer and Mewar, Abdur Rahim was summoned back to the court in 1580 or 1581. He was appointed shortly thereafter to the newly created post of Mir Ard or the master of petitions. Formally, the post entailed the processing of petitions addressed to the emperor. On the face of it, it appears to be one providing direct access to the emperor and therefore of great significance and influence. We know little, however, of how the system actually worked with Abdur Rahim at the helm. Certainly, the appointment itself can be taken as another sign of the emperor's affection and his high regard for Abdur Rahim's capabilities and potential.

Abdur Rahim was Mir Ard for about two years and then, at the age of twenty-six, was appointed ataliq to Prince Salim, the future emperor Jahangir. This mirrored Bairam Khan's appointment as Akbar's ataliq and we can again surmise that Akbar had not forgotten his old regent and felt that obligations remained to be discharged. The appointment, which he held for just under two years, no doubt conferred tremendous status and prestige, though again, its actual influence is hard to assess. Jahangir was then thirteen years old. The appointment suggests that Akbar, as well as the harem, felt that Abdur Rahim had all the suitable attributes for being the tutor-guardian of a prince of the realm, being possessed of military skills, well versed in etiquette, familiar with the classics, and with established literary qualifications. Some modern biographers of Abdur Rahim have traced Jahangir's well-developed sense of aesthetics and his appreciation of the arts to Abdur Rahim's influence at an impressionable age.[41] It is evident from his memoirs that Jahangir had a considerable affection for his tutor, although the relationship ended in bitterness and tragedy in the closing years of Abdur Rahim's life. At this time, however, the prestige the appointment conferred can be gauged from the description below:

> Mirza Khan [i.e., Abdur Rahim] held a grand feast in connection with the appointment on which occasion he invited the Emperor to grace it by his presence. The latter could not refuse the request. Numerous officers participated in the function. From the fort up to his [Abdur Rahim's] residential palace, flowers of gold and silver were showered and near his residence rubies were scattered. At the entrance satin and velvet were spread on the ground to walk on. Within the compound a dais was erected at the cost of one lac and twenty-five thousand rupees. When the Emperor took his seat on it, Mirza Khan put before him as an offering, precious jewels, costly garments and amazing types of weapons of war. The Emperor was so elated over the celebration that he bestowed on Abdur Rahim a drum, a *charqab,* banner and all the insignia pertaining to a prince royal as a mark of favour which were never given to ordinary officers.[42]

Abdur Rahim's career was thus progressing rapidly. His background, paternity, marriage into the Atka Khail, and finally the presence of Salima Sultan Begum as an increasingly important member of the harem would have been contributing factors. Salima Sultan Begum, in particular, is described as having been close to the future emperor Jahangir and there is evidence suggesting the existence of a personal bond between the two. Childless herself, she, it was said, 'seems to have attached herself especially to Prince Salim

(Jahangir)...'[43] Her relationship with Abdur Rahim and the fact that he was appointed as ataliq to the prince is unlikely to have been a coincidence. She was away between October 1576 and April 1582 on a pilgrimage to Mecca and Medina along with a number of other royal ladies. The appointment as ataliq was made a few months after her return to the court.

Between 1580 and 1584, Abdur Rahim appears to have entered a mature and creative phase; some of his greatest literary achievements are attributed to this period. Akbar's court at this time was characterized by intellectual ferment and religious controversy, and Abdur Rahim, given his own interests and his position in court, is likely to have been a close observer of, and greatly influenced by, all that was happening around him.

In 1575 Emperor Akbar ordered the construction of the Ibadat Khana as a place for religious discussions. For some time, these were limited to Sunni theologians but soon Shiites were also admitted. In the initial years, the debates were almost entirely monopolized by the established clergy and were, presumably, conducted on purely sectarian lines. Gradually, however, Akbar realized that the Ibadat Khana could serve as a check to the dogmatism of the Sadr or chief judge of the realm, Sheikh Abdun Nabi, as well as limit his ability to act as a power centre independently of the emperor. Akbar's own relationship with Abdun Nabi had begun as one of adulation and devotion but ended in alienation and antagonism. The process reflected Akbar's evolution as a ruler whose outlook became increasingly liberal as he engaged with the larger question of a state and regime with a largely Islamic identity that sought to coexist with a society that was principally Hindu.

A learned and highly educated family enters the drama at this stage: Sheikh Mubarak and his two gifted sons, Sheikh Abul Fazl (1551–1602) and Sheikh Abul Faiz or Faizi (1547–1595). Sheikh Mubarak had had run-ins with the ulema even in the court of Islam Shah, the son of Sher Shah. These were sharp doctrinal differences and the family was persecuted and faced some hardships. On account of Sheikh Mubarak's eclecticism, his position in Akbar's early years did not improve much with conservatives such as Abdun Nabi at the helm of ideological affairs. As Akbar's impatience with the conservatives grew, the family came into its own.

The learning, sophisticated wit and ambition of Abul Fazl and Faizi, backed by the formidable intellect of Sheikh Mubarak, became for Akbar the perfect foil for the ulema's dogmatism. In the Ibadat Khana, Abul Fazl led sharp attacks on the ulema with the emperor's acquiescence and both brothers rose swiftly in the emperor's favour and in the imperial hierarchy. Faizi was awarded the title of Malik-us-Shaura (Poet Laureate) by the emperor in 1589 and entrusted with important diplomatic assignments, especially to the kingdoms of the Deccan. Abul Fazl held a mansab rank of 1,000 by the mid-1580s, was steadily promoted thereafter and, towards the end of Akbar's reign, held the very high rank of 5,000. This, for a scholar and writer with no military accomplishments to his credit, was unusual indeed and very pointedly demonstrated the emperor's favour.

This spectacular rise inevitably led to jealousy in other courtiers and those also claiming the emperor's personal favour. The early signs of discord between the young emperor and Abdun Nabi can be seen in the episode described below, from a time when the status and power of the Sadr were unquestioned, and he could take unimaginable liberties with the monarch.

> … there came the birthday of His Majesty, the vice regent of God. Saffron was sprinkled on his royal dress. Sheikh Abdun Nabi flew into a rage and in the presence of the entire court, threw (his) rod at His Majesty, the vice regent of God; the rod having touched the skirt of his august dress tore it. He said, 'Why have you put on the dress of men of innovation (bidat), not sanctioned by religious code.'[44]

The emperor did not react then, but later complained to his mother: 'He hit me with a rod in the presence of the entire court; if his intention was to enforce the tenet of Command to do what is right in the eye of God, he should have advised me in private.' His mother consoled him by saying that the Sheikh was a man of God and that the incident would 'endure till the day of Resurrection that a poor Mullah carried out the command of God in this manner with an emperor'.

> Akbar then sought the counsel of Sheikh Abdul Fazl and Sheikh Faizi These (two) submitted, 'To what purpose is all this putting up with (such attitude of) these (people)? If it is on account of regard for learning or knowledge, learning and knowledge which we possess, they do not. If Your Majesty patronises and sides [with] us, they cannot take lead in learned discussion. First, in the matter of the saffron-sprinkled dress, for which they have shown such disrespect, feed them today with saffron-seasoned meals. Thereafter, we will make known our reasonable arguments.'

At their advice, a meal with a liberal use of saffron was fed to the Sadr, on a suitable occasion:

> After partaking of the saffron-seasoned meals, Sheikh Abu'l-Fadl told [Abdun Nabi], 'If saffron is lawful, why did you prevent His Majesty from putting on [a] saffron coloured dress, and if saffron is unlawful, then why did you take (it) in your food, for its effect will last for three days?' Sheikh Abdu'n-Nabi flung the rod at Sheikh Abu'l-Fazl's head.

These latent tensions were bound to come to a head and did so when Abdun Nabi ordered the execution of a rich brahmin in Mathura, who had built a temple with material seized from an Islamic teacher, which was meant for the construction of a mosque. When confronted, the brahmin had abused the Prophet in front of witnesses. While there were many who argued that he deserved the death penalty, others among the Muslim clergy suggested a more lenient punishment. Akbar, although not publicly declaring his own opinion, let it be known that he favoured the latter view. Perhaps he was prompted in this by the urgings of the Rajput women in his harem. Sheikh Nabi, however, ordered the brahmin's execution, an outcome that was deeply mortifying for the emperor.

This was the immediate context in which the Mazhar (or, as it has been termed, the doctrine of infallibility) was issued in 1579. In its essence, it gave the emperor the right to decide on a course of action in religious matters if opinion among the clergy was divided and a consensus did not exist. The document was signed, perhaps not entirely willingly, by the entire ulema, including Sheikh Abdun Nabi. It showed the emperor's determination to ensure that he would control sectarian differences and divisions. It also represented the growing influence of a group of scholars of liberal persuasion who were close to Akbar. At the head of this section was, of course, the family of Sheikh Mubarak and his sons, Sheikh Abul Fazl and Sheikh Abdul Faizi.

In this same year, a decree abolishing a separate tax – or the jizyah – on Hindus was issued. Abul Fazl wrote that earlier rulers had levied this tax to discourage other religions and also demonstrate the ruler's contempt for non-Muslims. Akbar, he wrote, made no distinction between followers of different religions. The abolition of the jizyah was a step of enormous significance as it – symbolically and visually at least – ended the distinction between a dominant Muslim court and subordinate Hindu society.

The episode of the capital punishment being awarded to the brahmin was followed by a swift undermining of the position of Sheikh Abdun Nabi, who was in late 1579 ordered to proceed to Mecca and not return without specific permission to do so. He returned, however, in 1582, anticipating that a rebellion brewing in the Punjab and Bihar would see the end of Akbar. The miscalculation led to his being imprisoned and thereafter, in 1584, strangled to death. Abul Fazl is believed to have been responsible for this. Sheikh Mubarak and his sons were now clearly pre-eminent and their rise in the last years of Abdun Nabi illustrates dramatically the winds of change sweeping the court. Only a few years earlier, in AD 1575–76,

Sheikh Mubarak had been a near supplicant before Abdun Nabi and Faizi had composed in Arabic the inscription that still adorns a mosque built by Abdun Nabi in Delhi; it refers to him as the 'mine of learning and the spring of beneficence'.[45]

The point, however, is that Akbar was moving in a liberal direction as is clear from the nature of the debate in the Ibadat Khana where, from 1578 onwards, religious discussions had been acquiring a new intensity. Initially limited to Sunni theologians, then opened to Shia clergy and scholars, it began to see the participation of Hindu scholars and Jain ascetics by the end of the decade. A group of Parsee priests is also described as having attended the Ibadat Khana in 1578, and in the same year we are informed of Christian participation. An encounter with a Jesuit priest had engaged Akbar's interest in Christianity that year and shortly thereafter, at the emperor's invitation, the Portuguese viceroy of Goa sent what was to be the first Jesuit mission to the Mughal court. This was led by Father Rudolph Acquaviva, a twenty-nine-year-old Italian 'of high social status and outstanding sanctity'. The mission was to spend three years in Fatehpur Sikri and Agra and also accompany the emperor on his expeditions outside the capital.

Apart from the developing chasm between Akbar's policies and those of the established clergy, the widening of the discussions in the Ibadat Khana reflected the deepening eclecticism of Akbar. In April–May 1578, in the midst of a hunt at Bhera in the Punjab, he is described as having received divine messages and gone into a mystical trance. One chronicler wrote of the emperor having obtained 'heavenly instructions and heard divine messages relating to certain affairs'. Subsequently, Akbar and those who followed him in this eclectic venture are described 'as voluntarily giving up certain practices and directed their attention to the essence of things'.[46]

Those were the years, excluding the brief period in Gujarat and the time spent in Ajmer, when Abdur Rahim was in constant attendance at the court. The religious and intellectual convulsions he was witness to would undoubtedly have had a formative influence on him. A fascinating glimpse of Abdur Rahim in the midst of this great intellectual churning is provided in 1582 at the commencement of a new regnal year.[47] The emperor used the occasion to announce the marking out of a select group of nobles as his disciples (*'celas'*) and decreed that each of them should 'submit their sentiments' about what was expedient and desirable for the empire.[48]

The ideas that emerged were interesting in themselves and also for the light they shed on those who advanced them. Prince Salim advocated that marriages should not take place before the age of twelve; Mirza Aziz Koka that provincial governors should not have the right to award capital punishment without the emperor's sanction and Akbar's brilliant revenue minister, Raja Todar Mal, felt that charities should be distributed daily. Other suggestions included that of Hakim Abul Fath, who suggested the establishment of hospices, and Sheikh Faizi, who wanted the appointment of inspectors of prices and markets, while others wished for the establishment of more serais (halting places for travellers) and so on.

This is, on the whole, a fairly practical, if high-minded, set of recommendations, the kind perhaps to be expected from those closest to Akbar and interested in enhancing the reputation and popularity of the monarch. Abdur Rahim's suggestion stands out, however, amongst them all for what may be called its essential other-worldliness. He said that '… it would be good if fragments of life such as small birds and creeping things were not taken and if many lives were not destroyed for a small benefit.'[49]

What could the twenty-six-year-old Abdur Rahim have meant by this? Was he going through an eclectic phase similar to the emperor's and seeking answers from diverse religious faiths and doctrines? Was he influenced by the Jain thinkers whom he may have come in contact with during his time in Gujarat, Ajmer or Mewar, or indeed at Akbar's court itself?[50] Or, more simply, was his esoteric idea a way of attracting the emperor's attention? Akbar was himself interested in elements of Jain philosophy and the Mughal court had hosted Hiravijay Suri, the chief pontiff of the Svetambara branch of the Jains, for about four years from 1583. There are also references to a group of some thirty-five Jain monks preceding the pontiff to the Mughal court, so the Jain presence possibly stretched over several years. Abdur Rahim may have had some discussions with them, and his understanding of elements of Jain doctrine and philosophy, combined with the desire to appear at one with the emperor's own thinking, could well have prompted his suggestion to spare the life of smaller animals and insects.

That Abdur Rahim was, or was trying to show the emperor that he was, open to influences other than the ulema's is also suggested by the reports of Father Acquaviva, the leader of the first Jesuit mission to Akbar's court. In a letter dated sometime in 1582 he wrote:

> One of the two leading personalities in the court, by name Mirza Khan [Abdur Rahim], endowed with great talents and very friendly to us, at the suggestion of the King wishes to learn the Portuguese and Latin languages and has already made a start in them. This has given me great joy, for he is fit for the Kingdom of Heaven. Since, dear Father, a door opens wide before us for great enterprises send us soon some more companions.[51]

We have additionally in this case the clear suggestion of the emperor's encouragement, perhaps even expectation, of Abdur Rahim's progress in a particular intellectual and spiritual direction.

—ꝏ—

Spiritual matters do not appear to have been the sole preoccupation of Abdur Rahim during these years in court. The composition of one of his important works of Hindi poetry, titled *Nagar Shobha* ('Adornments of the Town'), is dated to this time. A collection of brief verses of delicate but unmistakably erotic poetry, it is, at the same time, a fascinating aggregation of descriptions of women from different artisanal castes. The attempt in each couplet is to weave into the description of the physical attributes and sexual appeal of each woman a sense of the caste she belongs to, or the craft she practises. These two aspects, the sexual and the occupational, are present in each verse and are intended to reinforce each other: the woman in each case derives her sexuality and identity from the pride of belonging to a particular caste or trade.

The 142 verses in the collection describe women in sixty-six categories – a mixture of castes, occupational crafts and ethnic backgrounds. It begins with the higher caste brahmin, kshatriya and kayastha women and ends with descriptions of women from the lower castes of dhobis (washerwomen) and chamars (scavengers and those dealing in skins). In between lies a wide range: goldsmiths, jewellers, shopkeepers, traders, potters, vegetable sellers, butchers, silk weavers, dyers, ink makers, musicians, painters, prostitutes, dancing girls, shield makers, soap makers, gold beaters, etc.[52] How does Abdur Rahim describe these women? Here are some examples:

BAAJDARINI: THE WIFE OF THE HAWK KEEPER

The wife of the hawk keeper loves only the hawk and does not therefore adorn her body. The glow of love-making is as naturally present in her body as is the hawk's power to look down from a great height.

The wife of the hawk keeper uses her eyes like hunters to capture men as birds of prey. But she does not let the hawk sip of her juices.

DHUNIYAIN: THE WIFE OF THE COTTON CARDER

The cotton carder's wife works night and day with the ornaments of love-making adorning her. If you do not know the raga of your beloved, what and why do you card so loudly.

When she is fully aroused she goes tender at the touch and sticks to her lover's body much as carded cotton would.

Dabgarin: The Wife of the Shield Maker

Bursting with the energy of youth, she stays near her lover and tells him that her heart is not happy being away from him. Her well-formed breasts do not fit into her bodice. Her eye-shaped breasts under the bodice overflow from the influence of the oil of young love.[53]

Dalalin: The Wife of the Broker

The broker's wife shows off the splendour of her body, plays with her eyelashes, and showing the beauty of her lips captivates the client.

She is too conscious of what people think and of the pride of her community to say anything, but with her eyes shows her value to her lovers.

Mahavatin: The Wife of the Elephant Keeper

With her body perfectly balanced, she rides with her husband on the elephant. The exuberance of youth fills her as she roams freely with her lover.

She is wearing yellow clothes and holds a rope around the elephant's neck. Her husband's strength is the reason she roams freely slaying (captivating) all around her.

Kagdin: The Wife of the Paper Maker

Her body is like paper. She remains fulfilled with love. She, drenched by desire, becomes limp and weak like wet paper.

The paper seller's wife is like the string of the paper kite, high in the skies of love. She sights her distant lover and draws him in with her body close to her heart.

Lohari: The Wife of the Ironsmith

The beauty of the lohari woman at work radiates as if the fire of the furnace. Her body is itself a furnace in which the embers of loneliness burn arousing sparks in one's heart.

It is as if she is burning her loneliness to feed the furnace.

Gujarin: The Wife of the Gujar or Cowherd

The Gujarin, carrying a pot of curds on her head, is exceptionally beautiful. The spilling of the curd is like the nectar of the senses, but she does not give any.

She jokes with the customer and freely makes promises first stating her own price and then that of the curd.

Telin: The Wife of the Oil Presser

She has put on her body a scented oil made of the creeper's flower and the til seed. Her youth and the perfume make the eyes of the desirous move around her as the oil crusher's bull circles.

Bhattiyari: The Wife of the Innkeeper

Her nature is like that of Lakshmi. She welcomes the incoming traveller but does not spare a glance for those leaving much as Lakshmi is honoured when she arrives but not even spoken of when she has left.

The Bhattiyari gives her heart to the lover and speaks freely of her love. She is one during the day and another in the night.

Chhapin: The Wife of the Cloth Printer

Engrossed in passion's play, the Chhapin imprints the red of the paan in her mouth repeatedly on her lover.

Her love-making makes it as if she is Eros incarnate. Her beauty fills the eyes of the beholder with indescribable joy.

Descriptions such as these, with their erotic, pithy wit, characterize each of these couplets.[54] Some have suggested that the inspiration may have come from the Meena Bazar, the women's market within easy distance of the palace, which was often frequented by the emperor and his harem. However, the caste and occupational break-up of the women would have been true to the description of any prominent noble's household in Agra or Delhi, the principal capitals of Akbar's dominion. Women carrying out a range of occupations would also have been on the servants' roll of its harem. Craftsmen's wives making ink or paper, women belonging to the caste of bards, musicians and magicians, vegetable sellers, oil pressers, grass cutters and cowherds, singers and dancers – these would certainly have been part of the permanent domestic staff of Abdur Rahim's own household.[55]

The *Nagar Shobha* manuscript was discovered in the second decade of the twentieth century. Although the name Abdur Rahim or Rahim did not figure in any of the verses, the language and maturity of the compositions, the sentiment they conveyed, convinced scholars of the time that Abdur Rahim was the author.[56] The most direct confirmation of this is an inscription in Sanskrit at the beginning of the manuscript, which states that the *Nagar Shobha* has been written by the Nawab KhanKhanan.[57] The work is prefaced by a benedictory verse in Sanskrit, suggesting that it was composed as an integral whole:

> The light of the first man is in the heart of every being,
> But I cannot describe this infinite light because of my limited mind
> Seeing the beauty of the universe gives some solace since
> In each of its elements is reflected the primeval beauty of the first man.[58]

Perhaps the posts of Mir Ard and ataliq allowed for some leisure. Abdur Rahman was living in the capital city in the company of friends and equals, as also the presence of a multitude of scholars and poets. It could be that these verses were composed not as a serious literary venture but were rather the light-hearted attempts of a young man still discovering his facility for poetry and composing poems to amuse himself and his friends. The sophisticated eroticism of the verses also suggests that they may have been meant for an audience of cultured nobles, whether Rajput, Persian or Central Asian, and recited in largely masculine company. Half serious and half in jest, many of the verses in this collection vividly capture the life of Mughal nobles in an age of eclecticism and synthesis.

The four years that Abdur Rahim spent in court, between 1580 and 1583, were marked by awards and titles of distinction. They ended, however, with disturbing news from Gujarat. The foundations of Mughal power in the newly conquered province were being challenged once again by a revolt led by the ousted ruler, Muzaffar Shah. Mughal rule in Gujarat had been uneasy and troubled since the initial conquest of the region in 1572 by Akbar. Insurrections regularly punctuated the decade that followed, suggesting the inability of the Mughals to put down roots at any depth. The deposed ruler, Sultan Muzaffar Shah, had managed to escape Mughal control and surveillance in 1578, taking refuge in regions outside their reach. He waited and watched for a suitable opportunity, which was finally provided by the recall of the governor, Shihabuddin Khan, to the court and the appointment in his stead of Itimad Khan. The latter headed one of the factions in Gujarat, which had first invited Mughal intervention and had led to Akbar's original expedition against Muzaffar Shah.

When Itimad Khan was reappointed governor, he had to deal with a large body of troopers formerly in the employ of his predecessor, Shihabuddin Khan. His unwillingness to grant them more generous terms of service led to the beginnings of a full-blown revolt. The troops offered their services to Muzaffar Shah, thereby giving him the opening he was waiting for. The resistance put up by Itimad Khan was insufficient and despite an alliance somehow patched together between him and the outgoing governor, Shihabuddin Khan, a rout followed. Large parts of Gujarat passed out of Mughal control. Even as news of these developments reached Akbar, then busy with the building of a fort in Allahabad at the confluence of the Ganga and the Yamuna, Muzaffar Shah was making further advances with victories in Baroda and Broach. Patan alone remained firmly in Mughal control and was to emerge as the principal centre from where developments and events in the rest of Gujarat could be monitored.

Akbar decided, on hearing the news, that an army needed to be dispatched to Gujarat immediately. The noble picked to command the expedition for the region's relief and reconquest was Abdur Rahim. Despite his earlier experience in the Gujarat campaign, the choice was surprising. He was only twenty-eight years old and did not have the experience of commanding an army faced with such a politically sensitive task as the re-establishment of Mughal rule over an entire region. The early 1580s were, however, a period of some difficulty for Akbar and he was probably seeking a commander whose loyalty he could trust beyond any doubt. Not surprisingly, we find that in the farman of appointment, Abdur Rahim is addressed as Farzand or favoured son: 'The prop of the Kingdom, the pillar of sublime sovereignty, the trusted one of the glorious khilafat, worthy of royal favours, *farzand* Abdur Rahim.'[59]

Abdur Rahim was instructed to march towards Gujarat at the head of the contingent, taking a direct route via Jalor and Patan. A Mughal official, Qilij Khan, was instructed to bring in troops from Malwa and join up with this force, ensuring that lack of numbers would not be an issue when the enemy was faced.

Abdur Rahim reached Patan in late December 1583, spurred on, en route, by dispatches describing an increasingly grave situation. We have evidence of a council of war held around this time to decide on the future course of action. Abdur Rahim was advised by a number of nobles to halt in Patan till the contingent from Malwa arrived. Others, motivated by even greater caution, advised the consolidation of position and avoidance of a major engagement till the emperor himself could come. A third group, however, advised that it was best to press on ahead.[60]

It was the latter that Abdur Rahim was to pay heed to, although his initial inclination may have been to halt at Patan and wait for the reinforcements from Malwa.[61] The balance of forces was unfavourable to the imperial army by a ratio of at least three to four. The emperor's own advice appears to have been to await the arrival of the Malwa contingent led by Qilij Khan before engaging with Sultan Muzaffar Shah.

Abdur Rahim finally decided to press on with the battle after the prompting of an old Afghan noble, Daulat Khan Lodi, who was perhaps Abdur Rahim's closest companion as well as his principal commander:

> When after joining with Qilij Muhammad Khan and others you wage war he will emerge as the major partner, i.e., the credit of victory will go to him (being a senior). If you want to become KhanKhanan, fight Sultan Muzaffar with the greatest possible haste. If there is victory, you will attain yours father's rank and title and if defeat is (in store) you should die fighting, for to be killed in a battle is better than living in obscurity.[62]

Daulat Khan's advice was to seize the moment for himself if he wished to replicate the trajectory of his father and the other great nobles of the court. That the young Abdur Rahim heeded it shows that he was conscious of the emperor's expectations and the opportunity that the Gujarat campaign presented for him personally.

The council held in Patan has been dated to 31 December 1583 or thereabouts. Abdur Rahim is believed to have left Patan a few days later, marching towards Ahmedabad, where Sultan Muzaffar Shah had concentrated his forces; control over the city would decide the outcome of the war. The two armies were finally to engage near the settlement of Sarkhej, about 8 kilometres from Ahmedabad. Numerical superiority was certainly with the Gujarati forces and the engagement on 16 January 1584 was fierce. What seems to have decided the outcome in the Mughal army's favour was a tactic that had served them well since Babur's victory at Panipat. As the main body of troops engaged, a smaller force would undertake a flanking movement to the left or the right to attack the rear of the opposing army. Abul Fazl described the battle's crucial stage when the contingents of the rival commanders at the centre of their respective armies clashed and the Mughal left wing attacked the rear of Sultan Muzaffar Shah's force with a flanking movement:

> Mirza Khan with 300 warriors and 100 elephants kept his eyes on the marvels of daily increasing fortune. Muzaffar with 6,000 or 7,000 men came in front of him and was behaving insolently. Short-sighted well-wishers seized the Khan's [Abdur Rahim's] rein and sought to turn him back, but that fore rider of royalty planted more firmly the foot of courage. He snatched the reins from the hands of those who recognized not fortune and took the path of battle. He brought on the rank-breaking elephants, and the elephant Shermar and others distinguished themselves. Before they reached the foe the latter lost firmness. The breeze of victory refreshed the standards. Rai Durga went in that direction and inspired fear into the enemy's right wing.[63]

At this stage, rumours to the effect that the emperor himself had arrived with a large force, or that the army from Malwa had joined battle, led to a swift retreat by Muzaffar Shah's army. He was not, however, pursued and was able to regroup his forces at Cambay. Abul Fazl criticized the failure to seize him there and then:

> After that burnt out star had taken the road of flight ... he could have been seized if a little pursuit had occurred and that thorn would have been pulled up from the root. But in the joy of victory they did not attend to this, and the foolish talk of the wicked and the crooked in their ways was an additional obstacle.[64]

This cryptic reference to the 'wicked and the crooked' remains unclear. In any event, it is easy to imagine the jubilation in Abdur Rahim's camp at this first major victory for which the credit was solely his. A ceremonial entry was later made into Ahmedabad, but even more important must have been the penning of a dispatch to the emperor with news of the glorious victory. Akbar received the news on 8 February while still in the vicinity of Allahabad. Although the outcome of the battle of Sarkhej was of considerable significance to the Mughals and a personal triumph for Abdur Rahim, the description of Akbar receiving the news is somewhat subdued. Abul Fazl refers to the outcome demonstrating that 'The Shahinshah's knowledge of secrets became impressed on mankind.'[65] This may be construed as a vindication of the emperor's trust in Abdur Rahim, still largely untested with a major military command. Beyond this, however, we are not informed of any major celebration by Akbar, underlining perhaps that the task entrusted to Abdur Rahim was by no means regarded as complete.

On 14 February, after a halt of about a month at Ahmedabad, Abdur Rahim marched towards Cambay, where Muzaffar Shah had regrouped his forces. Perhaps this delay was the basis of Abul Fazl's critical remarks on the lack of timely pursuit. While one can only guess at the causes, a reasonable inference would be internal differences again, within the Mughal camp, over the future course of action. The debate that had taken place at Patan seems to have recurred with one section of the commanders advising that further military action should be left to the Malwa contingent, which had not so far faced the brunt of the fighting.[66]

Abdur Rahim was to join up with the Malwa force in Cambay but Muzaffar Shah avoided an engagement, withdrawing first to Baroda and then to Nandod across the Narmada in the Rajpipla Hills. It was here, around 10 March, that the second engagement took place, resulting in another convincing Mughal victory. Muzaffar Shah himself managed to flee again, but the back of the insurrection had been decisively broken and the expedition ended in an unqualified victory for Abdur Rahim. Although Gujarat remained prone to rebellion and insurrection as long as Muzaffar Shah was alive – he managed to elude Mughal forces for almost a decade – the danger of the province slipping out of Mughal control had passed. That this was now evident is demonstrated by the reaction in the court, then still in the vicinity of Allahabad, when news of the second victory was received. The atmosphere is best conveyed in the following description from the *Darbar-e-Akbarī*, the nineteenth-century best-seller on Akbar's court. The author of the account, Muhammad Husain Azad, claims that it is derived from a letter of Abul Fazl:

> ... it transpires from a reading of this letter that the absence of news for some days from Gujarat led to all kinds of loose talk. His and his father's enemies emerged from their hiding places and teased their friends, barely able to conceal their own glee about news from Gujarat. They even cast doubts on the emperor saying firstly this is a region in the Deccan and that, too, disturbed. When in such circumstances two experienced commanders [i.e., Itimad Khan and Shihabuddin Khan] have failed how could an inexperienced youth have been sent in their place? Is he a commander or an ornament of the court with little to do with battle and military matters? The well-wishers of Bairam Khan's family were quiet as indeed was the Emperor himself. For this reason, he hastened from Allahabad after laying the foundations of the new fort with the intention of proceeding to Gujarat and taking over the command himself. It was at this time that news was received of a glorious victory. The critics immediately changed their stance and started praising the Emperor's judgement in choosing the right commander despite others more experienced having been available.[67]

On receiving the news – first through banjaras (nomadic traders) and then via dispatches from the army itself – orders were passed that the victory be immediately announced through the music and drums of the Nukkad Khana. 'The Emperor praised Mirza Khan greatly and ordered that his father's title be awarded to Abdur Rahim.' He was also granted other honours: a mansab of 5,000, a robe of honour, a jewelled dagger and the right to bear a banner – *tuman tagh* – a standard of the highest rank. Military success had catapulted the young man to a status and position only just below that of the royal family itself, something his own father had achieved only in the closing years of his life.

That Abdur Rahim had hoped for these honours is evident from the counsel given by Daulat Khan Lodi on the eve of the battle of Sarkhej. Obtaining high rank and title was important not only because of the status they would confer, it was also a vindication of his father's and family's honour, and Abdur Rahim would have been encouraged to achieve this over the years by relatives, friends and retainers. Abul Fazl's letter to the noble mentioned that news of the victory 'had united enemies and friends alike' and that his being awarded the title of KhanKhanan was the very bounty of providence 'as it was the ultimate ambition of every Mansabdar of 5,000 Rank'.[68]

Abdur Rahim's own reaction to the victories and honours conferred on him is well documented. Before the battle of Sarkhej, he had taken a vow that 'if the bride of victory showed her face from behind the veil he would give all the goods and chattels that might be among the baggage as a thanksgiving … to the poor and needy…'[69] The legends that were to grow about the Khan-i-Khanan's generosity have their origin in this ceremonial gifting of all the property in his baggage train as thanksgiving for the victory. In the end, it was said, the Khan-i-Khanan had nothing to give to a trooper who approached him saying that 'A whole world has benefited by these gifts except me who has been left out.' Whereupon the Khan-i-Khanan took the silver inkwell he was using to pen a dispatch and gave it to the trooper.[70]

Military success, vindication of the emperor's trust, high honour and title – all this followed from the initial victories in Gujarat. It was undoubtedly a hard task for a young and still untested commander to lead an army into a region only nominally conquered, against a foe with some staying power. The prolonged debates over tactics and strategy in the councils of war before the battles at Sarkhej and Nandod reveal the enormity of the task Abdur Rahim faced in bringing about a measure of consensus over military tactics. In the presence of older, established nobles such as Itimad Khan, Shihabuddin Khan and Qilij Khan in the army, how did an inexperienced military commander obtain obedience, if not respect? We get a fascinating glimpse of these tensions as also of the atmosphere in the Mughal camp from the contemporary historian, Badayuni. He describes a situation where Abdur Rahim's retainers and those with personal loyalties to him find the condescension of the other generals irksome:

> And some domestics, who were servants of Mirza Khan, such as Daulat Khan Lodi, Mulla Mahmudi and others represented: 'Ever since we have been your attendants, we have not committed a fault. How comes it then that we should be so lorded and impressed by the imperial servants, when they are really our inferiors with respect to salutations and other points of court etiquette?' Mirza found these weak and fallacious arguments very agreeable and reasonable ...[71]

The context here is obscure, but the meaning is clear enough. We find Abdur Rahim seeking advice from Nizamuddin Ahmad, later to become a historian of repute, but at the time an important official in Gujarat. He is described as being married to Bairam Khan's foster-sister, though the exact relationship is not defined. Nizamuddin Ahmad's advice combined sturdy common sense with a full grasp of the intricacies of court hierarchy and etiquette. Abdur Rahim is told:

> These followers of yours are possessed by a spirit of wrong headedness; if the Emperor were to hear of it, what would be the order? As far as salutation on your part is concerned, what reason would there be in his ordering you to salute Shihabuddin Khan who is your superior both from the dignity in commanding 5,000 and also from being older in years? (since you would do it naturally without being ordered); and similarly how would it be right for him to order Itimad Khan, who once upon a time was commander of 20,000 horses to salute you?[72]

This argument evidently carried weight since Abdur Rahim followed the advice and 'gave up the pretension'. Itimad Khan and Shihabuddin Khan had both been humiliated by Muzaffar Shah by the time of Abdur Rahim's appointment as commander. Nevertheless, they remained important nobles. The irony of a young Abdur Rahim leading an army that included Shihabuddin Khan would not have been lost on others. Shihabuddin Khan was the son-in-law of Maham Anga, Akbar's wet nurse, who had been one of the principal agents of the plot against Bairam Khan. He had held important positions in court, and had also been governor of Malwa and of Gujarat. At the time of his recall from Gujarat and subsequent defeat and disgrace by Muzaffar Shah, he had been a *panch hazari* (5,000) mansabdar for at least seven or eight years. Itimad Khan was the governor of Gujarat at the time of Bairam Khan's murder when Abdur Rahim was an infant. Thus Abdur Rahim's appointment over the heads of senior nobles would have made the politics of command itself challenging, quite apart from the fact that there was a difficult military mission to accomplish.

Even earlier, during Abdur Rahim's attachment to the Mewar campaign in 1579, we have a sense of his rising status and the attendant swagger of his immediate attendants and followers. This was clearly hard for established nobles such as Shahbaz Khan Khumbu to swallow. At one stage in the Mewar campaign, Shahbaz Khan was the commander of the force and Abdur Rahim one of the many nobles who formed part of the army. Daulat Khan Lodi was Abdur Rahim's principal military captain. We have an episode in which Daulat Khan's innate aggression, coupled with the knowledge that his young master enjoyed the emperor's favour, rubbed against Shahbaz Khan's own notions of propriety. Shahbaz Khan insisted on his army marching in single file, while he rode at the head of it. No one was allowed to come abreast of him. Daulat Khan Lodi chose to ignore this convention and galloped to the head of the line, disregarding the protests of Shahbaz Khan's retainers. Outraged, Shahbaz Khan sent his brother, Abdal Khan, to stop him. When

Daulat Khan refused to fall back, Abdal Khan hit his horse with a stick, whereupon Daulat Khan unsheathed his sword and hit Abdal Khan's mount with its hilt. Faced with this insubordination, Shahbaz Khan ordered his soldiers to seize Daulat Khan, who 'displayed feats of valour' but could not prevent Shahbaz Khan's followers from attacking and plundering Abdur Rahim's camp. Perhaps realizing this elaborate game of one-upmanship had got out of hand, Abdur Rahim made a public display of penitence. He spread a mat and sat at the entrance of Shahbaz Khan's tent for a whole day and produced a 'credible witness' to testify to his lack of involvement in Daulat Khan's actions. This seems to have checked any permanent damage, though Daulat Khan Lodi retained a hatred for Shahbaz Khan to the end of his days.[73]

Abdur Rahim's rise and the many favours shown to him by the emperor would have been galling to many less favoured. Given the dense network of kinship, politics and intense jostling for position and power, all of which characterized the Mughal court, Abdur Rahim needed a major military success to cement his rapid and remarkable progress and to ensure continued appointments to important positions. The emperor's favour or the fortune of high birth could take him only so far. Individual enterprise, leadership, the ability to take risks were equally important, and the Gujarat campaign provided the opportunity for him to showcase all of these.

The clearest evidence of Abdur Rahim's enhanced stature is found in two letters that Akbar sent him in March–April 1586. The first of these is principally concerned with the death of Raja Birbal in an engagement with Afghan tribesmen on the Punjab–Afghanistan frontier. The emperor here shares his anguish with Abdur Rahim and reminds him that:

> ... after Birbal's death, he (KhanKhanan) was the most intimate and loyal friend, a grand gift of God. (He) assures him that he would soon realise how important he had become. (Akbar) Prays that he

(KhanKhanan) should receive favours from Akbar's everlasting glory and be a joy for himself (Akbar) through his own crowning facility.[74]

The second letter, written around the same time, contains a long description of some pigeons gifted by an ambassador from Central Asia and a number of statements testifying to Akbar's attachment to Abdur Rahim: 'a loyal friend like him could be absent from, and without the honour of attending imperial assemblies, but was always remembered by him (Akbar) particularly at moments of rejoicings such as these. The absence of KhanKhanan was felt when the pigeons were presented before him …'[75]

Abdur Rahim spent about five years in all as governor of Gujarat; for most of this time his residence was in Ahmedabad, although we hear of a few visits to the court for ceremonial occasions. Muzaffar Shah continued in his efforts to strike a military blow at Mughal power in Gujarat, sometimes seeking an alliance with the ruler of Junagadh, and at other times attempting to raise an army on his own. While these efforts did not result in any notable successes, he was nonetheless able to elude the Mughals and continued to constitute a very real threat to their position. This chapter in Gujarat's history was to close only with his betrayal and suicide in 1592 when Mirza Aziz Koka was governor a second time around.

Notwithstanding the fact that the final prize of Muzaffar Shah eluded him, the governorship of Gujarat was an important stage in Abdur Rahim's political career as it conclusively established his reputation as a military commander. The battle of Sarkhej, his first military victory, had a certain symbolic value for Abdur Rahim; to commemorate it he laid out a pleasure garden, the 'Fateh Bagh' or garden of victory, near Sarkhej on the banks of the Sabarmati. It was to remain 'for generations one of the chief attractions near the capital city. The grounds were covered with flowering shrubs and fruit-bearing and other shady trees, watered by several canals in the classic Mughal style.'[76] The site was apparently the battlefield where Muzaffar Shah was defeated and it covered an area of some 50 acres, surrounded by walls on three sides. Abdur Rahim and his family appear to have had a special affinity with the place and one of his daughters, Khair-ul-Nissa, was to entertain Emperor Jahangir there during his stay in Ahmedabad in 1618. The garden and the structures within it are described as having remained intact till at least the early eighteenth century. A few traces still remain in Sarkhej, although the pace of its urban expansion means that their final extinction is near.

Abdur Rahim's time in Gujarat was marked by important events in his personal life. It would appear that the absence of sons had been a cause of some worry to him and to Mah Banu for several years. This concern was evidently shared with the emperor, for we have Abul Fazl writing:

> He had always wished for a son and had been impatient in his seeking for one. When he was in Gujarat, HM said one night 'when you write the Farman styling him the KhanKhanan, say in it that the life giving deity will soon give him three sons and that he is to call them Iraj, Dorab and Qaran'. In a short time the saying was fulfilled and great and small had a new knowledge of hidden things.[77]

These lines were recorded in the description of the thirty-fifth regnal year (1590) in the context of a third son being born to Abdur Rahim, so Abul Fazl may well have retrospectively accorded the emperor the power of foresight. Nevertheless, the fact that Abdur Rahim and Mah Banu were greatly worried over the absence of male progeny is evident. For they did not have any male children till Abdur Rahim was nearly thirty years old and they had been married for at least a decade.

Military victory, great honour and prestige and, finally, male progeny, came to him almost together, and Abdur Rahim must have felt that the bounties of providence were visibly favouring him. The first son, Mirza Iraj, was born in Ahmedabad in 1585 and the second, Dorab Khan, in 1586. A third son, Mirza Qaran, was born in 1589 (or 1590), perhaps after Abdur Rahim's return to the court, for we are informed that he held a feast and 'begged for the presence of His Majesty who granted his request'. Four other sons, Mirza Rahmandad, Amrulla, Haydar Quli and Mirza Shah Pasand are mentioned. Of the seven sons, Mirza Qaran, Haydar Quli and Mirza Shah Pasand died either in infancy or before they could become grown men. Mirza Rahmandad was born of a princess from the Sohayya tribe in Sindh and we will take note of this alliance a little later.

Amrulla is described as the son of a bond maiden. We know little about him barring Jahangir's description of him seizing a diamond mine from a local ruler in Gondwana (central India) on the instructions of his father in mid-1618. The lack of information about him suggests he too may have died soon afterwards. Perhaps his being a bond maiden's son made him less interesting to the chroniclers of the time.

About Abdur Rahim's daughters the historical record is inevitably less explicit: we can put a name to only two of them, although there are references to a third. Janah Begum was the oldest and we will encounter her briefly on the occasion of her marriage to Emperor Akbar's son, Daniyal, in 1597 and later, during Abdur Rahim's imprisonment by Mahabat Khan. About Khair-ul-Nissa we know even less, barring an entertainment she arranged for Emperor Jahangir at the Fateh Bagh in Sarkhej in 1618. There is also a fleeting glimpse of her from the English traveller and ambassador to the Mughal court, Sir Thomas Roe, whose correspondence tells us that a kind of friendship grew between Khair-ul-Nisa Begum and Mrs Steele, the wife of one of Roe's companions. Were these girls the elder of Abdur Rahim and Mah Banu's progeny? It is possible to at least speculate this was so since two daughters in a row may well explain the parental anxiety for sons. We are also informed of a third daughter, who was married to a Persian émigré named Murad Safavi. Many Persians came to Abdur Rahim's court and Murad Safavi is described as having gained his heart's desire by marrying a daughter of Abdur Rahim.[79]

Gujarat thus completes one phase of Abdur Rahim's life: He has established himself in the court, vindicated the honour of his father and his family and is well on the way to becoming a family man. Our knowledge of his family life is, however, meagre. Certainly, the older sons were given the best education available; both Mirza Iraj and Dorab Khan, despite their principal interests being political and military, are described as expert calligraphists. There is an old tradition in Hindi literature which holds that the composition of the verses of the *Jahangir Chandrika* by the great poet Keshavdasa was a means of tutoring Mirza Iraj. This is unlikely but certainly it was composed at Mirza Iraj's request. Yet, at least one of the other sons, Amrulla, is said to have been illiterate, a discordant note, given the family he was born into. Was this because his mother was a bond maiden and so he was not given the education appropriate for a noble's legitimate son? Or was it because Abdur Rahim's household fell into some turmoil after the death of Mah Banu and the premature demise of two or three other children? But this is to anticipate the rest of the story. In any case, the children further reflect the close relationship between Abdur Rahim and the emperor, as we find the former seeking advice and support on relatively mundane domestic matters. In a letter to Abdur Rahim in March–April 1586, the emperor says:

> ... regarding KhanKhanan query as to where he should send his sons, or whether he should send them to the court, before himself proceeding to the Deccan, expresses his affection for children by emphasising that there was no one (so dear) as KhanKhanan and his sons in the family. Reassures him that even while they may be out of his (Akbar's) sight they could never be out of his mind. Expresses his insistent desire at the moment that KhanKhanan and his family should always be by his (Akbar's) side. Asks him to keep himself informed of the movements of the royal camp, and to send the children to the court if he (Akbar) returned to the capital early.

> Alternatively, to keep them in Gujarat or at any other proper place if his (Akbar's) return was delayed ...[80]

The immediate context of this letter appears to have been Abdur Rahim's proposal to launch an expedition against the Deccan kingdoms. Yet the letter illustrates also the position of Abdur Rahim in Akbar's affections and his continued ascendency within the imperial hierarchy. Akbar's concern comes through clearly in the advice to send the children to Agra only if he (the emperor) is present. If his return is delayed, the children are to remain with their father. The subtext is obviously of Akbar declaring his personal, particular concern for the children and, by extension, for Abdur Rahim himself. In another letter, the emperor refers to a new addition expected in Abdur Rahim's family. He writes almost jocularly:

> ... since a new guest was on his way to the house, suitable arrangements should be made, after which, some pigeons would be dispatched for him and the new guest. In the event of delay in the guest's arrival, the Emperor would still send him some pigeons but fewer than he expected.[81]

This was possibly in anticipation of the addition of another child to Abdur Rahim's family and reflects more clearly than anything else the personal, intimate affection that bound the two men.

Abdur Rahim's formal association with Gujarat as its governor ended with his recall to the court in 1587. The emperor had other plans for him and Abdur Rahim's own ambitions appear to have broadened. On at least two occasions, he had strongly hinted at wanting a change from Gujarat. In March–April 1586 there was correspondence with the emperor on a proposal from the Khan-i-Khanan for the conquest of the Deccan – evidently an issue of considerable interest to Akbar after the completion of the conquest of Gujarat. Similarly, in 1587, upon hearing that the emperor was marching towards Kabul for the projected conquest of Badakhshan, Abdur Rahim had represented that he should be permitted to join the campaign. Perhaps he was seeking an assignment that would enable him to deliver another victory. Pacification and administration of a region where a real military threat no longer existed could hardly have had the same appeal for a young man once the initial enthusiasm of being the province's foremost nobleman had receded. In both cases we have the emperor counselling patience in response to what were evidently repeated requests for a fresh assignment.

Abdur Rahim rejoined the emperor in Lahore in March 1587. Although he retained the designation of governor of Gujarat till at least January 1590, this charge now appears to have been largely a nominal one and he principally functioned as a courtier and high nobleman of the court. We come across references to court-related assignments given to him at this time. The first of these, in December 1587, pertained to a major Shia–Sunni dispute. An important nobleman, Mirza Fulad, had attacked and seriously wounded a Shia, Mulla Ahmed, on the grounds that he had made disparaging remarks about the companions of the Prophet. According to Badayuni, upon being asked 'Whether he had stabbed from religious hatred … said, "if religious hatred had been my motive, it would have been better to kill a greater one (i.e., the Emperor) than the Mulla". This was reported back to the Emperor, who said, "This fellow is a scoundrel; he must not be allowed to remain alive" and ordered his execution, though the people of the harem asked the Emperor to save him.' [82]

Abul Fazl, while not doubting that sectarian zeal was the reason for the crime, points out that Abdur Rahim, along with three other courtiers, was asked to investigate the circumstances of the murder. It was only after they had reported back to the emperor that the execution was ordered and carried out, despite pressure brought to bear by the harem. He also acknowledges that it was the catholicity of opinion permitted by the emperor that may have provoked Mulla Ahmed, who was 'a firm adherent of the Imami doctrines, and talked largely about them, continually brought forward discourse about Shias and Sunnis, and from a despicable spirit used immoderate language'.[83]

Investigating a matter such as this would have been a sensitive task. That Mulla Ahmed was intemperate and provocative in his language was not in doubt, but particular objection was taken in his case because 'he was an apostate, his father having been a Sunni'.[84] Was the real transgression that he had crossed the divide and although born a Sunni, had adopted the Shia creed? On the other hand, Mirza Fulad was a person of some eminence in the court and Akbar had, sent him as an ambassador to Turan in 1577. The sympathies of the harem appear strongly to have been with him, adding to the delicacy of the task of the investigating team, which included Abul Fazl.

On another occasion, in the summer of 1589, while forming part of the emperor's personal party during Akbar's tour of Kashmir, we find Abdur Rahim in the midst of what can only be called a royal tantrum, spurred on by a failing relationship between Akbar and his eldest son Salim.[85] The march was through difficult terrain and the emperor marched in conditions that Abul Fazl was to describe:

> The walking was over snow. Shall I describe the severity of the cold? Or shall I tell of the depth of the snow, and of the bewilderment of the natives of India? Or shall I describe the heights of the pass, or speak of the narrowness of the path, or of the heights and hollows of this stage. While crossing, it snowed and hailed.

The harem had remained with the main entourage at a camp at Bhimbhar. Prince Salim was asked to return and escort some ladies of the harem back to the emperor's party. Obviously concerned at the prospect of the women having to traverse this difficult terrain, Akbar dispatched Abdur Rahim to 'attend the Prince and assist him in bringing on the secluded ladies'.

At the designated place of the emperor's rendezvous with the prince and the harem, 'a cloud settled on the face of joy' since 'the Prince Royal arrived alone and reported that on account of the difficulties of the road it was not fitting that the Ladies should be brought, and that he had left them at Naushera'.

At this point, exacerbated perhaps by the strain of the journey and worry about the harem, we witness a spectacular show of Akbar's temper which is best described, if at some length, in Abul Fazl's words:

> ... the prince was not allowed to pay his respects and an order of censure was sent to the KhanKhanan. If the prince, owing to his evil propensities, behaved in this way, why did you allow him to exhibit such audacity? In his wrath, H.M. ordered, in the midst of the rain, and of the slipperiness of the ridges, that his horse should be brought. His whole thought was that he would go in person and bring the ladies. He took with him (a tiny group) ... (and) ... an order was given that no one except (these) persons should accompany him. He travelled that day up to evening and reached Hirapur. I was nearly losing my senses, and the dress of society was falling from my shoulders. By God's help the ebullition of my disposition did not prevail over my reason and discretion. The whole confusion was caused by thinking why at such a time should the Shahinshah of the Universe become so angry? And why did he take upon himself this task which could be accomplished by a minor servant? Why did he not accept the truthful speaking of his royal servants. The Prince shut himself in his tent and abstained from food and sleep. When the devoted servants petitioned (him), the wise sovereign yielded and returned. An order was given that the KhanKhanan should bring on the ladies.

Abdur Rahim's position in court and his intimacy with the emperor and others in the royal family are illustrated by these incidents. Yet, attendance on the emperor, his duties as an important courtier, and his political and administrative preoccupations do not define the totality of his existence in this period. He also has two important literary achievements.

The *Waqayat-i-Baburi* is perhaps Abdur Rahim's best known achievement in the Persian historical record and one of the most significant milestones in his literary career. Abul Fazl writes that on 24 November 1589, in the middle of the Kashmir–Kabul tour, '... the KhanKhanan produced before the august presence the memoirs of Firdaus Makhani (Babur) which he had rendered into Persian out of the Turki and received great praise.'[86]

Although some parts of the memoirs had earlier been translated into Persian, the larger text, as a whole, had remained inaccessible to a court that was increasingly dominated by the Persian language and fast losing touch with its Central Asian and Turkish heritage.[87]

The inability to read his grandfather's memoirs, or rather have them read to him, would surely have troubled Akbar. Not surprisingly, there is evidence of at least two other attempts in the 1580s to translate the memoirs into Persian. In 1584, 'Mirza Payadah Hasan Ghaznavi commenced its translation ... but he could not translate the account beyond the first sixth and a part of the seventh year. Subsequently, Mohammad Quli Mughal Hisari continued the work, and brought it down to 1528-29.'[88] Abdur Rahim's work appears to have been a fresh translation and '... it is almost certain that the KhanKhanan used Babur's own text to translate the work into Persian.'[89]

Was Abdur Rahim familiar enough with Turkish to undertake such a task? Abul Fazl in the *Akbarnama* and other contemporary or near-contemporary writers affirm that he was, as do later texts of the mid-seventeenth and early eighteenth centuries. It would be reasonable to assume, however, that Abdur Rahim put together a group of scholars in his own entourage and assigned them the task, retaining for himself overall supervision as well as the eventual credit. Indeed, such a hypothesis was put forward in the *Darbar-e-Akbarī*. Its author, Muhammad Husain Azad, despite his very obvious admiration for the Khan-i-Khanan, derides the possibility that Abdur Rahim would have personally translated the work himself:

> It is clear that this high-minded and premier noble would neither have strained his eyes nor burnt the midnight oil. There were a number of scholars who lived off his generosity and one of them would have been instructed (to do the translation). One or two helpers would have been assigned (to him). They would have worked together keeping the KhanKhanan informed of their progress. He would have supervised their work and a beautiful copy would have been prepared.[90]

Another nineteenth-century sceptic, this time a European, suggested that this may well have been the case:

> I think, too, it may reasonably be doubted if Abdur Rahim was competent to translate this work. His father probably knew Turki, despite the fact that he was born in Badakhshan, and was a Shia by religion; but he was murdered when Abdur Rahim was only four years old, and the latter was the son of a Hindustani mother, and was born and lived and spent all his life in India.

However, he revised his opinion later, to write:

> I did appear to have underrated Abdur Rahim's acquirements as a Turki scholar for in Hawkins' 'Voyages' ... Hawkins tells us that he had a three hours' interview with the KhanKhanan at Burhanpur and 'the language that we spoke was Turkish which he spoke very well'.[91]

The presentation of the translation to the emperor took place in Kabul just a few days after the emperor had visited the tomb of his grandfather. Evidently, it had been ready for some time and a suitable occasion awaited for its ceremonial presentation.

It is also to these years, when Abdur Rahim was in attendance on the emperor at court, that scholars of Hindi literature date a work of sensuous and occasionally erotic verse, the *Barvai Nayika Bhed*.

Although this is seldom popularly cited as one of his principal works, it is to literary theorists a minor milestone of medieval Hindi literature. It is an integral work consisting of 116 couplets – the first being a *doha*, followed by an invocatory verse and then 114 *barvai*s – the latter being an even briefer couplet than the doha.[92] The substance of the work is the classification of different kinds of *nayak* and *nayika* – heroes and heroines – and an exploration of the range of emotions felt by women in love.

This genre of literature has a complex antiquity in Sanskrit and has traditionally been classified as 'nayak nayika bhed', i.e., the different kinds of heroes and heroines, or lovers – male and female. Drawing on this tradition, a considerable volume of 'nayak nayika bhed' poetry was written in Hindi from the sixteenth century onwards. It was composed primarily, but not entirely, by poets associated with the courts and much of it drew upon imagery and emotions associated with Krishna and the gopis of Brindavan – in particular, Radha. Building on this Krishna-related theme, the genre lent itself easily to highly stylized, ornamental and erotic verse – a reason for the strongly puritanical and adverse nationalist reaction against it that emerged in the late nineteenth and early twentieth centuries.[93]

Abdur Rahim's *Barvai Nayika Bhed* consists largely of a classification of heroines, their emotions and other defining characteristics. Some ninety of the 114 couplets are devoted to these themes. The male lover or nayak receives less elaborate treatment, the types and classifications being covered in some fourteen barvais. The remaining barvais are devoted to descriptions of the nayika's friends (sakhis) and of particular situations, for instance, lovers meeting after a long separation, or being surprised during an assignation, etc. The classification of the nayak and nayika is largely based on categories derived from Sanskrit poetry and poetics. This characteristic is common to the entire genre in medieval Hindi literature, although the fact that Hindi poets greatly developed and experimented with the basic Sanskrit genre is widely accepted.

These English translations of a few of the barvais, each of which describes a particular nayika or a type of emotion, are illustrative of the work:[94]

(1) Svakiya: The heroine who is entirely content with her lover

A shadow of a glance hovers at the corner of her eye
When she moves you can't even hear her anklets.

(2) Mugdha: The still sexually immature, modest and bashful young girl

She is wearing a 'laharia' silken sari;
Its borders are set with pearls;
Her hair is spread all over her face.

As wind passes over her
It makes her sari and hair picturesque
The arrow of Love has gone deep into her heart
And so her breasts have become swollen and glances slanting.

(3) Agyatyovana Nayika: The young woman who is still unaware of her emerging sexual maturity

What is this malady that has enlarged my breasts?
There is a burning pain all over my limbs.

(4) Gyatyovana Nayika: The young woman who has become conscious of her sexual maturity

Youth has come upon me all of a sudden.
It has deprived me of the company of my friends.
It makes me terribly sad.

(5) Navodha Nayika: The heroine who is embarrassed and bashful when approaching her lover

She eagerly dresses herself with a chunni and chanderi to meet her
lover,
And puts on her ornaments and kohl on her eyes.

(6) Israbdha Navodha Nayika: The heroine who is fearful and repelled by her lover

That her lover not be able to touch the tip of her breasts
She sits rigidly with her thighs joined to her chest.

(7) Ganika Pravatsyatpreyasi Nayika: The courtesan saddened at her lover leaving

Give me a rosary of memories before you leave
To tell, my love, when I'm lovesick and find reprieve.

(8) Premagarvita Nayika: The woman who has subordinated her lover with her passion

She puts on her own collirium; weaves her garland;
Picks and wears a dappled mantle – my soul's foundation.

(9) Mugdha Agatpatika Nayika: The Mugdha woman whose husband is returning home from afar

After so many days my beloved comes home today!
Our young bride thrills at the thought as she works away.

(10) Parakiya Vasaka Sajja Nayika: The courtesan awaiting her lover

The elders at last are sleeping; she knows it well!
She opens wide the window, in passion's spell.

(11) Vacanacatura Nayaka: The man who invites a woman for love making, cleverly disguising his motive

In the dense mango grove's cool shade
The cuckoo comes with a challenge, but flies away.

Abdur Rahim's *Barvai Nayika Bhed* is a minor landmark in the history of medieval Hindi literature, not just because it was the work of a Mughal nobleman attempting a genre well known in Sanskrit poetics; it is, in fact, one of the earliest attempts to use this Sanskrit genre in Hindi poetry. While opinion is divided on whether it is the first or among the first of the genre, its reputation as a pioneering work is undisputed.

The second innovation for which the work has been praised is the use of the barvai couplet. Perhaps the most often quoted example of barvai is the great Tulsidas's *Barvai Ramayan*. It was one of the poet's minor works – a collection of sixty-nine couplets – although attribution to Tulsidas is itself far from proven. An early eighteenth-century hagiography of Tulsidas claimed that his use of the barvai couplet was suggested to him by Abdur Rahim, although a more rigorous examination of the construction of the couplet by the two poets has not supported such a hypothesis.[95]

The introductory verse of the *Barvai Nayika Bhed* is a doha – perhaps to underline the contrast with the body of the work and also to emphasize that the verse that follows is, in fact, novel. The doha is in Braj Bhasha, again to underline the distinct dialect – Avadhi – of the barvais themselves.[96] The conscious innovation is emphasized in the doha itself:

I composed poetry in doha and kabit metres
I did not get satisfaction from the chappay metre also
Realizing that the barvai metre is the most pleasurable
I am composing this work in this metre.[97]

What were the circumstances in which Abdur Rahim became acquainted with this obscure verse form? A Hindi literary tradition ascribes his interest in the barvai couplet to a charming story in which a munshi, or clerk, in his establishment overstays his leave. The Munshi's wife sends a couplet in the barvai metre to Abdur Rahim, seeking his indulgence on the grounds that her love for her husband needs constant tending. The brevity of the couplet captivates Abdur Rahim and leads him to experiment with the metre and thereafter compose the *Barvai Nayika Bhed*. The authenticity of this story cannot be proved, but it is interesting to note that it reflects both a feminine impulse to Abdur Rahim's interest in the barvai, as well as the idea of the separation of two lovers – a well-established idiom in classical Sanskrit poetry and one with which Abdur Rahim's familiarity can easily be imagined.

In sum, the *Barvai Nayika Bhed* incorporates two innovations: the use of the barvai couplet and the 'nayak nayika bhed' genre in Hindi. Abdur Rahim's use of the barvai has been praised for its economy and control and for the range of emotions expressed using the briefest possible metre. Early twentieth-century surveys of medieval Hindi literature's greatest names concluded without much difficulty that if the doha is synonymous with Bihari, the *chaupai* with Tulsidas and the *pada* with Surdas, the barvai couplet is the domain of Abdur Rahim.

What is the evidence that Abdur Rahim composed this work during the three years he spent in court, at the end of the 1580s, between his assignment in Gujarat and the future campaign in Sindh? The logic is that such a work could only be that of a relatively young man – Abdur Rahim was at this time in his early thirties – who was already adept at writing verse. How valid is such a proposition? We know that Abdur Rahim was exposed to a host of eminent Sanskrit, Hindi and other literary scholars and poets at court. The sensuous, often erotic themes imply an engagement with the court culture where every physical and emotional refinement was available. However, asserting a specific chronology to Abdur

Rahim's verse is, as we shall continue to notice, a hazardous undertaking.

The *Barvai Nayika Bhed*, despite its literary innovativeness and technical virtuosity, is by no means Abdur Rahim's most accomplished work. It is possible to imagine him striving for technical virtuosity by espousing classical Sanskrit prosody. While he was successful in pulling off this literary exercise, the work he produced, on account of its self-imposed classical character, is ultimately self-limiting. One critic has concluded that Abdur Rahim, 'despite having an eye for metaphor, tends towards the formulaic in his verse composition'.[98]

Abdur Rahim, the popular people's poet reflecting on the crests and troughs of life, is yet to emerge.

3

THE SENIOR COMMANDER

THE GUJARAT chapter of Abdur Rahim's life formally came to an end while he was still in Kabul, in attendance on Akbar. He was now an established figure in the court and trusted by the emperor. In January 1590, we are informed of 'the bestowal of the Vakilship on the KhanKhanan. As ability and disinterestedness shone on his forehead he was raised to this post and Jaunpur (in eastern India) was made his fief.'[1]

The appointment as vakil of the empire was part of a larger chain of imperial transfers, which saw Mirza Aziz Koka transferred back to Gujarat as governor. The post of vakil had fallen vacant on the death of Raja Todar Mal, Akbar's trusted advisor, and Abdur Rahim's elevation was a demonstration once again of the emperor's continuing high regard. Both this position as also the jagir of Jaunpur were to remain a transitory arrangement because, in early 1590, he was given Multan and Bhakkar as jagirs, with instructions to lead the army on an expedition to conquer Qandahar and Sindh.

The Sindh expedition and the build-up to it mark also the first major controversy in Abdur Rahim's relations with the court. According to Abul Fazl, Abdur Rahim's instructions were to first march on Qandahar and only thereafter embark on the Sindh expedition. Both regions were uppermost in the emperor's mind: he had effectively shifted his capital to Lahore in the Punjab from 1585 onwards to focus more closely on the northern and north-western frontiers of the empire. If the death of Mirza Muhammad Hakim, Akbar's half-brother and – to all intents and purposes – independent ruler of Kabul, provided the immediate context for this, there was also the need to keep a close watch on the Uzbeks, who had been active in instigating Afghan tribal activity and defiance against the Mughals in Kabul. In 1586, a pact between Akbar and the Uzbeks gave the Mughals the freedom to attend to the constant attacks by Afghan tribes and simultaneously initiate a determined military campaign to annex Kashmir and Sindh into the empire.[2]

The subjugation of the Afghans and the conquest of Kashmir dominate the next three to four years. Kashmir was finally settled in 1589 when Akbar travelled to Srinagar to receive the submission of the rebel ruling prince. The war against the Afghan tribes in early 1586, however, saw a significant defeat being inflicted on the Mughals when Raja Birbal, Akbar's great Hindu friend and a prominent nobleman in his court, was killed in battle. Over the next few years, the tribes were relentlessly pursued by Mughal armies and finally contained to the region which today comprises the border areas between Afghanistan and Pakistan. Meanwhile, Akbar had not forgotten Sindh. Muhammad Sadiq Khan was appointed governor of Multan and instructed to ensure the annexation or subjugation of Thatta, the capital of Sindh. However, Mirza Jani Beg, the ruler of Sindh, repelled the Mughal military assault in 1586, inflicting heavy losses. These could have been more severe but for Mirza Jani Beg's reluctance to provoke a full-scale Mughal attack.[3] For much the same reason, he also offered a face-saver to the Mughals by dispatching envoys and presents to the emperor and acknowledging Mughal suzerainty, even if only nominally. The military defeat was a real, if temporary, setback to Akbar's plans.

With the appointment of Abdur Rahim as governor of Multan and Bhakkar in 1590 came the next phase in the Mughal conquest of Sindh. The subjugation of Kashmir was complete and the position against the Afghan tribals was stable. Mirza Jani Beg's continued refusal, on different pretexts, to come to Lahore and offer submission in person, now became sufficient provocation for Akbar to make a major military move against him. It could also be that Akbar wanted under his control the region he was born in during Humayun's desperate flight from the pursuing Afghan army. Sindh was, moreover, a rich economic prize. It provided, then as now, access to the sea for the Punjab. Finally, the region offered an alternative route to Qandahar and this gave Sindh added importance in the Mughal strategic framework.

It was in this context, then, that Abdur Rahim set out on the expedition to Sindh. As Abul Fazl reiterates, he had been given a twin mandate: to first proceed to Qandahar and then to embark on the military expedition against Sindh. Qandahar, it may be recalled, was retaken by the Persians in 1568 after Humayun's death. It remained, however, a possession to be reclaimed.

In a letter to Abdur Rahim dated 25 December 1589, Abul Fazl asked him:

> Not to take any bitter remarks as of Abul Fazl's making, since they have been added at the Imperial command; advise(d) him not to bother much about his former Jagir of Jaunpur and the amount it had brought him in ... the KhanKhanan's complaints were presented to the Emperor in summary form, and his letter was not reported in detail: KhanKhanan is advised not to delay his departure to Thatta and the expedition to Qandahar.

It would appear that Abdur Rahim had complained to the emperor about the arrangement whereby he was assigned Multan and Bhakkar instead of Jaunpur. In fact, his association with Jaunpur had been brief. It was assigned to him in December 1589 or so, and we are informed in the *Akbarnama* that he was dispatched on the expedition to Qandahar and Sindh as early as January 1590.[5]

When he left Lahore, with what is described as a very large contingent, the emperor met him at the army's first halt, demonstrating both his affection for Abdur Rahim and the importance he assigned to the expedition. The instructions to Abdur Rahim at this stage, as set out in the *Akbarnama*, appear clear enough: first Qandahar via Baluchistan, and then Sindh.[6]

Yet Abdur Rahim appears to have taken a somewhat leisurely course, arriving in Bhakkar, which lay somewhere between Multan and Thatta, around December 1590, which suggests that he did not march directly there from Lahore. It is possible that he may have escorted his family back to Agra, or was busy outfitting the army for the proposed campaign. Equally, it could be that the tardy progress signalled Abdur Rahim's dissatisfaction with the new jagir arrangements or, indeed, with the instructions given to him.

In any case, his arrival at Bhakkar was at odds with the original instructions, at least according to Abul Fazl. The delay may well have been because he kept insisting, even while he was en route, on a change to the mandate given to him. Abul Fazl's disapproval of Abdur Rahim's tactics and probable motives is writ large in the *Akbarnama*:

> It has been mentioned that a choice army was appointed under the command of the KhanKhanan to take Qandahar. As Multan and Bhakkar were in his fist, he left the rear (i.e., the shortest) route … and took a long route in order to look after his jagirs. Meanwhile, mercenary people who did not understand what should be done represented the large spoil of Thatta and the little spoil of Qandahar. The commander took leave to conquer Sindh.[7]

The court, although we only have Abul Fazl's writings to confirm this, preferred an initial move against Qandahar. Abul Fazl, in his letters to the Khan-i-Khanan, constantly exhorts him not to postpone the Qandahar campaign and expresses displeasure over the early march against Sindh.[8] Notwithstanding these pressures, it appears that Abdur Rahim insisted on a rearrangement of the priorities set out for him. Against the allegation of Abul Fazl that his real motive for attacking Sindh first was simply a desire to plunder the riches of the region, Abdur Rahim offered logic, both financial and military: he was faced with an acute shortage of funds, and essential to the success of the Qandahar expedition was the submission of Mirza Jani Beg.

Finally, Abdur Rahim's insistence on getting to Thatta first paid off, and the court sanctioned a change in plans. It is possible that Akbar too was keen that Mirza Jani Beg be dealt with quickly. However, the Sindh ruler's resistance was fierce, and it was only after two closely contested riverine and land battles that he finally capitulated in mid-1592.

The first of these took place in Nasrpur, about 75 kilometres from present-day Hyderabad in Pakistan. Both sides had equipped themselves well with large masted boats and artillery. Mirza Jani Beg's considerable force included a contingent of Portuguese troops from Hormuz. He decided that the only way to take on the Mughal army, which had the resources of the empire behind it, was to attack in force and secure a quick victory. Accordingly, he dispatched a large flotilla of boats and troops. He did not, however, commit the rest of his army in support of this flotilla and after a fierce battle, the Sindh forces were defeated. The second engagement ended with a protracted siege of Unarpur, until Mirza Jani Beg capitulated and agreed to a treaty with the emperor. Daulat Khan Lodi, incidentally, was in the thick of the fighting in Unarpur. Throughout, Abdur Rahim was kept regularly provisioned with both money and supplies by the emperor, suggesting that Akbar had been keen all along that Thatta be dealt with firmly.

The terms of Mirza Jani Beg's surrender included his attendance in Akbar's court, the acceptance of a mansab rank in the Mughal hierarchy and the marriage of his daughter with Mirza Iraj, Abdur Rahim's eldest son, then about six years old. It has been said that Akbar gave permission for the wedding only after the political integration of Sindh into Mughal India.[9] This was, however, not the only marriage born of politics during the campaign. Abdur Rahim himself married a niece of the Raja of Umarkot, the town that was Akbar's birthplace. Mughal troops had been dispatched to that desert chiefdom in order to deprive Mirza Jani Beg of any support from his hinterland; Abdur Rahim's marital alliance with Umarkot may also have been a means of driving a wedge between Mirza Jani Beg and his neighbours. Another account, however, interprets the marriage differently:

> When Abdur Rahim KhanKhanan conquered Sind he might have heard about the beauty of Sodha women and wished to marry within the family of the Rana. As the Rana Megraj of Umarkot had no daughter suitable for KhanKhanan he offered the hand of his brother Man Singh's daughter.[10]

It is also possible that the marriage was meant 'to emphasize direct links with an important local ruler, till now mainly within the Sindh orbit'.[11] The Umarkot princess bore a son, Mirza Rahmandad, in AD 1600, who was later said to be 'very proud to be the son of a mother whose birthplace was the same as that of Akbar'.[12]

With the cessation of hostilities, Abdur Rahim made a grand entry into Thatta, Mirza Jani Beg's capital. A string of banquets and feasts followed, reciprocally organized by Abdur Rahim and Mirza Jani Beg, and inevitably accompanied by grand poetry recitals. In these Mirza Jani Beg's sardonic sense of humour is evident. During the recitation of the 'Saqinama', a panegyric in honour of the Sindh campaign and Abdur Rahim's victory by Mulla Shakebi, a well-known poet of his entourage, one of the verses referred to both Abdur Rahim and Mirza Jani Beg in highly complimentary terms:[13]

> A Huma (phoenix) which used to strut about in the celestial world,
> you captured and set it free from your net.

Mirza Jani Beg responded:

> May God's mercy be on him that he called me Huma;
> had he called me a jackal, nobody had tied his tongue.

Abdur Rahim's Sindh experience ends with his escorting Mirza Jani Beg to the court of Akbar, where he was confirmed as a mansabdar with the rank of 3,000. Mirza Jani Beg spent the rest of his life in the Mughal court as a subordinate noble but never stopped craving for his independence, or for Sindh. We have a glimpse of his unreconciled spirit years later, in the Deccan, where Akbar had personally moved to supervise operations. In 1599–1600 the Mughals besieged the great fortress complex of Asirgarh on the Malwa–Deccan frontier. Witnessing the fort surrendering without any real fight, Mirza Jani Beg is believed to have stated that 'had he been the lord of that type of fort, even if the vice-regent of God had, in his august person, come to Sind, victory would not have been possible'.[14]

When this comment was brought to the emperor's notice, Mirza Jani Beg is said to have fallen from grace and 'within a few days he died'. But this may well have been coincidental since a likely cause of death could also have been the Mirza's heavy addiction to alcohol.

With the presentation of Mirza Jani Beg in court in 1593, we come to the end of the Sindh chapter in Abdur Rahim's career. Till his next assignment to the Deccan, he remained in court, in attendance on the emperor, with numerous ceremonial and other duties. In October 1593, for instance, the ceremonial function of escorting a scion from the Safavid dynasty, who was seeking refuge in the Mughal court, to the emperor's presence, was assigned to him.

It is to this period that the composition of another lot of barvai verses has been attributed. No unifying theme runs through this collection of about a hundred verses. Some are erotic and sensuous, often inspired by the emotions arising out of the separation of lovers; a few have a stronger moral overtone and an emphasis on the virtues of an ethical life, as also a focus on faith and devotion. Many of the descriptions of separation – *virah* – are made more poignant by their being set amidst different seasons – *barahmasa*. The barahmasa was an established tradition describing the twelve months of the lunar calendar by dividing them into different seasons. Each season is then described alongside emotions of separation and loneliness. Both virah and barahmasa are favoured themes in medieval Hindi poetry. One can think of Abdur Rahim planning a larger work of barvai verse to illustrate the barahmasa but not completing it, and miscellaneous verses being added from time to time. This collection of barvais was found in the second decade of the twentieth century and seen then as an important literary discovery. It was announced in a prestigious literary journal, *Saraswati*, in 1926, in the following terms:

> The manuscript is written in very beautiful handwriting and on every page the margins are flowers and vines beautifully painted in the Persian style. Abdur Rahim's maternal grandfather was Jamal Khan Mewati and the manuscript was found in a place where the population of Mewatis is preponderant.[15]

The manuscript begins with the following annotation:

> 'Victory to Shri Ram'
> Barvais composed by Nawab KhanKhanan
> Begin[16]

The form of the six introductory couplets has led scholars to conclude that the compilation was meant to be an integral whole although there is, as we have noted, no single unifying theme. The first five verses are stylized invocations of the Hindu deities Ganesh, Krishna, Surya, Siva and Hanuman; the sixth verse is addressed to the guru or the teacher:[17]

GANESH

I salute the destroyer of obstacles, lord of success and attainment
Imparter of pure intellect, child of the one whose head wears the moon.

Krishna

With steadfast mind I rehearse the name of Nandakumar
The foundation of life for Vrasbhanu's daughter.

Surya

Worship the lord of animate and inanimate, the sun god
Giver of pleasure to afflicted folk, a very saviour.

Siva

I mediate upon the deliverer from grief, Girija's lord (Siva)
Maintainer of the skilful, three-eyed, having the Ganges on his head.

Hanuman

I meditate upon Hanuman, the breaker of adversity, son of the wind
Destroyer of the grove of the wicked demon, and dear to Raghubir.

The Guru

Again and again I salute the lotus feet of my preceptor
Through whose brilliance the darkness of my mind is removed.

The early barvai couplets that follow these invocations describe the pangs of separation in the context of changing seasons, and in particular the onset of the rains, when travel becomes difficult and the absent lover cannot return:

The clouds pour rain on all sides in increasing torrent
The month of Savan comes, O Nandakumar.

Still Ghanshyam has not remembered us and come, friend;
Some woman has settled somewhere and kept him.

How long will patience remain in my heart, my friend?
Even in Savan he does not come – where is Balbir?

Clouds gather all round, lightning flashes:
Lover and beloved swing together in Savan's Teej festival.

A day without seeing Manmohan has no charm;
I shall not forget his qualities, friend – just bring us together.

They pierce my inner heart and impale my soul,
poison-like, supreme amongst all, these eye arrows.

Constantly my mind stands on tiptoe, ever watching the door
Ever since Nandakumar left my friend.

O my heart, night and day worship lord Balbir
who removes people's pain without appraising them.

Surging from all sides, the rain pours down:
so too without my lover, friend, my body pines.

A breeze of threefold nature roams, pleasant and lovely;
in Hari's absence friend, it seems like a sword.

You spoke of coming, Kisor, at the beginning of Asarh;
[but now]clouds gather on all sides, the peacock dances.

The love-sickness in my limbs has grown, friend; slander has grown –
what cruel trick is this you have done, Nandanandan.

Amidst such verses of separation and unrequited love are also a few in which the poet's engagement appears to be entirely moral and ethical:[18]

What fate has written cannot be erased,
Just as the love birds in a cage sleep with their faces turned away (from each other).

Seeing the flour, so white and shining clean,
The customer asks the grocer the price even without any intention to purchase any.

All say 'Be strong of heart!', now Hari's gone away –
A stupid barren woman knows not the pain of childbirth.

There is, however, a lack of directness and purpose in these verses which contrasts with the practised ease with which the more conventional verses about pining lovers are rolled out. Clearly Abdur Rahim was still new to ethical and sententious poetry, although this was the genre that would come to be regarded as his most characteristic work.

The maturity of language and ease of composition suggest that the *Barvai Nayika Bhed* was composed prior to these verses. In many ways, the period immediately after the Sindh expedition marks the high point of Abdur Rahim's career. His victories in Gujarat and Sindh, the knowledge that he enjoyed the confidence of the emperor, the presence of his children, particularly his sons who were soon to reach maturity, would have given Abdur Rahim both self-confidence, prestige and – in the light of his own, uncertain early years – a sense of security and personal fulfilment.

He had had a lot to prove to the court, to the emperor, to his father's enemies, and he had to do it without a large and powerful family, such as most nobles in the court possessed. He had won an eminent and – it must have seemed – unassailable position by virtue of his own shrewdness, talent and discipline. It is considerations such as these that led some scholars to date these barvai couplets, with their brimming confidence and maturity, to this period in court when he was a little short of forty years of age.

There are many legitimate questions that can, however, be posed to counter this conclusion. The principal difficulty stems from the fact that in the entire corpus of Abdur Rahim's verse, we have little by way of historical markers in terms of references to datable events or persons. But again, this is common to most medieval Hindi poets. It was written of the great poet Kabir: 'I think that it is not at all impossible that no such person ever existed and that his name is mere cover to the innovations of some free thinker among the Hindus.'[19] This statement applies equally to Surdas and is, in fact, an overarching problem since the absence of clear chronological and historical references is notable in many significant works of medieval Hindi literature.

Abdur Rahim's life, unlike that of Kabir or Surdas, has identifiable biographical milestones, which are documented in detail. The frustration, therefore, is compounded. But there is one other characteristic that stands out too. Abdur Rahim's verse so far, quite apart from the absence of a historical imprint, shows also the complete absence of any sign at all that it is the work of a Muslim composing Hindu devotional verse. There is no apparent synthesis here, or even a passing reference to Islam, something that would have embedded these verses in real life. One could even conclude that the composition of these verses may have been a purely aesthetic exercise of playing with a literary form or genre, rather than an act inspired by faith or devotion.

Attributing Abdur Rahim's literary works in Hindi to specific periods in court would also imply that his literary pursuits were limited to the time spent in court. The evidence from Persian literature, however, suggests otherwise and the early 1590s is a useful point to locate him in the web of Persian poetry and patronage. We may do this by detailing the one aspect of his life, outside of the political, that is well documented by Abul Baqi Nihavandi, a contemporary biographer and hagiographer.

This Persian scholar, like many others, emigrated from Persia to India to seek patrons at the Mughal court. Like the others, he may have heard of Abdur Rahim's liberal patronage of Persian poets and writers and gone to Burhanpur on arrival from Persia in 1614. He seems to have been assigned the task, or may have suggested it himself, of writing about his patron, which he did at great length, producing the *Maathir-i-Rahimi* in Persian, which remains untranslated, although a critical edition was printed by the Asiatic Society of Bengal in three large volumes over a twenty-year period between 1910 and 1930.

The *Maathir-i-Rahimi* recounts Abdur Rahim's genealogy and biography, and the careers of his sons. Although a panegyric, the work is invaluable for the information it provides about the Persian poets and scholars who enjoyed Abdur Rahim's patronage and formed what has been called Abdur Rahim's 'literary circle'. From the details we have of these poets and their work, it has been possible to construct a fuller picture than might have been otherwise possible, of Abdur Rahim's literary personality and his court.

One of the best documented aspects of the life of Abdur Rahim is of him as a patron of Persian poetry and literature. In this he followed, to some extent, in the footsteps of his father, who patronized several well-known poets from Persia. Abdur Rahim built upon this inheritance and, during his own life, stories of the munificence of his court and his generosity became legendary. The narrow sectarianism of the Safavid court and the contrasting widening 'of the space for accommodating opposition and conflict' in Akbar's court provides a broader context for the migration of Persian intellectuals from Persia to India in this period.[20] The prospects for material improvement in Mughal India and the encouragement they received from the high nobility attracted many litterateurs from Central Asia and Persia. And Abdur Rahim was easily the greatest patron amongst the high ranks of the Mughal nobility.[21]

A poet at the Safavid court composed the following verse, described as a 'daring challenge' to Shah Abbas, the ruler of Persia, in which he declares that he 'expects no literary patronage in Persia' and that he would send his poems to the Khan-i-Khanan in India:

That in Persia no one comes within sight,
Who is a customer of the commodity of meaning;
In Persia the palate of my soul has become bitter,
Go I ought towards Hindustan;
Like a drop towards the ocean,
I may send my commodity to India;

For there is not among the learned of the age,
The customer of speech except the KhanKhanan.[22]

Another Persian poet, Rasmi Qalandhar, spoke of the Khan-i-Khanan's generous patronage of poets in the following terms:

Through auspicious praise of thee the fame of the perfection of the subtle singer of Shiraz (**Urfi**) reached from the East to Rum.

In praising thee he became conversant with a new style, like the fair face which gains adornment from the tire woman,

By the grace (fayd) of thy name **Faydi** like (his predecessor) **Khusrau** annexed the Seven Climes from end to end with the Indian Sword.

By gathering crumbs from thy table **Naziri** the poet hath attained a rank such that other poets

Compose such elegies in his praise that blood drips in envy from the heart of the singer.

Men of discernment carry as a gift to Khurasan, like the collyrium of Isfahan, copies of **Shakebi's** verses.

By praising thee **Hayati** found fresh life (hayat); yea, the substance must needs strengthen the nature of the accident.

How can I tell the tale of **Nau'í** and **Kufwi**, since by their praise of thee they will live until the resurrection dawn?[23]

Urfi, Naziri, Mulla Shakebi and Hayati were among the more prominent of the poets in Abdur Rahim's court at different points of time and they also count as among the great Persian poets of the time in India. Kufwi, in the stanza above, refers to Mir Husain Kufri, who consciously and provocatively chose to declare himself an infidel or non-believer with the nom de plume he adopted. According to Abul Baqi Nihavandi, Abdur Rahim's literary establishment could count over 130 scholars and poets, many from Persia, who attached themselves for varying periods of time to his court. This assembly of talent was legendary during Abdur Rahim's lifetime, as indeed were stories of his generosity and lavish patronage, and these were greatly celebrated in verse both in Persia and in India. It is likely that the reams of verse in praise of Abdur Rahim outweigh anything similar that was offered to any other noble or even prince of royal blood.[24]

We also see these poets and scholars performing a multitude of tasks: as ambassadors and envoys to the kingdoms of the Deccan, as regular soldiers and troop commanders, serving in judicial and administrative positions, or working in Abdur Rahim's celebrated library as compilers of the diwans of other poets, calligraphists and so on.

This library needs special mention, even though it was by no means unusual for Mughal nobles to have their own collections of books and acquire valuable manuscripts. But the scale of Abdur Rahim's collection and the establishment he maintained to look after it was quite unique. Clearly, he drew inspiration from Emperor Akbar in amassing a very large collection of books in different languages. One estimate of the size of the imperial collection, based on a stocktaking after Akbar's death, mentions a figure of 24,000 manuscript volumes. Abdur Rahim is believed to have started building his library as a young man when he was governor of Gujarat in the early 1580s. Abul Baqi Nihavandi, who served for some years as the superintendent of the library, after joining Abdur Rahim's court in 1614 or 1615, informs us that it 'was visited by nearly a hundred scholars daily who met there to have their doubts settled, their difficulties solved and their frontier of knowledge enlarged and extended'.[25]

Employed in the library were calligraphists and copyists, but also painters, paper makers, bookbinders, gilders and illuminators. Details about many of them are enumerated in the *Maathir-i-Rahimi*. The establishment, inclusive of translators, is said to have numbered ninety-five.[26]

Abdur Rahim also enjoyed a considerable reputation as a connoisseur of painting, as the following anecdote illustrates:

> When the KhanKhanan was going to the court of the Emperor, a painter came to him and handed over to him one of his pictures. The scene depicted therein was of a lady who was taking a bath and that a maidservant was rubbing the sole of her foot with a pumice stone. The KhanKhanan looked at the picture for a moment and then putting it in his palanquin went away to pay homage to the Emperor. When he returned, the painter reappeared. He ordered that a sum of five thousand rupees be paid to him. The painter said, 'My picture is hardly worth more than five rupees, but there is one artistic skill which I have employed in it. If your Honour has marked that, then I shall be glad to accept your reward, for then I shall have satisfaction that your Honour has really appreciated my work.' The KhanKhanan said 'Your skill lies in that you have expressed in the lady's face the feeling which is produced by the rubbing of the sole with a pumice stone.'[27]

Charming as this anecdote is, similar accounts are encountered with regard to other patrons as well. But the point of these stories is to establish Abdur Rahim's reputation as a generous and discerning patron. Reports of his lavish gifts to poets and painters are also numerous. For instance, it was said that '(W)hen Khwaja Muhammad of Gilan sent to the KhanKhanan a Persian poem which was copied by the well-known calligraphist, Amir Muizzuddin Muhammad of Kashan, he sent him a lakh of rupees'. Mulla Shakebi is described as having been given ten thousand rupees when he dedicated a collection to the Khan-i-Khanan. The poet Naziri is described as having once asked the Khan-i-Khanan what a lakh of rupees looked like; a heap of coins amounting to the sum was ordered to be placed before the poet and was thereafter given to him. Urfi was said to be so generously looked after by the Khan-i-Khanan that he never needed other patronage: '... he used to send to Mulla Urfi, without ever having seen him, so much money every year that he had not to knock on any other person's door'. [28]

The *Maathir-i-Rahimi* informs us that the first poet from Persia who was attracted by the munificence of Abdur Rahim's court was Maulana Naziri Nishapuri in 1583. He was ranked by his contemporaries as a poet of a very high order and his association with Abdur Rahim seems to have lasted till his death in 1612. Naziri was introduced to the imperial court in 1587 by Abdur Rahim, but did not have much success there and was to remain attached to his original patron. He did, however, receive high praise from Emperor Jahangir, who invited him to his court and wrote in the *Jahangirnama:*

> I had previously summoned Naziri of Nishapur, an expert in the art of poetry who lived as a trader in Gujarat. At this time he came to pay homage. He presented an ode he had composed in imitation of Anvari's ode that begins, 'What youth and beauty is this the world has regained'. I gave him a reward of one thousand rupees, a horse and a robe of honour.[29]

Naziri had earlier been attached also to the court of Prince Murad when the latter was governor of the Deccan, which is somewhat surprising given the less than harmonious relationship between Abdur Rahim and the prince. Naziri's relationship with Abdur Rahim was, by all accounts durable, and notwithstanding other attachments, he reappears periodically in Abdur Rahim's circle. Naziri had a strongly religious bent of mind and it has been said that 'in matters of religion he was somewhat of a fanatic'.[30] While accompanying Abdur Rahim to the Deccan in 1595, he stayed back in Mandu to study Arabic and theology. Abdur Rahim was later to help him perform the Haj in 1603 in response to the following verse:

> Through genius I cannot explain myself,
> like the Magian wine in the jar;
> the very garments are rent on my body,
> when my ideas ferment.
> Through thy beneficence I experienced all the pleasures of this world:
> what wonder if through thee (also) I should obtain provision for the other world?[31]

Since his religious views were orthodox, we find him, not surprisingly, on the opposite side of the divide with the Abul Fazl family and are informed that he wrote verses attacking 'the heretic Abul Fazl'. The latter's description of Naziri also reflects this tension: '... he possesses poetical talent and the garden of thought is open to him. Outwardly he is a good man but he also desires plans for the edifice of the heart.' Naziri's attachment to Abdur Rahim is demonstrated also by his entrusting his patron with his diwan or compilation of poetry in 1611, shortly before his death.

Wit, polished verse and elegant repartee were what made a literary reputation. We see all these in the brief career of Urfi Shirazi (1555–91), who was 'probably on the whole the most famous and popular poet of his century'[32]. On his arrival in India from Shiraz in Persia, Urfi had originally attached himself to Sheikh Faizi, Abul Fazl's brother and a greatly celebrated poet of the court. The contemporary historian Badayuni, whose dislike for Abul Fazl and his family is palpable even some four centuries later, described the falling out between Urfi and Faizi:[33]

> One day he went to Sheikh Faizi's house and found him fondling a puppy. Urfi asked, 'What is the name of this child of my lord's?' The Sheikh replied, 'His name is well known (Urfi)', and Urfi replied at once 'May it be auspicious'. The Sheikh was very angry but to no purpose.[33]

Wolseley Haig, the nineteenth century translator of Badayuni's history, explains how the pungency of the repartee is lost in translation:

> Urfi's question is not as pointed in the original Persian and might be rendered, 'What is the name of this highly born one'? Faizi replies by giving Urfi's *nom de plume* to the unclean animal. Urfi's retort is one of the commonest expressions of politeness, but its mordant wit cannot be reproduced in a translation. In its original it is '*mubarak bashad*,' i.e., 'may it be auspicious' or 'may it be *Mubarak*'. Mubarak was the name of Faizi's father.

Urfi was to attach himself to Abdur Rahim till his premature death in 1590. A Shia himself, his differences with Sheikh Faizi and Abul Fazl had less to do with doctrinal matters than with literary rivalry. Thus his verses have been held to be representative, along with those of Faizi and others, of the fact that Persian poetry was 'an important vehicle of liberalism in the medieval Muslim world (and) helped in no insignificant way in creating and supporting the Mughal attempt to accommodate diverse religious traditions'. The following verses are illustrative:

> Give up the path of the Muslims
> Come to the Temple
> To the master of the wine house
> So that you may see the divine secrets.
>
> Or
>
> The lamp of Somnath is (the same as)
> the fire at the Sinai
> the light spreads all around from that.[34]

Urfi's free-thinking liberalism contrasts with Naziri's doctrinaire orthodoxy. What unites them is their dislike of Abul Fazl and his brother, Faizi. The presence of both men – perhaps simultaneously – in Abdur Rahim's court points to an eclectic environment rather than a predisposition for one or the other point of view.

To his contemporaries, what was most striking in Urfi's personality was not so much his liberalism as his overbearing vanity, arrogance and conceit. He was to write of the great Sadi, also from Shiraz:

> Wherefore did Sadi glory in a handful of
> the earth of Shiraz,
> If he did not know that it would be my birthplace and abode.[35]

Vanity and conceit were necessary facets of a poet's identity. The patron was expected to play up to these in order to coax the poet to even greater literary heights. Illustrative of this is an episode from the life of Naziri, who wished to retire from court after performing the Haj and was waiting for an opportune moment to tell Abdur Rahim so. The opportunity presented itself when, in a letter to Anisi, also a well-known poet of his court, Abdur Rahim scribbled a few lines in the margin to Naziri. Pretending to be deeply hurt, Naziri sent some verses seeking retirement:

> Thou didst not scribble two or three madds [sentences] especially for our heart.
> A master has never noticed his servant in this slighting manner.
>
> We have erased our name from the margin, since we can no longer suffer ourselves to be the parasite of thy pen,
>
> Enjoying the favour that is really meant for someone else.[36]

In the same poem, he went on to give the real reason:

> The day on which I clothed the sacred house (Kaba) with the dust of thy gate,
> I was divested of all desires.
>
> Hence my firm resolve that by devoting myself to the worship of God,
>
> I shall renounce the company of my master and his servants.

Abdur Rahim's large literary establishment had at its heart his library, and a galaxy of scholars and poets. We are fortunate that at least a few of the physical products of this establishment have survived and careful historical research has shown that these did indeed emanate from Abdur Rahim's court. These provide us with fascinating insights into his interest in literature and his patronage of it. Brilliantly illustrated Persian translations of the principal Hindu mythological and religious texts, the Ramayana and the Mahabharata, a *Ragamala* collection of eighteen paintings with accompanying poetry, illustrated manuscripts of the Persian *Shahnama,* Amir Khusrau's *Khamsa* and the *Timurnama* are among the best known manuscripts that have survived of Abdur Rahim's great collection. These and other works 'constitute the most coherent corpus of Mughal painting produced for a patron outside the imperial family'.[37] Very evidently he was an ideal patron – wealthy and prepared to expend large sums of money on poets and artists, so that the circle around him and his library remained so large that it acted as a magnet for others.

The first three texts mentioned above exemplify Abdur Rahim's interest in Hindu scriptures and literature and the latter three locate him in the mainstream of classical Persian and Islamic traditions. The great library is, of course, dispersed and some of its greatest possessions are now known by the collectors or museums that acquired them in the aftermath of the decline of the Mughals, rather than by his name. Abdur Rahim's brilliantly illustrated Persian translation of the Ramayana is thus known as the *Freer Ramayana*. Similarly, his copy of Amir Khusrau's *Khamsa* is identified as the *Berlin Khamsa*.

The preparation of the Ramayana and Mahabharata manuscripts followed in the wake of Akbar's initiative of translating important Hindu scriptures into Persian. The *Ragamala*, known today as the 'Laud Ragmala', remains perhaps the earliest Indian manuscript to enter a European collection. It was presented by the Archbishop of Canterbury to the Bodleian Library in 1640. The subject of the manuscript itself was an innovation:

> Paintings of the *Ragamala* (literally, garland of ragas, or musical modes) are not illustrations in the usual sense of the word, but belong to an ancient Indian tradition in both music and poetry of creating personifications of the six basic melodies or modes of Indian music. Each of these major 'male' *ragas* are further divided into five minor expressions, deemed its 'wives' or *raginis*. These six 'families' are usually depicted in a series of thirty-six paintings, which are often accompanied by a brief identifying caption or verse.
>
> The origin of the iconography of these visual interpretations of musical modes is obscure. From the late-sixteenth century on, *ragas*

and *raginis* began to be represented by images of worship, seasonal activities, or emotional situations which seemed to correspond in mood. By the mid-seventeenth century, the iconography of *Ragamala* paintings had become relatively fixed, so that very coherent visual traditions were established over large geographical regions. Although Akbar had ragas sung at the Mughal court, the *Laud Ragamala* paintings have no known precedent in imperial Mughal painting.[38]

This innovation in Mughal painting style, of course, reminds us of two others attributed to Abdur Rahim: verse composition in the barvai metre and the migration of the nayika bhed genre from Sanskrit into the realm of what we today consider Hindi literature.

Two of these manuscripts contain long annotations in Abdur Rahim's own hand. One, in Khusrau's *Khamsa,* illustrates Abdur Rahim's love of books, the pleasure he derived from them and the persistence with which he directed efforts to acquire them for his library. Needless to say, he was also prepared to spend large sums of money:

In the year 1012 [1603–04], Mir Baqi of Samarqand brought from Gujarat several folios of this rare *Khamsa*, whereupon they were obtained. I asked him about the rest of the book. After much inquiry about the remainder of the book, it was ascertained that a book with several other folios was in the possession of Mirza Abd al-Malik, who generously presented it to me. We took it and the remainder of the book from him. After asking many questions, we heard that everyone in Gujarat had some folios. Mir Baqi was sent again with two or three thousand rupees so that he could buy whatever he wanted from whomever had [some folios], and thus he put his hands on several folios. In that way it happened by divine grace that all these five books were acquired save for several pages which had been lost. Among these [people], one person had fourteen or fifteen folios, thinking that if he brought them himself with a few other books ... set out from Agra. Those were the days when this humble servant, who together with Mahabat Khan was accused through the artifices of slanderers, had gone to court and thence to petition the king. Because my intentions were just and I went in truth and in a solicitous manner, I appeared in the court of His Majesty Sulayman Makani (Akbar) and was delivered from those afflictions. If the sword of the world should move from its place, it would not cut even a vein unless God so willed it. I have seen the meaning of this. In brief, the man who had brought the folios kept bringing others … He brought those ten or twelve folios. Anyhow, this book … whose writing is by Mawlana Sultan' Ali and whose paintings are by Bihzad, was complete … The paintings that had fallen out were [ordered to be] restored, and those other folios … too which had fallen out, Muhammad Mu'min was ordered to rewrite. The binding was tooled in gold and the borders were embellished. The work was done in ten or eleven years so that it reached completion on the date 1026 [1617]. Written by Abd-al Rahim son of Muhammad Bayram, may the two of them be forgiven.[39]

Given Amir Khusrau's stature in Mughal India, it is not surprising that Abdur Rahim had a copy of a principal work of his in the library. In this case we find the search for a manuscript of the *Khamsa* enduring over a decade, the final product emerging almost fifteen years after the first folios came into his hands. Restoring and repairing the manuscript and then improving it were very much part of the endeavour. But the references to enemies in Akbar's court around 1603–04 and to Mahabat Khan's involvement are intriguing. Even if, as we shall see, Abdur Rahim faced in Akbar's closing years a period of uncertainty, Mahabat Khan was to emerge as a noble of importance only after the installation of Jahangir as emperor. These lines were written in 1617–18, when work on the manuscript was completed, certainly a time when Mahabat Khan was a premier noble of the empire and also a rival power centre to Abdur Rahim. Had a bitter personal enmity with Mahabat Khan, which would mature and come to fruition some decade and a half later, already germinated in these closing years of Akbar's reign? Or could it be that Abdur Rahim deliberately erred in describing events of a decade and a half earlier, possibly to cast Mahabat Khan in a poor light?

The second annotation, on the flyleaf of the Ramayana, is even more fascinating. It is regarded as the longest specimen of Abdur Rahim's handwriting:

> This book, which is known as the *Ramayana*, is among the esteemed books of India. It is an account of Ramacandra, who was one of the great kings of India. His external and spiritual graces were exemplary, being manifestations of divine attributes. According to Valmiki, who was among the greatest darvishes of India, it is said that he [Ramacandra] is the son of Mahadeva [Siva]. [These] discourses are an account of his graceful attributes, pleasing virtues, great victories, and conduct, which show the magnificence of his being. At the order of the officials of His Majesty Akbar, Naqib Khan of Qazwin, who was among the high-ranking lords and became exalted in the companionship and service of the king of kings, was honoured and made eminent by the love of the king. He translated [this book] into Persian from the Sanskrit language, in which Indian literature was recorded at the time. There was a brahman by the name of Deva Misra who would interpret the meaning of the verses (*slokas*) and Naqib Khan would translate [that] into Persian. The desire of the king, that king of Jamshid-like magnificence, on this occasion was that paintings be executed in this book. Upon completion of that [work], this slave reared by the kindnesses of the Emperor, Abd al-Rahim, son of Bayram Khan (may he rest in peace), requested that as I had the privilege of seeing this book, I be allowed to have a copy made. By royal favour, permission was granted. This work was prepared and illustrated by the scribes and painters of this well-wisher of the king. Thus, it may be viewed by people. This work was completed in the year A.H. 1007 [AD 1598–99]. The beginning of the work and illumination of this work was made in the year 996 Hijra [AD 1587–88]. The total number of paintings is 135, and the number of leaves is 349 leaves. It was completed under the term of the supervision of the loyal and gracious Mulla Shakebi Imami, and reached completion by the mercy of God.[40]

This note, in many ways, unites the Hindi with the Persian Abdur Rahim, and again brings out the length of time it took to complete such a project – almost thirteen years in this case. But it does leave what has been called a 'troubling question':

> [the] erroneous identification of Rama as the son of Mahadeva, another name of Siva ... How could someone interested enough in Hindu culture to commission an illustrated copy of this text be unaware of an important belief of Hinduism, that is, Rama is an incarnation of Vishnu? That this point is emphasized repeatedly even in the Persian text of the Freer Ramayan raised doubts about how carefully Abdur Rahim actually read the manuscript or at what level he understood it.[41]

Was this a simple oversight? Or is there more to it?

Attached to Abdur Rahim was an establishment of Hindi and Sanskrit poets and scholars, parallel to the Persian. The details of this are sketchier and derive largely from poems composed in his honour. There are, however, numerous examples of such poetry that praise and admire his many accomplishments. The list of poets, much as in the case of the Persian, includes many of the premier poets of the time: Gang, Keshavdas, Narhari, Mandan, Harnath, Prasidh, among others.

The mainstream Hindi poet most associated with Abdur Rahim's name is Gang (c. 1533–1617), about whom we know little barring the fact that he was counted amongst the most accomplished Mughal court poets, and that he also eulogized Raja Man Singh, Prince Daniyal and Birbal. That he suffered at Jahangir's hands is widely cited and some accounts point to his having been trampled to death by an elephant at the emperor's orders. Apart from his scattered verse, what is best known of his life is an episode of how Abdur Rahim gave him 36 lakh rupees for one verse:

The beetle bee does not suck nectar from the lotus flower
The serpent does not hold the precious stone on his hood
The breeze and the cloud stand still;
The swan has deserted the pond;
The pheasant and its mate no more make love;
The most pretty maid has no attraction for man;
Sesnaga holds not the earth steady;
Even the chariot of sun stops in its sojourn;
When the son of Bairam KhanKhanan
Tightly straps the saddle to his horse.[42]

According to Hindi literary accounts, on receipt of this huge gift, the poet is said to have spontaneously recited:

How did you pick up
This habit of giving alms
As the hand goes up to give
The eyes go downward on their own.[43]

Abdur Rahim's equally spontaneous response completes the tradition:

The Giver is someone else
People needlessly give me credit
Hence my eyes are low in humility[44]

There are numerous verses of Gang in praise of Abdur Rahim and the following two translations convey some sense of them.

For Gang,
Bairam's son Abdur Rahim KhanKhanan
And his son Dorab
Are as valourous as
Kashyap's son Surya
And his son Karna
And the Ocean's son, the Moon.

Both are true sons of their fathers
As Ram of Dashrath
Samba of Krishna
Brahma of the Lotus
Ganesh of Shankar
And as Kalpraviksh is of the Ocean.
Hanuman of the Wind
Anirudh of Pradhuman.
So Abdur Rahim KhanKhanan and Dorab Khan.

Hearing Abdur Rahim's drumbeats in preparation for battle
The Turanis loose heart
The Christians are startled
Multan shivers
The Men of Maru stop all work
The Rana of Mewar begs for mercy

Portugal and the West
The North
Gujarat and the Deccan
Are all in turmoil
There is consternation in Arabia, Africa,
Rome, Syria and Khurasan

That Abdur Rahim KhanKhanan marches into battle.

What is striking, of course, is that Gang situates Abdur Rahim's attributes of valour and generosity in the context of Hindu mythological and epic traditions. At the same time, we encounter other references to be expected in a Mughal context: Khurasan, Bhakkar, Multan, Turan, Rome, and so on.

In the work of other Hindi poets of the time we find more conventional descriptions of Abdur Rahim's martial qualities. Such is the case of the poet Prasidh (c. 1534) about whom we know little beyond the comment in a nineteenth-century anthology of Hindu poetry that he was a poet in Abdur Rahim's patronage.[45]

When the vanguard of Abdur Rahim's army marches
The Seven Seas and the Seven Continents tremble.
Kuber shivers
The Meru Mountain shakes
Hanuman's hair falls
The Earth sinks and cracks
The pillars of the palaces of Khurasan shake
The thousand hoods of Sheshnag
Splinter into pieces.

We encounter similar descriptions by the poet Mandan, who possibly composed his verses between the 1590s and the 1640s, and was from Jaitpur in Bundelkhand.

Your bow, KhanKhanan
Behaves with you as you do with your enemies.
For your qualities
Reach the ears of your wicked enemies
Just like the bow string reaches your ear.

You unsheath your sword and extract tribute
It fearlessly holds on to your hand.

You march on the world
It rides on your shoulder.

There are other poets too, about whom we know even less, though their panegyrics to Abdur Rahim have endured.

Harnath

Abdur Rahim son of Bairam
Has only two masters
Always uppermost in his mind

For Harnath

I have seen his devotion to Jahangir the ruler of Delhi
And to Siva

Around Siva's head he places vines and leaves
On Jahangir's feet he offers the heads of his enemies.

ALA KULI

Seeing the amount the KhanKhanan gifts
It would seem as if all of Lanka had been looted

As if the peak of the Sinhal Island has been broken
And he has received multitudes of elephants, camels, horses and treasure.

As if he is friends with Kuber
And has received thus countless treasures.

O KhanKhanan, have you found some limitless mine?
Or have you found the paras stone?

KESHAVDAS

The most valuable verses in praise of Abdur Rahim come, however, from the poet Keshavdas, also a court poet from Bundelkhand, in the kingdom of Orchha. Keshavdas (1555–1618) is believed to have been technically the most advanced and certainly the most famous medieval court poet in north India. His best-known works include *Kavipriya* (Handbook of poets), *Rasikpriya* (Handbook for poetry connoisseurs) and *Ramchandra Chandrika* (Moonlight on Ramachandra). Two other works draw him closer to the Mughal court: The *Virsimhdevcharita* (The Deeds of Bir Singh Deo, 1607) and the *Jahangirjaschandrika* (Moonlight on the fame of Jahangir, 1612).[46]

The former is a panegyric to Prince Bir Singh Deo, Jahangir's friend and the assassin of Abul Fazl. Some Hindi literary traditions have maintained that the *Jahangirjaschandrika* was composed for Abdur Rahim's son, Mirza Iraj (Shah Nawaz Khan). The opening verses of the work are in praise of Iraj, Abdur Rahim and Bairam Khan. Possibly the work was commissioned by Iraj as a gift for

Jahangir. The year of its composition broadly coincides with the time that Mirza Iraj was acquiring an important position in the imperial hierarchy and was moreover highly regarded by the emperor.[47]

In general, we find in Keshavdas's verses describing Abdur Rahim the same qualities and attributes that we noticed in the other poets: a Hindu mythological framework, occasional glimpses of Krishna and Siva devotion and finally, references also to the Persian and Central Asian universe, perhaps to reiterate that this was, after all, a Mughal nobleman who was being so eulogized.

The fame of his (Abdur Rahim's) sword
Has crossed the seven seas.
He has the blessing of both Siva and Vishnu.

In the battlefield
He has the pace of Rudra.

With the boundless nectar of love
Like the Kalpraviksha
He is the support of Akbar's empire
And also its guardian.

* * *

His son's fame has spread over the world
He has emerged as the protector of Jahangir.

Abdur Rahim protected Akbar's sovereignty in every respect.
He was as dutiful as the brave Hanuman towards his one master.

Abdur Rahim's charisma dazzles the entire earth, its splendour like the milk ocean.
And his pure motives and limitless nobility are respected everywhere, just like Ganges water.

The Khan of Khans is like Rama's arrow.
It destroys evil and protects the world.[48]

* * *

He has won Bhakkar
And made its king a beggar.
Brought the king of Khurasan in chains
Brought back from the thieves like fair Turks
The kingdom they stole
In the same way as God in the Varaha avatar
Rescued earth by cutting down Hiranyakshu [sic].

He cut down the Gujaratis
As the Lion does the deer.
And the Deccani Rajas
As the Lion with the Elephant.

Man Singh and Abdur Rahim guard Akbar's court
As two lions.

Were poets such as Gang, Keshav, Mandan and Harnath permanent fixtures in Abdur Rahim's court? Or were they in the nature of itinerant visitors or, perhaps, long-distance recipients of gifts and awards for verses that appealed to him? We can surmise that at least some of them worked in his library, which had in its collection both Hindi and Sanskrit works. Similarly, we can only guess at the relationships between the Hindi and the Persian poets but that there was some degree of interaction between them is suggested by the mixed verse – in Persian and Hindi – with which Abdur Rahim continued to experiment. In the barvai collection dated to the period spent in court after the Sindh conquest in 1591 and mentioned earlier in this chapter, we find four barvais that consist almost entirely of Persian words. We find in them descriptions of the pains of separation, so evident in much of Abdur Rahim's sensuous verse, but also reminiscent of sentiments expressed in the Persian poetry of the time:

Dear friend, each beat of my lovelorn heart
Passes like a thousand years.

In your absence, even drowning myself a thousand times
In this world of wine does not give any solace.

My beloved has shot arrows that can see into my heart
And so you hear its anguished moans.

Dear friend, how do I tell my lovelorn state to my beloved.
When I never see him alone and my mind remains frustrated.[49]

In these barvais we find a simplicity and freedom from excessive ornamentation and obtrusive philosophizing that are, as we shall see, the most characteristic features of Abdur Rahim's mature dohas, which built his reputation as a poet of standing in Hindi literature.

Abdur Rahim, as we see him at this time, is at the peak of his mental and physical powers. His military and political reputation had been established with his participation in the major expeditions of the empire into Gujarat and Mewar in the 1570s and '80s and Sindh in 1591–92. He had already held appointments with great symbolic power, as vakil and as ataliq to Prince Salim. He had also an enviable reputation as a man of letters, with many Persian poets of distinction having composed verses in his praise and with many of them in his court. His facility with Hindi verse and some knowledge of Hindu religious and cultural practices and doctrine would have similarly endeared him to the powerful Rajput nobles in the emperor's court. His friendship with Raja Man Singh is one indicator of this, in addition to the numerous literary traditions that speak of the intimacy Abdur Rahim enjoyed with other Rajput nobles. We can imagine the heady magic of this period for him, as his father's life story as well as his own would have been part of the lore of the court and the empire. Bearing the highest title of the empire, as his father had before him, and being an intimate of the emperor, at ease with the other high nobles and with the royal family, he was at this time amongst the most prominent personalities of Akbar's India.

These accomplishments and honours were matched by a personal life that was equally gratifying. His marriage to Mah Banu had bound Abdur Rahim to a family with great intimacy to the emperor himself, and this further cemented his own ties to the Timurids. By the time of his assignment to lead the Deccan campaign he had at least three – perhaps four – sons, with two more to follow. He had also at least two daughters. A large family was important as it would become over time a further source of strength and new alliances. We know also that his friendship with Raja Man Singh had strengthened:

> An intimate friendship existed of old between KhanKhanan and Raja Man Singh. When Mirza Dorab and Iraj were young, the Raja out of affection had fixed a daily allowance for both the brothers. When they had attained maturity and were appointed to high Mansab, one day both the brothers jokingly said to the Raja: 'Dadaji, what if we attained youth and mansab. Why have you withheld our daily allowance?' The Raja calculated it from the beginning till end and gave two lakh rupees to the mirzas.[50]

The great ideological issue of Abdur Rahim's youth was perhaps that of the balance of moral authority between the ulema and the emperor. This reached its climax by the end of the 1570s and early 1580s as the strain between the Sadr, Abdun Nabi, and the emperor reached a point when a new equation became inevitable. The exile and subsequent killing of Abdun Nabi was a resolution of the issue and the defeat, in some sense, of religious orthodoxy. Akbar was, at this time, also moving towards a more inclusive notion of sovereignty and authority with the abolition of the discriminatory jizyah, an exaltation of the Rajput alliance, marriage with prominent Rajput families, the public celebration of Hindu festivals in court and so on.

Where did Abdur Rahim stand on a matter that, in retrospect, appears to have been an important divide of his time? Any response to Akbar's liberalism and eclecticism was in many ways so closely tied to the question of personal loyalty to the emperor that it would have required both recklessness and doctrinal conviction of a high order to have spoken against it. If Mirza Aziz Koka could do so and survive, it was entirely on account of his special relationship with the emperor (Even in Mirza Aziz's case, the orthodoxy of his views was tempered in the later years). We cannot say with any certainty that Abdur Rahim felt the same way as Mirza Aziz Koka did, nor do we have any reasons for doing so. The eclecticism of his poetry, his capacity to engage with Hindu devotional themes, even if within the literary genre he adopted, the range of opinions expressed by the poets attached to him, and his intimacy with and perceived sympathy towards the Rajputs suggest, in fact, just the contrary. Moreover, the difference in age and Abdur Rahim's personal obligation to the emperor make the possibility of his having a critical or opposite point of view towards Akbar's religious innovation an unlikely one.

By the same token, however, is it not remarkable that we do not see Abdur Rahim in the forefront as a keen protagonist of such innovation? Why is it that, despite the rapidity of his advancement and his favoured status in court, we can find no evidence of Abdur Rahim being an initiate in the emperor's experiments with new forms of devotion?

At the same time, there are reasons to infer that the monochrome impression of Hindu devotionalism in Abdur Rahim's personality needs to be tempered. Sometime in the second decade of the seventeenth century occurs the following incident concerning Mian Fahim, one of Abdur Rahim's most prominent retainers and, in all probability, virtually a member of his immediate family:

> ... one day, Raja Bikramajit came to the house of Darab Khan and sat on Darab Khan's divan (*masnad*). Darab Khan was showing a multi-coloured[sic] stone to him, and the Raja was reclining against the round cushion with legs stretched in front. In the meanwhile, Miyan Fahim came to the assembly. He immediately opened his tongue with abuse saying, 'How can a Brahmin supplicant like you dare sit in the presence of a grandson of Bairam Khan (and) a son of KhanKhanan in this disrespectful manner?' The Raja immediately

> assumed a deferential posture and offered excuses. Then Miyan Fahim addressing Darab Khan said, 'I wish you had died in place of Mirza Iraj, so that you would not have committed such an act of disgrace.'[51]

Mian Fahim had, in fact, been brought up in Abdur Rahim's household from the time he was a young boy and is described as being a Rajput, although we do not know when his family converted to Islam. It is difficult to say whether the outburst reflected a Rajput prejudice against Bikramjit – apparently a brahmin from eastern India – or was on account of a non-Muslim or non-Mughal showing such familiarity. We do know this about Fahim:

> As long as he was alive, he did not miss (any of the) thirty days' fast of the auspicious month of Ramadan; and all the five compulsory daily prayers along with (voluntary) ones of sunrise (*ishraq*), forenoon (*duha*) and midnight (*tahajjud*) were offered at their prescribed time. He was without exception an early riser. He would cry a lot out of fear of God. He was ungrudgingly liberal and a lover of scholars, learned men and saints.[52]

Abdur Rahim's coming to adulthood and maturity – the period from the 1570s to the mid-1590s – coincides also with the presence in Akbar's court of the pugnacious and acute observer, Mulla Abdul Qadir Badayuni (1540–1615) whom we have encountered earlier in this story on more than one occasion. A learned scholar in his own right, Badayuni has in the centuries since continued to be regarded as Akbar's most prominent and independent critic. Assigned relatively minor translation jobs, including of the Hindu religious epics, through much of Akbar's reign, Badayuni was to carry out a sustained and bitter polemic against the liberalism of Akbar's thought and policy. This, for fear of the emperor, he did largely silently by means of a secret history, the *Muntakhabu-t-Tawarikh,* which he completed in the first half of the 1590s. Incidentally, Badayuni appears to have disliked the task of translating Hindu texts. The protagonists of liberal

Plate I: The assassination of Bairam Khan.

(Bairam Khan is murdered by an Afghan at Patan. Painted by Tulsi and Triyya; Victoria and Albert Museum IS.2:5-1896.)

Plate II: Humayun being received by Shah Tahmasp.
Photo by Khosrow Bozorgi.
Courtesy: The Aga Khan Documentation Center at MIT.

Plate III: The arrest of Shah Abul Maali

The Art Institute of Chicago. E 10879.

Plate IV: Bairam Khan's widow and child are escorted to Ahmedabad, c. 1590-95.
Artist Mukund. Victoria and Albert Museum, No IS.2.6-1896.

Plate V: Presentation of the young Abdur Rahim at Court.
Victoria and Albert Museum. IS.2.7-1896.

Plate VI: Abdur Rahim as an old man. Portrait by Hashim, c.1626

Freer Gallery of Art 39.50. Folio 38 by 26 cm. Painting 14.9 by 8.2 cm

Plate VII: The tomb of Shah Nawaz Khan. Burhanpur.
Courtesy: The Archaeological Survey of India

Plate VIII: Gate of the Nawab Abdur Rahim Khan Masjid, Burhanpur
Photo: Nayan Kapadia, Chetna Studio, Burhanpur

Plate IX: The tomb in Nizamuddin built over the grave of Mah Banu. Abdur Rahim was also buried within this tomb

Photo: Narendra Swain Courtesy: The Aga Khan Trust for Culture

Plate X: A mural in the Parliament House, New Delhi. A scene from Emperor Akbar's court showing, apart from the Emperor, Todar Mal, Tansen, Abul Fazal, Faizi and Abdur Rahim

Plate XI

Turkmenistan coin depicting Bairam Khan

An advertisement by the Madhya Pradesh government in *Seminar*, May 2001

The young Akbar and Bairam Khan: a still form the film *Bairam Khan* by Gajnan Jagirdar (1946)

tendencies in Akbar's court – Abul Fazl and his brother Faizi – bore the brunt of his invective and sarcasm in the *Muntakhab.* Yet others, seen to be participants in what Badayuni clearly believed was Akbar's vainglory and megalomania, were not spared either. He saw them as time-servers deviating from the Islamic path to please the emperor as he progressed from excess to excess.

Ironically, Badayuni's career at the imperial court began in the mid-1570s as a 'young and scathing' critic of the established ulema. Akbar, keen to weaken Sheikh Abdun Nabi's position at the head of the orthodoxy, encouraged Badayuni just as he had Sheikh Abul Fazl and Faizi. However, Badayuni's usefulness to the emperor diminished over time, perhaps because he was himself orthodox and doctrinaire. The contrast of his career with that of Abul Fazl and Faizi was obvious and clearly a source of deep jealousy to Badayuni. The atmosphere in the court, discussions in the Ibadat Khana, Akbar's liberal propensities and his supporters, who joined in to strengthen these tendencies, are the subject of the bitter critique and history which make up the *Muntakhabu-t-Tawarikh.*

It is striking, however, that Badayuni's references to Abdur Rahim are respectful and warm, in sharp contrast to his treatment of Abul Fazl. Did Badayuni not know of Abdur Rahim's Hindu devotional compositions? Or did he see them as the work of a nobleman playfully experimenting with a literary genre and employing all the stylized techniques that form required? In other words, could it be that the aspect of Hindu devotionalism that is embedded in Abdur Rahim's verse did not in any way reflect his personality and religious outlook, which remained firmly and demonstrably tied to an Islamic world view?

Although quick to seize upon and expose in others any sign of compromise with religious conviction for career advancement, Badayuni speaks of Abdur Rahim with admiration. Abul Fazl and his brother Faizi were to him the evil geniuses behind much of the emperor's liberal experimentation and eclecticism which, he believed, weakened the Islamic foundations of the empire and were at the root of the political revolts that periodically punctuated Akbar's reign. Although his history ends before the murder of Abul Fazl and the death of Akbar, it does cover the death of Faizi. The bitter jealousy Badayuni harboured against Abul Fazl's brother is reflected in the description of his death in 1595–96: 'And since he had ... associated and been mixed up with dogs day and night, they say that at the moment of death they heard him bark like a dog.' To Badayuni, Faizi's death meant also that 'The pillar of heresy is broken'.[53]

Similar descriptions abound of those whom Badayuni regarded as protagonists of the new thought in Akbar's court. The description of Mirza Aziz Koka on his change of heart and joining the fold of the emperor's disciples drips with irony:

> At this time A'zam Khan returned from Makkah, where he had suffered much harm at the hands of the Sharifs, and throwing away the blessing which he had derived from the pilgrimage, joined immediately on his return, the Divine Faith, performing the *sijdah*, and following all other rules of discipleship; he cut off his beard, and was very forward at social meetings, and in conversation. He learned the rules of the new faith from his reverence Allami, and received Ghazipur and Jhajipur as *jagir*.[54]

On his part, Badayuni was keen to enter Abdur Rahim's service and almost succeeded in doing so:

> ... Nizam-ud-din Ahmad wrote a letter to me from Gujrat, saying that since the KhanKhanan at the time of setting out [for Fathpur] made a promise, that if he got the Emperor's leave he would at this time bring with him Mulla Ilahdad Amrohah, and yourself from court. Consequently, it is right that he should treat you both with every proper politeness, and having got leave for you from Court should bring you at once hither. As a wise man has it: 'And afterwards, whatever may be best.'
>
> So I saw at once the KhanKhanan, when he came into the writing office, which had been set apart in Fathpur as the translation

> department. But he, as quickly as possible, was sent off to Gujarat, and then immediately afterwards Kabul came in the way, and so my hope of employment, which I had looked on as the key of salvation, and a secured provision for life, became clouded over: 'wish for nothing, but what God wills.'[55]

The impression we get is that entry into Abdur Rahim's court would have been deliverance for Badayuni from the atmosphere in Akbar's court, and secured faster advancement. The references in the *Muntakhabu-t-Tawarikh* do not suggest any striking eclecticism of approach in Abdur Rahim's character. On the contrary, he comes across as a man whose Islamic moorings were intact and unblemished by the 'free thinking' of the Mughal court. Take, for instance, this account by Badayuni of a case relating to a scholar, Haji Sultan of Thanesar, who had been accused of killing a cow and was consequently in trouble with the court:

> He was employed for four years, alone and without any co-adjutor in the translation of the Mahabharata which is known as the Ramza Nama ... On account of an accusation of the crime of cow killing which was brought against him by the Hindus of that area (Thanesar) an order was issued of his banishment to Bhakkar, and the KhanKhanan who was in those days in charge of the Suba (of Multan) treated him with great consideration and kindness, and applied ointment to the wounds of his soul. After that land had been completely subjugated, the KhanKhanan took Haji Sultan with him thence and promised to procure the reversal of the sentence of banishment. Haji Sultan returned secretly to his native place and the KhanKhanan after conquering the province of Asirgarh and Burhanpur prayed in one of his petitions for the reversal of the sentence against him. His request was granted ...[56]

Does this episode illustrate the Khan-i-Khanan's effort to ensure a reversal of what he believed was an unjust sentence? Or was it sympathy for a co-religionist that made him act thus? That there is more to this is suggested by the fact that Haji Sultan was the father-in-law of the Islamic revivalist, Sheikh Ahmad Sirhindi, whom we shall encounter in greater detail later.[57]

Abdur Rahim's religious viewpoint and his personal beliefs remain enigmatic. Could it be that he maintained a careful distance from both sides of the divide, so much so that neither could claim him as one of their own? Was this a deliberate and conscious choice of the middle path, born of a belief in moderation as best practice, or was it a calculated position arising from the realization that rapid and continued advancement could best be secured in this way?

To get into a discussion on this subject would be to anticipate the story. For now, it is the Deccan campaign, to which he was assigned in 1593, that we must accompany the Khan-i-Khanan.

4

THE DECCAN

WITH THE assignment to the Deccan in 1593, Abdur Rahim was to enter a phase of his life that extended for the next three decades; in fact, this period comprised virtually the rest of his life. If the military situation and the politics of the Deccan were to remain a dominant feature of his career, his personal life too now enters more pronounced intervals of light and shadow. The contrast between the quarter-century before the Deccan assignment and the period after that is striking. The year 1593, or thereabouts, is therefore a useful point to evaluate his life so far and situate it within a broader matrix before it is gradually but inexorably alters from the early seventeenth century and the beginning of the end of Akbar's reign.

Abdur Rahim in his late thirties was, like most nobles of his standing and age, entering a period of less certainty. The most obvious reason for this was the coming of age of the emperor's sons. In 1593 the oldest, Salim, was twenty-four, the second son, Murad, was twenty-three and the youngest, Daniyal, twenty-one. Each of these princes was emerging as a power centre with separate courts and favourites. Decision making would now be inevitably more complex than in the 1570s or 1580s as the individual personalities and ambitions of the princes would be a factor in each emerging political situation.

Akbar, now entering his fifties, was at the zenith of his powers. The north and north-west were secure as the Safavids and the Uzbeks posed no immediate threat. These frontiers had in any case been strengthened by the conquest of Sindh and Kashmir and the re-establishment of Mughal supremacy over Qandahar in 1595. Qandahar continues to feature in the Mughal–Safavid duel, but the next phase of this conflict would only be in the 1620s. At the close of the sixteenth century, Akbar's long stay of over a decade in the Punjab and Kashmir had served its purpose of securing the northern frontier for the remainder of his reign. Expansion into Malwa and Gujarat in the 1570s and 1580s had also set the stage for an intrusion into the immensely complex politics of the Deccan. However, with the three princes coming of age and with an emperor in his fifties, the vortex of succession loomed like a spectre over any imperial initiative. Even as early as 1589 or 1590, Akbar is said to have accused Prince Salim of trying to poison him.[1] In the subsequent decade and a half, up to Akbar's death, we see Salim as a perennial malcontent, either in open rebellion or sullen discontent. The other two princes too were jostling for advantage and making every attempt to gain their father's favour. The emperor's displeasure with Salim and the prince's excesses held out the hope of an opportunity which, with any luck, could catapult one of them to the throne.

The Mughals inherited their aim of imperial expansion into the Deccan from their predecessor sultanates of Delhi. The Deccan Muslim sultanates – the Nizam Shahis of Ahmednagar, the Imad Shahis of Berar, the Adil Shahis of Bijapur, the Barid Shahis of Bidar and the Qutb Shahis of Golconda – provided opportunities but also great difficulties and challenges for Mughal ambitions. For a start, the ruling elite in each of them was predominantly composed of either Persian Shia nobles or Sunni Afghans, along with less powerful Indian Muslim converts. Each had an inherited suspicion of the Mughals, quite apart from the natural disinclination to submit to an outside force.[2]

We may digress here briefly to go into the Deccan camp and consider the life and career of the remarkable Chand Bibi of Bijapur and Ahmednagar. Daughter of Husain Nizam Shah, who ruled Ahmednagar (r. 1554–65), she was married to Ali Adil Shah I (1543–80) of Bijapur. The marriage was one of a number of matrimonial alliances reached in 1563 to cement an alliance of all the five Muslim sultanates against the Hindu kingdom of Vijayanagar, and was thus of enormous significance in the region's political history. Vijayanagar had hitherto been successful in cherry-picking alliances at will with one sultan or another, against the rest. Ahmednagar, in particular, had been a victim of Vijayanagar aggression on more than one occasion. The five-ruler alliance led to the battle of Talikotta in 1565, which saw Vijayanagar being decisively defeated and its capital sacked. The kingdom survived but was fatally weakened and no longer a real factor in Deccan politics.

This, in turn, meant that, in the absence of any external glue, rivalries among the Deccan sultans grew and acquired even greater intensity. Berar was thus annexed by the Nizam Shahis of Ahmednagar in 1574, and Bidar went into a steady decline from the 1580s and was finally annexed by the Adil Shahis of Bijapur in 1619. Chand Bibi's husband Ali Adil Shah I was assassinated in the course of a Bijapur–Bidar tussle in 1579, leaving her regent to a nine-year-old king, Ibrahim Adil Shah II. In the endless intrigue that characterized the internal affairs of the kingdoms, Chand Bibi emerged as a factor to reckon with in Bijapur as well as Ahmednagar, her skills in diplomacy and war setting her apart from the army of squabbling and ultimately self-destructive faction-ridden nobles of the region. She was a good horsewoman, an adept polo player and evidently possessed of a strong personality, given that she was a woman in a largely male world. Her life would evoke for the British in nineteenth-century India a comparison with England's Elizabeth I whose contemporary she was.

> Few in England know that the contemporary of our Queen Elizabeth, in the Deccan Kingdom was a woman of equal ability

> of political talent, equally, although in a different sense, education and accomplishments, who ruled over a realm as large, a population as large, and as intelligent, and as rich as England, a woman who, surrounded by jealous enemies, preserved by her own personal valour and endurance her kingdom from destruction and partition, who through all temptations and exercise of absolute power was at once simple, generous, frank and merciful as she was ...[3]

We will encounter her in late 1595, defending a siege by a determined Mughal army led by Abdur Rahim. Ahmednagar was then in the midst of a succession struggle and all its neighbours were involved in the strife, as indeed were the Mughals.

Alliances between the more powerful of the Deccan states – in particular, Bijapur, Ahmednagar and Golconda – could, and did, deter Mughal expansion for prolonged periods. But mutual rivalries and competition were the Deccan rulers' passion and all-consuming interest; they rarely acted in concert. Mughal military strategy had to be coordinated with diplomacy so as to preclude the emergence of any cooperation between the kingdoms or to detach one or the other sultanates from a larger alliance. The rivalries between the sultanates provided opportunities for inroads but equally, a determined bid by the Mughals could lead to these rivalries being temporarily set aside.

The combination of political and diplomatic efforts with the application of military force formed the broad parameters of Mughal expansion in the Deccan. Its eventual success in the late seventeenth century was to coincide with the beginnings of the disintegration of the imperial edifice itself as this political and military expansion created and unleashed forces that it was not equipped to contain. The great historian of the eighteenth-century Indian decline, Jadunath Sarkar, called the Deccan the 'Spanish ulcer' of the Mughal Empire, borrowing a term from Napoleon's description of the resistance put up by Spain to French expansion in Europe.

Notwithstanding Akbar's preoccupation with the north and north-west of his empire and his long presence in Lahore, events in the Deccan were kept under constant imperial scrutiny. A succession strife in Ahmednagar provided the opportunity for Akbar to assist a scion of the Nizam Shahi dynasty, Burhan-ul-Mulk, who had earlier sought refuge in the Mughal court, to defeat his rivals. However, once enthroned as the ruler of Ahmednagar in 1591, Burhan-ul-Mulk refused to be a pawn in the hands of the Mughals, and was not prepared to act as a vassal either. As signs of this became evident, Abul Fazl was to record:

> When Burhan prevailed over Ahmednagar he should have increased his devotion and gratitude and been an example of obedience to the other rulers of the Deccan. The wine of success robbed him of his senses and he forgot the varied favours he had received from the Emperor.[4]

Soon thereafter, we find the dispatch of four diplomatic missions – to Khandesh, Ahmednagar, Bijapur and Golconda. The Mughal envoy was directed to go to Khandesh first and then to Ahmednagar – a clear indication of Mughal priorities. This was natural as the Faruqi dynasty in Khandesh, with Burhanpur as its capital and the nearby fortress of Asirgarh as its garrison, straddled northern India and the Deccan. None of the four kingdoms accepted Mughal suzerainty; the ruler of Khandesh, however, sent a daughter to be married to Prince Salim and those of Golconda and Bijapur sent gifts. But in Ahmednagar, Burhan-ul-Mulk's behaviour with the Mughal ambassador was not even conciliatory. When he returned to court and reported this to the emperor, the stage was set for a military assault in 1593.

Prince Daniyal was appointed to command the expedition and Abdur Rahim was assigned to accompany him. Abdur Rahim was perhaps the obvious choice for this role: he had approached the emperor several times since his Gujarat days for permission to lead a campaign into the Deccan. Simultaneously, Prince Murad – then governor of Malwa – was ordered to 'make preparations for the conquest of the Deccan Kingdoms and that when the soldiers had been gathered together from every side near him, he should carry out the order'.[5]

There were delays on the part of both the princes and an impatient Akbar contemplated leading the Deccan campaign himself. When Abdur Rahim was summoned by the emperor to account for the delay, he suggested that it was better for the rains to cease before beginning the march: '... the KhanKhanan ... represented that the time for the army to enter the Deccan was after the rains. Water and forage would then be plentiful and corn cheap. On this account there was slowness of movement.'

It is more likely that the delay was on account of Abdur Rahim's reluctance to proceed with a military expedition with an impossible command structure of two princes in the army and the younger one (Daniyal) in charge. It is possible that Akbar had assigned the command to both the princes since he felt that the Deccan was too big a potential prize to leave to one alone; victory would have elevated the strength and prestige of that prince greatly. Did the emperor fear that this would set up a rival power centre to him? More likely, he may have felt that credit for victory in the Deccan to either of his younger brothers would provoke Prince Salim into further acts of defiance. Whatever the compulsions, Akbar decided to lead the campaign himself, then changed his mind and appointed Prince Murad as the leader of the expedition. The representations of Prince Murad, that as the older brother he could not be expected to serve under Daniyal, may have prevailed. Subsequent events, however, demonstrated that this too was not a tidy arrangement.

The task assigned to Prince Murad and Abdur Rahim was to bring the weight of their combined forces to bear on Ahmednagar. Providentially for the Mughals, Burhan-ul-Mulk died in April 1595. Soon afterwards, his heir and eldest son Ibrahim was killed in a battle against the ruler of Bijapur, who had marched on Ahmednagar to avenge an insult to his envoy when he arrived to offer felicitations to the new ruler! At this stage a struggle broke out within the Ahmednagar court itself, between Prime Minister Mian Manju and

Ikhlas Khan, a prominent noble supported by Chand Bibi, who was the sister of the former ruler and now in Ahmednagar. Mian Manju installed a young boy, who claimed to be a descendent of the Nizam Shahi rulers, on the throne and set himself up as the regent. Ikhlas Khan and Chand Bibi supported the claim of Bahadur, the infant son of Ibrahim. Mian Manju then sought assistance from Prince Murad, who saw this as an opportunity for decisive intervention and a quick victory.

Although Abdur Rahim was the designated commander of the main expeditionary force, Prince Murad, as governor of Gujarat, perceived the future action as falling solely within his jurisdiction and sent word to the nobles to join him. The prince, in fact, embarked on his march in early June 1595 and was incensed at Abdur Rahim's more leisurely consolidation of forces. That a number of nobles and their forces chose to join Abdur Rahim in Malwa rather than converge in Gujarat, further angered the prince.

Murad's intent from the very beginning was to directly mount an assault on Ahmednagar. The possibility of an early and quick victory was obviously predominant in his mind. Abdur Rahim's approach appears to have been more cautious. He preferred to first ensure that Khandesh joined the Mughal expeditionary force so that the army's flanks and rear were not vulnerable and, secondly, allow Ahmednagar's internal feud to fester further. A decade earlier, Abdur Rahim had witnessed first-hand as governor of Gujarat the difficulties Mirza Aziz Koka had faced in his Deccan expeditions because of a lack of cooperation or outright opposition from the Khandesh ruler, Raja Ali Khan. Although Khandesh had technically accepted Mughal suzerainty from the 1570s, on occasion paying an annual tribute, such suzerainty was nominal. Raja Ali Khan had a shrewd insight into Deccan politics, was well acquainted with the other rulers of the region and had also been instrumental in Burhan-ul-Mulk's ascent to the Ahmednagar throne. Abdur Rahim, therefore, considered him a potentially invaluable ally in the move against Ahmednagar. At the same time, he did not entirely trust Raja Ali Khan and was keen to ensure that the Mughals did not provoke or encounter any act of duplicity.

The fundamental issue in these differing tactical approaches was that of command. Prince Murad, a son of the emperor, would have found the presence of a high noble in joint command a threat to his own position and ambitions from the Deccan campaign. This resentment was further exacerbated by feuds between important nobles in the two armies, which finally converged in November 1595 near Ahmednagar. Raja Ali Khan had by this time formally declared his allegiance to Akbar and joined his forces with Abdur Rahim's. Abdur Rahim, having heard that Prince Murad had already begun the march on Ahmednagar, set off with a light force, along with Raja Ali Khan, leaving his principal army, elephants and artillery to follow. The meeting between the prince and Abdur Rahim was less than cordial and subsequent events did not portend well either:

> From want of experience and evil teaching, the Prince did not admit them (i.e., Abdur Rahim and Raja Ali Khan) to pay their respects. He (assumed) a distant manner and only after much discussion granted an audience. When the army came up afterwards it was not treated in a soothing way. The KhanKhanan and many of the auxiliary troops became disgusted and he withdrew his hand from the work.[6]

What had originally appeared a relatively easy task on account of the internal divisions within the Ahmednagar court was becoming increasingly difficult. Some troops in Abdur Rahim's command plundered the suburbs of the city despite the assurances given by Prince Murad to the Ahmednagar nobility. This had the effect of uniting the different Ahmednagar factions against the invading army. Mian Manju now appealed to Chand Bibi to assume the regency and defend the kingdom against the Mughals. He himself, along with the boy pretender, managed to escape to summon help from Bijapur and Golconda. Abul Fazl comments that he should have been captured but 'escaped owing to the neglect of the Generals'. Clearly, he blamed Abdur Rahim for the lapse.

Meanwhile, news of the dissension within the Mughal command structure, as also Chand Bibi's success in enthusing factions within the Ahmednagar nobility to unite against a common foe, galvanized those defending the fort. The siege of the Ahmednagar fort began in mid-December 1595 and, in the words of Abul Fazl, 'became a tedious affair'. It was suggested to Chand Bibi that she appear before the defending troops to inspire them and she did so in glittering armour, mounted on an elephant and, disregarding the barrage from the Mughal guns and archers, moved around among her troops. The impact of this is to be gauged from the fact that henceforth, even her foes referred to her as Chand Sultana instead of Chand Bibi.

The high morale of the defenders can be gauged from the partial success of a daring night attack they mounted on the strongly defended positions of Abdur Rahim. Although beaten back, the raiding party made it safely to the fort. We find Abul Fazl saying: 'If the success had been a little prosecuted they would have been taken or active men would have entered the fort with them.'[7] Athough cryptic, his suggestion is clear enough: Abdur Rahim was not putting everything into the enterprise.

The siege dragged on amidst reports of the assembling of reinforcements from Bijapur and Golconda. To the Mughal command it would have appeared that their nightmare – an alliance among the Deccan powers – was becoming a reality. This emerging threat focused minds. A council of war between Prince Murad and Abdur Rahim led to an agreement that the fort needed to be attacked quickly and a decisive victory achieved before the armies from Golconda and Bijapur arrived. Shortly thereafter, a determined assault was mounted on the fort, with mines being laid up to the fortifications to breach them. The plan miscarried. The defenders came to know of it and the mines were destroyed. Lack of tactical coordination between Abdur Rahim and Prince Murad, coupled with the latter's impatience, led to his forces being beaten back. The main force inexplicably delayed its attack, allowing the defending force to concentrate men at those points where the mines had in fact weakened or breached the fortifications. A determined defence was led by Chand Bibi, 'clad in armour' with 'her green veil … seen everywhere and her voice was heard, echoing in its sharp treble her late husband's battle cry'.[8] To quote Abul Fazl again: 'The end of the day shone upon failure …'

This failure, news of the advance of the Bijapur and Golconda forces, attacks on the Mughal army's rear and flanks by Ahmednagar troops, combined with interceptions of supply caravans from Gujarat, made the Mughal position untenable. At this point, Prince Murad and Abdur Rahim held another council and decided to open negotiations with Chand Bibi. Whether the initiative came from the Mughal camp or from Ahmednagar is difficult to say, but both sides agreed in February 1596 on a treaty that was nominally a face-saver for the Mughals. The region of Berar was ceded to the Mughals and prince Bahadur was recognized as Nizam-ul-Mulk, free to rule Ahmednagar while recognizing Mughal suzerainty. Abul Fazl, in his description of the Ahmednagar expedition, pulled no punches. Describing the inconclusive siege by a large force of a garrison whose morale should have been at rock bottom, he writes:

> Things became difficult on account of dissensions in the army, the closing of the roads and the want of food. Though ingenious and right thinking persons represented that three great armies (those of the KhanKhanan, Prince Murad and Raja Ali Khan of Khandesh) had assembled and that each should take upon itself one of three things: first to take the fort, second to conquer the country; third, to guard the roads, not one was done.[9]

Of the terms of the treaty and their acceptance, he has this to say:

> A party of men, owing to ignorance, and some from interested motives, accepted these improper proposals. Though able men represented the want of food, the dismay and the trickery of the garrison, it was of no avail. Owing to the influence of bribes, and the listening to idle tales, the peace proposals were accepted and fighting was laid aside.[10]

On 23 February 1596, the siege was abandoned. Prince Murad moved eastwards into Berar and Abdur Rahim established himself in Jalna, roughly midway between Burhanpur and Ahmednagar. Mughal morale had seriously eroded following the failure to achieve a clear military victory. The private and not-so-private recriminations on either side resonate through the chronicles of the period with Abdur Rahim, as the senior noble and army commander, coming in for a major part of the blame. Prince Murad was told by his advisors that the failure was entirely due to the acts of omissions and commission of Abdur Rahim, who did not wish that he (Murad) should gain the glory of being the conqueror of Ahmednagar. The suggestion clearly was that Abdur Rahim was a partisan of Prince Salim. This was by no means the only time, or only quarter from which such a charge would be made. There were also insinuations of treachery, that some of his commanders had been secretly helping the besieged garrison.

Even after the treaty, the situation on the ground was by no means satisfactory from the Mughal point of view. The Bijapur–Golconda force led by the Bijapuri noble Suhail Khan Habshi was reinforced by forces from Ahmednagar. Accusations that the Mughals were occupying territories beyond what had been ceded in Berar provided the pretext for the next engagement, which took place early in February 1597. According to some accounts, Prince Murad was reluctant to get involved this time around. We find Abdur Rahim leading a force of some 20,000 cavalry against a vastly superior Deccan army. The battle began on 8 February in the environs of a town called Ashti, south-east of Ahmednagar and lasted for two days. The result was uncertain till virtually the very end. The odds faced by the Mughals and the anxiety about the outcome are conveyed in the following account:

> It is related that KhanKhanan had placed in the vanguard of the army … the Barha Sayyids, who enjoyed high Mansabs and Miyan Daulat Khan his commandant and stationed them ahead. The venerable Sayyids said to Miayn Daulat Khan, 'You and me are Indians and

> have taken place in the vanguard. There is no alternative or any other way except being killed. But you try to fathom the mind of KhanKhanan as to what his intentions are.' Miyan Daulat Khan came to KhanKhanan and told him 'Miyan Suhail has come with that much large force, many elephants and artillery. Victory is from heaven but if we have to retreat, indicate one place where we may find you.' KhanKhanan said '(Find me) under the corpses of the killed. Rest assured there is no other errand (before me) but to die.'[11]

Clearly, this suggests a degree of uncertainty among his own commanders about Abdur Rahim's conduct and political aims. That he would not wish to gain a victory for which the credit might go to Prince Murad was perhaps widely discussed even among those who were close to him. His reply conveys both a sense of frustration as also the determination that recent events would not be allowed to mar his reputation as a military commander.

The battle ended with a spectacular victory for the outnumbered Mughal force. Abul Fazl's account of the battle is cryptic and he says as little as possible about Abdur Rahim's victory.[12] Other sources inform us:

> The KhanKhanan having offered prostration before God in thanksgiving, danced (out of Joy) in that battlefield and whatever holdings he had, had it all plundered by (his own) soldiers ... It is said that when KhanKhanan returned to his home after the victory all his workshops ... comprised of just two camel loads. He took Miyan Daulat Khan in his embrace and kissed his head and shoulders and showed such courtesies to him as is beyond one's imagination.[13]

The emperor himself is believed to have asked a daughter of the Khan-i-Khanan 'as to how much holdings the Khan had thus gifted away', and the figure she responded with was Rs 75 lakh. In his dispatch on the battle, the Khan-i-Khanan is said to have credited the victory to his old commander, Daulat Khan Lodi.[14]

The victory did much to restore Mughal prestige, the morale of the army, and also the reputation of Abdur Rahim. Yet causalties in the battle were heavy and included Raja Ali Khan. His story, in fact, has an even sadder end. He had fallen in battle, unknown to the Mughal generals, but his absence was seen as evidence of Deccani treachery and it was claimed that the Raja had crossed over to the enemy.[15] His camp and possessions were looted by the victorious Mughals. When the body of the dead king was discovered shortly thereafter, in the words of Abul Fazl, 'the evil-thoughted [sic] and the foolish talkers were ashamed'[16]. Mughal suspicions of the Khandesh ruler and the plunder of his camp had adverse effects, which would affect Mughal–Khandesh relations over the years, resulting finally in the annexation of Khandesh into the empire.

Notwithstanding this victory, differences in the Mughal command structure were to persist and even grow. Prince Murad preferred pressing on with another attack on Ahmednagar, but Abdur Rahim counselled patience and consolidation of the position in Berar. Both petitioned the emperor, Murad complaining about the commander, while Abdur Rahim sought his own recall given the differences with the prince. It was evident that Mughal expansion had ground to a halt because of these differences. At this stage Abdur Rahim, using as a pretext the emperor's instructions for an inquiry into disturbances caused by a local zamindar in his jagir, withdrew from the campaign.

Akbar was now seriously concerned, perhaps more so because of the reports he was receiving of Prince Murad's excessive consumption of alcohol. In March 1598 two courtiers were dispatched – Raja Salivahan, who was also a physician, to persuade Murad to come back to court and Rup Singh to Abdur Rahim, with instructions that he should return to his command. A sense of the court's frustration and exasperation at the situation and, of course, Abul Fazl's own growing differences and personal dislike of Abdur Rahim are evident in his account:

> When it became known that Prince Sultan Murad regarded the winning of people's affections an easy matter, and went somewhat aside from propriety, and that the KhanKhanan owing to the evil success of his evil wishes, had gone back to his Jagir, that conscientious servant (i.e., Raja Salivahan) was sent off to bring the Prince back to Court in order that HM might send him back again with good counsels. Rup Khwas was appointed to rebuke the KhanKhanan and to make him return in order that he might take charge of the army and the country till the Prince arrived back.[17]

These efforts did not succeed. The courtiers returned to inform the emperor that the prince refused to return on the grounds that there was a real danger of an uprising were he to do so. Abdur Rahim said that he would return only after the prince had left, and to distance himself further from the campaign, set off for Lahore where the emperor was. In October 1598, according to Abul Fazl, Abdur Rahim 'came to Court and was exalted by paying homage. The gracious sovereign forgave his crooked ways and summoned him to his presence. Perhaps counsels might make him straight.'

In court, Abdur Rahim had the opportunity to explain to the emperor his difficulties with Prince Murad. News of the prince's ill health and excessive drinking had been reaching the emperor. His displeasure, however, extended to Abdur Rahim too, and he was kept waiting for some length of time before being granted an audience. It was nevertheless clear that the recall of the prince – both to retrieve the situation in the Deccan and also for the sake of his health – could not be delayed any further. In January 1599 Abul Fazl was dispatched to bring him back to court. The emperor himself had returned to Agra by then.

The failure to take Ahmednagar, the certainty of his own recall in dishonour and the death of an infant son had led Prince Murad into what was almost certainly a state of deep depression. He avoided meeting Abul Fazl and marched towards Ahmednagar, but fell terminally ill en route and died in May 1599.

Abdur Rahim's own return to court had also been tragic. A young son was accidently burnt to death. Shortly afterwards, his wife Mah Banu died at Ambala. It would appear that both these tragedies occurred in December 1598, in the course of Akbar's march back to Agra from Lahore. Possibly, Abdur Rahim was with the emperor on this journey. The son, Hydari, is said to have died in a serai. During the journey, Mah Banu had been left behind in Ambala since she was ailing, and died there.

We know frustratingly little about Mah Banu. The chronicles tell us that she was 'distinguished for her intellect and purity' but little else. If Hydari was her son, although we do not know this for certain, perhaps his accidental death was too much for her weakened constitution to bear. But our questions about Mah Banu and her relationship with her husband are so numerous that the silence of the historical record is frustrating.

What survives is the mausoleum Abdur Rahim constructed for her grave – a well-known monument to this day in Delhi, at walking distance from the shrine of Nizamuddin Auliya. It is a landmark structure and architectural historians see in its dome a midway point between that of the nearby tomb of Humayun and the famous Taj Mahal, to be built several decades later by Emperor Shah Jahan, in memory of his wife and queen, Mumtaz Mahal. Mah Banu's mausoleum is usually referred to as Abdur Rahim's, when in fact it was built by him in memory of his wife. Amongst the numerous such structures which remain as the heritage of the Mughals in India, it is one of the very few in memory of a woman – even rarer if we exclude Mughal queens and important princesses. It is certainly testimony to Mah Banu's status: she was, apart from being the wife of the Khan-i-Khanan, the daughter and sister of nobles who enjoyed a great deal of importance in the first half-century of Mughal rule. The scale of the complex and the size of the mausoleum are a reflection of Abdur Rahim's own position and prestige in the empire, apart from an indication of his personal wealth. It may not be inappropriate to surmise that this magnificent mausoleum also symbolized real affection in a relationship of which we know so little. The attention and resources that it would have demanded may well have been a source of solace to the grieving husband.

—ʬ—

These four years in the Deccan form a watershed in Abdur Rahim's life. The victory in February 1597 may have salvaged his military reputation, but there is little doubt of an erosion in his overall reputation and profile. What is at work here is quite clearly the politics of succession and it is to this factor that the impetus and motives behind the events that crowd these years must be traced. There is an obvious and marked deterioration in Abdur Rahim's relations with Abul Fazl. While differences had existed earlier as well, as evidenced during the Sindh campaign, the language used in the *Akbarnama* to describe Abdur Rahim's conduct in the Deccan may have had much to do with Abul Fazl's difficulties with Prince Salim, quite apart from his growing prejudice against the Khan-i-Khanan.

It is possible that Abul Fazl felt, as others did, that Abdur Rahim was shifting his loyalty to Prince Salim in anticipation of a succession crisis and judged his acts in the Deccan through this prism. Equally, it is possible that after the two fell out, as favourites are prone to, Abul Fazl himself spread this canard in order to alienate Akbar from Abdur Rahim. Akbar's impatience and irritation with Salim, from at least the early 1590s, would have provided a fertile ground for such a whispering campaign. The fit of anger against Salim and Abdur Rahim in Kashmir in the summer of 1589 described earlier, when the prince did not carry out instructions on escorting the harem to the letter, was perhaps an early indication of these growing tensions and does provide some credence to such an angle. It is, however, useful to bear in mind that nowhere in the *Jahangirnama,* is there a mention of Abdur Rahim as someone who helped or stood by the prince during his estrangement from his father. Similarly, the great nineteenth-century popularizer of Mughal history, Muhammad

Husain Azad – an admiring but not uncritical commentator on the life of the Mughal nobles and one who had access to a wide range of personal correspondence exchanged between prominent nobles and their families – does not claim that Abdur Rahim acted in concert with Salim to deny a victory for Murad. Nevertheless, the charge that Abdur Rahim deliberately subverted the campaign has a certain credibility given its fairly wide contemporary acceptance. We have, for instance, a letter to Philip III from the Portuguese viceroy in Goa, Don Francisco de Gama, written in December 1599:

> ... some people are of the view that it would have been better for this Estado if Xamorad (Shah Morad) had not died, for on account of the ill will he and his older brother bore to each other there would have been such wars among them that they would have gone at each other so much after the death of their father ... and for the same reason would have also put a halt to the conquest of the Kingdom of the Melique on account of the secret dealings that the Prince (Salim) had with Canacan (KhanKhanan) ...[18]

And a little later, in the same letter: '... Equebar (Akbar) ... called back Canacan on account of the dealings he had with the Prince'.

We need not give too much credence to a Portuguese viceroy's sources of information or indeed, his interpretation of events. Nevertheless, it is obvious that doubts about Abdur Rahim's intentions were widespread, and quite regardless of the truth of the matter, which appears now impossible to decipher, his reputation suffered. There is thus real displeasure, although temporary, in Akbar's response to him. For the balance of Akbar's reign, it would appear that extra efforts were made to bind Abdur Rahim more securely to imperial aims so that his loyalties were not buffeted by the looming succession.

But first, Murad's death necessitated changes in the Deccan command. Akbar's youngest son Daniyal was now appointed to lead the campaign, with Abdur Rahim being appointed a little later as his commander-in-chief. Daniyal was also made governor of

Khandesh and Berar; Abul Fazl and Abdur Rahim were deputed to establish Mughal control over Berar and the remains of the Nizam Shahi kingdom of Ahmednagar respectively. Abul Fazl's assignment away from court, incidentally, was a sop to Prince Salim, who traced to this important courtier his father's poor impression of him.

Either dissatisfied at Daniyal's slow pace or to ensure a definite outcome, the emperor himself moved in September 1599 to Malwa. Abul Fazl had, in the meantime, been receiving messages from Chand Bibi in Ahmednagar. The situation there had reverted to one of factional dispute and conflicts within the nobility, and Chand Bibi as regent sought some accommodation from the Mughals to prevent an internal coup against her. In parallel, pressure on the Mughals in Berar had increased.

Abul Fazl decided to move on Ahmednagar to explore whether Chand Bibi could be made to join up with the Mughals. However, a somewhat peremptory message from Prince Daniyal, possibly at Abdur Rahim's instance, advised him to await the arrival of the main army. Meanwhile, the situation in Khandesh had also deteriorated. The successor to the unfortunate Raja Ali Khan had assumed a position of defiance and moved into the formidable Asirgarh fort, ready to withstand a Mughal siege. This refusal to acknowledge Mughal suzerainty had to be addressed, especially since it took place in the proximity of the emperor himself. Akbar therefore sent Daniyal and Abdur Rahim to Ahmednagar and proceeded to Burhanpur to attend to Khandesh.

The presence of the emperor, the overwhelming might of the Mughal army, the absence of a larger Deccan alliance, with Golconda and Bijapur staying aloof, and dissension in Ahmednagar and Asirgarh, led to decisive Mughal victories in both these sieges. Chand Bibi, now seeking an arrangement with the Mughals, was assassinated by a rival faction that inisted on fighting on and rejected her more pragmatic approach. Her end was particularly brutal. A mob inflamed by the deliberately planted rumour that she was secretly in league with the Mughals entered her private apartment and killed her. The Mughal advance, as she had correctly foreseen was however unstoppable. Ahmednagar fell in August 1600 and Asirgarh in January 1601, after a siege of four and nine months respectively.[19] Having brought his last major military campaign to a successful close, Akbar became anxious to return to Agra quickly, primarily on account of Prince Salim's increasingly open postures of defiance and rebellion.

It must be said here that despite these victories, the difficulties in the Deccan continued to grow. Mughal control over the Ahmednagar fort and the neighbouring areas did not mean the total extinction of the Nizam Shahi kingdom. There were new threats represented by two emerging leaders who were spearheading local resistance to Mughal encroachment: Malik Amber and Raju Deccani. Raju had been in the service of a premier Ahmednagar noble. When his master defected to the Mughal side, Raju stayed with the Nizam Shahi cause and soon acquired control over enough of the kingdom to become a force in his own right. Malik Amber was a former slave of Abyssinian descent and a military commander and war leader with whom Abdur Rahim would remain militarily and politically engaged for the next two decades. His ultimate lack of success against Amber anticipated the larger failure of the Mughals in their Deccan endeavours over the rest of the seventeenth century. Incidentally, Raju and Malik Amber, while professing loyalty to what remained of the the Nizam Shahis, were themselves bitter rivals.

Thus, if a unifying thread runs through the period, it is the inability of the Mughals to establish themselves in the territories they conquered outside of the fortified garrison towns. They faced a largely hostile populace, with Malik Amber recruiting war parties to harass and disrupt Mughal supply lines and carry out swift raids on Mughal posts before withdrawing and regrouping some distance away and repeating the same pattern at some other point. This was anticipating tactics that the great Maratha leader Shivaji would master and use against Mughal armies half a century later.

The threat posed by Malik Amber and Raju Deccani after the fall of Ahmednagar and the possibility of an alliance of the Deccan powers was one part of the problem. The other was internecine conflicts and jealousies within the Mughal nobility, and the absence of the emperor – or his preoccupation with affairs in north India. Together they showed up the political and military weaknesses of the Mughal position.

It would appear that Akbar was sensitive to these weaknesses. Some of the steps taken by him appear to have been directed towards addressing precisely these infirmities. Most prominent was the effort to prevent any issues in command, such as had effectively paralysed the Deccan campaign earlier. A marriage was arranged between Prince Daniyal and Janah Begum, Abdur Rahim's daughter. Abul Fazl, unsurprisingly, does not mention this alliance. Other sources confirm it, although it remains unclear whether it took place at the time of Daniyal's appointment to the Deccan or just before Akbar's departure for Agra, after the fall of Asirgarh. The purpose is clear enough: to bind the two in a close familial alliance, thereby reducing the possibility of other nobles conspiring to create differences. We also find Daulat Khan Lodi, Abdur Rahim's commander, being taken into the prince's court, perhaps with a similar intention. A second alliance, aimed this time at securing Bijapur's neutrality, was also cemented through a marriage between Daniyal and the daughter of Sultan Ibrahim Adil Shah in June 1604. Although the initiative for this may have come from the Bijapur court, which was keen to conciliate the Mughals, it was by all accounts an alliance greatly to the liking of the Mughals.

Despite all this, events were moving far too quickly and the situation on the ground was deteriorating rapidly, primarily on account of the swift movements of the light cavalry of Malik Amber and Raju Deccani. Malik Amber had set up a minor princeling of Nizam Shahi descent as Murtaza Nizam Shah II, to serve as a rallying point for other nobles, with some assistance from Bijapur. With Ahmednagar fort in Mughal control, Parenda, to its south, was made the new capital. To strengthen this alliance, Malik Amber married his daughter to the new king and himself took the title of Vakil-i-Sultanat, becoming in effect the principal minister and advisor. These developments in the southern part of the former Ahmednagar state were matched by those in the western parts bordering Gujarat. Here, Raju Deccani gathered around him a force strong enough to seriously threaten Mughal positions. He also formally accepted the suzerainty of Murtaza Nizam Shah II, although this did not in any way reduce the intensity of his own rivalry and conflict with Malik Amber.

In the military arrangements made after Akbar's departure, Abul Fazl was given responsibility for the operations against Raju Deccani. Abdur Rahim was charged to act against Malik Amber in the south and consolidate Mughal positions in Berar and Telingana. Notwithstanding their conventional superiority, the Mughal armies were hard pressed to show substantive progress on the ground, caught as they were between Malik Amber and Raju Deccani. Success against one army enabled the other to consolidate its position. It would appear that the presence of Abdur Rahim and Abul Fazl in the same army was also the cause of some lack of coordination given their now embittered relationship. Certainly, Muhammad Husain Azad ascribes to Abdur Rahim a not unnatural feeling of triumph upon finding Abul Fazl in a position subordinate to his. Although written two centuries later, the following description conveys some flavour of the state of their relationship:

> The KhanKhanan again used a trick. He praised Abul Fazl's abilities and capacity greatly and sought his services for the army. The Sheikh's position in this arrangement thus became very delicate. The Prince was the ruler of the Province, but the KhanKhanan his Commander in Chief and also his father in law. The Sheikh had to subordinate himself to him and the KhanKhanan had complete authority to deploy and use him as he wished. The Sheikh would sit in his camp, look over his shoulder, and burn with jealousy.[20]

At one stage the Mughal armies inflicted two successive and severe defeats on Malik Amber. Afterwards, Abdur Rahim adopted a conciliatory position, indicating his willingness to negotiate a treaty with the proxy Nizam Shahi ruler, Murtaza Nizam Shah II. The agreement was eventually concluded in January 1602 and was severely criticized by Abul Fazl: 'Some by love of sedition, some by shortness of thought and some by simplicity were led into the sleep of neglect by the artifices of the son Shah Ali [i.e. Murtaza Nizam Shah II].'[21] His own recommendation was that both Malik Amber and Raju Deccani should be fought against till their elimination.

The disinclination to eliminate Malik Amber and other allegations of double dealing against Abdur Rahim need to be seen in a broader context. The terms of the agreement with Malik Amber were similar to the treaty of 1596 with Chand Bibi, when the siege of Ahmednagar was lifted by Murad and Abdur Rahim: Mughal suzerainty would be recognized, some territory ceded, and the Nizam Shahi ruler would be given his own territory distinct from the Mughals. Thus imperial aims remained limited to securing some territory and recognition of Mughal suzerainty but did not extend to the annexation and extinction of Ahmednagar. The threat posed by Raju Deccani, the difficulties in conducting a campaign simultaneously against him and Amber, and finally, the realization that an agreement with Amber would isolate Raju Deccani, are certainly valid grounds for not too readily accepting the view of some of his contemporaries that Abdur Rahim was either acting in bad faith or exercising poor judgement.[22]

Events subsequent to this agreement also worked to some extent in favour of the Mughals. The forces of Raju Deccani and Malik Amber fought a series of largely inconclusive battles, weakening each other in the process and giving the Mughals the respite to consolidate their position. The continued neutrality of Bijapur, reinforced by the matrimonial alliance with Prince Daniyal, further helped the Mughal position. In any case, the focus of Mughal attention was now north India. This was not simply on account of the emperor's departure for Agra but because the endgame of the succession struggle had begun. Abul Fazl was murdered en route to Agra in August 1602 on Prince Salim's instructions. The latter's impatience to assume the throne,

Akbar's disillusionment with him, the conspiracy of Raja Man Singh and Mirza Aziz Koka to promote Prince Salim's son Khusrau (who was nephew and son-in-law respectively of these two power centres) in the emperor's favour so as to supersede the father, must have been the stuff of gossip and discussion throughout the empire. Perhaps such speculation would have been more intense in the Deccan army led by Prince Daniyal, who was himself in the main line of succession and who could still, given favourable circumstances, find his way to the throne.

That this did not happen was on account of the same agent that had been the cause of the early death of many Mughal nobles and princes: alcohol. In Daniyal's case too, his addiction had been a cause of worry to the emperor for some time. In February 1602, the prince's lack of interest in the task assigned to him was noted in the following terms:

> ... the jewel of the diadem of the Caliphate did not apply himself to the work of administration and that he left this to some avaricious, short-sighted people. How could work go on in this turmoil of carelessness and envy?[23]

Of course, this comment is as much a reproof of the prince as it is a dig at Abdur Rahim, the senior noble and commander in the Deccan. Yet the prince's drinking appears to have continued unabated. A few months later,

> it was reported to His Majesty – (that the Prince) who in accordance with the insistence of His Majesty had for a time given up wine drinking and had broken his wine vessels ... had ... broken his vow (to Akbar) and again fallen into drinking habits and that in consequence his disposition became immoderate.

In March 1603, Akbar appears to have decided to call Danyial back since it was 'reported that (he) never quitted hiccups and that he had become weak and ill from constant wine ...' The prince sent back an evasive reply:

> When I was informed of my being summoned, inasmuch as the time was not proper for sending for the KhanKhanan to Burhanpur I went off rapidly to interview him in order that I might instruct him about what was fitting to be done, and might give him advice...

His father was not so easily fooled.

> When H.M. learnt this, his mystery-knowing mind perceived that the prince was not inclined to come, and that his going from Khandesh to the Deccan was a pretext. Accordingly, an order was issued to the effect that his not coming was due to his habits of drinking and self-indulgence. What need was there for the KhanKhanan's receiving instructions from him? If he wrote such things again H.M. would be a thousand times more displeased.[24]

In March 1604, we are informed of the emperor's anger at continued reports of the prince's drinking and the dispatch of another imperial physician to attend to him. A little later, the emperor was to dispatch one of the prince's old wet nurses 'in whose bosom the Prince had been born and grown up and who was not afraid to speak strongly' with the added instruction that 'by every possible means the Prince should be brought to him'. Reports, however, kept coming in that the prince 'was in a bad state from excessive drinking and that he was becoming weaker day by day'. In March 1605, after a long alcohol-induced stupor, the prince died.

For Abdur Rahim, this meant the loss of a royal son-in-law. Prince Daniyal's marriage with Janah Begum was, by all accounts, more than a political alliance of convenience. The prince, we are informed, was 'wonderfully attached to Janah Begum ...' She had given him a son in late 1601 or early 1602, but the child did not live long. Of Jana Begum's grief at the death of Daniyal, the description that has come down to us is unusually graphic:

> That excellent and faithful lady became inconsolable after this catastrophe and wished to go to the other world with the Prince. She did not get this boon and submitting to the prohibitions and

> advices of others she remained in this abode of sorrow. But she was consumed with grief for the departure of the Prince. She lived for many years but till her last breath, each day of her widowhood was the first day.[25]

The death of the prince was also a major political setback for Abdur Rahim, given the nature of his responsibilities in the Deccan. With Daniyal's matrimonial alliance in place to ensure the neutrality of Bijapur, Abdur Rahim had been following essentially a holding policy against Malik Amber and Raju Deccani. Mughal strategy was limited to ensuring that neither party grew excessively in strength so as to be able to move beyond their spheres of influence. This also meant that neither grew disproportionately at the cost of the other. Thus we have occasion to find Abdur Rahim dispatching contingents of troops to help Malik Amber when he was in a precarious position against Raju. A little later we find the positions reversed and Mughal troops assuming a threatening posture to reduce excessive pressure on Raju from Amber. Given the emperor's preoccupation with Prince Salim, the sense of looming uncertainty over the succession, and the general infirmity of the Mughal position in the Deccan, such action, while hardly satisfying from the point of view of the court, was perhaps the only stable equilibrium achievable at that point of time.

Prince Daniyal's death upset this balance. It led to Abdul Rahim's appointment as governor of the Deccan and his move to Burhanpur, further away from active campaigning. This gave Malik Amber the space he was waiting for. It also weakened the Mughal alliance with Bijapur. Finally, it may have led to a further erosion of Abdur Rahim's standing in the court. There is, first, the absence of major victories since 1596 under his leadership. Secondly, the death of two young royal princes occurred in a command in which he was very much the senior noble and military leader, and there were rumours that the absence of political or military success had driven both to excessive drinking. Third, the rumours and insinuations about Abdur Rahim acting in concert with Salim never quite disappeared, even after the death of Murad and the appointment of Daniyal. Even if there was a more restrained quality to the allegations, they continued during Daniyal's tenure, with the prince's occasional but muted dissatisfaction with Abdur Rahim's policies and lack of quick action.[26]

Thus, if one issue is to be highlighted as dominating the court subsequent to Akbar's return from the Deccan, it would be the succession. Prince Salim's march on Agra fort while the emperor was still in the Deccan, in an unsuccessful bid to secure it, having coins struck in his name in May 1602, and the murder of Abul Fazl – each of these episodes reflects a situation fraught with continual stress. A few months after Abul Fazl's murder, a rapprochement with his son was attempted by the emperor by dispatching Salima Sultan Begum to Allahabad to persuade the prince to return to court. The reconciliation was to be temporary, and Salim returned to Allahabad in defiance of his father's command that he proceed for a campaign against the Rana of Mewar.

In Allahabad, Salim's excesses of alcohol and opium coupled with repeated bouts of drunken sadism continued. One episode stands out, illustrating his lack of moderation and control as also the struggle that Salim at that stage may have anticipated against Daniyal.

> … one of the Prince's reporters was smitten with a khanzad who was in the circle of the elite, while the brazen khanzad became infatuated with another servant. All three ran away together hoping to get themselves to the Deccan and live under the protection of Prince Daniyal. When the reality of the case was presented to His Highness, he immediately assigned troops of mounted patrols to seize them. By chance all three were caught and bought before the Prince while the flames of his wrath were high. By his order the reporter was skinned alive in his presence, one servant was turned into a eunuch, and the other was lashed.

When this incident was reported to the emperor, no doubt with embellishments, he said: 'We have conquered a whole world by the sword, but until today we have not ordered so much as a sheep to

> be skinned in our presence. My son is unimaginably hard-hearted if he can have a man skinned in his presence.'[27]

The death of Akbar's mother in August 1603 provided the opportunity for another reconciliation between father and son. But Salim's presence in court brought to the foreground another greatly troubled relationship – with his firstborn son, Khusrau. Raja Man Singh, Khusrau's uncle, and Mirza Aziz Koka, whose daughter he married, were among the premier nobles of the court at the time. They saw in Khusrau a possible candidate for emperor, motivated, no doubt, by the desire to install on the throne a prince who was their intimate, genuine outrage at Salim's continued acts of rebellion and, finally, a real concern over the fate of the empire given the stories in circulation about Salim's lack of moderation and excesses of wine and opium. The reports of Daniyal's ill health and the general expectation that he would not recover gave to their efforts an added urgency. Akbar's rage at Salim's behaviour and outrage at his excesses were tempered by the realization that Salim might well be the only son he would soon have left.

Abdur Rahim in the Deccan would probably have been a mere observer of these events. It is true that he had good relations for many years with Raja Man Singh and Mirza Aziz Koka, the two nobles at the centre of the machinations in court. However, there is no reference to be found of his partiality for Prince Salim, or otherwise, in the context of the Khusrau–Salim duel. Evidently, Abdur Rahim took pains not to get sucked into this imbroglio. The fact of his physical absence plus preoccupation with the difficulties of governance in the Deccan would have helped him to avoid taking sides. His relationship with these two premier nobles had also evolved – the carefree friendship of their youth giving way to the more cautious dealings of seasoned courtiers.

Akbar's death in October 1605 was a great personal loss for Abdur Rahim. The emperor was just over sixty-three years of age and had ruled for half a century. For so great a ruler the last few years were sad from a personal point of view. Two sons died in their prime – victim to drink. His close confidant Abul Fazl was murdered at the orders of another son, Prince Salim. Akbar's last weeks were particularly distressed – as clashes between the supporters of Salim and his son Khusrau took place increasingly in the open. Abdur Rahim heard of the death while near the great Deccan garrison fortress of Daulatabad. Dressed all in black, he addressed an assembly of notables who collectively expressed their condolences. A message of homage and gifts were dispatched to the new emperor.[28] But there was now the anxiety of gaining favour with the new dispensation.

There was certainly an old relationship going back to the time when Abdur Rahim was Salim's ataliq. But we do not observe any special favour being bestowed on him after Salim's accession (as the Emperor Jahangir), which would have been expected had there been some credence to the stories about his having been a partisan of the prince. The impression we have is that rather than being marked out for special favour, the new emperor sought to reassure Abdur Rahim by sending an envoy:

> After my accession because of the absolute trust I had in him (the envoy – Shaykh Hussain Muqarrab Khan) I sent him to Burhanpur to bring my brother Danyal's sons and family and to deliver detailed advice to the KhanKhanan. Muqarrab Khan performed this service well in a short time removing the fears that were clouding the minds of the KhanKhanan. and the Amirs there ...[29]

A little later, we are informed of the dispatch of a jewel-studded sword hilt to the Khan-i-Khanan. In December 1607, Abdur Rahim's gifts to the new emperor were presented:

> He had sent forty elephants, a gem, jewelled utensils, Persian textiles and cloth made in the Deccan and that area. In total it was worth

> one hundred and fifty thousand rupees. Mirza Rustom and most of the couriers appointed to the above mentioned Suba also sent offerings. I like several of the elephants.[30]

These exchanges do not suggest anything more than the accepted protocol between the sovereign and an important noble and provincial governor. A similar exchange of gifts is, for instance, reported with Raja Man Singh, who had allied himself with Khusrau against Salim. There is no sign of either great favour or prejudice on the part of the new emperor as far as Abdur Rahim is concerned. For some three years after the accession, no particular attention is paid to the Deccan either, nor any determined effort made to assist the army, though the situation continued to worsen for the Mughals.

A strong move against Qandahar by the Persians and a preoccupation with Khusrau's attempts to undermine the newly installed emperor through open revolt were obvious reasons for this. The lack of initiative provided an opportunity for Malik Amber. A reduction of Mughal forces due to the redeployment of some troops for the Qandahar front may have also provided a favourable opening on the ground. Malik Amber moved rapidly from one stronghold to another and up to the environs of Burhanpur itself. In parallel, a major operation against Raju Deccani saw the latter suffer a humiliating defeat. He was captured and the great Daulatabad fortress fell to Malik Amber. Control of Daulatabad enabled Malik Amber to pose a threat to Gujarat as also to Burhanpur. In brief, Malik Amber now threatened every gain made by the Mughal forces since at least the 1580s.

It is around this time, towards the end of July 1608, that we find Abdur Rahim being summoned to the court and granted an audience. In Jahangir's words:

> ... the KhanKhanan who held the high post as my ataliq came from Burhanpur to pay homage. He was so happy that he did not know whether to walk on his feet or his head. In confusion he threw

himself at my feet but I kindly raised his head, embraced him warmly and kissed his face ...[31]

If this description of Abdur Rahim is correct, it hardly suggests the behaviour of a confidante of the emperor, or one who had conspired to advance his claim over that of his brothers. The emperor is certainly well disposed towards the noble, but this is more on account of their previous association. In any event, Abdur Rahim's visit to the court was not about the past, but to consult the emperor about the position of the Mughals in the Deccan. The outcome of these consultations was recorded by the emperor on 22 September 1608:

... the KhanKhanan undertook to smooth things out in the Nizam-ul-Mulk's territory where some disturbances had occurred since His Majesty's death. Having written his pledge he gave it to me saying, 'if I do not discharge this task within two years I will be guilty of a fault' – provided that in addition to the army that was already in the suba, twelve thousand more soldiers and a treasury of Rupees 10 lacs be assigned him. I ordered that the troops and a treasury of 10 lacs of rupees be assigned him. I ordered that troops and treasury should be quickly made ready so that he could be quickly sent off.[32]

A few weeks later, in November 1608, Abdur Rahim returned to the Deccan with due honour, after being rewarded with 'a jewelled girth sword, a robe of honour and a royal elephant'. And yet, only a little while earlier, the matter of his permanent recall from the Deccan was being considered and Raja Man Singh had been appointed to command an expeditionary force to the region. Abdur Rahim was able to persuade the emperor to retain him in the position by undertaking to complete the job within two years. And so it came to pass that Man Singh was deputed to serve under Abdur Rahim – the first time since 1586 that the Raja was to serve under another noble.[33] The following conversation adds pungency to this situation:

One-day Man Singh asked the KhanKhanan about the slow pace of military progress in the Deccan. The KhanKhanan replied: You have

> come back after concluding the affairs of Usman Afghan in Purab (East) and have been appointed as my subordinate. If I end the present war quickly under what noble would I be deputed to serve?[34]

One can only speculate on the strain this situation would have placed on the relationship between Man Singh and Abdur Rahim.

The return of Abdur Rahim with additional resources and troops made little difference to the Mughal position and their capacity to contain Malik Amber. Jahangir decided to send further reinforcements and appointed his son, Prince Parvez, as governor of the Deccan and a senior noble, Asaf Khan, as his advisor. These reinforcements, however, made the situation more difficult as the familiar issue of the chain of command surfaced again. Assistance from Bijapur, whose ruler was worried at the large Mughal armies being deployed in the Ahmednagar territories, further helped Malik Amber. Surprise night attacks, disruption of supply lines and swift withdrawals to regroup and strike at another location remained tactics which the Mughal commanders were unable to deal with. Abdur Rahim was again accused of lack of cooperation, indifference and incompetence as Prince Parvez's efforts failed to cope with this element of tactical surprise employed by Malik Amber's light cavalry. Finally, an accusation of treachery would be made.

A plan involving a large force that would strike deep into Ahmednagar failed disastrously in 1609 and Malik Amber continued to make major inroads into areas hitherto held by the Mughals. According to some contemporary accounts, Abdur Rahim had been cautious about the enterprise and had 'advised that the campaign should be put off in view of the impending rainy season. But the impetuosity of the generals could not be controlled and it was decided to make a march.'[35] Others, however, paint a different picture:

> The KhanKhanan … had devised an elaborate plan of delivering a surprise attack on Malik Amber. The rainy season had already started. Against the better judgement of his followers the KhanKhanan made a dash into the Nizam Shahi territory. To a certain stage his plan

> worked according to his expectations, but ended in tragic failure on account of rains ...[36]

Lack of provisions, the enemy's avoidance of head-on battles, relying instead on surprise night attacks, make up the rest of the story. The charges of negligence, rashness and treachery mounted as Abdur Rahim was forced to make whatever terms were possible before retreating to Burhanpur.[37]

There is a ring of truth in the account that the disaster occurred on account of misjudgement on Abdur Rahim's part. Did frustration at the lack of progress, and the realization that the two-year limit promised by him to the emperor was running out, provoke him into a rash undertaking? Worse was to follow. Malik Amber's forces, in an ironical reversal of roles, now besieged Ahmednagar fort. Abdur Rahim's efforts to relieve the defenders failed and the garrison had to be surrendered, a setback to the Mughals on which no gloss could possibly be put.

The army in the Deccan was then strengthened by one of Jahangir's closest favourites, Khan Jahan Lodi, and other prominent nobles and they, in turn, added to the chorus against Abdur Rahim. His final recall was decided upon after Khan Jahan Lodi's complaints against him grew to a crescendo.

> ... all our supporters considered the confusion and turmoil to be the fault of the KhanKhanan's uncooperativeness. And they sent reports to this effect to court. Although all this was not to be believed absolutely, still it made a bad impression on my mind until Khan Jahan's report arrived saying that the confusion had all occurred because of the KhanKhanan's lack of cooperation. 'Either turn the mission over to him', Khan Jahan wrote, 'or summon him to the court and assign the mission to this protégé of yours'.[38]

Mahabat Khan, another premier noble, was tasked to carry out an investigation into recent Mughal failures and escort Abdur Rahim back to court.

We may pause to take note here of the two high nobles mentioned in the preceding narrative. First, Mahabat Khan. The juncture at which he is charged with escorting Abdur Rahim back to court is the first time we encounter him and the Khan-i-Khanan together. That Abdur Rahim ascribed to Mahabat Khan a feeling of enmity is clear and that he was being investigated rankled deeply. We can do no more than recall Abdur Rahim's inscription about Mahabat Khan in his copy of Khusrau's *Khamsa* and wonder whether this feud had an older history.[39] In the years that follow, their lives would be intertwined to a greater extent than either man could have imagined. If the beginning is hardly propitious, the rest of their interactions would be even less so and, in the case of Abdur Rahim, the end would be tragic.

Secondly, Khan Jahan Lodi. This Afghan noble was none other than the son of Abdur Rahim's faithful commander and advisor Daulat Khan Lodi. After the latter's death, at the turn of the century, Pir Khan, as the Khan Jahan was then known, was also in Abdur Rahim's service. Soon after Jahangir's accession, we find Pir Khan summoned to court, rapidly promoted and given the title of Khan Jahan. This may have been on account of Jahangir's desire to ensure that capable Afghan nobles were personally indebted to him, but also because of a personal liking for him and the Khan Jahan's own charm. In any event, his was a spectacular rise and he was soon one of the most powerful nobles in court. That the hand of the son of his own subordinate general, Daulat Khan Lodi, was writ large in Abdur Rahim's recall is only one more indication of the constant jostling for position that constituted court politics.

We could also pause to introduce two other contrasting frames in the life and career of the Khan-i-Khanan. The first of these is a remarkable Sanskrit poem from around this time, composed in honour of Abdur Rahim. The second is his interface and relationship with Sheikh Ahmad Sirhindi, who in the judgement of many at that time and in the centuries since, represented the Islamic backlash to the forces of liberalism and eclecticism in Akbar's court.

There are numerous stories of Abdur Rahim's close relationship with the Rajputs. Some are historically documented, such as his friendship with Raja Man Singh. Others are oral traditions and celebrated in verse, such as those of the poet Jada seeking help on behalf of his master Jagmal, or describing Abdur Rahim's admiration for Rana Pratap. The *Nawab Khankhanan Charitam* is a petition addressed to Abdur Rahim and covers both categories and forms part of the body of evidence and literature positing a close relationship and sympathy for Rajput ruling houses. One of its verses has a precise date – Saka 1531, AD 1609 – and we can therefore locate it to the time when Abdur Rahim is hard-pressed in the Deccan but obviously still of a standing when he can help old friends. It is a Sanskrit work with a mixed prose-and-verse composition and written by the poet Rudra Kavi, the court poet of Pratap Shah, a Rathore Rajput prince who ruled the minor kingdom of Baglan, near modern Nashik in Maharashtra, and who is important in this story. Other panegyrics composed by Rudra Kavi include *Rastraudhavamsamahakavya* – a work on the ruling Rastraudha dynasty of Baglan, composed in 1596; the *Danasahacaritam* – a composition on the Mughal prince and Akbar's son, Daniyal, in AD 1603; and the *Kirtisamullasa* – a panegyric to Prince Khurram in AD 1616.[40]

While Rudra Kavi is otherwise described as a poet of great merit, in these compositions he is said to have been 'much handicapped; firstly, he had to compose poems on order; secondly, for the members of the Royal family, for which he may not have a genuine fondness ... As the subject matter of the above mentioned works is about the same, some verses occur ... with occasional changes here and there. "Danasaha" and "KhanKhanan" have metrically the same characteristics and, therefore, with regard to these two names, he simply substituted one word for the other.'[41] For the work on Khurram, he had to change the title and the text a little.

The *Nawab Khankhanan Charitam* consists, in all, of forty-one verses unevenly distributed in three sections. The first contains nine verses besides some prose, the second, twenty verses and the third, twelve. The last five verses of the third and final section, which set out the context as also the real purpose of the panegyric. The body of the *Charitam* itself has highly stylized descriptions in praise of Abdur Rahim. The opening verses describe him as a chief among all kings, one who has conquered all parts of India such as Anga, Kalinga, Vanga, Magadh, Panchal and Koshal. In these descriptions, 'the poet's eye is more upon the rhythmic alliteration in country names than the truth of the statement'. He is one who is well versed in all arts of war and peace and spends his time hunting, sporting, studying, painting, etc. The second and third parts continue in much the same way – praise of his courage, his generosity, magnanimity, and long descriptions of his horse. The work, as a whole, has been described 'as a fine specimen of Sanskrit ornate prose and poetry but is curiously silent about the historical aspect of the hero under description'.[42]

Baglan had been bound by feudatory ties to the Mughals since at least the mid-1590s. Perhaps the relationship was forged by Abdur Rahim himself as the commander of the Mughal expedition against Ahmednagar. The circumstances in which the original friendship, or at least some kind of relationship, between Pratap Shah and the Khan-i-Khanan was born are clarified in the *Rastraudhavamsamahakavya*, which describes Pratap Shah's valorous deeds during the storming of the Ahmednagar fort, as part of the army of the Khan-i-Khanan and Prince Murad.[43]

There are also other details available about Pratap Shah, adding flesh and bones to his character. We have, for instance, a description by Emperor Jahangir of Pratap Shah coming to pay homage to him in September 1617:

> On Friday the twenty fourth Raja Bharjiu, the Zamindar of Baglana came and paid homage. His name is Pratap, but all those who become Rajas there are called Bharjiu ... The province of Baglana is situated in the midst of Gujarat, Khandesh, and the Deccan ... The Raja has never failed to act with gentle caution with the rulers of Gujarat, the Deccan, and Khandesh but has never gone to see

> any of them. Whenever one of them has desired to stretch forth a hand to usurp his territory he has availed himself of the protection of one of the others.[44]

This attendance in Jehangir's court took place about eight years after the composition of the *Nawab Khankhanan Charitam.*

What explains the composition of the *Khankhanan Charitam?* Clearly, a court poet putting together a panegyric on instructions from the ruler, who was keen to supplicate the Mughal commander-in-chief. It is the brief final verses which, however, illuminate the text and 'characteristically allow us a glimpse of the scene behind the curtain':

> The rising passion in the form of the valour of Emperor Jahangir has upset the fawn eyed lady in the form of the southern direction. If KhanKhanan, the ornament of the earth, extends his hand to touch her garments, she is pleased.[45]

These verses suggest that Pratap Shah was in some difficulty and expected help from Abdur Rahim, who is reminded 'of the old relations that existed between him and Pratapa, whom ... KhanKhanan had treated as his own son and honoured as a great warrior'. It is also pointed out that the Baglan chiefs had always paid tribute to the Delhi emperor. Rudra Kavi employs for the Khan-i-Khanan metaphors such as 'protector of the weak' and 'one who checks powerful monarchs', suggesting that Baglan was threatened in some way by imperial forces and the appeal to him was on the basis of an older relationship. The *Nawab Khankhanan Charitam* was thus a 'petition of succour' and the main body of the work was in the guise of a panegyric. Evidently, Pratap Shah saw a Sanskrit poem as the most appropriate means to ask help from Abdur Rahim.

Was this on account of Abdur Rahim's own fondness for poetry and his knowledge of Sanskrit, and because it was felt that this cultural medium would be appreciated the most? One is tempted to answer with a resounding yes. Incidentally, this work is reminiscent of the verses composed by the Rajput bard Jada, seeking intervention in favour of his master, which we encountered earlier.[46] Similarly, we had James Tod attributing to Abdur Rahim verses addressed to Maharana Pratap, praising his valour and perseverance.

In fact, some two-and-a-half decades after Rana Pratap's epic struggle against the imperial advance, we find another oral tradition in which Abdur Rahim is described as offering solace to a beleaguered Rajput prince. The pressure of the Mughal armies on Maharana Amar Singh, Rana Pratap's son, was intense. The constant clashes, the need to seek refuge in the inaccessible and hilly parts around Mewar and the regular enticement from the imperial army to surrender had taken a toll on the resolve of the Maharana as also his principal nobles. The *Vir Vinod*, a history and gazetteer of the kingdom of Mewar, composed in the late nineteenth century, tells of Maharana Amar Singh seeking Abdur Rahim's advice through a brief verse – a doha in eleven words, a literal translation of which would be:

> The Gonds, Kachhwahas and Rathors are in their luxurious palaces.
> Tell the KhanKhanan that we wander like men of the forests.

The allusion obviously is to the easy life of the ruling clans of Amber and Jodhpur, now subordinates and allies of the Mughals. The question is an obvious one: should Mewar also not compromise and submit to the Mughals? The reply attributed to Abdur Rahim is an equally brief verse of twelve words:

> Land and faith will remain, the Khurasanis destroyed. Maharana Amar should have faith in the protector of the Universe.[47]

Khurasanis refers to the Mughals and the meaning is quite clear: Amar Singh should fight on and not compromise. Evidently, this Mewar tradition, which the *Vir Vinod* captured, attributes to Abdur Rahim such a degree of sympathy and admiration for Mewar that he asks its Maharana to continue resisting the Mughals and advises that the almighty would secure his victory. Thus Abdur Rahim is in effect taking sides against his own side.

There is no reference to this exchange in the Mughal chronicles and the main chronology of Abdur Rahim's career would find him totally engrossed in events in the Deccan during this period, far removed from anything to do with Mewar. Also, Maharana Amar Singh did move to a settlement with the Mughals around 1616 and surrendered to Prince Khurram, the future Shah Jahan; for Emperor Jahangir, this was a considerable achievement given the resistance that Mewar had mounted against the Mughals for half a century. For Prince Khurram too, it was a political and military triumph.

Of significance, however, in the context of our story, are the allusions to Abdur Rahim as an intimate and sympathetic friend of the Rajputs while they were in the midst of a bitter life-and-death struggle against the imperial forces and pondering the options of submission or continued resistance. Whether true or not, this image of Abdur Rahim has persisted and consolidated in the centuries since. The oral traditions and verses linking Abdur Rahim with Rana Pratap, such as those in the *Rajprashisht Mahakavyam* and *Amar Kavyam*, from whence they travelled to Jayashanker Prasad's *Maharana ka Mahatva*, or as recounted in Rudra Kavi's *Nawab Khankhanan Charitam* and Shyamaldas's *Vir Vinod* have each played their part in this. Did these reflect a real sense of empathy that, in turn, shows the communal consensus and synthesis emerging in and at the heart of Akbar's India? Or was the image deliberately but discreetly built up by Abdur Rahim himself over the years, as an asset that could have some use, but equally one that could be denied if so required? We may speculate, but we also need to look at other evidence which points to a different kind of image.

We have encountered the secret history of Badayuni and his bitter invective against the eclecticism and departure from Islamic moorings of many of Akbar's courtiers as well as the emperor himself. In Badayuni's estimation, Abdur Rahim stood out as one whose Islamic moorings were strong and immune to the liberal vagaries of the court. The closing years of Akbar's reign and the early years of Jahangir's rule did see a conservative reaction to Akbar's liberal policies. This included the claim that the emperor had a deliberately repressive policy towards conservative practitioners of Islam. Prince Salim, in the midst of one of his rebellions against the emperor, is believed to have issued a farman in 1601 that reads:

> At the instigation of some mischievous persons, my father has abolished the arrangements for the maintenance of khatib, mu'ázzin, and imam in the mosques and has prohibited the performance of namaz in congregation. He has converted many of the mosques into store houses and stables. It was improper on his part to have acted in this manner.[48]

The charge is bizarre. Salim, however, felt that there was a groundswell of repugnance at the extent to which Akbar had gone in his eclecticism and liberalism and this outrage could be harnessed in his support, against his father.

The panegyric on Abdur Rahim, the *Maathir-i-Rahimi*, refers at one stage to an incident which appears to corroborate the general impression that Akbar was implacably opposed to Islam:

> ... after Danyal's appointment to the newly conquered Suba of Deccan and Khandesh (1601), Akbar had written to him to destroy the jama masjid at Asirgarh and raise (in its place) a temple of the pattern of Hindus and (other) infidels of Hindustan.

Daniyal, however, was wise enough, continues the text:

> ... not to enforce the order by ignoring it and whiling away the time so that the demolition of a mosque and building of a temple in its place during the time of the king of kings of Islam was avoided.[49]

This story has no other corroborative evidence, but in Abdul Baqi Nihavandi's narration of it, 'there is an implicit suggestion ... that the credit for ignoring Akbar's extraordinary order should partly go to the KhanKhanan who was then next in command to Danyal'. Certainly, the *Maathir-i-Rahimi* has all the elements required of an authorized and official biography. It has, therefore, been suggested that the source of the story was possibly Abdur Rahim himself and that:

> Such a story being recorded in a text identified with Abdur Rahim Khan-i-Khanan tends to suggest that at the time of its writing (1614), Akbar's restrictive measures against orthodox Islam were such common knowledge that an allusion to it in a historical text's passing observation was not expected to be considered offensive by Jahangir as well as his couriers.[50]

Contemporary with these issues are the teachings of Sheikh Ahmad Sirhindi (1563–1624), who is regarded by his followers as the one responsible for correcting the liberal tendencies unleashed by Akbar and finally also responsible for inspiring Aurangzeb in his religious policy.[51] His title, *Mujadid-i-Alf-i-Thani*, by which he remains well known to this day, means literally 'Regenerator of the second Millennium'.

The Sheikh is said to have reversed the heretical trends of the period of Akbar and restored the pristine purity of Islam. His work is credited with inspiring the orthodox reforms of Aurangzeb, whose main objective is thought to have been the imposition of the shariah on the state.[52] Also:

> He is portrayed in the history textbooks currently published in Pakistan as the restorer in the early seventeenth century of Sunni 'orthodoxy' after the innovation, even apostasy of the Emperor Akbar ... Hence his active role as *Mujadid-i-Alf-i-Thani* ... saved Indian Islam from self-perpetrated annihilation and serves as a model today for those responsible for determining the role of Islam in the contemporary state.[53]

In these assessments, Sheikh Ahmad Sirhindi was the ideological fountainhead of a large number of Muslim nobles who were dissatisfied with the growing influence of Hindu nobles and even more with the eclectic and syncretic winds that had swept the court under Akbar. To an extent, this group prevailed following Akbar's death since it 'turned the scales in favour of Jahangir during the controversy between Salim and Khusrau for succession'. Such support for Jahangir came, it is argued, after a promise was extracted, at Sheikh Sirhindi's insistence, from Salim that he, on becoming emperor, would defend Islam. Situating him in a broader context of Islamic history in the Indian subcontinent, it has been argued that 'long before British rule and long before modern political notions of Muslim nationhood, the consensus of the Muslim community in India had rejected the eclecticism of Akbar and Dara Shikoh for the purified Islamic teachings of Sheikh Ahmad of Sirhind …'

Such an assessment has been contested by others who argue that there is no evidence suggesting that Sheikh Ahmad Sirhindi had any great influence with the nobles of the day, or in other sections of the Mughal court, and indeed had no real role to play, ideological or otherwise, in the succession crisis in the last years of Akbar. The elevation of Sheikh Ahmad Sirhindi as the leading ideologue of seventeenth-century Mughal India is thus described as being without evidential basis and his current 'glorification is only a part of the modern separatist tradition'.[54]

Similarly, it has been argued that:

> Sirhindi's present significance for the Indian and Pakistani Muslims is a result of his image as a restorer of orthodoxy and a reviver of 'pure' Islam. This image … reflects twentieth century developments in the Indian subcontinent rather than the seventeenth century thought of Ahmad Sirhindi …[55]

The details of this debate need not concern us here. What remains part of the historical record is a body of letters that Sheikh Ahmad wrote to a number of Mughal nobles including Abdur Rahim. While the Sheikh's supporters argue to this day that this establishes his great influence over the Mughal nobility, others argue that there is no evidence in them to suggest any kind of spiritual or ideological influence over those whom the Sheikh addressed his numerous epistles to.

Sheikh Sirhindi's views were certainly opposed to the dominant trend in Akbar's court and, in fact, even Jahangir's. He had 'no patience with those who might suggest an identity between the higher beliefs of the Bhakti Movement and Muslim mysticism'. To Hardai Ram, a Hindu who had written devotional tracts, the Sheikh wrote a letter condemning the extreme stupidity of believing Ram and Rahman to be the same and comparing Ram and Krishna to the lowliest of sweepers.[56]

Similarly, he wrote:

> The glory of Islam consists in the limitations of infidelity and the infidels. Anyone who held an Infidel in esteem caused humiliation to Islam. Holding in esteem does not simply mean that one pays respect to them or seats them in higher position. Giving a place to them in one's company, sitting and talking with them are all ways of showing esteem. They (the infidels) should be kept at a distance like dogs.

And again:

> ... the real purpose in taking the *jiziya* (poll tax) is to humiliate them (the non-Muslims) and this humiliation should reach the stage where owing to the fear of the *jiziya*, they should not be able to wear good clothes and should never enjoy any peace of mind and be in constant dread and fear of the King taking away their property.[57]

Sheikh Ahmad Sirhindi wrote some twelve letters to Abdur Rahim. It is not possible to date them accurately, but it would not be unreasonable to place them in the early years of Jahangir's reign. These letters certainly do not always suggest that he was writing to someone who shared his particular view in its entirety or one he could count amongst his disciples. Thus:

> It is my duty to say what is proper and becoming and must be communicated to you. It is for you to either accept my word of advice or take offence at it. All your three letters had an air of indifference about them ... I am not unmindful of my obligation to you but some things which I say are not palatable and appear to be unpleasant. Flatterers you have galore so let some plain talking suffice from my side. The purpose and advantage with the *faqirs* that is to say, the humble folks, is that they frankly point out your weakness and defects to you. In this way, a man becomes conscious of hidden blemishes and weakness of character ...[58]

This letter is believed to have been written around 1607–08 when Abdur Rahim had visited the court at Agra to wait upon the emperor. Sheikh Ahmad Sirhindi had also gone to Agra but was unable to have access to the Khan-i-Khanan, for which he blamed the latter's servants. 'Some benefits which this journey could give you would really have fulfilled the purpose for which it was made but the "friends and well-wishers" that you have did not allow that to happen,' he wrote.

Even from the distance of four centuries, it is easy to imagine the scene. The Khan-i-Khanan's visit to the court would possibly have been his first major audience with the emperor. Anxieties on that score would have coupled with those arising from having to convince the court of the next steps to be taken in the Deccan. This was hardly the time or the occasion for receiving a discourse on the true path from a philosopher.

It is useful to recall also the help Abdur Rahim gave to Haji Sultan Thanesari, Sheikh Ahmad Sirhindi's father-in-law, who had been punished by Akbar for allegedly slaughtering a cow. In fact, Sheikh Sirhindi's letters to Abdur Rahim, as indeed to other nobles, were also frequently accompanied by recommendations of particular persons for employment, help, promotion, etc.

> Syed Ibrahim has had a long and lasting attachment with your house. He is one of your well-wishers. It is incumbent upon your

> gracious obligation to help him out. He may thus be enabled to lead his last days of life in peace and security and may be assisted to overcome want and poverty. He will thus pray for your success in both the worlds.[59]

That there was a correspondence and exchange of letters between Sheikh Ahmad Sirhindi and Abdur Rahim is beyond doubt, and some of the Sheikh's teachings may well have found an attentive reader. For, elsewhere, we find the Sheikh writing:

> Praise be to Allah and blessing on the holy prophet. The letter you sent to me through Maulana Muhammad Siddique was received by me with gratitude. May God bless you and reward you for the good you do. You have shown courtesy and grace and paid the respect due to poor religious mendicants. The holy prophet has said that whosoever adopts a condescending attitude towards the people who are *faqirs* is elevated in merit by the Almighty. I am sure your treatment to the humble ones will raise you high in both the worlds. In fact you have attained that high station already. This is good tidings. You have talked of returning to the true faith and coming back to the fold of religion and I surmise that it is now a *fait accompli* due to the interceding of some man of God. You may justly await a good reward.[60]

On the whole, the tone of Sheikh Ahmad Sirhindi's letters to Abdur Rahim is respectful and carries all the deference due to a great noble. Clearly, the message in these is quieter and more restrained than in some of the other epistles he wrote. Knowing something of Abdur Rahim's personality, he may have concluded that a harder enunciation of views on Islam in India would fail to find favour. In any case, Abdur Rahim's interest and fascination for Hindu idioms and genres as an aesthetic or even devotional pursuit did not imply his inability to engage also with the strongly conservative and orthodox, even bigoted, such as Sheikh Ahmad Sirhindi, amongst his own co-religionists. If Abdur Rahim's frequently cited Hindu devotional verses and friendship with prominent Hindus is one frame of reference, the view of Sheikh Ahmad Sirhindi and of Abdul Qadir Badayuni that Islam and another faith such as Hinduism were antithetical and contradictory forms another. Accepting either one to the exclusion of the other would preclude the possibility of a personality with multiple layers. Alternatively, we could argue that here again is a case of careful positioning by Abdur Rahim, so that he remained at the centre even in the midst of changing political – ideological divides and tensions, rather than at either end.

5

THE TWILIGHT YEARS

AFTER HIS recall to the court in October 1610, we can imagine Abdur Rahim waiting and watching. There were strong rumours that he had secretly helped Malik Amber and there was, consequently, some indignity involved in the initial period of his return. An investigation was entrusted to Mahabat Khan by the court. There was also an accusation by a former trusted servant that a highly regarded attendant, Sheikh Abdus Salam Lakhnawi, had in his possession all the letters exchanged between Abdur Rahim and Malik Amber. He was summoned, but neither bribes nor promises of promotion or threats could get him to divulge anything. Sadly, 'ultimately he was tortured and killed, and having thus shown utmost loyalty, brought honour ...'[1]

Abdur Rahim spent at least some part of the next two years or so in Kannuaj, then his jagir, attending to matters there. Since he had no other administrative charge of substance during this time, we do not know whether the stints in Kannauj were interspersed with periods spent in Agra. Was this time spent happily in the company of his sons and their families? Did he wait philosophically for the tide of events to turn and to have an important charge allotted to him again? Or was this a period of frustration and lobbying with those close to the emperor? Certainly there was intense anxiety about his position vis-à-vis the emperor and a keen need to keep abreast of the news of the court.

> KhanKhanan was so much anxious of hearing the news of court that Mahmud Khan, the Agent, Uttam Chand, the first assistant, and Mian Babu Kalal, each of them used to send separately a report containing the news of the court every day by relay post. One courier each was stationed at the court house, at Kotwal's platform, and royal *kacheri* and they used to write down and communicate to him the happenings of the events of that place in detail. One person was assigned to move about in the lane and market place; he would write down the public gossip circulating there. In the evening after having studied these reports himself he would consign them to fire.[2]

That the emperor's displeasure did not run deep and indeed, was temporary, is clear. In March 1611, Abdur Rahim's oldest son, Iraj, was awarded the title of Shah Nawaz Khan. Jahangir described him as a 'worthy and talented Khanazad'.[3] A little later, in April 1611, the emperor almost decided to dispatch Abdur Rahim and his sons to Kabul to deal with an insurrection. Although the assignment did not fructify, it is apparent that he had been forgiven.[4]

To place this stage of Abdur Rahim's life in context, it is useful to recall some other events that changed the dynamics of the court. In 1611 Jahangir married Mehrunissa Begum (1577–1645), daughter of a Persian émigré, Muhammad Ghiyas Beg, who was to receive the title of Itimad-ud-Daulah. Mehrunissa Begum – as empress she was given the title of Nur Jahan – was to be Jahangir's most important confidante and advisor for the duration of his reign. Her close relations, in particular her father and her brother Abul Hasan Asaf Khan (later given the title of Iqtiqad Khan), were rapidly promoted.[5] Nur Jahan, Ghiyas Beg, Asaf Khan and finally Jahangir's son, Prince Khurram (the future emperor Shah Jahan) formed a quartet that may well have exercised a veto over decisions emanating from the emperor, or been the source of all new initiatives and policies. Coins minted during this time bore the names of both the emperor and Nur Jahan. This group would, over time, develop their own differences and contradictions and the alliance finally collapsed over the issue of succession. But that was still some years away and in the aftermath of Abdur Rahim's recall, the quartet had a considerable, if not preponderant, say in most important imperial assignments and appointments. Nobles such as Khan Jahan Lodi, Mirza Aziz Koka and Mahabat Khan were at different times to come into imperial disfavour partly on account of the fact that their relations with Nur Jahan and her family were not cordial. With Mirza Aziz Koka, a supporter of Khusrau during Jahangir's own succession, relations were strained virtually the whole length of Jahangir's reign, till the noble's death in 1619–20. It was said of Mirza Aziz Koka at this time:

> He never had any dealing with or would not flatter, try to please or cultivate acquaintance with, any one out of any selfish motive. Khan Azam did not go to the house of even any member of the illustrious and sublime house of Itimadud Daula who were the mine of magnanimity. Nor did he send his sons or his wakil, too, to the threshold of the palace of Nawwab Nur Jahan Begum, unlike KhanKhanan who would personally go to the house of Rai Govardhan, diwan of the late Itimadud Daula.[6]

This provides another useful illustration of the differing personalities of Mirza Aziz Koka and Abdur Rahim, which has been commented upon earlier. Mirza Aziz Koka's sense of entitlement, as also a peculiar sense of integrity, are evident. Abdur Rahim, on the other hand, saw Nur Jahan and her family, not as inimical to his interests but, rather, as powerful entities to be courted if imperial favour was to be regained. Nevertheless, for Abdur Rahim and his family, this would have been a time of some stress. After decades of being at the centre of events and counted among the highest of the land, it could not have been easy falling out of that circle. But even after making these allowances, it is disappointing to find that:

> Towards the closing years of his life, KhanKhanan's nature had undergone change. His lofty disposition had taken a turn for the worse, for he subjected a person like Miyan Fahim to the accounting of the faujdari of the Sarkar of Bijanagar and was demanding an amount (of dues) from him. Hafiz Nasru'llah who had become the Agent (vakil) with absolute power, of the Nawwab, behaved harshly with Miyan Fahim in the presence of the Nawwab. Miyan Fahim slapped the Hafiz and also spoke harshly to KhanKhanan, and taking affront came out of the city, saying 'I would not stay in this place now.'

Thankfully, this is only temporary and we are relieved to find Abdur Rahim making amends.

> KhanKhanan riding a palanquin (doli) at night, went to Miyan Fahim's camp house, declared his identity there and said, 'I have come to turn you back'. Miyan Fahim, looking to such affection of the Nawwab, agreed to return.[7]

It is to this period of waiting, removed from the power politics of the court and the military action of the Deccan, that the best known aspect of Rahim's life and works have been traced to.[8]

Abdur Rahim lives on today in north and central India, as also in countless school primers, essentially because of his dohas. There is little doubt that these dohas are the work of a man looking back at the crests and troughs of an eventful life. To most of his literary critics and hagiographers, they can only be the work of a man fully engaged with all aspects of life – they could not have been composed by a scholar, a recluse, or even one inspired by a divine revelation or only the spirit of bhakti. Thus, whether it is the undeniable presence of the ideas and similes of Tulsidas, or the imprint of the technical virtuosity of Keshavdas, Abdur Rahim's dohas are regarded as unique to him, not only for their simplicity of language and brevity of expression, but also because they are suffused with the spirit of practical everyday life and the difficulties, as equally the inevitability, of making choices. Laconic but direct, they embody a patrician voice speaking through the centuries of the experience and heartbreak of a life lived to the full, from which fundamental principles of behaviour can be extracted and distilled.

Abdur Rahim's dohas did not come down to us as a single work. Dispersed and scattered over different – oral and written – collections, these were, as we shall see, painstakingly and incrementally gathered in the course of the nineteenth and early twentieth centuries – an endeavour of research and literary scholarship, powered by intense devotion to language and political advocacy. Definite authorship was problematic in cases where the verse does not refer to 'Rahim' or 'Rahiman' and in these cases the language used and traditional attribution were evaluated before ascribing the verse to Abdur Rahim.

In the lexicon of Hindi poetry Abdur Rahim stands with Surdas, Tulsidas or Keshavdas in popularity and esteem. His dohas encompass the full range of human emotions. In that sense they are a departure from the structured and controlled sensuousness of the *Nagar Shobha* and the conventional classifications in portraying different dimensions of love – engagement, fulfilment, parting, loneliness, jealousy, etc. – which was the hallmark of the *Barvai Nayika Bhed.*

Many of Abdur Rahim's dohas are the poetry of everyday life – its disappointments, elation, and the moral compromises it demands. In substance they are in the nature of moral aphorisms and there is scarcely a situation for which one cannot find an appropriate couplet from his corpus. Themes of love, friendship, honour, fame, knowledge, prosperity, time, fate, greatness, generosity, meanness, helpfulness, selfishness, worry, betrayal, gratitude and ingratitude form the basis for a moral or a lesson that is conveyed in an exquisitely brief couplet, the full sense of which is often impossible to capture in translation.[9]

> To instruct one who says what should have been left unsaid
> Is as vain as trying to wake one who pretends to be asleep.

The core idea here is by no means original and virtually the same idea and language are found in a couplet of Tulsidas too. Verses on the theme of the impossibility of waking someone pretending to be asleep or instructing someone who pretends to be wise abound in classical Sanskrit and also in Hindi poetry contemporary to Rahim.

The doha itself does not explain; it preserves its integrity of brevity. A great deal is thus unsaid and the assumption, of course, is that the meaning will be easily understood. For instance, a common idiom, or at least a great familiarity with the story of the Ramayana, are the basis of this and many other dohas.

> Ram obtained great fame by obeying his father's command
> Bharat obtained even more by disobeying Ram's command.

A doha on the theme of achievement again presumes intimacy with at least the better-known stories of the Ramayana.

> Krishna is called Giridhar
> Hanuman's achievements are wondrous, yet no one calls him Giridhar.

The doha itself does not contain any details and it is presumed that the listener would know that while Krishna lifted up a mountain, Hanuman flew with a whole mountain across the continent to Lanka, to bring the medicinal herb – the Sanjivani – to Lakshman when he lay wounded in battle. But Hanuman has never been specially named Giridhar for his feat.

Other examples of a Hindu religious fable becoming a vehicle for expressing an everyday moral or truth include this one:

For Rahim, evil persons look at fickle Lakshmi with desire,
She is Vishnu's consort, so her fickleness is natural.

Here the reference is to Lakshmi, the goddess of wealth, and the allusion is to the transitory and passing nature of wealth. The same idea is contained in another doha:

Everyone knows that Lakshmi is fickle, and why not
Would not the consort of God Vishnu be fickle?

A story from the Mahabharata is used to emphasize the idea that wealth and power are no armour against the storms of fate.

If power alone could bestow wealth, then who would accept fate
Did not the mighty Bhim work as a cook in Virat's palace?

In contrast to the use of stories from religious texts to underline essentially secular, moral or pragmatic everyday lessons, we also have dohas conveying religious or spiritual devotion.

Hari resides in Rahim's own eyes.
Then what need does he have to apply kajal?

This is Krishna bhakti of the kind one would expect to encounter in the work of Surdas. Similarly, a widely prevalent theme within this genre, of liberation from worldly desires stemming from devotion to Hari, is expressed in some of the dohas.

For Rahim, Hari will help you to overcome
The arrows of desire from the beautiful nymph's eyes.

Yet, not all of Abdur Rahim's dohas are suffused with a Hindu religious idiom or mythological similes or indeed, with the spirit of devotion or bhakti. Secular moral themes also abound, expressed in similes from the experience of everyday life. For instance, there are many dohas on the theme of honour: What constitutes it, what are its parameters, and what defines one's personal sense of honour?

An honourable man does not express a selfish sentiment even to himself
Just like a high born woman does not even enter another's house

He who guards jealously his honour and that of his family's elders
For Rahim, this person will attain God.

Honour here is not abstract but a daily routine and an infringement on it would be self-evident. A related theme is of the importance of tradition:

One who remains within the traditions of the past, endures
For Rahim, the water, which spills over the pond just flows away.

The nature of friendship and the difference between true friends and friends of good fortune are also recurrent themes in Abdur Rahim's dohas, as is the related aspect of the importance of the company one keeps. Thus:

If a broken pearl necklace must be restrung with each bead found
A good friend must be appeased, even if he gets angry a hundred times.

A related aspect is of friends turning into foes.

In good times there are many friends; in bad, none
Preserve for life the friends who stay when things are bad.

The scarf which shields the lamp is itself burnt during a storm
So Rahim, when hard times come, good friends become foes.

The most fascinating of the dohas are those that appear to have been crafted even more directly on the basis of personal experience.

In common with the rest of Abdur Rahim's poetry, there is no mention in his dohas of historical events, or even of persons who were part of his life – nothing, for instance, on Akbar or Jahangir. Yet, it is tempting to see a verse on the loss of a son as derived from Abdur Rahim's own experience. As we shall see, he outlived all his male progeny.

A lamp lights all around it, like a good son a family
Darkness follows when the lamp is extinguished.

The contrast between good and bad sons with the simile of a light and an extinguished flame is encountered again:

The death of a son extinguishes the light in a family
Just as darkness follows when a flame goes out.

A bad son when young is the apple of his family's eye
But as his character becomes known, darkness spreads in the family.

Reflections on the highs and lows of life can be found in a number of dohas and it is tempting to date their composition to the period after his recall from the Deccan.

For Rahim, many years are spent only a few remain
Like the man who repents a lifetime in pursuit of Maya and love;
I repent too.

My expenses have increased, my income reduced. The King is displeased
So Rahim, how does a fish live in so little water?

Heat, cold, and rain – the earth bears it all
So Rahim, Man too must endure whatever Fate ordains.

Strangely, there is nothing in Abdur Rahim's verse that is intended to inspire men into battle. Instead, we find verse that is almost pastoral, preaching the simple morals of everyday life. These absences have led many to speculate that what has survived are only a section of Abdur Rahim's dohas, perhaps only those with a broadly moral theme or those inspired by the spirit of bhakti. Could other dohas, including those with a more erotic flavour or on subjects such as love and martial endeavour, or with historical themes, have been lost? A widely circulated theory suggests that a *satsai* (a collection of 700 verses) of Abdur Rahim's dohas has been lost and what remain are only some 280 dohas from the original collection.

If it is frustrating not to encounter any real-life references, there are other problems too. Did age dissipate entirely the sensuous poet we encountered in the *Nagar Shobha* and the *Nayak Nayika Bhed*? It certainly appears so, although occasionally we come across a doha that is clearly a comment on the earlier mischievous verses, such as this one, on looking at the breasts of a young woman:

> A wrong act will result in its own hubris
> Eyes which glance at the girl's breasts darken their own face.

The allusion may well be to another verse in a collection titled *Shringar Sarotha*, which is lost but for six verses that have survived and are widely attributed to Abdur Rahim. One mischievous verse, in particular, stands out:

> The bride holds the lamp close to her bosom; her scarf protects its flame
> The flame itself flickers with agony – if only I had hands for these breasts.

But such verses and sentiments were, we can imagine, far from Abdur Rahim's thoughts as he awaited the emperor's discretion to exercise itself again.

In April 1612, the period of Abdur Rahim's life when he was without an important responsibility ends. Meanwhile, dispatches from the Deccan continued to paint a dismal picture. Khan Jahan Lodi had been unable to retrieve the Mughal position in any discernible manner. Jahangir's strategy had, in essence, been a straightforward one: change commanders and forge a closer relationship with Bijapur. Accordingly, Abdur Rahim had been recalled and Khan Jahan Lodi dispatched in his place. Secondly, in response to feelers from the Bijapur court, Khan-i-Azam Mirza Aziz Koka was sent to Bijapur as a high-level envoy. The Bijapur sultan was concerned about the growing strength of Malik Amber, and the Khan-i-Azam found the sultan amenable to an alliance that would at least ensure his neutrality in Mughal offensives against Malik Amber.

The military situation continued to be unpredictable, however, and we find the Mughal army unable to cope with Malik Amber's tactics. A major offensive involving a two-pronged attack on Amber was planned in 1610. The essence of the campaign was to launch a simultaneous attack on Malik Amber with two separate armies, one from Gujarat and the other from Berar and Khandesh. A galaxy of nobles was associated with each column. The plan is best described in Jahangir's own words:

> In summary, it had been decided that Abdullah Khan would set out from Nasik Trimbak with the Gujarat army and emirs who had been assigned to him … From the other side, Raja Man Singh, Khan Jahan … and many commanders were supposed to set out from Berar. The two divisions would keep abreast of each other's movements until they caught the enemy in a pincer on the agreed upon date. Had they followed this procedure and been united, and had selfish interests not intervened, it is most probable that God would have granted them victory.[10]

The offensive failed. The Gujarat army, with its commander keen to secure victory on his own, moved prematurely without coordinating with the main Mughal force from Khandesh and Berar. Malik Amber defeated it decisively, forced it to retreat with heavy losses and pursued it to the very borders of Gujarat. Hearing of this debacle, the main force held back, not joining battle at all. The presence of a number of eminent nobles, including Man Singh and Khan Jahan Lodi, made for poor coordination, given the mutual jealousies and rivalries. Success may have been possible, but it required a centralizing force in the form of a powerful prince or the emperor himself. We thus find Jahangir saying: 'When I received these reports in Agra, I was very upset and wanted to go myself and pull out by the roots these slave boys who were acting like lords.'[11]

It was at this time that Abdur Rahim's name was suggested for reappointment to the Deccan command by Nur Jahan's brother, Abul Hasan Asaf Khan:

> No one else understands the affairs of that area the way the KhanKhanan does. He should be sent to get the disorganized campaign back into shape. Let him make a temporary truce to give himself time to get the campaign back on track.[12]

The decision appears to have been taken quickly and Abdur Rahim was dispatched to Burhanpur, this time with a rank of 7,000. This was the first time in Mughal India that a noble was being given such a high rank.

What explains Abdur Rahim's reappointment? It is possible that his efforts to cultivate Nur Jahan's family paid off. Equally, the Deccan was becoming a quagmire and Abdur Rahim was probably the only senior noble capable of executing a complex holding operation of the kind the emperor had approved. Perhaps, also, no other noble of seniority or stature was interested in a venture of this nature. In this context, we should take note of two marriage alliances that were worked out around this time, or perhaps just a little earlier: Asaf Khan's daughter, the future empress Mumtaz Mahal, was married to Prince Khurram, the future Shah Jahan, and a granddaughter of Abdur Rahim – the daughter of Shah Nawaz Khan – was married to Asaf Khan's son. For Abdur Rhim, this meant an alliance with a premier family in Jahangir's innermost circle.

In his latest tenure in the Deccan, Abdur Rahim enjoyed a position and authority far greater than in the past. That he was solely and completely in charge does not seem to have been in doubt. Although Prince Parvez, Khan Jahan Lodi and Man Singh also continued in the Deccan, the high rank awarded to the Khan-i- Khanan, the failures of these earlier commanders and the emperor's palpable displeasure with them, gave to him a greater autonomy than would have otherwise been possible. The English traveller, Thomas Roe, was to write in 1615 while visiting Burhanpur:

> Here lives Sultan Parvez, the Emperor's second son, holding the state and custom of his father, and the KhanKhanan, being the greatest subject of the noble, general of his armies, 40,000 horses are with him. The prince has the name and state but the Khan governs all.[13]

Abdur Rahim, at fifty-six, would have been regarded as an old man. Perhaps for the first time since his heady victories in Gujarat and Sindh, he was sure of his principal commanders since they were his own sons. With their father holding the unprecedented rank of 7,000, Shah Nawaz Khan, Dorab Khan and Rahmandad were also promoted to high ranks at the time of Abdur Rahim's departure, or soon thereafter.

Yet, these advantages had to be balanced against the continuing difficulty of bringing about any real change in the situation on the ground. Mughal tactics focused essentially on insulating Malik Amber from Bijapur and Golconda while trying to simultaneously entice away with bribes, land grants and offers of high rank in imperial service as many as possible of the old Ahmednagar nobility that supported him. These diplomatic moves were intended to facilitate military action aimed at defeating Malik Amber. The difficulty though lay elsewhere. Even when these measures were successful – and they often had been in the past decade of Mughal campaigning in the Deccan – a reduction in Malik Amber's strength inevitably caused concern over Mughal expansion in Bijapur and Golconda and they would revert to assisting him against the imperial army. Each military victory was thus a political step backwards.

The Ahmednagar nobles who were enticed away remained, at best, uncertain allies of the Mughals. A revival in Malik Amber's fortunes would enable him to win them back. Mughal military gains thus proved to be difficult to translate into political advancement. No matter how convincing the victory in the battlefield, Mughal supply lines and outposts remained vulnerable to ambushes and raids by Malik Amber's forces, which were increasingly made up of local Maratha troops and cavalry. Mughal weaknesses, whether on account of internal tensions in the chain of command or the court's preoccupation with other matters, could quickly lead to their principal centres, Burhanpur and Ahmednagar, being threatened.

How much of this overview did Abdur Rahim comprehend? In many ways, the situation he faced against Malik Amber was similar to that which, half a century later, Raja Jai Singh, the ruler of Amber and Aurangzeb's foremost Deccan commander, would encounter with the Maratha leader Shivaji. The Rajput general realized that, notwithstanding Aurangzeb's and the court's objections to his approach, the only plausible solution was political. It lay in co-opting Shivaji into the Mughal hierarchy and giving him sufficient space, in the hope that the arrangement would crystallize and with the passage of time finally acquire permanence. These were, after all, the very tactics employed by Akbar when the Rajput alliance was forged from the 1560s. And it is hardly surprising to find Mirza Raja Jai Singh – the most prominent product of the Mughal–Rajput alliance – seeking to replicate this in the Deccan, even if often in the face of Emperor Aurangzeb's displeasure.[14]

It is easy to surmise that Abdur Rahim too sought to apply to Deccan politics the same principles he had, as a youth, seen Akbar so successfully use in relation to the kingdom of Amber and other Rajput states. The strong similarities between Malik Amber's challenge to Abdur Rahim and Shivaji's to Jai Singh are numerous, but one in particular stands out: Shivaji's grandfather Maloji was Malik Amber's right-hand man in his campaigns against Abdur Rahim.[15]

In Abdur Rahim's final command in the Deccan, the patterns established earlier would be repeated. Only cautious and careful diplomacy combined with a calculated use of force could enable a military success, and the translation of this into permanent political gains would remain a much more difficult enterprise. We find Abdur Rahim reaching Burhanpur, where he patiently bided his time, waiting for a suitable opportunity. One was to come in 1613 in the form of intense factional infighting in Malik Amber's camp, enabling some prominent followers to be enticed over to the Mughal side. An unsuccessful assassination attempt on Malik Amber followed – it cannot be said for certain that the Mughals were directly involved in the plot. Desertions to the Mughal camp continued, severely weakening Malik Amber, and in early 1614 the Mughal army decided to march on Amber's capital at Khirki (modern Aurangabad). A major battle took place at Roshangarh, near Jalna, in February 1616, resulting in a clear military victory for Abdur Rahim and his son Shah Nawaz Khan, who had actually conducted the campaign.

The victory came as a vindication for Abdur Rahim and restored his reputation. His care and caution in pursuing the military option is illustrated by the fact that it took place almost four years after his arrival in the Deccan – time spent, no doubt, in reinforcing his own troops as also in securing the maximum possible defections from Malik Amber's camp. The defeat was a considerable setback for Malik Amber: his force of artillery and elephants was lost and his newly established capital at Khirki was plundered and destroyed. Abdur

Rahim's prominent field commanders were his sons – Shah Nawaz Khan and Dorab Khan. Both were promoted by the emperor – the former to the rank of 5,000 mansab and the latter to 4,000.

Yet, it has been said with some accuracy that 'the battle of Roshangarh was a battle without any aims'.[16] Even before the Mughal victory, Malik Amber had been successful in securing assistance, in the form of troops and treasure, from Bijapur and Golconda. The Mughal march had deepened the apprehensions of these kingdoms and Malik Amber's defeat intensified their concerns. Soon after Roshangarh, Amber was able to win back many of those who had defected, with financial assistance from the Bijapur sultan. We also find Malik Amber reoccupying Khirki soon after the Mughals' withdrawal. As his forces regrouped, rumours about Abdur Rahim's treachery began to circulate again.

But the factor that would change Mughal policy in the Deccan once again had largely to do with the internal dynamics of the court. There is a curious anecdote narrated by Thomas Roe.

> The Prince [i.e., Khurram] who entended to build his honour on the warrs of the Decan which his elder brother [i.e., Parvez] had left with disgrace and great Commander *Chan Chanan* did not prosper in (which doubtlesse was a practiser with the Deccanis, from whom he received Pension) caused his father to recall *Chan Chanan*, who refusing to come, desired the King not to send Sultan Corronne [Khurram] to that warr, but one of his youngest sons about fifteen years of age. This Corrone [Khurram] took to heart, but prosecuting his purpose of the warr, promised to Abdela Chan the command of the army under him by displacing *Chan Chanan.* The king, fearing troubles, and knowing all the ambitions and factions of this sonne, the discontent of his two elder, the power of the *Chan Chanan*, was desirious to accommodate all by accepting peace and confirming *Chan Chanan* in the government he held and closely to that end wrote a lettre of favour and Purposed to send a vest acording to the Ceremony of reconciliation to *Chan Chanan.*

> But before hee dispatched it he acquaynted a kinswoeman of his liueing in the zereglia of his purpose. She whether false to her friend (wrought by Sultan Coronne) or out of Greatnes of hart to see the Top of her familye after so many merittes stand on soe fickle terms answered playnly that shee did not beleeue *Chan Chanan* would weare anything sent from the king, knowing his Majestie hated him and had once or twice offered him Poyson, which hee putting in his bosome instead of his Mouth had made tryall off. The king offered to ware it himself before her for an hower and that shee should write to testefy it. She replyed he would trust neyther of them both with his life, but if hee might liue quietly in his Command would doe his Majestie true service. Wherevppon the king altered his purpose and resolved to proceed on the sending sultan Coronne and to Countenance his reception would follow after with another Armie.[17]

The story does seem bizarre and, in brief, amounts to this: Prince Khurram persuades his father to appoint him as commander in the Deccan in place of Abdur Rahim. He wants to cement his path to the throne with a Deccan victory, which has eluded his brother Pervez. Abdur Rahim is unwilling to be replaced. The emperor, not wanting to take on Abdur Rahim frontally by dismissing him, decides instead to kill him by sending him a poisoned vest. A relative of Abdur Rahim in the king's harem is informed about the plot so that she can lull Abdur Rahim's suspicions. This relative, however, informs the emperor that, given Abdur Rahim's state of mind in view of two earlier attempts to poison him, he would never trust the emperor enough to wear a vest sent by him. The emperor has perforce to give up this plan.

Diplomatic accounts and those of foreign travellers, despite their claims to gravitas, are not always reliable. But even discounting such narratives, the court's dissatisfaction with the Deccan situation is clear enough. We can identify some of the elements at least, in this cluster of motives and forces. Notwithstanding the military victory at Roshangarh, the Mughal offensive thereafter, at least in the view of the court, was tardy in its progress. Abdur Rahim may have wanted to proceed cautiously; perhaps work again on weakening Malik Amber politically by enticing defections before committing himself to military action. But in the court there was great impatience. This had much to do with the new alliance that had emerged between Nur Jahan's family and Prince Khurram, the future emperor Shah Jahan. A victory in the Deccan was what Khurram needed – to ensure his own place in the hierarchy and the path to the succession. The presence of Prince Parvez in the Deccan, no matter how nominal, was obviously a threat to this plan. Parvez was the older brother and a victory in the Deccan during his tenure could well elevate him to the throne.

A short while after the victory at Roshangarh, therefore, it was decided that Khurram would head for the Deccan. Parvez was recalled and assigned to Allahabad as governor. Roe's account, as quoted above, would have us believe that Abdur Rahim was reluctant to accept the change and his preference would have been for a minor son of the emperor to be made the nominal commander-in-chief. If this is true, it certainly implies a replay of the situation of a decade and a half earlier between Abdur Rahim and Prince Murad, and then with Prince Daniyal.

It is more likely that Roe's interpretation is incorrect. Certainly, Asaf Khan's role, as Shah Jahan's father-in-law, in the dispatch of Abdur Rahim to the Deccan suggests otherwise. Abdur Rahim's reappointment to the Deccan command had the full support of the clique around Nur Jahan and may have been the very reason for the appointment. Prince Khurram was very much a part of this alliance and so there is reason to doubt Roe's view that Abdur Rahim had reservations or objections to Khurram being appointed as commander of the Deccan forces. A more credible possibility is that Abdur Rahim was, given Khurram's position and growing strength in court at that time, in no position to have or voice such reservations.

In any event, we find a greater focus on the Deccan in the Mughal court now than at any time since Akbar's departure from Burhanpur in 1601. Khurram's departure for the Deccan was followed soon afterwards by Jahangir's own progress to Mandu in October 1616. The presence of the emperor in Mandu and of Khurram in Burhanpur meant a concentration of Mughal forces, which radically altered the situation with Bijapur, Golconda and, of course, Malik Amber. The former two rulers offered their submission and accepted Mughal suzerainty. Such a powerful Mughal presence, backed by the emperor and an impatient prince, obviously rendered any overt encouragement of Malik Amber near-suicidal. Malik Amber was left with no option but to make substantial concessions and this was done by the surrender of the Ahmednagar fort, as also other areas taken from the Mughals in the past. The Mughals could now, finally, declare a grand victory.

Khurram had no interest, however, in staying long in the Deccan. Having secured the diplomatic victory, he made the administrative arrangements to keep the Deccan secure after his departure. Abdur Rahim was made governor of Berar, Khandesh and Burhanpur. Shah Nawaz Khan was placed with a large force in areas recently ceded to the Mughals, suggesting that the arrangements were by no means stable and the Mughals expected to ward off attempts to undo the gains that had been made.

The most interesting of the arrangements made by Khurram was a matrimonial alliance with Abdur Rahim's family. He married, with Jahangir's permission, a daughter of Shah Nawaz Khan. This, of course, brings to mind the marriage of Prince Daniyal with Abdur Rahim's daughter. The marriage was clearly a recognition of Shah Nawaz Khan's importance and the position he occupied in the Deccan. Equally, one may speculate that it had to do with Khurram wanting to bind to his side a premier family. With one granddaughter married to Asaf Khan's son and another to Prince Khurram, Abdur Rahim's own coordinates in the politics of the Mughal court appeared firm. That the alliance between Nur Jahan and Khurram, to which he had evidently declared himself, would itself splinter with dramatic and disastrous consequences for him and his family is something he could not have anticipated. But a succession crisis was looming and it forms the last and most tragic chapter of his life, set again in the backdrop of the Deccan.

The humiliating treaty he forced Malik Amber to conclude gave to Khurram the success he had wanted. He left the Deccan in triumph and his arrival in Mandu in October 1617 was celebrated in a manner befitting a victorious prince. Jahangir awarded him the title of Shah Jahan and it is by this name that we will henceforth refer to Khurram. No fundamental change had, however, occurred in the Mughal situation in the Deccan, nor indeed had the balance of forces altered decisively in their favour. Malik Amber waited for his moment and for Mughal attention to waver. In 1618, by means of a direct threat, he secured the assistance of Bijapur and Golconda to restart a campaign to recover territories lost or conceded to the Mughals. Marshalling a large force, he laid siege to the Ahmednagar fort and then marched into Berar. Notwithstanding victories in direct engagements, the Mughals remained incapable of breaking the mould of their campaigns in the Deccan. Thus, despite their advantage in face-to-face encounters, the problem remained of how to control territory and deal with an enemy that could retreat, regroup, harass and break supply lines, and finally attack whenever an opportunity arose. If Abdur Rahim's endeavours during his two decades in the Deccan to arrive at a political settlement remained unsuccessful, the period after the departure of Prince Shah Jahan again demonstrated that a comprehensive military victory was equally elusive.

In many ways, this was a traumatic period for Abdur Rahim. He had been permitted to leave Burhanpur and pay homage to Jahangir, then still in central India, in the vicinity of Ujjain. The meeting took place in November 1618 and Abdur Rahim spent some three weeks in the imperial camp. Jahangir writes:

> When my old ataliq was taking leave of me, I told him in all seriousness that I had heard repeatedly that Shah Nawaz Kahn was

> overly fond of wine and drank too much and if it was true it was a pity for him to kill himself at such an age. I told the KhanKhanan not to leave him as he was but to take him in hand and rectify his conduct. If he could not he was to report it to me frankly and I would summon Shah Nawaz Khan to court and straighten him out myself.[18]

But this was not to be, and Jahangir informs us in April 1619 that 'the arrival of the death of the Sipahsalar KhanKhanan's son Shah Nawaz Khan … caused me much sorrow … I greatly regretted hearing this dreadful news. He was really a fine Khanazad who should have rendered excellent service and performed great things for the empire.'

Not only was Shah Nawaz the oldest, he was also the most capable of Abdur Rahim's sons. The victory in 1616 over Malik Amber owed a great deal to his generalship. Earlier, in 1601, during Abdur Rahim's first tenure in the Deccan, he had played a significant role in the military advances of the Mughals. Jahangir mentions his age at the time of death as thirty-three, suggesting that he was very young when he first began campaigning with Abdur Rahim in the Deccan. We know little about him except that he was regarded as a 'staunch Sunni' and as one 'who combined wisdom with courage' and also that 'he was stingy and dressed poorly'.[19] This parsimonious nature, if true, is certainly a contrast to the quality of generosity uniformly ascribed to his father. But we may also recall that he was the patron who had commissioned the poet Keshavdas to compose the *Jahangirjaschandrika* and we also find him extolled in verses praising his father and grandfather.[20]

The death of his firstborn son was devastating for Abdur Rahim. We find Jahangir sending 'Raja Sarang Deo, one of my most intimate servants, to (my) old ataliq, to offer (my) condolences and sympathy', and 'Shah Nawaz Khan's rank of 5,000 was added to his brother's and sons' rank.' Two sons of Shah Nawaz Khan are mentioned – Minuchihr and Toghril – in Jahangir's account.

The tragedy of Shah Nawaz's death occurred at a time when Malik Amber was again seeking to reorder the situation in the Deccan. Abdur Rahim was to constantly petition the court for assistance as Malik Amber's cavalry paralysed the Mughals and confined them to their fortified camps. Abdur Rahim's second son, Dorab Khan, who had been in attendance at court, was sent to the Deccan following his brother's death. Jahangir's intention was evidently to strengthen Abdur Rahim's forces and commanders. The pressure on the Mughals was unrelenting and often, Malik Amber's raids brought his troops up to the fortifications of Burhanpur itself.

In the midst of this, a second tragedy occurred. Rahim's third son, Rahmandad, also died. Rahmandad was the son of the Umarkot princess whom Abdur Rahim had married during the Sindh campaign in the early 1590s. No one in the family had the courage to report the news to the father and, finally, it was broken to Abdur Rahim by a sage, at the request of the ladies in the family. The emperor himself recorded at some length the details of how Rahmandad died:

> ... he had a fever for several days, and then one day while he was recuperating, some Deccanis appeared in a troop. Rahmandad's elder brother Dorab Khan mounted, intent upon battle, and when the news reached Rahmandad, he too mounted in bravery and valour despite his weakness and illness and joined his brother. After crushing the foe, he returned to camp but failed to take sufficient precaution when he was divesting himself of his armour padding. Once the air got to him, he went into convulsions and could not speak ...

Jahangir's response to this second tragedy is certainly more emotional than might be expected of a faraway and dispassionate ruler. He wrote:

> Although, as they say, 'death and fire burn wet and dry alike', it was hard for me to take. Imagine what it was like for his poor broken

hearted father. He hadn't recovered from the loss of Shah Nawaz Khan when he was afflicted with this new wound.[21]

The emperor's sentiments are in stark contrast to his feelings in the future about Abdur Rahim as the pillars of his life further crumble in even greater tragedy and pathos. All this unfolds against the backdrop of an imperial crisis with the rising spectre of a struggle over succession, civil war and a near breakdown of Mughal positions against the renewed attacks of Malik Amber.

The compact between the emperor, Nur Jahan and Prince Shah Jahan had started weakening with a decline in the emperor's health. The marriage of Nur Jahan's daughter Ladli Begum to another son of the emperor, Shahryar, in early 1621 heralded this, but it was against the backdrop of the Deccan that the conflict would play itself out. By 1620, Malik Amber had recovered sufficiently from the earlier setbacks and had carried his raids up to Burhanpur, apart from incursions into Malwa and Gujarat. The emperor was in Kashmir but Abdur Rahim's appeals for reinforcements soon became too incessant to be ignored. 'They say that … petition after petition from him (the KhanKhanan) were produced before the King to the effect that he was in a difficult position and he had determined to follow the custom of *johar* (self-immolation)'.[22] A powerful injection of additional forces and the presence of one of the princes was now essential and Shah Jahan was again dispatched. Jahangir is believed to have said to the prince that 'as Akbar had by a hurried march rescued the Khan Azam when besieged by the Gujaratis, he should now rescue the KhanKhanan from his dangerous position'.[23]

The succession issue, however, now coloured all perspectives. To Shah Jahan it appeared that the motive for sending him to the Deccan was to ensure his removal to a distant unwinnable campaign while Shahryar consolidated his position at court with the help of his mother-in-law, Empress Nur Jahan. But the appointment was also seen, at least by some, as the result of a deeper conspiracy between Shah Jahan and the Khan-i-Khanan. This alternative reading of the situation, not surprisingly, comes from a near-contemporary Deccan source obviously keen to depict the anticipated Mughal advance in as unfavourable a light as possible. The Bijapuri writer Fuzuni Astarabadi thus says that the Khan-i-Khanan worked actively to ensure Shah Jahan's assignment to the Deccan as a means to eliminate Prince Khusrau:

> KhanKhanan, in concert with Khurram, in order to bring that prince to the Deccan (and kill Khusrau), sent a man to Amber-jiu telling him to totally ravage all the country from the bank of the Narmada to the frontier of the Nizam Shahi kingdom … KhanKhanan repeatedly wrote to the Emperor that unless a prince was sent to the Deccan the situation could not be saved.[24]

Certainly, Shah Jahan was sensitive to the possibility that being far away from the court and north India at a time when Jahangir's health was fragile could very easily result in a rival prince succeeding to the throne. He insisted, and Jahangir appears to have had no choice but to agree, that Prince Khusrau be sent with him – for all practical purposes, as a hostage. There were other rivals too – Shahryar, Parvez and, of course, Empress Nur Jahan and her machinations. But Khusrau was the emperor's firstborn son and thus impossible to discount.

Khusrau is one of the more tragic figures in Mughal history, with the vortex of succession defining his life. Son of Prince Salim, the future Jahangir, and a Kachwaha Rajput princess, Khusrau was, from his early boyhood, a victim of his father's claim to the throne. Salim's excesses and a deteriorating relationship with his father, Emperor Akbar, led a number of powerful nobles to promote Khusrau as a possible alternative. Prominent among these were Mirza Aziz Koka, Akbar's foster-brother, and Raja Man Singh – Khusrau's father-in-law and maternal uncle respectively. Salim went so far as to attribute Khusrau's mother's suicide, through an overdose of opium, to her anguish over Khusrau's ambitions and the ensuing bad blood between her husband and her son. In the end, Khusrau and those supporting him were unable to prevent Salim's succession, although some sources suggest that they very nearly succeeded. For the rest of his life, Khusrau's life was to alternate between rebellion and imprisonment, and he remained a sullen, brooding presence on the margins of the Mughal court.

Shah Jahan's arrival in the Deccan in March–April 1621 saw yet another repetition of an older pattern. The assemblage of a large Mughal army and its victories in a number of tactical engagements forced Malik Amber to concede areas he had seized and, in sum, revert to positions defined in the peace treaty of 1617. Shah Jahan, on his part, wished to secure the terms of this agreement and no more. His real concern was the succession. Getting sucked into the quagmire of the Deccan was hardly a desirable option at this stage.

Predictably, in early 1622, while in Burhanpur, Shah Jahan ordered his half-brother's death by strangulation while he himself was conveniently away on a hunting trip.

Jahangir recorded the news baldly, almost as if it were a foregone conclusion: '... a report was received from Khurram containing the news that Khusrau had died on the 8th of the month [circa 16 February] after an attack of colic pain'.[25]

At least one contemporary source, albeit a foreign traveller, records that Abdur Rahim was also a party to the murder of the prince. But Abdur Rahim only appeared resigned to the state of affairs. Such things were inevitable in a succession struggle and his own granddaughter was, after all, married to Prince Shah Jahan. If the emperor could hand over his firstborn to an almost certain death, there was little he could do or say that would make a difference.[26]

He is, however, believed to have penned this exquisite couplet:

The leaves of the lotus spread and screen off water,
The moon with its cold causes the leaves to contract.

In the family of the lotus it is difficult to say
Who is friendly and who is the enemy.[27]

Whether he actually composed this verse in the aftermath of Khusrau's murder is uncertain and, in a sense, immaterial. A vast corpus of Hindi literature considers he did, and that, in doing so, he penned the epitaph of the Mughal empire and, ultimately, his own role in it.

Khusrau's tragic history does not end with him. When the imperial crisis erupted after Jahangir's death, the eldest son of Khusrau, Dawar Buksh, was briefly crowned emperor in October 1627. The supporter and choreographer of this move was none other than Asaf Khan, the father-in-law of Shah Jahan. In fact, the enthronement of Dawar Buksh was a ploy, a stratagem on behalf of Shah Jahan to gain time for himself. Once he was assured of the support of the important nobles and was crowned on 8 November 1627, Shah Jahan ensured that all other possible rivals and pretenders were eliminated. Dawar Buksh was killed in January 1628.

By March 1622, the problem of the Deccan had again receded in the priorities of the court in the wake of an impending move by the Persians against Qandahar. Jahangir sent instructions to Shah Jahan to lead an expedition to deter the Persians. The choice was an obvious enough one – the prince was the ablest of the emperor's sons, with proven military victories to his credit. Moreover, he commanded, at the time, the cream of the Mughal forces. To Shah Jahan, however, the summons to proceed to Qandahar seemed like one more of Nur Jahan's machinations to keep him engaged at the extremities of the empire, out of the way of the other emerging rival, Sharyar.

Shah Jahan marched north as instructed, with senior generals and nobles including Abdur Rahim. When they reached Mandu, he wrote to the emperor, laying down his conditions for accepting the Qandahar command. These included absolute command over the army and control over the Punjab; he also demanded Ranthambore fort for his family to stay in. However what precipitated an imperial crisis was also a clash between Shah Jahan and Sharyar's men over control of the jagir of Dholpur – both princes claiming it had been allotted to them by the emperor. Nur Jahan certainly had some part to play in the breakdown of relations between father and son and, shortly afterwards, we find Shah Jahan in full-blown revolt. The immediate and most obvious result of this was the loss of Qandahar to the Persians.

One contemporary record informs us that after the Persian move on Qandahar, Shah Jahan called on the important Mughal nobles in the Deccan to take an oath of loyalty to him: 'He wanted to rebel against his father and expected that they would gird him with the sword of his father.'[28]

The rebellious force, however, faced setbacks almost immediately upon its entry into north India from the Deccan, when it encountered a strong imperial army under the command of Mahabat Khan and Prince Parvez. Shah Jahan's army could not proceed further than the environs of Agra, where they were beaten back and defeated in a battle near the village of Bilochpur in March 1623. Amidst the military activity, efforts by both sides to entice important nobles to their side continued. In this Shah Jahan relied on the presence of his father-in-law, Asaf Khan, who continued in his important position in the court.

The behaviour of Abdur Rahim, his son Dorab Khan, and his grandsons confirms – with different sources ascribing loyalty or treachery to an extent that it appears impossible to make any judgement – that the family, while certainly in Shah Jahan's camp, were desperately trying to reduce the risk to themselves in the event of either party becoming victorious in the contest. Abdur Rahim was easily the most prominent Mughal noble in Prince Shah Jahan's army. Inevitably, blame for the defeat in the battle at Bilochpur was put 'on the head of Dorab and KhanKhanan … (since) when victory was near, Dorab withdrew from the battlefield in obedience to a hint from KhanKhanan to do so'.[29] Shortly after the defeat of Shah Jahan's army and his return to Mandu, with Prince Parvez and Mahabat Khan in pursuit, we find Minuchihr, the Khan-i-Khanan's eldest grandson (and son of Shah Nawaz Khan) deserting to join the imperial forces.

It is impossible to disentangle this web entirely. Abdur Rahim's treachery as an explanation of the defeat does appear somewhat bizarre since it is unclear what he or his son would have expected to gain from Shah Jahan's defeat at this stage. We can, however, see attempts by all parties to leave open as many options as feasible, to minimize the damage to themselves from this latest round of royal bloodletting. However, the judgement pronounced by Jahangir on Abdur Rahim could not have been more damning:

> … if *Amirs* like the KhanKhanan, who had been singled out for the exalted post of *Ataliq*, could so dishonour himself at the age of seventy with such insurgence and ingratitude, what complaint could one have of others? It was as though insurgence and ingratitude were part and parcel of his nature. At the end of his life his father had done the same thing to my exalted father. Following in his father's footsteps, he had made himself eternally accursed at this age.[30]

And finally, Jahangir quotes from the *Gulistan*: 'In the end, a wolf cub becomes a wolf, even if it has grown up among humans.'

Shah Jahan's defeat and return to Mandu, and thence further south, was accompanied by the constant and heavy pressure on his rear by the army led by Prince Parvez and Mahabat Khan. There was also a steady haemorrhaging from his army of men and nobles. As Shah Jahan crossed the Narmada, a letter was intercepted, by all accounts from Abdur Rahim to Mahabat Khan, which contained a verse in Persian: 'A hundred eyes keep me under surveillance, otherwise due to uneasiness I would have flown.'[31] Abdur Rahim and his entire family, including Dorab Khan and his sons and nephews, were then summoned to Shah Jahan's presence. Abdur Rahim denied that the letter was his; not surprisingly, Shah Jahan did not believe him and the family was placed under close surveillance as the march towards Burhanpur and Asirgarh continued. Jahangir was to write sardonically in his diary, at this point, that just as Abdur Rahim had predicted, 'a hundred persons keeping watch' had come true.[32]

After having been commander for so many years, the aged noble found himself in the custody of that same army. Worse still, he was viewed by both the emperor and the rebel prince as treacherous. We have very little to go by to gauge Abdur Rahim's frame of mind at this moment. Some trace one or more of his most poignant dohas to this time. One of them, in particular, poses the eternal question of personal integrity against worldly advancement:

> For Rahim, you have to choose one of two paths,
> With truth, you lose the world,
> With deceit, you never get Ram.[33]

If this, as a guide to Abdur Rahim's frame of mind, is speculative, we do have a note in his own handwriting on a copy of the Quran, written on 28 August 1623 while at the village of Khargoan, in Khandesh, en route to Burhanpur. The noting, part of a well-known Islamic tradition called *fal,* is on how to obtain omens or an augury from the Quran:

> ... before taking the fal one must recite the Surah Fatiha [the first and opening verse of the Quran] and thrice the Surah Qul Howalah and Ayat al Kursi [both parts of the Quran], pray for the holy Prophet and his family, thereafter taking the Quran in hand and opening it count the names and qualities of Allah [As each word has a number attached to it]. To the total reached add three (3) more to it and recite the ayat of this number. The meaning of the ayat will answer your query.[34]

It is unnecessary to belabour the point but is this perhaps the tired dependence on superstition of an old man whose world is collapsing around him? Or is it, at a time of adversity and trauma, about relying on deeply ingrained notions of how daily life is to be conducted in accordance with the tenets of Islam?

Worse is to follow.

According to Jahangir, Shah Jahan had marched to the fortress at Asirgarh, intending to imprison Abdur Rahim and his son there, but on arrival changed his mind and carried on to nearby Burhanpur. His own position was getting increasingly more precarious and we see further ironies unfolding as he dispatched envoys for help to Malik Amber and the Bijapur ruler Adil Shah. Both were spurned, possibly insulted, for Shah Jahan's own assaults on the Deccan kingdoms could hardly be forgotten. Shah Jahan's options had become limited now to the extent that he opened communications with Mahabat Khan, the commander of the imperial forces, who was camped on the opposite bank of the Narmada. Mahabat Khan insisted that no terms could be discussed unless the negotiations were led on Shah Jahan's side by the Khan-i-Khanan. The events of September 1624 are best described in Jahangir's words. Shah Jahan here is called *bedawlat* or the luckless one:

> Bedawlat sent Rai Bhoj Hada's son Sarbulandi Rai, a valiant Rajput Chieftain. Mahabat Khan said, 'Unless the KhanKhanan comes, peace is impossible'. Of course, his main intention was to separate that wily leader of the forces of corruption from him by this means. There was nothing Bedawlat could do but release the KhanKhanan from detention and make him swear an oath of allegiance on the *Koran*. Then, to appease him and for the reaffirmation of his oath, he took him into his *harem* and made him an intimate. Bringing his wives and children before him, he extracted through tears and pleading all sorts of binding oaths from him. Finally he stated his purpose. 'Time is running out, and I am in a difficult position. I turn myself over to you, and the safety of our honour is in your hands.

> Something must be done so that I not suffer any more misery and humiliation.'[35]

This may have been the version that was conveyed to Jahangir, but it has a ring of truth to it. Abdur Rahim too had been suggesting to Khurram that he could negotiate a peace:

> Since the times have turned unfavourable, if during these few days of setback, truce is unopposed, it will certainly bring about peace in the world and wellbeing of God's creatures. If by arresting us, you can attain kingship, this humble servant along with (his) sons is prepared to sacrifice (themselves) for His Excellency's illustrious name. Otherwise, set us free and keep my sons, family and children so that having approached Sultan Parvez and Mahabat Khan, I may (bring about and) strengthen and consolidate truce. And if they do not agree to come to terms, I shall (manage) to gather fifty six thousand horsemen and footmen of Adil Khan of Bijapur, Qutb-ul-Mulk of Golkonda, Nizam-ul-Mulk of Ahmednagar, Malik Amber and the Karnatka Army, etc., to enter the Jahangiri kingdom.[36]

The latter possibility is clearly far-fetched. But Shah Jahan was desperate – perhaps clutching at straws – and Abdur Rahim was undeniably the senior statesman of the empire with half a life spent in the Deccan as the Mughal commander. An assurance of this kind from him would have carried some weight, perhaps even some conviction. After all, Abdur Rahim was known to be intimate with all the rulers in the Deccan. If an honourable exit seemed the best alternative, he was obviously the most effective instrument to secure it. The taking of oaths by Abdur Rahim inside Shah Jahan's harem conveys both a sense of Shah Jahan's desperation and also his doubts about Abdur Rahim. The latter's granddaughter from Shah Nawaz Khan would have been present – as a young wife of Shah Jahan – to shame, but also to secure.

Abdur Rahim's stated intent was to stay on the south bank of the Narmada – Mahabat Khan being on the north. Negotiations were to be carried out by correspondence and messengers. Mahabat Khan, however, secretly sent a body of troops across the river and effectively cut off Abdur Rahim from his main force and made him a prisoner. One version of events is that Shah Jahan's local commander at the Narmada, Bairam Beg, relaxed his vigilance on learning of the impending truce:

> When the news of the truce and departure of KhanKhanan reached the Shahi troops (of Shah Jahan), (their) firm resolve began to wane and the precaution which they had taken in the blockade of the ferries did not retain its original state. One night, (when they were) in deep slumber of carelessness, a group of zealous young men, induced by Mahabat Khan, plunged the horses of courage into the river and valiantly crossed it. In the middle of that night, on account of the dread of this commotion and disturbance, the pillars of resolution of many a person got shaken and Bairam Beg was unable to put up a fight or defence. Many persons crossed the river and KhanKhanan with an eye on loyalty to (lit. salt of) Jahangir, washed away the roll of truth and fidelity with water and joined Mahabat Khan.[37]

Mahabat Khan had, in brief, outflanked Shah Jahan and taken his emissary into his custody. Some suggested that Abdur Rahim was complicit in this latest move and Bairam Beg had, in fact, acted in concert with him. If this fits with an impression of Abdur Rahim's duplicity, it is of interest to find that Jahangir's description of the episode suggests that Abdur Rahim was outmanoeuvred and, more significantly, confused; Bairam Beg, similarly, is not so much duplicitous as incompetent:

> Bairam Beg, unable to maintain an offensively rebellious stance began a defensive array. By the time he got himself together, many men had crossed the river, and that very night the miserable rebels were sent scattering into flight. The KhanKhanan was left totally dumbfounded, outmanoeuvred by our unfailing fortune and unable to make a move.[38]

The treatment of Abdur Rahim in Mahabat Khan's camp hardly suggests the picture of a fellow-traveller.

> ... since they were not completely reassured in regard to KhanKhanan ... they kept KhanKhanan under watch through expediency and advise of well-wishers of the government and it was decided that a pavilion be erected for that dear one (i.e., KhanKhanan) adjacent to the royal quarters of the pearl scattering prince (Parvez) and his daughter Janah Begum who was married to Prince Danyal and who was an apt pupil of her father, live there along with him, and a group of trusted servants kept watch around his pavilion.

We are informed also of Mahabat Khan's attempts to win over Abdur Rahim by first trying to entice the trusted Mian Fahim:

> ... when Mahabat Khan wanted to arrest KhanKhanan, he first tried to wean away Miyan Fahim with (an offer of) high rank if he left KhanKhanan. Miyan Fahim did not agree to this and going to the KhanKhanan apprised him of the latest position in the matter ... (and) advised (KhanKhanan), 'You should arm yourself and set out for the royal court. It would not matter if any disgrace befalls there; we should not get killed here in disgrace.' KhanKhanan did not agree and said, 'The Emperor will not be sincere to me.'[39]

Again, while Abdur Rahim continued under house arrest, we find Fahim being summoned to Mahabat Khan and told:

> If you want a royal mansab, I shall give you a mansab of 1000 person and horse in addition to some fief ... And if you take up service under me, I shall pay every year without fail 1,00,000/- rupees and 30,000/- rupees in cash respectively to you and your son Firuz Khan, and also make you commander of my entire army.[40]

Mian Fahim, true to character, rebuffed the offers, provoking Mahabat Khan's anger: 'How long will you boast of your valour?' Fahim replied: 'My courage and valour are such that if I here and now put my hand to arms, nobody can face me.'

Fahim and his son were to continue to stand up to Mahabat Khan, as is illustrated by an incident, the circumstances of which highlight the indignity of Abdur Rahim's position and also argues against the possibility that he was, in fact, hand in glove with Mahabat Khan and Prince Parvez.

> ... the daughter of Burhan-ul-Mulk (of Ahmadnagar) who was in the bond of marriage with Dorab Khan was summoned to the royal presence. Mahabat Khan sent some *Khwajasaras* (eunuchs) to escort her to the royal court. Very probably, KhanKhanan also permitted her to be taken. Miyan Fahim used impertinent language in his talk to KhanKhanan and sent his own son Firuz Khan with the instruction that he should not allow the wife of Dorab Khan to be taken away. Firuz Khan gave a determined fight ...[41]

It is difficult to say why Dorab Khan's wife was separated from Abdur Rahim in this manner. Was it to increase pressure on Abdur Rahim, or perhaps detach Dorab Khan from Shah Jahan, or to ensure that Dorab Khan and Shah Jahan did not reach a compact with the ruler of Ahmednagar? Or were there more sordid motives? In any event, we soon find Fahim and his son in conflict again with Mahabat Khan, when he sends troops to confiscate Abdur Rahim's possessions and arrest Fahim. Ironically, the latter's steadfastness moved even those in the emperor's camp and Fahim's last engagement sometime in May–June 1625 is described thus: 'He refused to give himself up without a fight to anyone, made a valiant stance along with his son and several liegemen, and sacrificed himself to honour.'[42]

For Abdur Rahim, the grief of separation from his remaining son, the indignity of arrest, not only of himself but also the females of the family, and the death of Fahim happened alongside the public disgrace of being seen as a time-server and turncoat. Yet, worse was to follow as both the parties – Shah Jahan and Jahangir – now turned on the ageing noble. The vengeance they wreaked on him clearly stemmed from their own sense of frustration and anger against each other. The very nightmare Abdur Rahim had striven to avoid for himself and his family was upon them.

Mahabat Khan's capture of Abdur Rahim left Shah Jahan with no choice but to retreat deeper south, leaving Mughal territory. He was desperate for shelter and assistance from one or the other of the Deccan kingdoms. In February–March 1624, he reached the kingdom of Golconda and not getting assistance there, was forced to turn eastwards towards Orissa and Bengal. Dorab Khan was now released on oath and assigned as governor of Bengal. His son Aram Baksh and nephew Shakar Shikan, son of Shah Nawaz Khan, were also promised high mansabs. Shah Jahan then proceeded towards Allahabad with these two of Abdur Rahim's grandsons as hostage. Clearly he had no choice but to use Dorab Khan, though he did not trust him.

Shah Jahan was defeated again near Allahabad and forced to turn back. In Benares, he summoned Dorab Khan to join him with all his forces, an order that Dorab could not comply with as, according to him, he himself was besieged by refractory zamindars. Shah Jahan was, on his part, convinced of Dorab's treachery since letters had been intercepted between Abdur Rahim and him, which pointed to plans of rejoining Jahangir.[43]

In the last quarter of 1624, Shah Jahan turned back to return to the Deccan. Dorab's son Aram Baksh and nephew Shakar Shikan were handed over to a noble in his camp, who had them killed. The final act in the tragedy had begun.

The murder of the grandsons of Abdur Rahim does appear as a deliberate act of Shah Jahan. One source describes the episode:

> To a madman a suggestion is enough and so Abdullah cruelly put both of these innocent ones to death. Afterwards, when Sultan Parvez and Mahabat Khan heard of this they sent strict orders to the Zamindars of Bengal to refrain from interfering with him [Dorab Khan] and to send him to them.[44]

Dorab Khan also finally jettisoned Shah Jahan and joined the imperial side. If the preceding quote suggests that Dorab was regarded by Prince Parvez as being one of them, subsequent events proved otherwise. When the news of Dorab's capitulation – sometime towards the end of 1624 – reached Jahangir, he sent an order to Mahabat Khan: 'What is the sense in keeping this wretch alive? As soon as this imperial decree arrives, send the head of that ill-starred wanderer in the valley of perdition to court.'[45]

Dorab Khan was executed. Mahabat Khan sent his head to Abdur Rahim – still his prisoner – wrapped in a piece of cloth, as a gift of a melon. Abdur Rahim, on seeing it, is believed to have said, '*Tarbuj Shahidi*' or 'True; a beautiful melon' – a play on 'shahidi', which means martyred but also beautiful. Afrasiyab, another son of Dorab, was also put to death at this time.[46]

The charge of duplicity and double dealing against Abdur Rahim has some merit. But he was in an impossible situation. It could be that Mahabat Khan was also intent on suggesting to the emperor that Abdur Rahim was the lynchpin of the rebellion, while simultaneously seeking to entice him over from the prince's army. Did some old enmity, never recorded, perhaps dating back to the time when Abdur Rahim was a star of Akbar's court and Mahabat Khan was yet to make his mark, lie at the heart of this? Sending the head of Dorab Khan in the form of a gift suggests a deep personal enmity rather than only the expediencies of imperial service. Similarly, why did Mahabat Khan send a party to seize Dorab Khan's wife when Abdur Rahim was already a prisoner and why, indeed, did Fahim so fiercely resist this move? Recall also Abdur Rahim's noting on the illustrated manuscript of Amir Khusrau's *Khamsa*, in which he referred to Mahabat Khan as his enemy as early as 1604–05, much before the historical record suggests the crossing of the paths of these two noblemen.[47]

Abdur Rahim's tragedy was now complete and what we get is the picture of a great house breaking up in disarray. However, the wheel of fortune was to turn again, even if what followed could only be described as a pyrrhic victory.

Khusrau's murder in August 1621 and Shah Jahan's refusal to march on Qandahar shortly thereafter had heralded the beginning of the revolt. Successive defeats, first in his march on the capital, then in Bihar and Orissa, and the consequent haemorrhaging of troops and nobles, as well as a determined pursuit by Mahabat Khan and Prince Parvez remain the rebellion's enduring milestones. Towards the end, Shah Jahan was forced back to the Deccan and into an alliance with the Mughal's old foe, Malik Amber. Yet, this was only a temporary respite and by March 1626 Shah Jahan was left with no option but to seek reconciliation on whatever terms and conditions the emperor imposed. The civil war had preoccupied the empire for at least three years.[48] The loss of Qandahar to the Persians was its most obvious consequence. There were others too.

The consequences for Abdur Rahim are evident and devastating. In the space of a few years, his family, never very large, was virtually wiped out and erased from the upper echelons of the nobility – with the death of Shah Nawaz Khan and Rahmandad, the execution of Dorab Khan and almost all of Abdur Rahim's grandsons. One – Minuchihr, a son of Shah Nawaz Khan – did survive. He had, as we saw, crossed over to the emperor at the early stages of the revolt, but he would never reach the levels achieved by his father or even his uncle Dorab Khan, leave alone his grandfather.

The physical decimation of the family was accompanied by its very public humiliation. Abdur Rahim's son and grandsons had been executed by decree of the very court and of the princes they had grown up with. Stripped of dignity and title, the aged Abdur Rahim was in much the same state as his father had been in the last months of his life. Yet, however partial and meaningless, it would be imperial discretion again that would try to make amends. In October 1625 we find Abdur Rahim summoned to the court and into the presence of the emperor:

> For a long time he remained with his forehead on the ground in humility and shame. Finally in order to comfort him, His Majesty

said 'what has happened was done by fate and destiny and not chosen by you or us. Do not let yourself be shamed or alarmed in this regard.' After the KhanKhanan had performed the ritual of kissing the ground, His Majesty mentioned for the Bakshis to bring him forward and stand him in a suitable position.[49]

Jahangir restored to Abdur Rahim the title of Khan-i-Khanan, earlier taken from him and awarded to Mahabat Khan. At this time Abdur Rahim is believed to have had the following verse inscribed on a ring:

By the help and assistance of God, the kindness of Jahangir has given me a second life and for a second time the title of KhanKhanan.

Abdur Rahim's rehabilitation was related to the emperor's failing health. It appears that en route to Kashmir, in Lahore, he remembered his old tutor (Plate VI) and sent for him. But with the putting down of Shah Jahan's rebellion and the consequent end of the civil war, a larger reordering of Mughal court politics was also taking place. In this context, the stature of Abdur Rahim remained an obvious asset, especially since he was the least likely to be in Mahabat Khan's camp. For, ironically, after the defeat of Shah Jahan, the very instruments used to quell the rebellion needed themselves to be discarded. The Prince Parvez–Mahabat Khan combine constituted a threat to Nur Jahan's ambitions, now invested in her son-in-law Prince Sharyar. Separating Parvez from Mahabat Khan seemed the obvious next step. Mahabat Khan was accordingly transferred to distant Bengal, and another noble was appointed in his stead as guardian of Prince Parvez. Mahabat Khan was now himself to rebel – and in spectacular fashion. In March 1526, when the court was in the Punjab, he and a determined group of Rajput warriors took the emperor and empress prisoner.

During the period of this coup, Mahabat Khan was extraordinarily sensitive to the danger Abdur Rahim could pose to him. Amongst his early orders were that Abdur Rahim be seized. Abdur Rahim was then in Delhi and was taken into custody. He, on his part, had wholly resigned himself to whatever was in store; 'resigned himself to the decree of fate' is how one chronicle puts it.[50] He had, after all, lost so much already.

Certainly, Mahabat Khan feared Abdur Rahim's revenge. Besides the emperor and many nobles, he also had in his custody the son of Asaf Khan, Abu Talib, who was married to the daughter of Shah Nawaz Khan. We find Jahangir too playing on Mohabat Khan's fear. Despite the extent of the outrage committed against his person, we are informed of Jahangir's attempt to secure his position by winning Mahabat Khan's confidence. One manner of doing so was to warn him about Abdur Rahim's granddaughter: 'And Shah Nawaz Khan's daughter ... says, "Whenever I have an opportunity, I will shoot Mahabat Khan with my musket."'[51]

The curious situation of Jahangir as a virtual prisoner was to last for over three months. It ended with Mahabat Khan's flight, largely as a consequence of being outwitted by the empress and Asaf Khan, her brother. By June 1626, the coup had collapsed and there was a churning under way by which all equations were again to change. Prince Parvez died in October 1626, opening up the possibility of a new alliance between Shah Jahan and Mahabat Khan. Both grasped the opportunity since Nur Jahan and her ambitions were the common enemy. We now find Nur Jahan summoning Abdur Rahim to lead the force that would award retribution to Mahabat Khan. She gave him:

> ... by way of assistance 300 Iraqi horses, 9 furious elephants, 20 she elephants, 1200 camels, 300 wagons, carpets and beddings and pavilions ... Thus, having made good his losses and deficiencies, he was sent to pursue Mahabat Khan, with great elation and pride and with a hundred fold pomp and grandeur. His main wish was to take revenge against the latter.[52]

Revenge was, however, to be denied. At seventy-two, Abdur Rahim fell ill at Lahore and died soon after reaching Delhi, in mid-1627.

His end was painful, as one chronicler relates on the basis of the testimony of the physician who attended to him:

> At the time of death agonies KhanKhanan showed great distress and pain. I had asked him, 'Nawab is a perfect man, then what all this distress and pain' to which he replied, 'for a period of fifty years, this body has enjoyed the position of KhanKhanan; now, at the time of separation between the body and the soul, the body on the whole is in the state of turmoil.[53]

Abdur Rahim Khan-i-Khanan was buried in Nizamuddin by the side of his wife, in the mausoleum constructed by him at her death.

6

AFTERLIFE: RAHIMAN AND ABDUR RAHIM

IN ONE of the labyrinthine by-lanes of the ancient city of Benaras is the building which houses the Nagari Pracharni Sabha. The Sabha was, in the late nineteenth and early twentieth centuries, in the forefront of the politics of language in north India. Its members and office-bearers were the vanguard of the movement to establish Hindi as India's national language, with Devanagari as its authentic script, and to displace Urdu from what was believed to be its high pedestal. Today, the building looks rather forlorn; the library is deserted; the portraits of the Sabha's illustrious founders look down severely on empty desks, although the bookshelves are full and well dusted. The more precious manuscripts are kept in large steel almirahs upstairs. The institution's reputation, however, is not forgotten. Some years ago a study of language and nationalism, for instance, referred to the 'entrenched elites' of the Nagari Pracharni Sabha, although 'embattled', or even 'embittered intellectuals' would perhaps have been a more accurate description.[1]

Within one of the steel almirahs, wrapped carefully in soft red cloth, lies a copy of an early edition of a seminal text on Abdur Rahim, the *Rahim Ratnavali* by Pandit Mayashankar Yajnik. Carefully pasted on to one of its inside pages is a translation in Hindi of a brief news report by a staff correspondent of the *Hindustan Times* datelined New Delhi, 2 January 1966. It describes a function organized by the Jangpura branch of the Hindi Sahitya Sammelan to commemorate the 410th birth anniversary of Bairam Khan's son, Abdur Rahim Khan-i-Khanan. The report states that 'The uncertainty about the date of birth of Nawab Abdur Rahim Khan-i-Khanan, a poet warrior of Akbar's times, has been cleared.' A horoscope discovered recently in Ujjain, the report said, had established that Abdur Rahim was born on 3 December 1556 and not in January 1557. The horoscope, cast by Krishna Derajna, a celebrated astrologer of Akbar's court, established also that Abdur Rahim was born in Lyallpur, formerly known as Labhpur, and not Lahore as hitherto assumed.

This was challenged a few days later by an indignant letter to the editor of the *Hindustan Times* from Mrs K.N. Hasan of Aligarh. The letter, published on 6 January, pointed out that according to the *Maathir-i-Rahimi* written by Abul Baqi Nahavandi on the instructions of Abdur Rahim Khan-i-Khanan and later published by the Asiatic Society, the birth took place on Wednesday, 10 Safar, 964 Hijri era (13 December 1556). Mrs Hasan also contested the change in birthplace. Lyallpur, she wrote, was founded in AD 1886 and its site was previously uninhabited. Labhpur was, therefore, definitely a corruption of Lahore.

The dispute, if it can be called that, over the date of birth of Abdur Rahim has its own history. His earliest Hindi biographer, Munshi Devi Prasad of Jodhpur, encountered it in two forms: one, the horoscopes cast at his birth carried a different date from that given in the Persian sources, and two, Munshi Devi Prasad found not one but three horoscopes of Abdur Rahim and they differed marginally from one another.

> Horoscopes are also of utility in history as they clarify the past. Muslims do not have, as do Hindus, the practice of casting horoscopes, nevertheless important persons did have horoscopes

made. With this in mind, I undertook a search for Khan-i-Khanan's horoscope and found one in the archives of Bikaner, another in an astrologer's collection and a third in a friend's library. But the first differed from the second and the third.[2]

Munshi Devi Prasad traced some of these differences to two different astrological calendars, as differences between the Marwar and Delhi *panchangs* were inevitable and might well explain the divergence in dates. His investigations unearthed yet another horoscope, which reconciled the differences in the earlier horoscopes. Nevertheless, the difference between the Persian chronicles and the Hindu horoscopes remained.

The exchange of letters in 1966, in fact, repeated the divergence Munshi Devi Prasad had encountered and reported at the close of the nineteenth century. This is, however, the smallest of the discrepancies we repeatedly encounter between Persian and Urdu accounts on the one hand, and Hindi narratives on the other. These differences reflect, in their own small way, how Abdur Rahim's legacy and heritage were claimed and contested by different literary cultures and communities in nineteenth and twentieth-century north India.

Devi Prasad was the most prominent of the early biographers of Abdur Rahim and we will dwell on his work on the nobleman at some length. The period between Abdur Rahim's death and Devi Prasad's interest in him can be called one of light and shadows. We find baffling and enigmatic absences, failures to encounter him or his poetry where most expected. From the early twentieth century, on the other hand, there is a steady expansion of knowledge about the Mughal noble and a determined effort to reconstruct his literary canon as he is built up as a social and national icon. In this transition from shadow to light are larger forces and changes at work, very distant from Abdur Rahim's own life and times.

Given his background and prominence, Abdur Rahim's history and biographical details figure in most Mughal chronicles. Three of these stand out, first among them being the *Maathir-i-Rahimi* of Maulana Abul Baqi Nahavandi (1570–1637). Nahavandi was of Kurdish origin and, on migrating to India, he attached himself to Rahim's court in Burhanpur. He completed work on his patron's biography possibly around 1616. It is, therefore, a primary source of contemporary detail on Abdur Rahim as a literary patron and on the poets and scholars attached to his court. Unfortunately, it remains untranslated from the original Persian, although the Asiatic Society of Bengal edited and published the work in three volumes between 1910 and 1931 and it has been widely consulted by medievalists.

Thereafter, Abdur Rahim features in a dictionary of Mughal nobles, the *Dhakhiratul Khawanin*, written some twenty-five years after his death. The author, Sheikh Farid Bukhari was a middle-level officer of the Mughal court and worked for many years in the Deccan, often for nobles who were subordinates of Abdur Rahim. Some of his descriptions would thus have been based on eyewitness accounts and from these we can get a flavour of the Khan-i-Khanan's personality. The *Dhakhirat* itself became the source for another dictionary of Mughal nobles, the *Maathir-ul-Umra,* originally written in the 1740s by Samsam-ud-Daulah Shah Nawaz Khan Nawab, who, like Sheikh Farid Bukhari, was a Mughal official who spent many years in the Deccan. The work was amplified and completed by his son Abdul Hayy in 1780. All these Persian sources mention Rahim's patronage of literature and also that he composed poetry in Arabic, Persian and Hindi, although no examples are cited of his verses in Hindi.[3]

Abdur Rahim's Hindi verse was also mentioned in the mid-eighteenth-century *Kavi Nirnay* ('The Verdict on Poets'). The work was composed in AD 1746 by Bhikharidas from Pratapgarh, in modern Uttar Pradesh, who is regarded as one of the great scholastic poets of Braj Bhasha. In the introductory verses of the *Kavi Nirnay*, Bhikharidas mentions the prominent Braj Bhasha poets of the past and distinguishes four (overlapping) categories of poets: those such as

Tulsidas and Surdas, distinguished for religious merit; those rewarded by patronage – Kesavdas, Bhusan and Balbir; those seeking fame – Raskhan and Rahim; and the scholastic poets, Tos, Rasraj, Raslin and himself.[4]

Bhikharidas's mention of Abdur Rahim is brief, but seeking fame is certainly a categorization with some lasting value. Mah Banu's tomb stands out as one of the few, in the very long list of Mughal structures that was built by a noble to remember his wife. The *Maathir-i-Rahimi* is one of the very few panegyrics inspired by, and devoted to, a Mughal noble rather than a monarch. The work was obviously composed at Abdur Rahim's own instance and designed with an eye to both his contemporary and posthumous reputation. Much the same purpose was also achieved by the unquestionably large corpus of verse composed in his praise by Persian, Sanskrit and Hindi poets.

The notice in the *Kavi Nirnay* suggests that Abdur Rahim's Hindi poetry survived to be noticed a century and a quarter after his death. One must remember, however, that Bhikharidas was a scholar-poet and would have delved deep into manuscript sources and oral traditions, and the fact that he mentioned Abdur Rahim cannot in itself be taken to imply that his verses were popular or even known outside a small fraternity of scholars at the time the *Kavi Nirnay* was composed.

Certainly, we have little evidence of widespread familiarity with Abdur Rahim's verse in the early nineteenth century. For example, Thomas Broughton, a British army officer who spent many years in India, compiled a collection of poems and songs popular among the soldiers in his command. His compilation titled *Selections from the Popular Poetry of the Hindus* was published first in 1814 and is possibly the first printed anthology of Braj Bhasha poets.[5] The sample of poets included is large and among the better-known medieval poets we find Surdas, Keshavdas, Bihari, Giridhar, Kaviray and Mandan, apart from lesser-known ones. There is, however, no Abdur Rahim. Most of the verses in the anthology are on the theme of amorous dalliance, in particular the Radha–Krishna legend. It also includes some dohas. Given these categories, Abdur Rahim's absence is noteworthy. There are other striking omissions in the collection, including Tulsidas and Kabir. Broughton's collection cannot, therefore, be said to be fully representative, but it assumes significance given Rahim's absence elsewhere too.

Another influential collection of its time was put together by William Price in 1827. It is amongst the earliest of anthologies 'put together as Readers, initially for the use of young British civilian and army students of Fort William College, but later for Indian schools as well'. *Hindee and Hindoostanee Selections* contains some 200 poems in categories such as Rama and Krishna bhakti, virah (separation), mythological references, *niti* or moral dohas, secular love, etc.[6] The poets included in this collection are Kabir, Tulsidas, Gang, Keshavdas, Mira Bai, Parmanand Das and Haridas Swami. The themes of the poems are such that some inclusion of Abdur Rahim's verses could have been expected but, once again, we do not encounter him and the absence continues.

Let us now look at two early books in 'Hindi' as it emerged in the nineteenth century and at the very beginning of its great divide from Urdu. The origins of this divide itself are usually traced back to the linguistic efforts of instructors at the College of Fort William:

> The institutionalization of Hindustani and Hindui as two autonomous linguistic entities came about when the Fort William College was founded in Calcutta in 1800 for the benefit of young British civilians entering the service of the East India Company … John Gilchrist was the natural choice as Professor of Hindustani, Colebrooke for Sanskrit. From the beginning, the Hindustani department taught the language in the Perso Arabic script; which according to the understanding of the times was identified specially with the Muslims and their culture and literature. Gilchrist realized that some arrangement needed to be made to teach Hindui or Bhakha, as was appropriate, in the Nagari script … On 19 February 1802 … the College Council approved the demand by Gilchrist for a Bhakha Munshi (and) Lallooji Lal was appointed to the post.[7]

The process by which such excision began and sustained itself is interesting:

> (t)he pundits and munshis found themselves coerced, possibly as much by the bureaucratic necessity of justifying their separate institutional existence as by any intrinsic characteristics of the language itself, into developing two gradually diverge registers, one leaning towards the Sanskrit end of the lexical spectrum, the other towards the Perso Arabic…[8]

At the end of this process we find that:

> … the important thing that emerged from Fort William is the idea of twoness, of linguistic duality. Fort William College gave institutional recognition to the notion that there were in fact two ways of doing Hindustani – one which used the available and mixed language, and another from which the Arabic Persian words (i.e., words of 'Muslim' origin) had been removed in order to produce a language more suitable to Hindus.

A parallel process was under way for Urdu too: 'The books printed for the use of the students of the college meant … that a literary corpus was also, willy-nilly, being established and that the past literary canons of Hindi and Urdu were henceforth to be viewed as mutually exclusive.[9]

Lallooji Lal (1747–1824) was described in later years as having 'practically newly invented modern Sanskritized Hindi by excising "alien" words from the mixed Urdu language of Akbar's camp followers…', as also having a pioneering role in the crafting, identifying and consolidation of Hindi as the 'language of the Hindus'. He brought out a collection of Hindi poetry in 1817, the *Sabha Vilasa*, an anthology of verses and the first of our two seminal texts.[10]

In the *Sabha Vilasa* is included a doha that is unmistakably by Abdur Rahim. This suggests that at least some of his verses were still in circulation in the early nineteenth century, scattered across different manuscript collections or oral traditions which Lallooji

Lal would have had access to. Yet the presence of this single verse should not necessarily prompt us to conclude that Lallooji Lal had any great familiarity with Abdur Rahim or his work. The fact that the *Sabha Vilasa* included a whole section titled 'Barvai' would lead us to expect a larger representation from Abdur Rahim since that was unquestionably a verse form that he dominated. Yet, none of the barvais in the *Sabha Vilasa* can be definitively ascribed to Abdur Rahim and we again encounter a relative fading of memory and a loss of his work by the early nineteenth century.

From Lallooji Lal, let us move rapidly to the mid-nineteenth century and to our second text. We look now at Raja Shiva Prasad – another important figure in the emergence of modern Hindi literature. 'Raja' Shiva Prasad Singh (1823–95) – his title an honorific bestowed by the government – was an inspector of schools and a prolific textbook writer with a pragmatic and non-doctrinaire attitude to the propagation of Hindi. He saw the dissemination of the Devanagari script as the way ahead in this endeavour, rather than the weeding out of Persian and Arabic expressions or vocabulary. By the 1860s and '70s, however, the process of codification into the straitjackets of Hindi and Urdu was far advanced and 'Shiva Prasad was too late in his attempt to bring the two languages together.'[11] He was, in fact, much pilloried by his co-religionists for his efforts to retain the Arabic–Persian phraseology that had passed into common usage. Equally, he was criticized by the eminent Muslim educationist and social reformer Sir Syed Ahmed Khan for his advocacy of the Devanagari script.

Among Raja Shiva Prasad's works is an anthology of prose and poetry, titled *Gutka* (1867).[12] This was an influential collection, not least on account of the importance of its author; it came to replace William Price's *Selections*, which had been in circulation for some decades. The verse selections in the *Gutka* include the work of Bihari, Kabir, Malik Muhammad Jayasi and Tulsidas amongst the medieval Hindi poets as also a selection from Lallooji Lal's *Sabha Vilasa*. But, once again, Abdur Rahim is conspicuously absent.

It can, of course, be argued that Abdur Rahim, whatever the political dimensions or significance of his inclusion, does not rank among the very greatest of medieval Hindi poets, especially if only a handful are listed. But his absence remains noticeable in other important collections too.

Gracin de Tassy (1794–1878) acquired his early training in oriental languages in Paris, but was perhaps also largely self-instructed. In 1828 he occupied a chair in Urdu at the Ecoles des Langues Orientales Vivantes, and wrote and published prolifically in French, his principal interest being Islam and Islamic literatures.

Gracin de Tassy's work remains largely untranslated into Hindi and English. One influential and important publication on the history of literature in Hindi and Hindustani was translated into Hindi only as late as 1953 and then too with abridgements. The original work, the first edition of which was published in two volumes between 1839 and 1847, contained a listing of over 730 Urdu and Hindi poets. The second edition in three volumes, published during 1870–71, was an even larger work listing some 3,000 poets and writers. De Tassy's compilation of poets and writers ranks as one of the earliest of its kind. That it was in French, and was not translated into Hindi till the 1950s and then only in part, obviously diluted the impact it had on other writers on the history of Hindi literature.[13] To many early historians of Hindi literature, de Tassy was a partisan figure closely aligned to Sir Syed Ahmed Khan and thus a clear protagonist of the opposite camp in the early years of the Hindi–Urdu controversy and split. According to Ram Chandra Shukla, one of the foremost Hindi writers and critics of the early mid-twentieth century, Gracin de Tassy had begun from an objective and non-partisan position but in later years, and under the influence of Sir Syed Ahmed Khan, moved to a doctrinal and hard-line position in favour of Urdu.[14]

A considerable part of de Tassy's vast corpus of writings is contemporaneous with the maturing of the language conflict in north India in the nineteenth century. He, on his part, recognized and participated fully in the ongoing process of identification of language with religion. For the purpose of our narrative, however, what is significant is the lack of reference to Abdur Rahim in the otherwise comprehensive listing of writers contained in the *History of Hindi Literature*. In the French text, Gracin de Tassy mentions three Abdur Rahims without giving the date of birth or death of any.

One such reference reads: 'Abd ur Rahim Khan of Lucknow, son of Dost Muhammad Khan, captain of cavalry, distinguished pupil of Mir Áli Bekhud, is the author of poetry circulated only among his friends, but of which Muhsin gives a sample.' The other two references are, first, to Abdur Rahim, a contemporary of Wali (c. 1665–1707) and second, to Abdur Rahim Buksh, without any accompanying details.

None of them has the title of Khan-i-Khanan and from the details provided, none can even remotely be identified with Abdur Rahim Khan-i-Khanan of the sixteenth- and seventeenth-century Mughal court.[15] The absence is certainly striking, given the length of de Tassy's treatment and the large number of poets he listed and also, of course, his interest in the Hindi–Urdu, Hindu–Muslim interface. At the very least, it can be surmised that knowledge about Abdur Rahim in Gracin de Tassy's time was still non-existent or very limited. His poetry, and in particular the dohas and barvais, may have remained in usage as aphorisms and the poetry of everyday life. Gracin de Tassy may well have encountered them en passant in collections such as the *Sabha Vilasa* of Lallooji Lal, but without any knowledge of its author, and relied on hearsay in collecting the details of the three Abdur Rahims he describes.

We encounter other texts where the enigma of Abdur Rahim's absence, or the confusion surrounding him, is pronounced. One of the foundational texts of Hindi poetry is a comprehensive anthology of Hindi poets, the *Shiv Singh Saroj*, first published in 1887 and reprinted regularly for nearly a century.[16] The intention of the compiler, Shiv Singh Sengor, was to provide historical details on the 800 major and minor poets included in the anthology. Despite its many deficiencies, the *Shiv Singh Saroj* is still regarded as an important source text for subsequent histories of Hindi poetry. The entry on Abdur Rahim is brief, but it does contain the gist of all the relevant information:

> This great scholar was a master of Arabic, Persian, Turkish and other foreign languages and also one of Sanskrit and Braj Bhasha. He was the apple of Akbar's eye. It was on account of his father Bairam Khan's role that Humayun could regain the throne of Delhi. KhanKhananji was especially regardful of priests, poets, mullahs, shayars, astrologers and all persons of good qualities. His court was brimming with scholars. His slokas in Sanskrit are very difficult and dohas in bhasha very beautiful. The dohas with homilies are so good that the reader can never tire of reading them. His Diwan in Persian is of a very high order. He translated Babur's autobiography from Turkish into Persian. He died at the age of 72 in 1036 Hijri.

The *Shiv Singh Saroj* then proceeds to give a few examples of Abdur Rahim's work. The brevity of the entry on Abdur Rahim is by no means unusual since the *Saroj*, on the whole, did not allocate attention proportionate to the reputation of the poet. Yet, some lack of clarity is evident as the work contains also an entry on a 'Rahim Kavi' and the assertion that it is difficult to separate 'the verses of Rahim KhanKhanan and this Rahim'. It would appear that at the time of the compilation of the *Saroj*, a knowledge of the corpus of Abdur Rahim's work had not yet crystallized to the extent of establishing his reputation as a medieval poet of Hindi and there was some doubt about the work that could be attributed to him. Shiv Singh Sengor's claim of a second Rahim was influential and we encounter it also in the work of the nineteenth-century

English linguist George Grierson who, following the *Saroj*, says: 'It is difficult to distinguish between the works of this poet and those of his illustrious namesake.'[17]

We encounter Abdur Rahim in greater detail in an equally important anthology of poetry, the *Misra Bandhu Vinod* (1913). The *Vinod* was composed by Ganesh Bihari (b. 1864), Shyam Bihari (b. 1872) and Sukhdev Bihari (b. 1876), three brothers known collectively as the Mishra Bandhu and distinguished for publishing all their work together.[18]

The *Vinod* has a comprehensive entry for Abdur Rahim, which summarizes the extant knowledge of him in the early twentieth century. Some aspects are noteworthy; for instance, the representation of him as an ideal man, with almost divine attributes: 'It is said that all his life he never acted in anger against anyone;' and 'all his life he spent in doing good to others'. These features would acquire greater prominence in twentieth-century portraits of Abdur Rahim. We also have an unambiguous assertion that 'despite being a Muslim he was a complete devotee of Krishna and Ram'. In its understanding of Abdur Rahim's works, however, we find that the *Misra Bandhu Vinod* is both less comprehensive and accurate. The *Nagar Shobha* and the barvais outside of the *Barvai Nayika Bhed* are prominent omissions in works attributed to him. Also, the *Raspanchadhyayi* is attributed to Abdur Rahim when it is actually the work of the Krishnabhakt poet Nand Das in the 1580s.

The complete Abdur Rahim was clearly yet to emerge – the historical character as well as the poet. But some knowledge about him was spreading and it advanced incrementally over the nineteenth century. In the early decades of the twentieth century, three seminal contributions would fill in the historical details about the Khan-i-Khanan and his literary work. This part-historical, part-literary endeavour was prompted by, and took place, amidst a wider nationalist and linguistic ferment in north India in the late nineteenth and early twentieth centuries, leaving its own indelible mark on scholarly efforts to excavate the identity and work of Abdur Rahim.

The Nagari Pracharni Sabha, or the Society for the Propagation of the Nagari Script, was the crucible of this ferment. The establishment of the Sabha in 1893 in Benaras constitutes a milestone in the movement for the promotion of Hindi literature as a whole and not just the movement to establish the primacy of the Nagari script, which was the society's avowed aim. The Sabha drew to it a body of committed and gifted scholars and public personalities. It spearheaded an agitation for the official recognition of Hindi and its use in government and court proceedings. Simultaneously, it conducted searches for old Hindi manuscripts, and published numerous books on history and literature including compilations of the works of the great Braj Bhasha and Awadhi poets of medieval India.

This exercise was intended to establish the antiquity of Hindi, to subsume within it the Braj Bhasha and Awadhi literary traditions and thereby establish the richness of its literature and the seamless continuity of its traditions from ancient times. The demand for the recognition of Hindi as the principal official and literary language of the majority of the population of north and central India had, integral to it, the parallel implication of the displacement of Urdu. The divide between the two grew over the second half of the nineteenth century and crystallized in the twentieth century as literary competitiveness was increasingly influenced by growing tensions between the Hindu and Muslim communities.[19]

The three protagonists I detail now, in the task of the resurrection of the literary and historical Abdur Rahim, were all intimately associated with the Nagari Pracharni Sabha. The elevation of Abdur Rahim due to their efforts becomes indistinguishable henceforth from the larger Hindi movement, and indeed from the great Hindi–Urdu debate of the nineteenth and twentieth centuries.

Munshi Devi Prasad belonged to a Kayasth family, long resident in Delhi in the service of the Mughal court as scribes and accountants. The Persian language, calligraphy and accountancy were the tools of their trade and the decline of the Mughals witnessed the dispersal of the family to smaller northern and central Indian courts in Bhopal, Sironj (in present-day Madhya Pradesh), Tonk, etc. Devi Prasad was to join the service of Tonk but had to leave the state apparently on account of his advocacy of Hindu causes. The efforts of his family led to his being offered a post in the Appeals Court of Jodhpur in 1879 and he remained in that city till his death in 1923.[20]

In Jodhpur we find the Munshi serving in a variety of posts – initially in the courts and then in government departments where his interest in history and research stood him in good stead. In 1888 we find him in a department established to write the history of Marwar state and thereafter, in 1891, as assistant census director, a position he held at the time of the 1901 census. Yet, government employment does not wholly define the Munshi's activities. Social reform, advancement of the status of women and historical research and search for antiquities, all formed part of his interests in Jodhpur.

Despite these varied preoccupations, he accorded priority also to the pursuit of Hindi and its propagation. In this commingling of history and language we can see the full range of the Munshi's endeavours. In his lifetime he wrote some fifty books and almost a hundred essays in Hindi, quite apart from his Urdu writings. His most important historical works include the *Shahjahanama, Aurangzebnama,* and the lives of Sher Shah and Akbar. Munshi Devi Prasad was equally a prodigious writer in Urdu and one source lists some twenty-seven publications in the language. These include a number of histories and writings on education and social reform.

Literary activity in Urdu forms an important part of the first phase of Munshi Devi Prasad's life, but it fades over time. His early works were principally in Urdu, then he moved on to using both the Urdu and Devanagari scripts and finally, only the latter. In some senses then, the move from the 'Muslim' princely state of Tonk to 'Hindu' Jodhpur was more than geographical. The advancement of Hindi and Devanagari, both locally and nationally, through the Nagari Pracharni Sabha was to become an inseparable part of the Munshi in Jodhpur.

Combining interest in history with commitment to the establishment of Devanagari Hindi as the national language of India is common to Devi Prasad and many other historians of the time, notably Gauri Shankar Ojha, Bisheshwar Nath Reu and Kasi Prasad Jaiswal. The establishment of Hindi in the Devanagari script was, in the eyes of its protagonists, an act of historical research and discovery as well as of political and public advocacy. The search for manuscripts of old Hindi poetry, establishing the identity and biographical details of its poets, tracing their mutual influences and establishing their historicity, were thus as important as petitioning the government or seeking to influence government decisions on the greater use of Hindi in courts, government offices and educational institutions.

We find in the second half of the nineteenth century numerous demands to allow the use of Nagari in courts. The principal sites of these agitations in British India were the towns of the United Provinces (now Uttar Pradesh) and the Central Provinces (now Madhya Pradesh). We find the Munshi in the midst of a similar conflict in princely Jodhpur.

> At that time Urdu was the language used in Jodhpur's courts. The influence of Dayanand Saraswati had led to Sir Pratap Singh developing deep regard for the Vedic Religion, Hindi language and the Devanagiri script. He, therefore, wanted to propagate the use of Hindi in courts in Jodhpur. But at that time, Muslim employees were predominant in the Jodhpur court. Because of this Sir Pratap Singh's wish could not be fulfilled immediately. He found, however, in Munshi Devi Prasad, someone who had good knowledge of and commitment to Hindi. With his cooperation within one or two

> years, Hindi began to be used widely in the court and decisions began to be given in it. Then one night, while hearing petitions addressed to him, Sir Pratap Singh ordered Munshi Devi Prasad to tear up 50–60 petitions in Urdu. From that day, all the work began to be transacted in Hindi, and for this the Munshi had to work even harder. Consequently the supporters of Urdu and Persians regarded the Munshi as their enemy.[21]

Devi Prasad, notwithstanding his very strong Marwar and Rajasthan roots, requires thus to be placed against a larger cultural and political landscape. His mature work – written between the 1880s and the second decade of the twentieth century – coincided with the movement for the establishment and recognition of Hindi in the Devanagari script. The different dimensions of this are now well known. A recent study has described the process as comprising two distinct aspects:

> The process of differentiation which was to lead to the formation of Hindi thus had two distinct aspects. The first was a process of creating internal cohesion, that is, the standard language which was being created set itself off, though at the same time it drew from the several spoken varieties, by seeking to create not only uniform orthography and grammar but also a standard literary idiom. It thereby appropriated to itself space occupied by former literary languages such as Braj Bhasa and Avadhi, which in their contemporary variety were now increasingly regarded as 'dialects' and consequently as substandard. The second aspect had to do with marking an external distinction. It consisted of a process which demarcated Hindi as arya or sadhu bhasa, the language of the Hindus, from the language of the Muslims. It was a development more religious than linguistic.[22]

In Munshi Devi Prasad's *Khankhanan Nama* (1906) we find the first modern full-length treatment of Abdur Rahim (and of his father Bairam Khan).[23] The book is in three segments. The first examines his political life and military achievements – in brief, the historical Abdur

Rahim Khan-i-Khanan; the second his verses in Sanskrit and Hindi, the gathering of which required considerable original research. In the third segment, Abdur Rahim is located within the wider landscape of seventeenth-century Hindi literature by presenting traditions and anecdotes of his interaction with other literary personalities of that period, in particular, giants of Hindi literature such as Tulsidas and Gang, and also by reproducing poetry about him by other Hindi poets of the time.

The historical sections of the *Khankhanan Nama* are largely, but not wholly based on the *Maathir-ul-Umra*, supplemented with other Persian texts such as the *Jahangirnama* and the *Akbarnama*. These enabled Devi Prasad to establish the broad chronology of Abdur Rahim's life, its political vicissitudes, his principal achievements, and so on. A subtext of this narrative is the lament that while the Persian texts mention Abdur Rahim's literary achievements in Persian, few or no details are given of his work in Hindi or Sanskrit.

Devi Prasad's Abdur Rahim is the scion of a family that had played a pivotal role in Mughal India, since Humayun's time. Devi Prasad describes a great general and commander, his part in the conquest of Sindh and Gujarat, and the major role he played in the Deccan for about a quarter-century. Finally, he describes Abdur Rahim as a connoisseur of literature and a fine poet in Persian and Hindi, one who knew many languages and whose command over Persian and Arabic was admired by his peers even given the high standards of the time.

In all this, Devi Prasad remained faithful to the Persian texts and histories and, in particular, to the *Maathir-ul-Umra*. He remained faithful also in presenting all the evidence in these texts about Abdur Rahim as a courtier. There is no gloss put over its often scathing remarks on Abdur Rahim or indeed over the *Maathir*'s assessment of his deviousness and manipulative behaviour. He remains circumspect over what, to later writers, appeared profoundly striking and important about Abdur Rahim's Hindi and Sanskrit poetry: its frequent and pronounced invocation of an obviously

Hindu cultural and religious paradigm and the absence of an Islamic 'accent'. The emerging divisions between Hindi and Hindu and Urdu and Muslim were known to Devi Prasad. The categories of Hindi and Hindu in their oppositional sense to Urdu and Muslim were evidently employed by him in full knowledge of their implications. What explains then, his extremely restrained treatment of Abdur Rahim, a premier Mughal noble who composed bhakti verses in Hindi? A simple explanation could be that for Devi Prasad, all such speculations were foreign to the territory of the historian. Since the sources he used did not enter into these issues, he saw no need to do so either. This circumspection then reflects the seriousness and commitment Devi Prasad brought to his endeavours as a historian.

Coupled with this was his determination to ensure that the history he wrote was based on evidence: 'Hindus have rarely written history of their time and such past (ancient) history they have written is very often not correct because if writing contemporary history is difficult, it is even more difficult to write of past periods as memories fade and get mixed up with hearsay ...'

Some two decades after Munshi Devi Prasad's *Khankhanan Nama* was published, we come across two other major works on Abdur Rahim. Brij Ratna Das and Mayashankar Yagnik both wrote full-length books combining history and literature to illuminate the life of Abdur Rahim. The triad of Devi Prasad, Brij Ratna Das and Mayashankar Yagnik has left an imprint on perspectives and perceptions of Abdur Rahim that remain definitive to this day.

In common with Munshi Devi Prasad, Brij Ratna Das brought to his study of Abdur Rahim a considerable scholarship in Persian as also a strong commitment to the cause of establishing Hindi as the national language of India. A nephew of Bhartendu Harishchandra, he devoted a lifetime of service to the Nagari Pracharni Sabha. A prodigious writer, his published books include a history of Hindi literature, one of Urdu literature, biographies of Henry Lawrence, Humayun and Harishchandra. His knowledge of Persian is demonstrated by his translation into Devanagari of the *Maathir-ul-Umra* and the *Humaynama*; these translations remain the standard versions of the Persian texts in Hindi to this day. The works he edited and compiled also cover a vast range: collections of Amir Khusrau's Hindi poetry and of Tulsidas, Inshaullah Khan and Bhushan, among others. This is in addition to numerous literary and historical articles published in the Sabha's journal.

For the *Rahiman Vilas,* published first in 1923 and again in 1929 in a revised and enlarged edition, Brij Ratna Das relied on the *Maathir-i-Rahimi* and one visible result of this is the many details he provides about the Persian poets and scholars patronized by the Khan-i-Khanan. Secondly, Brij Ratna Das wrote with the full benefit of the wide search for Hindi manuscripts initiated by the Nagari Pracharni Sabha since the end of the nineteenth century. This endeavour led to the discovery of hitherto unknown verses and poets and, in particular, of new verses by Abdur Rahim or credited to him. Devi Prasad had included in the *Khankhanan Nama* only forty dohas of Abdur Rahim while mentioning the existence of about a hundred; Brij Ratna Das reproduced 289 dohas in the *Rahiman Vilas* – close to the entire known corpus of Rahim's dohas.

Even a cursory reading of Brij Ratna Das brings out the contrast between his and Devi Prasad's Abdur Rahim. For the former, Abdur Rahim's Hindi works exemplify the 'nationalism' or the 'Rashtriyata' of Hindi:

> His veins had pure Turkish blood, but leaving aside his mother tongue and the Persian of his Emperor's court, by expressing his thoughts in Hindi he fully supported its nationalism.[24]

The reference to pure Turkish blood was a deliberate exaggeration since Brij Ratna Das would have known that Abdur Rahim's mother was a Mewati princess whom Bairam Khan had married after the battle of Panipat. Such assertions would have been foreign to Devi Prasad, with his restraint and evident desire to stick to the facts and refrain as far as possible from generalization. But in Brij Ratna Das's work we find more than an affirmation of Hindi's intrinsic merit and national status:

> Abdur Rahim was a follower of Islam but was influenced by the teachings of the Sufis and the liberal atmosphere of Akbar's court to such an extent that in the field of literature it appears more possible that he was a Hindu rather than a Muslim. Pick up any of his works – in every sentence you will find Indian love, bhakti, generosity, experience, civilization, etc. Similes, literary techniques, sceneries, etc., whatever there is, is full of the essence of hindutva. This could only be the work of a person such as Abdur Rahim who despite being the follower of one faith could have such a liberal attitude towards another that he started to appear as its devotee.

Abdur Rahim's verse thus provides a contrast in terms of the poetic techniques and metaphors employed by Urdu poets.

> From earliest times up to the end of the 19th century you can see each Urdu poem but you will never find a reference to the Ganga which has given them nourishment, but plenty of references to the rivers of Persia even though these poets never set eyes on them. The only reason for this is a feeling of religious superiority. Now compare this with the respect with which Abdur Rahim describes the Ganga.[25]

The contemporary character of Brij Ratna Das's narrative is evident, whether in the critique of the borrowed similes used by Urdu poets or in demonstrating the empathy that Abdur Rahim had for Hindi and Hinduism.

This brings us to the other important work on Abdur Rahim in the third decade of the twentieth century.[26] Mayashankar Yajnik's *Rahim Ratnavali,* published first in 1928, is structured on the same lines as Brij Ratna Das's *Rahiman Vilas* and Munshi Devi Prasad's *Khankhanan Nama*. However, there are visible differences in his treatment of his subject. Firstly, it is very evidently a compilation by a Hindi literary scholar rather than a historian using Persian sources. Such references as there are to Abdur Rahim's life history, his genealogy, Mughal court politics and political developments are based on Yajnik's reading of Devi Prasad and Brij Ratna Das and he makes no claims to originality in these areas. We do not know whether he knew Persian or even Urdu, unlike Devi Prasad and Brij Ratna Das. Yet he was, like them, closely associated with the Nagari Pracharni Sabha and was to gift his entire manuscript collection of medieval Hindi literature, gathered from different places in Rajasthan, to the Sabha library. Mayashankar Yajnik's interest in Rahim is evident from his discovery of two important verse collections of his: the *Nagar Shobha* announced in the Hindi magazine *Madhuri* in March 1925 and a miscellaneous collections of barvai, announced in the literary journal *Saraswari* in June 1926.

If Mayashankar Yajnik's interest in Abdur Rahim is more literary in character, this does not mean that he is devoid of contemporary relevance. Why is Abdur Rahim important? For Yajnik, the answer to this is located in the history of the development of Hindi in Mughal India, when a momentum was building up in its favour under Akbar, primarily because the spirit of Vaishnavism and bhakti expressed itself in Hindi. This momentum, he argued, was interrupted by none other than Raja Todar Mal, when he made Persian the state language. For Yajnik the regret is that 'a Hindu made the mistake whose consequences the entire nation has to bear today'. But for this error 'it is possible that Hindus and Muslims today would not have claimed two separate languages and Hindi would have been everybody's single language …'

Again, to Yajnik, Abdur Rahim is important because he served the cause of Hindi and its literature 'in a way that he did not do for any other language … Rahim did not see Hindi as being lesser than Arabic, Persian, Turkish, etc.' There is then a logical extension: 'From the name of incarnations, the glory of Mahadev and Ganga, etc., – from all this it becomes clear that Abdur Rahim's sentiments towards

Hindus were not one of dislike. There was great respect for the Hindu religion and he was a follower of Vaishnavism and a devotee of Krishna ...' Devotion to a language thus fuses with religious identity – in much the same way as we observed in Brij Ratna Das.

Brij Ratna Das's *Rahiman Vilas* and Mayashankar Yajnik's *Rahim Ratnavali* are only the most prominent and detailed of the many works that have led to the 1920s being described as the 'decade of Rahim'.[27] Through these years we have an explosion of titles on Rahim. *Rahiman Sataka* (Benaras, 1926) by Lala Bhagwandin, *Rahiman Vinod* (Allahabad, 1928) by Pandit Ayodhya Prasad Sharma, *Rahim Kavitavali* (Lucknow, 1926) by Surendranath Tewari, *Rahim* (Allahabad, 1921) by Ramanaresa Tripathi, *Rahiman Chandrika* (Benaras, 1924) by Rama Natha Lala 'Suman', *Rahiman Lalitya* (Calcutta, 1928) by Anant Sarana Ojha 'Lalita', *Rahiman Sataka* (Allahabad,1927) by Siva Sankara Misra, *Rahiman Sudha* (Patna, Allahabad 1928) by Anupa Lala Mandala, *Rahiman Sataka* (Mathura, 1924) by Navanita Chaturvedi, etc. There were many reasons for this plethora of titles apart from the nationalist mood sweeping the country: the expansion of Devanagari publishing houses, the commercial demands of a growing market for books to be used as texts in schools and colleges, and the requirements of school curricula for which Rahim's dohas in Hindi with their moral aphorisms were eminently suited. Not surprisingly, many of these publications focused almost entirely on Abdur Rahim's dohas to the exclusion of his other works. This abundance of books in the 1920s gave a certain completeness to the characterizations of Abdur Rahim and the portrait that emerged was of a symbol of 'Indianness'. Abdur Rahim as a literary or historical figure is thus overtaken by Abdur Rahim as a national icon.

An illustration of this is found in the work of Govind Das, a prominent political and literary figure in central India between the

1920s and the 1970s. Seth Govind Das was the scion of one of the premier landowning and moneylending families of the Narmada Valley that came into prominence in the erstwhile Central Provinces on account of the assistance it gave to the administration during the events of 1857. His grandfather, Gokul Das, was honoured with the title of Raja in 1889. The city of Jabalpur in Madhya Pradesh has numerous landmark buildings that owe their existence to the munificence of Raja Gokul Das and later, to his son Diwan Bahadur Jiwan Das. The possession of a vast moneylending business and agricultural estate, close relations with the colonial authorities and the demonstration of public-spiritedness through investments in charities and public works defined their life stories.

Govind Das's life, however, followed a different trajectory: He joined the Indian National Congress and in the 1920s and '30s was a prominent Gandhian and freedom fighter in central India. He was frequently in jail for his involvement in the national movement and later became a member of independent India's Constituent Assembly. He was reelected as a member of parliament from Jabalpur, representing the Congress party, till his death in 1974.[28]

Govind Das combined his active political career with an equally strong commitment to the cause of Hindi as India's national language; he was a prime mover in the Constituent Assembly of a resolution that Hindi be recognized as the national language of India and Devanagari as the national script. Amongst his many works of literary criticism, drama, historical fiction and poetry is a play entitled *Rahim*. First published in 1955, it presents the Khan-i-Khanan at different stages of his life: in the aftermath of his first victory in Gujarat, in Akbar's court at Fatehpur Sikri, on different Deccan battlefields, in Delhi and in Lahore, in custody during the civil war during Jahangir's reign, and in Tulsidas's ashram.[29] The ashram is particularly important in Govind Das's portrayal since his assessment of Abdur Rahim's life is of one pulled by contradictory impulses – a desire for political and military power befitting an important courtier on the one hand, but also, on the other, a yearning for the life of a recluse who finds fulfilment in religious devotion and literature; in other words, emulating the life of Tulsidas. In the closing scene of the play, we have Abdur Rahim on his deathbed telling his daughter Janah Begum of his regret that he could not lead the life that Tulsidas did. Abdur Rahim, the play suggests, realized that his enduring legacy would be that of a devotee and a poet rather than of a courtier and a general. For Govind Das, Abdur Rahim's life lies thus revealed:

> Despite being a true Muslim, Rahim was a devotee of Ram and Krishna and the spirit of this devotion suffuses his entire poetry … Although a Muslim, Rahim was a real follower and practitioner of Indian culture (Bharatiya Samskriti). Because of this his heart had tolerance and for this reason he viewed Hinduism and Islam, Hindus and Muslims equally.[30]

These remarks again remind us that Rahim's reputation as the sage statesman of Hindi literature was wholly formulated by the end of the third decade of the twentieth century and only grew as the national movement progressed. His status was derived in considerable measure from his Hindu devotional verse and this aspect of his work was viewed as indisputable evidence of his Indianness, even as communalism, separatism and the partition took their toll on the national psyche. The synthesis, believed to have been achieved in the past in Akbar's court, became also a road map for India's future and in this too Abdur Rahim was to be a major national figure.

It is now time to consider Abdur Rahim's afterlife in the other great literary tradition of north India, as Urdu's great split from Hindi matured and permeated all aspects of political's and social life in north India towards the end of the nineteenth century and in the first half of the twentieth.

In our encounter with Munshi Devi Prasad, his considerable expertise and knowledge of Urdu has been noted. In his preface to the *Khankhanan Nama* in 1906, he informs us that many years ago he had written a book by the same name in Urdu. The *Khankhanan Nama* in Urdu was, in fact, first published in 1898 and was itself based on an earlier publication of 1879, titled *Swanih Umri Nawab Khan-i-Khanan*. The 1898 *Khankhanan Nama* in Urdu was republished in Karachi, in Pakistan, in 1990. It is a measure of the gulf that now separates Urdu and Hindi as also the literary cultures in India and Pakistan, that authorship of the Urdu *Khankhanan Nama* is ascribed in the Karachi edition to a Munshi Devi Prasad 'Sehar'. However, this Munshi, an Urdu poet of repute himself, was from Badayun, and a person completely distinct from Munshi Devi Prasad of Jodhpur.[31]

The Urdu text is considerably shorter and almost sketchy when compared to the Hindi volume. As in the Hindi work, there is no effort to embellish Rahim's personality with imagined virtues. Instead, the narrative adheres faithfully to what the sources and chronicles say. The difference in the length of the two books arises principally from two reasons. Firstly, the historical part of the narrative is longer in the Hindi text and it also contains information that was found after the Urdu book had been published – in particular, details of the horoscopes of Abdur Rahim and of his sons, translations of letters addressed to him by Akbar and Abul Fazl, descriptions of the monuments constructed by him, and a host of other information. Secondly, much of the new material in the Hindi text is about the literary, rather than the historical aspects of Abdur Rahim's life.

The Urdu *Khankhanan Nama* notes that Abdur Rahim composed poetry in Turkish, Persian and Hindi and at one point says: 'We have already mentioned before that the KhanKhanan also used to compose poetry in Hindi and Sanskrit. This is ascertained from books in Hindi also. His slokas and kavita are famous among Hindus. More than amongst Muslims, his name is encountered in literary gatherings of the Hindus.' But apart from a few stray references to Rahim's Hindi verse and his patronage of Hindi poets, there is little about the Hindi heritage of Abdur Rahim and not a single example of his Hindi verse.

What explains this silence? Was Devi Prasad unware at the time he wrote the book in Urdu, of the full extent of Abdur Rahim's prodigious output in Hindi? It is possible that such knowledge came to him incrementally, as his own engagement with Hindi grew and also as literary research and knowledge of Abdur Rahim's work in Hindi expanded. Alternatively, it could be argued that some information about Abdur Rahim's Hindi work would have certainly been available to a scholar as committed as Munshi Devi Prasad. He had, after all, been writing in Hindi from at least the early 1870s.

So did he consciously exclude Abdur Rahim's Hindi poetry because the book itself was in Urdu? Perhaps the Munshi felt that beyond a point, the languages were not only distinct, but even the briefest sample of Abdur Rahim's devotional verse could disconcert or perhaps even offend some sections of the Urdu readership. There are no markers to help us decide which of these possibilities actually influenced the Munshi, and if at all. Nevertheless, we encounter the same question even more pointedly in the work of another great literary personality of the nineteenth and early twentieth centuries, Muhammad Husain Azad.

Muhammad Husain wrote under the pen name of 'Azad' (Free); he was born in Delhi in 1830 and grew to maturity in the afterglow of what is sometimes called the 'Delhi Renaissance'. After studying at the Delhi College, he joined his father in editing the first Urdu newspaper of north India. The revolt of 1857 and its violent suppression cut short this trajectory. His father was executed by the British on suspicion of helping the rebels and Azad, along with the rest of his family, was driven out of Delhi. In the 1860s we find him in Lahore in a clerical post at the postmaster general's office, and then at the Department of Public Instruction. By the mid-1860s, an acquaintance with Dr G.W. Leitner, principal of the newly set up Government College, Lahore, led to his association with the *Anjuman-e-Punjab*, the Punjab Literary Society. This also provided him the opportunity to re-establish his loyalties with the colonial authorities. Thereafter, Azad visited Central Asia twice on their behalf, on information and intelligence-gathering tours.

In his more literary endeavours, Azad's rise within the hierarchy of the *Anjuman* was accompanied by pronounced calls for the reform of Urdu poetry and poetics, so as to bring them closer to approved English models. Many contemporaries accused him of trying to create 'a language that was outwardly Urdu and inwardly English, such as the present rulers want to create'. His rejection of traditional Urdu similes and metaphors was likened by them to stripping 'some beautiful woman … of her jewellery and clothing and … (making her) stand absolutely naked'.[32] While conservatives may have found Azad's endeavours distasteful, he was supported by the modernists, most prominently the great Muslim social reformer, Sir Syed Ahmed Khan. From the late 1880s, Azad's life was overtaken by a series of personal tragedies. The death of several of his children and other close relatives triggered attacks of insanity, which grew in intensity and frequency until his death in 1910.

The *Durbar-e-Akbari* is a voluminous work composed in the lucid intervals between these attacks. During its writing, we are told, on one occasion 'he managed to reach Aligarh where he appeared without warning at the house of the amazed Sir Syed Ahmad Khan. He told his host that Abul Fazl and other spirits had been speaking to him dictating a book, which he was taking down in their own words.' The *Durbar-e-Akbari*, first published in 1898, is a voluminous work and in essence is an early attempt to animate and romanticize the Mughal Empire. It is a long and leisurely description of Akbar, his court and prominent courtiers; an 'immense, extravagant hymn of praise to Akbar … colourful, anecdotal, repetitive, full of long authorial asides – and so seductively written that it had immediate popularity and remains a favourite today'.[33]

After the emperor, Abdur Rahim is easily one of the most prominent characters in this book, which gives us a detailed account of his pedigree, upbringing, political and military achievements, the grandeur of his court, and his command over and patronage of the

Persian language, as well as the highs and lows of his personal and political life. Azad's Abdur Rahim epitomized the strengths of the Mughal Empire: he is the true scholar statesman, distinguished by birth, intellect, generosity, courage and sense of service to his emperor and the empire. What some other writers – both earlier and later – were to present as personal failings, in particular his inconsistent and devious conduct in the struggle between Shah Jahan and Jahangir, are for Azad no more than the natural complexities of choosing from a menu of bad options at a time of great trauma for the empire and its premier nobles.

The *Maathir-ul-Umra* quotes at one stage the following verse, which it says was composed about Abdur Rahim:

> A span in height and a hundred twists in the heart
> A tiny handful of bones, and a hundred frauds

It also says that Abdur Rahim was 'malevolent, worldly and time serving to a very great extent'. Azad's response to these criticisms and comments is spirited:

> But I say shame, shame on this heartless world and these hard hearted worldly persons. Those who live in holes and rot in hovels and make up stories about those who live in palaces; what do they know about the difficult and complex issues that came up before this noble who had rubbed shoulders with the Emperors of the realm or the manner in which he had handled issues confronting the empire.[34]

Azad's defence of Abdur Rahim is thus a defence of those bearing the burden of high office against uninformed criticism from the street. He presents the Khan-i-Khanan's actions not in terms of his personal gain or interest, but in terms of how he saw his duty towards the empire.

Yet, despite this long, detailed and measured evocation of Abdur Rahim, Azad is almost entirely silent on his accomplishments as a Hindi poet, beyond quoting Jahangir's assertion in his autobiography that Abdur Rahim composed very good poetry in Persian and Hindi. There is also a brief reference in *Akbari Darbar* to an astrological work of Rahim to the effect that he (Abdur Rahim) had 'obtained knowledge of the wisdom of Sanskrit. He has a poem which has one couplet in Persian and one in Sanskrit.'[35]

The absence of any further references to Abdur Rahim as a Braj Bhasha or Avadhi poet is therefore intriguing. Do we read Azad's omission of Abdur Rahim's Hindi poetry as evidence of the insularity between the Urdu–Persian and Hindi–Braj Bhasha cultural idioms and traditions in the late nineteenth century?

Yet Azad was not solely a scholar of Urdu and Persian, insulated from the world of Hindi poetry. He is best known in the history of Urdu literature not for the *Darbar-e-Akbarī*, but for an earlier work, the *Ab-e-Hayat,* regarded for a long time as the definitive history of Urdu poetry. Published in 1880 and predating the *Darbar-e-Akbarī* by almost two decades, the book remains both a canonical and controversial text. It has been described as the most often reprinted and most widely read Urdu book of the nineteenth century.

Azad remains, moreover, a remarkably controversial author. To a recent American scholar, he is the 'literary historian as gunslinger … ready to use fair means or foul, real texts or fakes, truths or falsehoods'. He is thus 'powerful' yet 'totally unscrupulous' and if classical Urdu poetry is not dead today, it is 'despite Azad's best efforts'. So what drove this modern scholar of Urdu poetry to employ such a bitter polemic against a long dead author? Essentially, the frustration with Azad derives from his basic postulate and hypotheses on the history and development of the Urdu language. His fundamental premise is summarized in the very opening sentence of *Ab-e-Hayat*: 'Everybody knows this much – that our Urdu language has emerged from Braj Bhasha.'[36]

To many Urdu scholars, this is absurd, since both languages are 'quite distinct'. Azad, his critics argue, used every ploy and argument possible to try and establish the wholly incorrect and impossible – but did so with spectacular success. The point relevant to our narrative is that Azad gives to Braj Bhasha an unmistakable primacy. Many illustrations can be cited from the *Ab-e-Hayat* of the familiarity Azad shows with the works of poets such as Malik Muhammad Jayasi, Tulsidas, Surdas, Kabir and Nanak. In his treatment of their works, he details the use of Persian and Arabic words in Braj Bhasha verses and describes how a non-Persian metaphor was employed by these poets. This familiarity with the great Hindi poets contrasts with the complete silence on Abdur Rahim in the *Ab-e-Hayat*. In turn this makes the silence on his Hindi poetry in the *Durbar-e-Akbari* even more mystifying.

It is impossible not to notice that for the purposes of Azad's own polemic against the Persian metaphor of Urdu poetry, the Hindi works of Abdur Rahim would have been a powerful argument in favour, and Abdur Rahim himself a formidable personality to produce in strengthening his case. Can it be that while writing the *Ab-e-Hayat* Azad may have come across references to the Khan-i-Khanan being a Hindi poet but not the actual verses, since Abdur Rahim's poetry was excluded from an Urdu-speaking milieu, or indeed had never been part of it? Or could it be that the *Durbar-e-Akbari* was written with an entirely different purpose to that of *Ab-e-Hayat* and, therefore, references to Abdur Rahim's Hindi verse were incongruous? This would be a difficult argument to sustain given the space devoted to Abdur Rahim in the *Durbar-e-Akbari*. Unfortunately, we can do no more than speculate, but before we do so, let us delve further into this strange amnesia.

Muhammad Husain Azad was first and foremost a popularizer, writing less for a literary or academic purpose than to reach as wide a readership as possible. We have a contrasting figure, broadly contemporaneous, in Allama Shibli Nomani (1857–1914). He was born near Azamgarh in Uttar Pradesh. Azamgarh was a town that had suffered greatly during the events of 1857 and restoration of the glories of Islamic intellectual achievement underwrites the whole of Shibli's life.

Apart from religious books such as those on the life and mission of the Prophet, and a biographical study of the second Khalifa, Shibli devoted a great deal of effort to correcting the impression created by the writings of English and European historians that Islamic rule was a tyranny inflicted on non-Muslims. His works include discussions of the concept of jizyah, studies of Aurangzeb, and investigations into the Turkish massacre of Armenians. He also produced detailed works on the history of Persian literature in India, and his book, the *Sherul Ajam*, a study of Persian poetry and poets in Mughal India, is regarded as a prominent study of the subject. In this survey too the central motive is to establish that Mughal history in India, far from being solely a narration of conquest and political domination, is a period of refinement, literary skill and intellectual achievement.

Allama Shibli Nomani first encountered the Khan-i-Khanan's works in December 1906 when, during a visit to the library of the Asiatic Society in Calcutta, he read the original manuscript of the *Maathir-i-Rahimi*. He reproduced details in summary form, in the Urdu magazine *Al Nadwa*, on the Khan-i-Khanan's patronage of poets, his love of poetry, his personality, and his numerous political and other achievements. Shibli concluded that viewing Mughal history as one of conquest and domination would be to overlook their enormous civilizational contribution to India and the reference to the Khan-i-Khanan's Hindi poetry is significant here: 'It is a matter of regret – and deepest regret – that the author of the *Maathir-i-Rahimi*, on account of being a Persian, does not give examples of KhanKhanan's Bhasha poetry since it would have then been possible to determine the effect Urdu had on Bhasha in those days'.[37]

Elsewhere in the essay, he observed that a search for the Khan-i-Khanan's Hindi poetry had yet to begin.

In the *Sherul Ajam,* Abdur Rahim Khan-i-Khanan figures

prominently as a patron of the great Persian poets, Urfi, Shakebi and Naziri, and also as a gifted litterateur in his own right. Nomani quotes a contemporary opinion that if the Khan-i-Khanan 'had been a poet he would have been of the status of Urfi and Naziri'. His admiration of Abdur Rahim is illustrated by his assessment of the Khan-i-Khanan as the perfect exemplar in the Mughal world of a man both of the sword and of the pen. In the descriptions of the Khan-i-Khanan, we are given details of his great library in Ahmedabad, his fondness for poetry and the fact that he used to recite poetry himself, his liberal and vast patronage of many Persian poets and scholars, and his friendship with the great scholar and poet of the first half of Akbar's reign, Abul Fath Gilani.[38]

At the same time, Maulana Shibli does not mention in the *Sherul Ajam* that the Khan-i-Khanan had an interest in Hindi and Sanskrit, was a patron of poets in these languages and composed poetry in them. This could well be because references to this interest may have been considered irrelevant to the principal subject of the *Sherul Ajam*: Persian poetry. In a work on Persian literature, the Khan-i-Khanan's literary forays in Hindi and Sanskrit may have been considered of little account. This silence bears noting, however, as we turn to the Dar-ul-Musanafeen, literally the House of Writers, an institution Shibli Nomani founded just before his death in 1914.[39]

After Shibli Nomani, the Dar-ul-Musanafeen in Azamgarh continued with its scholarly work on Islamic literature in India, and also further pursued his interest in correcting distorted views of Islam and Islamic history. This effort was spearheaded by Syed Sabahuddin Abdur Rahman (1911–87), a prolific author and historian. As an able successor to Shibli Nomani, he steered the fortunes of the Dar-ul-Musanafeen in the testing period after 1947.

Syed Sabahuddin wrote over thirty-five full-length books apart from numerous articles. His historical works include studies on Amir Khusrau, Ghalib, the cultural contribution of Mughal emperors to India, poetry in Mughal India, the military achievements of the Mughals, and so on. Syed Sabahuddin, in much the same way as Shibli

Nomani, sought to establish that British rule was facilitated by British historical writing about Islam and India, and that the distortions in such history writing meant that the history of Islam in India was itself distorted and presented as a history of conquest, tyranny and exploitation. One study by Syed Sabahuddin is of particular interest to us here as it broadens the scope of Shibli Nomani's *Sherul Ajam*. It is a study of court poets and court poetry – and not only Persian poetry, which was the focus of the *Sherul Ajam* – and the patronage it received in Mughal India. It covers Mughal emperors from Babur to Bahadur Shah Zafar as also their prominent nobles. The *Bazm-i-Taimuri* was Syed Sabahuddin Abdur Rahman's first major work and was to establish his reputation as a scholar of Persian, Urdu and Mughal history. The first edition of the work was published in 1938. The second edition was considerably delayed as the text required very substantial additions and finally three volumes were published over an eight-year period (1973, 1980, 1981) totalling, in all, over a thousand pages. These were intended to provide a comprehensive view of the literature associated with the Mughal court.

The section on Abdur Rahim in the 1990 reprint comprises some 130 pages. Along with brief details of his family background and political career, it is very largely a listing and description of the Persian poets and philosophers in his court, who enjoyed his patronage, based essentially on the *Maathir-i-Rahimi* of Abul Baqi Nihavandi. There is an occasional comment from Maulana Shibli Nomani indicating that much of this ground had been traversed earlier.

Sabahuddin Abdur Rahman encountered in 1944 Mayashankar Yajnik's *Rahim Ratnavali* and spells out his argument regarding Abdur Rahim's Hindi verse in the preface to the second edition of the *Bazm-i-Taimuri:*

> Abdur Rahim Khan-i-Khanan has been described in great detail. In this his Hindi poetry has also figured. Some books on his poetry which are now available have led me to have some doubts that these Hindi verses are his. The evidence is in the book. If someone can remove this doubt I would be grateful to him.[40]

The reason for this doubt is that no Persian work actually quotes Abdur Rahim's Hindi verses. Based on the details in Yajnik's *Rahim Ratnavali*, he describes the Khan-i-Khanan's generous patronage of eminent Hindi poets including Gang, Keshavdas, Mandan and Prasidh, outlines how he was influenced by Kabir, Surdas and Tulsidas, and portrays Abdur Rahim's influence on Mati Ram, Girdhar and Bihari. Mayashankar Yajnik is also cited as saying that more Hindi poets have praised Abdur Rahim than have Persian poets, an assessment with which the author of *Bazm-i-Taimuri* does not, however, fully concur. Examples of his sententious verse in the dohas, his expertise with the barvai couplet, as also a listing of his Hindi works then follow – again, largely following Mayashankar Yajnik's *Rahim Ratnavali*. Sabahuddin Abdur Rahman's description of the mixed Sanskrit–Hindi poetry incudes a comment that the aim of such poetry was to bring Hindus and Muslims closer together. The *Bazm-i-Taimuri* also says that in Abdur Rahim's Hindi poetry, we frequently encounter Persian words.

At this point in the narrative, some more verses of Abdur Rahim are cited in praise of Rama, Krishna, Vishnu, Shankar, Hanuman, the purity of the river Ganga, and he points out:

> This kind of poetry can only be said by someone who was greatly influenced by the Bhakti Movement *but was Abdur Rahim Khan-i-Khanan actually influenced by it?* [Emphasis added.][41]

Sabahuddin Abdur Rahman proceeds to point out historical reasons why this could not be so and these merit being quoted in full:

> The *Maathir-i-Rahimi* is a very comprehensive description of his life. There is no reference in this that he was a Krishna or Ram devotee. Its writer, in fact, says that the KhanKhanan was always concerned about advancing his Islamic beliefs … He would spend the whole nights in prayers and would perform his duties according to the Sunnah. He did not, in fact, get influenced by Akbar's *Din-i-Ilahi*

despite the great honour Akbar gave to him and there is never any reference that he was one of the *murids* of the Din-i-Illahi.

This logic is then strengthened by the argument that:

> ... if Sheikh Ahmad Sirhindi had even an inkling that he had moved away from Islam and believed in other faiths he would never have addressed him as 'My Makhdoom (My lord)' or instructed him on the nuances of the Sufi tradition. Sheikh Ahmad Sirhindi had high hopes of Abdur Rahim that in Jahangir's reign he would render all manner of assistance to the true faith.

Finally, the *Bazm-i-Taimuri* argues:

> Abdur Rahim's court had in it a large collection of ulema and because of them the Islamic spirit was well established in his durbar. Along with their names, Abul Baqi Nihavandi had prefixed Maulana and Mullah; it follows from this that there was no possibility of poets of other beliefs ... Many of the Persian poets associated with him were also distinguished from the religious angle. Naziri left Akbar's court because he found in it the spirit of infidels instead of an Islamic atmosphere. Naziri thus targeted Faizi and Abul Fazl and praised Murad because the Prince was not influenced by the Din-i-Ilahi. He [Naziri] remained an ardent admirer of the KhanKhanan till the very last days of his life. Had he even a remote doubt about the KhanKhanan he would not have praised him in his way.

These historical arguments are then buttressed by a literary and aesthetic one:

> It should also be understood that KhanKhanan's poetic aesthetic was of a very high order. He composed Persian poetry in the presence of Naziri, Shakebi and Urfi and maintained his own amongst them. If you compare his Persian poetry with other verses such as in the *Nagar Shobha* and the *Barvai Nayika Bhed* then an obvious, very huge contradiction is visible in his poetic approach and is a

> matter of surprise. Therefore the thought arises whether it can be another Hindi poet by name Rahiman, who was a Krishna and Ram Bkakht. His poetry may have got mixed up with the Hindi poetry of KhanKhanan's. This matter certainly requires research.

He, however, goes on to say:

> It is a fact that KhanKhanan's Hindi poetry and patronage of its literature is[sic] famous in its history in the same way as in the *Maathir-i-Rahimi* his position in Persian literature is celebrated.

Doubts on the provenance of verses attributed to Abdur Rahim are to be seen in the context of similar and real problems with respect to other medieval poets too. However, the numerous oral and written traditions which attribute these verses to Abdur Rahim, just in terms of their sheer volume, are a powerful argument to establish their provenance. In fact, Sabahuddin Abdur Rahman does not deny that Abdur Rahim composed poetry in Hindi. Indeed, his ability to craft poetry of a high order is fully accepted. What is questioned is the fact that a staunch Muslim like him could have written poetry so obviously suffused with the spirit of bhakti. The second part of this denial is that, given his accomplished Persian aesthetic, the Khan-i-Khanan could not have composed the sensuous and often explicitly erotic verses in the *Barvai Nayika Bhed* or the *Nagar Shobha*.

If we follow this line of thinking and exclude works with a bhakti flavour, the list would cover much of his scattered barvai and other verses, the *Madanashtak*, and his Sanskrit verses (apart from the early astrological work, the *Kheta Koutukam*). Excluding sensuous and erotic verses would mean excluding the *Barvai Nayika Bhed* and the *Nagar Shobha* among others. Excluding both categories would leave us with only his dohas, but not all the dohas are purely moral or ethical in nature: some are, but others are straightforwardly bhakti-inspired and others use a Hindu religious fable or parable to illustrate a moral or secular theme. Excluding those with a strongly bhakti flavour or based entirely on Hindu mythological or religious fables would reduce the number of dohas that can be attributed to Abdur Rahim very substantially. What would be left of Abdur Rahim would be a minor poet of parables, everyday morality and the virtues of an ethical life – far from the dashing courtier, the exuberant and generous patron and the accomplished litterateur, politician and general we know.

With this reading we come full circle and encounter in their full maturity two divergent and opposing views on the heritage of Abdur Rahim. In both trajectories we see the influence of forces far removed from Mughal history and, in fact, related entirely to inter-community relations and contestations in the nineteenth and twentieth centuries. In one of these trajectories we see a determined effort to recover Abdur Rahim's Hindi literary heritage and simultaneously aggregate that heritage to a Hindu identity. In the other, we encounter a silence, then some ambiguity, and finally a rejection of a significant part of that literary heritage, largely because it was felt this could not be reconciled with his Muslim identity.

Neither set of protagonists in this divide appears willing to explore the somewhat obvious possibility that adherence to literary convention in itself does not amount to either devotion or apostasy. Moreover, neither fully sees the requirement of a public personality to consciously acquire different layers as the best means to navigate specific challenges. Abdur Rahim had, from his early childhood, to confront a court which retained memories of his father not just as a rebel but also one who was ambitious and ruthless. His formative years coincided with the emperor's eclectic and liberal approach, which set the dominant trend of the court but created in its wake numerous enemies bitterly opposed to such thinking. In his years of maturity and greatest power, the question of the succession emerged as a factor to be considered and calibrated at all times; and in this too there was no saying when the religious element could come to the forefront.

Ensuring that neither side in each of these divides, present or future, saw him as a permanent feature of the other camp, while simultaneously retaining the emperor's favour, constituted the key to survival and promotion. To aggregate the complexities of the Mughal court in the sixteenth and seventeenth centuries with the politics of the twentieth erases the very real efforts Abdur Rahim made to be a man of different parts. That his life ended tragically, as he finally failed to protect himself and his family, has less to do with his accomplishments or the rich texture of his life, than with the unforgiving nature of the world he lived in.

If the Hindi–Urdu controversy was the terrain of the contest between different readings of past history and future nationhood, by the third and fourth decades of the twentieth century, more than language had parted ways. Revisiting this contest decades later, one can only regret that the lack of convergence between these epistemic communities caused the rich contours of Abdur Rahim's life to suffer some neglect as his afterlife overshadows his life story.

EPILOGUE

SUBSEQUENT TO Abdur Rahim's death in 1627, we can follow the threads of his family for another six to seven decades, after which the record quietly stops. The last direct trace of the family was uncovered in the early twentieth century and so, in a sense, it serves as a useful point to end this story that began with Bairam Khan joining Emperor Babur in Kabul.

From the decimation wrought on Abdur Rahim's family during the civil war and succession strife of 1622–26, the sole survivor was Shah Nawaz Khan's son, Minuchihr, who as we saw had defected to the imperial forces during Prince Khurram's revolt. He and his son Mohammad Munim were the remnants of Bairam Khan's family and they bring its story up to Aurangzeb's reign. Both had respectable, if unspectacular, careers largely in the Deccan: Mohammad Munim was governor of the fort of Ahmednagar early in Auranzgeb's reign; his father too appears to have spent long years in the Deccan.

The connection with Mewat, however, remained and this was to be unearthed by the most prominent of Abdur Rahim's early biographers. Munshi Devi Prasad found a document from Aurangzeb's reign pertaining to a property dispute in Alwar over a structure called the 'tirpolio', which in the late nineteenth and early twentieth centuries was still known as the Khan-i-Khanan's tirpolio. This document was executed by an agent of Nabib-ul-Nisa Begum, described as the owner of Khan-i-Khanan's estate and who, Devi Prasad speculated, was the daughter of Mohammad Munim. She would certainly have had a claim over some of the Khan-i-Khanan's properties in Mewat and, in particular, over the tirpolio.[1] Alwar's tirpolio or other structures associated with Abdur Rahim are hard to trace and identify now. His association with Mewat was, in any case, through his mother and his long years in the Deccan would have weakened these ties.

In central India, and more particularly in Burhanpur, you do not have to be an archaeologist or even a historian to encounter Abdur Rahim. Burhanpur is today a newly established district headquarters on the Madhya Pradesh–Maharashtra border. The bustling mofussil town, with its dusty roads, garbage dumps and shabby administrative buildings, bears little resemblance to the erstwhile viceregal headquarters of Mughal India, the last bastion of Mughal Hindustan before the then still unconquered Deccan. Yet numerous buildings attributable to Abdur Rahim continue to dot the townscape. Most prominent in these is the mausoleum of his eldest and most able son, Shah Nawaz Khan, on the banks of the river Utaoli on the outskirts of the town. The design of this handsome structure unifies elements of Gujarati, Tughlaq, Lodi and Bijapur styles (Plate VII). Its dome rises about 18 metres from the ground and under it, on a raised platform, is the grave of Shah Nawaz Khan. Next to it is a smaller grave, that of Prince Jahan Afroz, Shah Nawaz Khan's grandson, who died as an infant in 1621 in Burhanpur. He was born to Shah Nawaz's daughter, who was married to Shah Jahan in August 1617. What better place to bury the infant than by his grandfather's side?[2]

Near Shah Nawaz's magnificent tomb, on the northern side, one of two tombs remain, the other having been washed away by the river. Whose tombs they were is not known. It is not unlikely that Rahmandad, Abdur Rahim's third son, who died soon after Shah Nawaz, may have been buried here. On the eastern side is a damaged but once splendid tomb, again unidentified. Locally it is referred to as Bibi ka Maqbara or 'Tomb of a Lady', and is said to be of a relative of Shah Nawaz Khan. Given the length of time Abdur Rahim and his family spent in Burhanpur and the Deccan, there are numerous theories regarding her identity. One of the possibilities, almost certainly, is Abdur Rahim's own mother, the Mewati princess, who died in Burhanpur in 1617.[3]

For those looking for it, Abdur Rahim's presence can be found all over the town. He is credited with establishing an outstanding water supply system for Burhanpur, not from rivers but from mountain springs in the nearby hills. Subterranean wells in the suburbs of the city were linked by conduits, in turn leading to masonry reservoirs called *Mul Bhandar*, *Subha Bhandar* and *Chintaharan.* Underground tunnels from the reservoirs, some at a depth of about 30 metres, led the water to a large reservoir at Lal Bagh, about 4 kilometres from the city. The reservoir itself is called Jali Karnaj and, from this point, a pipeline, about a kilometre and half in length, supplied water to residential buildings. The entire arrangement worked with gravity flow. The waterworks are described as having functioned successfully for two-and-a-half centuries and a description in the 1950s has the author relying on living memory to establish its superiority over the municipal water supply of the British administration.[4]

Equally impressive are the remains of a public bath or *hamam* near the Akbari Serai. The bath has a number of chambers whose domed ceilings were once covered with fresco paintings. An inscription, found at the hamam and now preserved in a museum at Nagpur, records that it was constructed in 1607–08 on the orders of Abdur Rahim Khan-i-Khanan and the construction was supervised by Muhammad Ali Kark.[5]

The Jama Masjid in Burhanpur, easily the city's most spectacular medieval monument, was built by the last independent ruler of Khandesh, Raja Ali Khan, and is a source of pride to its custodians as much for its architectural beauty as for a handsome inscription in both Sanskrit and Arabic, recording the details of its construction. Abdur Rahim is credited with having ordered expensive repairs to the mosque, which were completed in 1615–16, as also giving it a secure water supply by means of an underground canal.

Most appropriate to Abdur Rahim's memory, however, is a smaller mosque in one of the labyrinthine streets of Burhanpur's old city. It is now an entirely modern structure with no trace remaining of its medieval origins, except for a notice prominently and proudly inscribed on the gate: Masjid Nawab Abdur Rahim Khan Burhanpur (See Plate VIII).

Elsewhere too, Abdur Rahim's name resonates across time and often in the most unexpected of ways. The intellectual and politician, Maulana Abul Kalam Azad, one of the great leaders of the Indian freedom movement, was arrested in 1942 and sent to the Ahmednagar fort – then a jail. A Persian scholar of repute, he was familiar with the major medieval histories and therefore was well informed about Ahmednagar's history and, in particular, the epic history of Chand Bibi and Abdur Rahim. His jail memoirs are a juxtaposition of Mughal history and contemporary events interspersed with poetry from the sixteenth and seventeenth centuries. During his imprisonment, he would often try and imagine life in the fort: the generalship of Abdur Rahim, his love of poetry and music, the determination of Chand Bibi, and so on. He named the jailor in charge 'Cheetah Khan' after one of Chand Bibi's commanders who had put up a fierce resistance to the Mughal army. What happened to the 35-metre-wide moat around the fort, which Abul Fazl had described as constituting the main defence against the Mughals, he wondered.[6]

Incarcerated in a sixteenth-century Nizam Shahi fort famous for its defence by its regent princess against the Mughals, Abul Kalam saw himself as a link in the wider timeline of history:

Turn from time to time the pages of past history
If you seek to reopen the wounds of damages sustained

> I thought if this place has been selected for our imprisonment; it is appropriate beyond doubt. The inebriated ones like us serve only such a ruin:
>
> *For malice of the world there is no better place.*[7]

In Delhi, near his wife's magnificent mausoleum (Plate IX), Abdur Rahim had two more tombs built. We cannot say whether he saw them completed; possibly these were finally finished only after his own death. They may well have been within the original grounds of Mah Banu's tomb but subsequent constructions in the area and the expansion of the Nizamuddin residential area have obliterated the original layout and design of the gardens and grounds. One of these two still survives. This structure with an exquisite blue dome is close to Humayun's tomb and is now known, appropriately enough, as the 'Nila Gumbad'. Its proportions and overall aesthetics enable it to hold its own even in a part of Delhi that has some of the best surviving examples of Mughal architecture. The Nila Gumbad, although the grave has disappeared, may be the tomb, many experts say, of the faithful Mian Fahim; he was buried, appropriately enough, close to his master. Squeezed between the demands of a growing metropolis and the adjoining Nizamuddin railway station, access to Fahim's tomb[8] was, till recently, difficult. The restoration of the entire Nizamuddin area currently under way may soon remedy that and Fahim's tomb will be visible again as a small jewel in the Mughal graveyard.

The second tomb has a sadder ending. It used to house the grave of Dorab Khan, Abdur Rahim's second son, who was executed on Jahangir's orders. The monument was known locally as the 'Chamariwala Gumbad'. A description from the late 1920s says:

> The tomb stands on an elevated piece of ground and is built of stone. It is an irregular octagon in plan, the broad sides containing lofty arches, each provided with a doorway opening into the central chamber. On each of the narrow sides, there is a double storied

> octagonal room furnished with arched openings. The central apartment was originally covered by a dome, but this has now fallen filling the building with its debris. It was originally surrounded by a walled enclosure of which only the southern wall now remains.[9]

Post-independence, the condition of the structure deteriorated even further. The demand for residential housing in Nizamuddin was increasing as the population of Delhi swelled dramatically with the influx of a large number of partition refugees. An application was moved to the government by the Nizamuddin Extension Colony Association that the structure be demolished:

> This old dilapidated structure which probably has little historical background has been allowed to fall into ruins since a very long time, the roof has completely collapsed, a considerable part of the masonry has fallen off and the stone walls are also giving way gradually. The damage of the falling stones hitting the residents of the adjacent houses, which have indeed been built very close to this structure are very great. The structure is infested with snakes and other reptiles ...
>
> Besides, the very existence of this old fossilized and dilapidated structure right amidst in the otherwise neat and clean colony ... not only presents a ghostly sight both to the residents and visitors alike, but it is also hardly a matter of pride to the archeological department ...

The application was then referred to the Archeological Survey of India for an expert opinion and it minuted:

> ASI is of the view that as the central dome has already collapsed, the building is not so very ideal but even the lofty arches with inscriptional medallions in plaster on the spandrels are interesting features. Its instantaneous collapse cannot be advised under the circumstances and instead the place should, however, be well kept and all debris removed by those responsible for building of colony amidst the group of monuments. If properly kept and fenced it should serve as a first rate 'Retreat' or Rendezvous for the locality.[10]

While the removal of the tomb was not recommended, this limited support for retention of the structure did not carry enough weight. It was, in any case, not a protected monument, so not directly within the ASI's mandate. The demands of the local residents, on the other hand, must have been loud and forceful enough to be heard and the disappearance of one tomb from the multitude in Nizamuddin was not seen as of any great significance.

There is no better way to end this story of two lives in Mughal India than to bring it even closer to our age. We encounter Bairam Khan in the very last days of colonial India and in the final months before the country's partition, in a Gajanan Jagirdar film of 1946.[11] This compresses within it the story of Bairam's loyalty to Babur and Humayun; his refusal to serve Sher Shah despite many entreaties from the Afghan; Akbar's upbringing and the instruction the boy emperor received from the regent on the rules of government. There is also time for a detailed love story, for in the film the relationship between Princess Salima Sultan Begum and Bairam Khan is shown as one of true and everlasting love. Salima Sultan is also, in the film, the mother of Bairam's son Abdur Rahim. Notwithstanding this considerable latitude with history, the dominant narrative of the film is that his regency was the precursor of the Akbari dispensation of interfaith harmony in India. The clear message is that this is the path the nation must follow after independence.

Early in the film, Bairam Khan, then an important noble in Babur's court, is shown politely refusing the emperor's gift of the jagir of Malwa after the conquest of Hindustan. He advises the emperor that the nascent sultanate needed a strong and united centre of authority, which would be eroded if Hindustan were divided into small fiefdoms. If a Mughal noble were to descend from the stirrup of the horse to the throne of jagirs, (this) would weaken the sultanate. 'Different jagirs would split Hindustan into small parts when it has instead to be strung into a strong necklace.' This earned Bairam the animosity of many powerful nobles eager for the prizes of victory. Devotion to the emperor and loyalty to the empire is Bairam's defining characteristic in the film, and he maintains this in the face of the most overwhelming odds.

The Rajputs in the film are Bairam's friends during his years of adversity. Mitter Sen, a Rajput chief, gives him refuge during his flight from Sher Shah, risking his life and the destruction of his kingdom. Mitter Sen's certain defeat and death at the hands of Sher Shah's generals is staved off only when Bairam overrides his host with the argument that 'Hospitality does not give you the right to play with the blood of Prithviraj Chauhan's descendants'. The reference here is to the last Rajput ruler of Delhi, whose defeat and death led to the establishment of the Delhi Sultanate from the early thirteenth century.

Mitter Sen appears periodically thereafter in the film as it takes Bairam's story further after the Mughal restoration. He sends gifts on the occasion of the infant Abdur Rahim's first birthday and again, when he is the cause of a rift between Bairam and Akbar's foster-mother, Maham Anga. Maham Anga objects to the dispatch of treasure to Mitter Sen, Bairam insists on it, and the boy emperor rules in favour of his guardian. Bairam is here teaching the emperor the importance of an alliance with the Rajputs, but his own time is running out. His enemies at court, led by Maham Anga, prevail and convince Akbar to move against Bairam, who leaves in disgust for the Haj. En route, the film shows different Rajput chieftains honouring him. Bairam rejects their advice that he march against his enemies in court, saying that they should instead husband their strength for Bairam's hopes of a united Hindustan of one voice, one spirit and one body. His enemies from the imperial court continue their pursuit and the ageing noble finally takes up arms against the boy emperor at Salima Sultan Begum's urging. She tells him that as ataliq it is now Bairam's responsibility to teach his ward another lesson in statesmanship: that of not listening to courtiers who mislead him and do not have the interests of the empire at heart.

Mitter Sen makes his final appearance in aid of an embattled Bairam Khan as he is under siege in the mountain fortress of another friendly Rajput king. Mitter Sen's army and Bairam's leadership bring the rebel forces to the verge of victory. But Bairam draws back from a final victory – distraught at the loss of life of those who were once his followers in the emperor's service but also because the aim of his rebellion was not to defeat the emperor, but to instruct him. The climax is Bairam's appearance in court where he exposes his enemies as being the enemies of the empire. He then, despite Akbar's entreaties, departs for the Haj, arguing that his final lesson as ataliq has also been rendered as Akbar understands the importance of wise courtiers.

History weighed heavily on the film, made as it was amidst a growing Hindu–Muslim gulf and as fears of a bloody and violent partition loomed ahead. Clearly, as India's independence dawned, the film sought inspiration from an earlier period of Indian history which could yet provide guidance to the new India. That the new state would need wise leaders is the obvious subtext, but the Muslim Bairam's friendship with the Hindu Mitter Sen is also a dominant theme.

We come across another Bairam Khan some sixty years later in the Mumbai production *Jodha Akbar* – a historical that also did well at the box office.[12] In this, Bairam is the faithful and loyal advisor and guardian to a young emperor, but he is also single-minded and ruthless. The empire, he believes, can only be secured with strength and by not tolerating any opposition. At the battlefield in Panipat, a wounded Hemu is brought before Akbar, and Bairam instructs his ward to kill him in order to send this message across clearly. Akbar is reluctant to kill a wounded enemy, at which Bairam, in exasperation beheads the hapless Hemu himself and announces Akbar's victory and status as a great Ghazi. Later, in campaigns against the Rajput kingdoms, a similar situation arises when Bairam advises Akbar to kill a defeated Rajput prince so that the other Rajput kingdoms may be intimidated enough to submit to the Mughals. Akbar's differences with Bairam Khan are traced to this: Akbar is keen on treating Rajputs with respect and enter into an alliance with them. Bairam thinks otherwise. This time around, a more mature Akbar prevails and Bairam is prevented from killing the Rajput prince; Akbar goes on to forge the Rajput alliance.

There are multiple readings and interpretations possible in the Bairam of 1946 and of 2008, but the story continues in other ways too.

Sukumar Ray, a student of the great historian Jadunath Sarkar, was an emerging young academic in Calcutta in the 1940s. His book, *Humayun in Persia*, was published in 1948 by the Asiatic Society of Bengal and very well received. In his introduction to it, Sir Jadunath Sarkar wrote that Sukumar Ray had embarked on a study of Bairam Khan and his son Abdur Rahim, and *Humayun in Persia* was the necessary first part of this. By the mid-1950s, the book on Bairam Khan was ready and in press. However, a domestic tragedy intervened and the book, as also the planned work on Abdur Rahim, was abandoned.

Abandoned but not forgotten. An old associate of Sukumar Ray, now in Karachi, remembered the project and mentioned it to a British amateur historian of Pakistani origin, M.H.A Beg. Beg travelled to India, searched out Sukumar Ray's widow in Calcutta and found his handwritten manuscript. The book was finally published in 1992 by the Institute of Central and West Asian Studies of the University of Karachi.

Even while this minor odyssey was in progress, Beg found a copy of Munshi Devi Prasad's Urdu *Khankhanan Nama*, published in 1898. This was the very same copy that Ajmal Khan, the famous hakim of Delhi, had picked up during a visit to Jodhpur. From his library, it travelled safely to Lahore during the partition of India. M.H.A. Beg obtained the book from Hakim Ajmal Khan's family and got it reprinted in Karachi in 1990. Serendipitously, a minister in the government of Turkmenistan chanced upon a copy and, keen to popularize the life of Bairam Khan, he arranged for it to be translated into Turkmen and published in Ashgabat, Turkmenistan, in 1998, with a forward by no less a personage than the then president of Turkmenistan. Turkmenistan had by then become an independent nation following the break-up of the Soviet Union. Independence was accompanied by a revisiting of its pre-Soviet and pre-Tsarist past for national icons to buttress a new identity. The logic of nation building in this newly created country entailed a mining of its older tribal history for suitable figures which could then be woven into the narrative of the modern state. The president of Turkmenistan spoke of his desire to see that:

> ... work is done to restore the old and proud history of Turkmenistan and offer it fully to the people. (The President) created the State Commission on Research on the History of Turkmenistan and himself headed the Commission. On (his) instructions, the work on collection, study and publishing of sources about the history of the Turkmens is underway. Several research trips were made to many countries to collect and bring back valuable historical sources to Turkmenistan. The books about Bairam Khan and his son Abdur Rahim were among the historical sources brought from India.[13]

With Turkmenistan's identification of Bairam Khan as a national hero, he has become immediately recognizable and popular in the new nation. A walk around the city centre of the capital, Ashgabat, reveals a statue of Bairam Khan, Khan-i-Khanan. In the 1990s, his name was invoked through objects as varied as strains of cotton to a motorized infantry division of the Turkmen army. His memory was also invoked to inspire Turkmen athletes going to the 2004 Olympic Games in Greece and the new nation's stamps and coins depicted Bairam Khan (see Plate XI top) often with the Turkmen president sharing space with the nobleman.[14]

This is not to say that Bairam Khan's new role as a modern Turkmen icon in the post-Soviet era was not contested. The Turkmen writer and journalist Abdur Rahim Esenov, who wrote a novel on the life of Bairam Khan, was taken into custody in early 2004. He was accused of 'committing a number of crimes, including smuggling copies of his novel *The Crowned Wanderer* into the country and publishing it abroad without official permission. The charges included inciting national and religious hatred by his publication which leads to destabilization of the situation in the country'. In his defence the author stated that 'a novel describing events which took place in the 16th century cannot contain any state secrets ... and the allegation of inciting national and religious hatred is absurd'. The authorities used 'quotes from the characters of the novel regarding events which took place 500 years ago as grounds for their accusations'.

The novel, set during the time of the Mughal Empire, portrays Bairam Khan as a great Turkmen poet, philosopher and general who saved the empire from disintegration. It was written possibly about a decade earlier, but not published because in February 1997 President Saparmurat Niyazov of Turkmenistan had publicly denounced the author for 'historical errors'. Esenov refused to change his manuscript and his detention followed the publication of the book in Russia. The principal charge against the book was that it portrayed Bairam Khan as a Shia rather than a Sunni Muslim. Shortly after Esenov's detention in March 2003, the president again denounced the author:

> The President justified the requirement for vigilance with the example of the illegal distribution in the country of the historical novel by the Turkmen writer Abdur Rahim Esenov. '*The Crowned Wanderer*' ... according to the President contains an incorrect interpretation of historical facts and could be used by those who are interested in provoking inter-tribal discord in the country, weakening the Turkmen state and breaking its friendly relations with the neighbours.[15]

The resurrection of Bairam Khan in Turkmenistan demonstrates yet again the double-edged nature of history, and how different aspects of the same life can be seen to unite a fledgling nation and also weaken it. Abdur Rahim Esenov was thus to say: 'They accused me of stirring up animosity. You know I write about the 16th century! I write about tribes that were fighting against each other in the 16th century. And they take all of that and they project it onto the present day.'[16] This strident dismissal of those who project the present into the past or the past into the future is hardly rare. But the past does invariably intrude into the present and that is what makes it so interesting.

Abdur Rahim's eminence as the sage statesman of Hindi literature only grew as the national movement progressed. Unlike the state-driven process that made his father Bairam Khan an icon in Turkmenistan, Abdur Rahim's installation was the outcome of a more spontaneous literary endeavour combined with strong public advocacy for Hindi as the national language of India. His dohas came to be viewed as indisputable evidence of his 'Indianness' and the capacity to accommodate and be syncretic. Akbar's court became also a road map for India's future. A large mural adorns the walls of India's Parliament House illustrating a scene from Akbar's court where Todar Mal, Tansen, Abul Fazl, Faizi and Abdur Rahim loom large while Emperor Akbar is depicted in the foreground (see Plate X).[17]

Abdur Rahim's verse covers a vast canvas – from decorative and sensuous court poetry to devotional verse, but it is because of his moral aphorisms which draw on the simple lessons of everyday life that Abdur Rahim as Rahim or Rahiman is so embedded in popular consciousness today. His sensuous poetry, despite its beauty and complex sociology, is now less well known. It is his mastery at conveying a moral aphorism pithily through a doha, and his frequent use of a pronouncedly Hindu devotional idiom that simultaneously elevated and established him as a harbinger of Hindu–Muslim unity for a nation seeking to define and consolidate itself while first combating foreign rule and then building a new, although divided, India. This is the image of Abdur Rahim that has endured. Rahim the sage, the Mughal statesman, the ethical exemplar exists in the popular imagination, but most resonant of all is Rahim, the national symbol of religious and secular unity.

In the process, Abdur Rahim has transcended the metaphorical and real meanings of his own poetry; his name itself constitutes the message. An advertisement carried some years ago in the highbrow, left-of-centre Delhi magazine, *Seminar*, prominently used Abdur Rahim's name and the opening words of a doha, *Rahiman pani rakhiye* (Plate XI, middle).[18] The advertisement, placed by the government of Madhya Pradesh, associates Abdur Rahim with ecologically sound practices, in particular water conservation, which sums up the sense of 'pani rakhiye' in this graphic. The foreground shows farmers irrigating their fields along with a large earthmoving machine. The advertisement in the May 2001 issue coincided with a major popular agitation in central and western India against the construction of the Narmada dam.

But all this, or indeed the need for water conservation, has little to do with the original doha, which reads:

Rahiman pani rakhiye, bin paani sab sun
Pani haye na ubrai, moti manush chun.

The doha is based on a play of words and meanings. The most commonplace meaning of 'pani' is water – but it also means lustre, fervour or prestige. And so, a loose translation would be:

Always keep water, for without it nothing exists,
Without water there is little use of pearls, men and flour.

Thus, a man without honour (lit. pani), a pearl without shine (lit. pani) are as useless as flour without water (lit. pani), since you cannot make dough without water. The association of the most commonplace meaning of pani, i.e., water, with Rahim is enough to marshal him into the worthy cause of water conservation and rural development. Abdur Rahim thus becomes a political symbol of national integration and unity.

As in the case of Bairam Khan, but even more so in Abdur Rahim's, there is a risk that the political statement may supersede and even diminish the texture of the life story, with its many facets, tensions and contradictions, which allow us to navigate the distance separating us from them. For it is their ambitions, accomplishments and flaws, interfacing with difficult choices, rightly or wrongly made, that give us the point of entry to use our own present to understand their long-past lives. And in doing so, we understand our own times better.

NOTES

1. BAIRAM

1 Plate I. Bairam Khan is murdered by an Afghan at Patan. Painting by Tulsi and Triyya, Victoria and Albert Museum, IS.2:5-1896. The Sahasraling Talav is so named apparently because of the thousand temples, dedicated to Lord Siva, once ringing the lake. The construction of the lake is credited to the Solanki ruler Siddhraj Jaysimha (1093–1143). The *Imperial Gazetteer of India* describes the condition of the lake in the early twentieth century thus: 'But of this nothing now remains but a large field with the ruins of a Muhammadan building in the centre, constructed on the site of a temple. Bairam, the minister of Humayun and Akbar was assassinated on the bank of this lake in 1561, while on his way to Mecca'. *Imperial Gazetteer of India* (1908), Vol. XX, p. 24.

2 Sukumar Ray, *Bairam Khan,* edited by M.H.A. Beg, Karachi: Institute of Central and West Asian Studies, 1992, p. 1 (henceforth Sukumar Ray, *Bairam Khan*).

3 V. Minorsky, 'The Middle East in Western Politics in the 13th, 14th and 15th Centuries', *Journal of the Royal Central Asian Society,* Vol. XXVII, October 1940, p. 440.

4 Sukumar Ray, *Bairam Khan,* p. 19.

5 Ibid., p. 8.

6 The quote is from the preface to Wheeler M. Thackston (ed.), *Baburnama,* New York: Oxford University Press, 1996, p. 23 (henceforth *Baburnama*).

7 Stephen P. Blake, 'Courtly Culture under Babur and the Early Mughals', *Journal of Asian History,* Vol. 20, 1986, p. 194.

8 V. Minorsky, 'Jahan Shah Qara Qoyunlu and His Poetry', *Bulletin of the School of Oriental and African Studies*, Vol. 16, No. 2, 1954, p. 273.

9 Abdul Qadir Ibn-i-Muluk Shah (known as Al Badaoni), *Muntakhabu-t-Tawarikh,* translated and edited by Sir Wolseley Haig, Vol. III, Delhi: Renaissance Publishing House,1986 reprint, pp. 266–67. Henceforth Badayuni, *Muntakhabu-t-Tawarikh*. That Bairam Khan wrote verses in Hindi is mentioned in the *Dhakhiratul Khawanin* of Sheikh Farid Bukhari, translated and edited by Ziauddin A. Desai, Delhi: Idara-i-Adbiyat, 1993, p. 14. (Henceforth, *Dhakhiratul Khawanin.*) No examples of these survive. Bairam Khan's extant poetry is in S. Hussamuddin Rashdi and Muhammad Sabir (eds), *Diwan of Bairam Khan,* Karachi: Institute of Central and West Asian Studies, 1971.

10 Sukumar Ray, *Bairam Khan,* p. 17.

11 Kishori Saran Lal, *Twilight of the Sultanate,* New Delhi: Munshiram Manoharlal Publishers Pvt. Ltd, 1980, p. 221.

12 Gulbadan Begum, *Humaynama,* translated and edited by Annettee S. Beveridge, London: Royal Asiatic Society, 1902, p. 105 (henceforth Gulbadan Begum, *Humaynama*).

13 Ishwari Prasad, *The Life and Times of Humayun,* Bombay: Orient Longmans, 1956, p. 23.

14 Ibid., p. 32.

15 Sukumar Ray, *Bairam Khan,* pp. 36–37.

16 A detailed account of the battle, the Mughal rout and what transpired thereafter in the Mughal camp is in Ishwari Prasad, *The Life and Times of Humayun*, pp. 125–97.

17 Sukumar Ray, *Bairam Khan,* p. 47, citing Abul Baqi Nihavandi's *Maathir-i-Rahimi.*

18 *Tarikh-i-Sher Shahi or Tuhfat-i-Akbar Shahi* of Abbas Khan Sarwani. *The History of India: As Told by Its Own Historians, The Posthumous Papers of the Late Sir H.M. Elliot,* edited by Sir John Dawson, Calcutta: Susil Gupta (India) Ltd, 1957, p. 101 (henceforth *Tarikh-i-Sher Shahi*).

19 Catherine B. Asher, *Architecture of Mughal India,* The New Cambridge History of India, Cambridge (UK): Cambridge University Press, 1992, p. 28.

20 *Tarikh-i-Sher Shahi,* p. 101.

21 Ibid. Lukhnor is also identified in Irfan Habib, *An Atlas of the Mughal Empire,* Delhi: Oxford University Press, 1982, Map 8A.

22 Nawwab Shamsam-ud-Daula Shah Nawaz Khan (translated by H. Beveridge, revised by Baini Prashad), *The Maathir-ul-Umra; Being*

Biographies of the Muhammadan and Hindu Officers of the Timurid Sovereigns of India from 1500 to about 1750 A D., Delhi: Low Price Publications, 1999 reprint 2 vols, Vol. I (henceforth *Maathir-ul-Umra*), p. 369. *The Akbarnama of Abul Fazl,* translated by H. Beveridge, 3 vols, Delhi: Low Price Publications, 1989 reprint, Vol. I, pp. 381–82 (henceforth *Akbarnama*).

23 Sukumar Ray, *Bairam Khan*, p. 58; *Tarikh-i-Sher Shahi,* p. 102.

24 Ishwari Prasad, *The Life and Times ...*, p. 159.

25 Gulbadan Begum, *Humaynama,* p. 155.

26 Sukumar Ray, *Bairam Khan*, p. 66.

27 Sukumar Ray, *Humayun in Persia*, Calcutta: Royal Asiatic Society of Bengal, 1948, pp. 2–3.

28 Riazul Islam, *A Calender of Documents on Indo-Persian Relations* (*1500-1750*), Karachi: Institute of Central and West Asian Studies, 1979, p. 71.

29 Sukumar Ray, *Humayun in Persia*, p. 58.

30 The very detailed instructions the Shah sent to the governors of different provinces in Humayun's route have survived and stand out for the extent to which care was taken to impress the Mughal emperor in exile. Riazul Islam, *A Calender of Documents ...*, pp. 73–78.

31 Plate II. Humayun being received by Shah Tahmasp, photo by Khosrow Bozorgi, Courtesy: The Aga Khan Documentation Center at MIT, Massachusetts, USA See also Sukumar Ray, Humayun in Persia, p. 25; S. Hussamuddin Rashdi and Muhammad Sabir (eds), *Diwan of Bairam Khan*, p. 6.

32 Stephen F. Dale, *The Garden of the Eight Paradises. Babur and the Culture of Empire in Central Asia, Afghanistan and India (1483-1530),* Boston: Leiden, 2004, p. 460 (henceforth Dale, *The Garden of the Eight Paradises*).

33 Mohammad Kasim Ferishta, *History of the Rise of Mahomedan Power in India,* translated by John Briggs, in 4 vols (bound in two). Delhi: Low Price Publications, 1997 reprint, Vol. II, p. 95, (henceforth Ferishta, *History of the Rise of Mahomedan Power in India*).

34 Sukumar Ray, *Humayun in Persia,* p. 21; S. Hussamuddin Rashdi and Muhammad Sabir (eds), *Diwan of Bairam Khan*, p. 6.

35 Ferishta, *History of the Rise of Mahomedan Power in India,* Vol. II, p. 110.

36 Ishwari Prasad, *The Life and Times ...*, p. 231.

37 Sukumar Ray, *Humayun in Persia*, p. 354.

38 Riazul Islam, *Indo-Persian Relations: A study of the political and diplomatic relations between the Mughal Empire and Iran,* Tehran: Iranian Cultural Foundation, 1970, p. 175.

39 Sukumar Ray, *Bairam Khan*, p. 81.

40 Sukumar Ray, *Humayun in Persia,* p. 53.

41 The references to the seizure of the fortress from the Persian army are from Ray, *Humayaun in Persia,* pp. 54–55. See also Sukumar Ray, *Bairam Khan,* pp. 90–93.

42 These suggestions are made by Sukumar Ray, *Bairam Khan*, pp. 93–95.

43 S. Hussamuddin Rashdi and Muhammad Sabir (eds), *Diwan of Bairam Khan*, p. 10.

44 *Maathir-ul-Umra,* Vol. I, p. 376. Bairam's reply is also translated by Hadi Hasan, *A Golden Treasury of Persian Poetry,* Delhi: Indian Council of Cultural Relations, 1972, p. 336. Abul Baqi Nihavandi is said to have included in his *Maathir-i-Rahimi* 365 Persian and fifty-five Turkish verses. 'A larger selection of verses (613 Persian and 346 Turkish) which formed the basis of Dennison Ross's edition of the Diwan was made earlier (i.e., before Nihavandi's selection for the *Maathir-i-Rahimi*) in 1605 at Jalnapur in Berar for the Library of Mirza Abdur Rahim KhanKhanan'. S. Hussamuddin Rashdi and Muhammad Sabir (eds), *Diwan of Bairam Khan*, pp. 17–18.

45 Ibid., p. 17. For a description of Bairam purchasing a poem and passing it off as his own see pp. 55–56.

46 Badayuni, *Muntakhabu-t-Tawarikh,* Vol. II, p. 2.

47 Ibid., pp. 2–3; *Akbarnama,* Vol. I, p. 611.

48 *Akbarnama*, Vol. I, p. 614. The meaning of the verse is obscure but possibly refers to the crescent moon. H. Beveridge, the translator and editor of the *Akbarnama* explains: 'The second line of the couplet is obscure but possibly *hilal* has the meaning of the young moon, a spear point and also an arrow.' Badayuni cites the same couplet in Vol. I, p. 622 of his work. His translator and editor George S.A. Ranking has translated the second line as 'Thy meteor with the aid of the crescent moon has erased the form of the Pleiades'.

49 Badayuni, *Muntakhabu-t-Tawarikh*, Vol. III, p. 267.

50 Ibid., Vol. II, p. 43.

51 Sukumar Ray, *Bairam Khan*, p. 102.

52 Badayuni, *Muntakhabu-t-Tawarikh,* Vol. I, p. 588.

53 Iqtidar Alam Khan, *The Political Biography of a Mughal Noble: Munim Khan Khan-i-Khanan*, Delhi: Munshiram Manoharlal, 1973, p. 5.

54 Ibid., p. 20.

55 *The Baburnama*, p. 388.

56 Ibid., 353.

57 Badayuni, *Muntakhabu-t-Tawarikh*, Vol. I, p. 447.

58 Abul Fazl, *The History of Akbar*, Vol. II, edited and translated by Wheeler M. Thackston, Harvard: Murty Classical Library of India, 2016, p. 443.

59 Sukumar Ray, *Bairam Khan*, p. 117.

60 *Akbarnama*, Vol. II, p. 28.

61 Plate III, 'The arrest of Shah Abul Maali', The Art Institute of Chicago, E 10879.

62 'Akbar Learning to Shoot', by Govardhan, British Library, Record No. 20080. This has been used on the front cover.

63 This detail and that he conveyed news of Akbar's birth to Humayun are in Gulbadan Begum, *Humaynama*, pp. 154, 158.

64 The available evidence is reviewed in detail in Sukumar Ray, 'Execution of Tardi Beg Khan', *Indian History Congress Proceedings, 1951*, pp. 183–89.

65 Iqtidar Alam Khan, *The Political Biography of a Mughal Noble*, pp. 48–49.

66 Sukumar Ray, 'Execution of Tardi Beg Khan', *Indian History Congress Proceedings*, 1951, p. 188.

67 S.K. Banarjea, 'Tardi Beg Turkistani', *India History Congress Proceedings, 1945*, pp. 335–36.

68 Sukumar Ray, 'Execution of Tardi Beg Khan', *Indian History Congress Proceedings*, 1951, p. 184.

69 Quoted in Sukumar Ray, *Bairam Khan*, p. 144.

70 Douglas Streusland, *The Formation of the Mughal Empire*, Delhi: Oxford University Press, 1989, p. 53.

71 Iqtidar Alam Khan, 'The Mughal Court Politics during Bairam Khan's Regency', in K.A. Nizami (ed.), *Medieval India: A Miscellany*, Bombay: Asia Publishing House, 1969, Vol. I, p. 33.

72 *Akbarnama*, Vol. II. pp. 91–92.

73 Ibid., pp. 98–99.

74 Gulbadan Begum, *Humaynama*, pp. 278–79. We will encounter Muhammad Husain Azad and his immensely popular *Darbar-e-Akbarī* in detail later in Chapter 6.

75 H. Beveridge, 'Salima Sultan Begum', *Journal of the Asiatic Society of Bengal,* Vol. II, No 10, December 1906, pp. 509–10.
76 Iqtidar Alam Khan, 'The Mughal Court Politics during Bairam Khan's Regency', p. 33.
77 Ferishta, *History of the Rise of Mahomedan Power in India,* Vol. II, p. 118.
78 Badayuni, *Muntakhabu-t-Tawarikh,* Vol. II, p. 20.
79 *Dhakhiratul Khawanin*, p. 9.
80 Ferishta, *History of the Rise of Mahomedan Power in India,* Vol. II, p. 118.
81 Iqtidar Alam Khan in 'The Mughal Court Politics during Bairam Khan's Regency', uses the term coup d'etat. See p. 33.
82 Ibid., 119.
83 Badayuni, *Muntakhabu-t-Tawarikh,* Vol II, p. 28.
84 Ibid, p. 24.
85 *Akbarnama*, Vol. II, p. 168.
86 Quoted in Iqtidar Alam Khan, 'The Mughal Court Politics during Bairam Khan's Regency', 1969, p. 34.
87 Kausar Chandpuri, *Muhammad Bairam Khan Turcoman*, Agra: Agra Akhbar Press, 1931, p. 42.
88 Badayuni, *Muntakhabu-t-Tawarikh,* Vol. II, p. 36.
89 *Akbarnama,* Vol. II, pp. 139–40.
90 Aziz Ahmed, *Studies in Islamic Culture in the Indian Environment*, New Delhi: Oxford University Press, first published in 1963, 1999 reprint, p. 176.
91 S. Hussamuddin Rashdi and Muhammad Sabir (eds), *Diwan of Bairam Khan*, p. 71, Turkish verses 323–25. I am indebted to Dr Mubarak Ali in Lahore for arranging their translation.
92 Sukumar Ray, *Bairam Khan*, p. 213; *Dhakhiratul Khawanin,* p. 13.
93 *Maathir-ul-Umra,* p. 374.
94 *Akbarnama,* Vol. II, p. 181.

2. THE YOUNG NOBLE

1 *The Akbarnama of Abul Fazl,* translated by H. Beveridge in 3 vols, Delhi: Low Price Publications, 1989 reprint, (henceforth *Akbarnama*), Vol II, p. 202.

2 Plate IV, Bairam Khan's widow and child are escorted to Ahmedabad, c. 1590-95. Artist Mukund. Victoria and Albert Museum, No IS.2.6-1896.

3 *Akbarnama,* Vol. II, pp. 203–04.

4 Plate V: Presentation of the young Abdur Rahim at Court. Victoria and Albert Museum, No IS.2.7-1896.

5 Wheeler M. Thackston (ed.), *Baburnama,* New York: Oxford University Press, 1996, p. 388 (henceforth *Baburnama*).

6 Cited in Shail Mayaram, 'Oral and Textual Discourses: An Enquiry into the Meo Mythic Tradition', Unpublished Report, Delhi: Centre for the Study of Developing Societies, 1995, p. 17.

7 Shail Mayaram, *Resisting Regimes: Myth, Memory and the Shaping of a Muslim Identity*, Delhi: Oxford University Press, 1997, p. 46 citing the 1878 *Gazetteer of Ulwar* (Alwar).

8 Ibid.

9 *Akbarnama*, Vol. II, p. 163.

10 Afzal Husain, *The Nobility under Akbar and Jahangir: A study of Family Groups*, New Delhi: Aligarh Muslim University/Manohar, 1999, p. 21.

11 Ray, Sukumar, *Bairam Khan*, edited by M.H.A. Beg, Karachi: Institute of Central and West Asian Studies, 1992 (henceforth Sukumar Ray, *Bairam Khan*), pp. 220–21, 246–47.

12 Afzal Husain, *The Nobility under Akbar and Jahangir*, p. 26.

13 Ibid.

14 *Akbarnama*, Vol. III, pp. 8–9.

15 Ibid., p. 17.

16 Ibid., pp. 68–69.

17 Balkrishna Akinchan, *Bhartiya Niti Kavya Parampara Aur Abdur Rahim*, Delhi: Alankar Prakashan, 1974, p. 243.

18 Jatindra Bimal Chaudhuri, *Contributions of Muslims to Sanskrit Learning, Vol. II, KhanKhanan Abdur Rahim and Contemporary Sanskrit Learning*, Calcutta: Prachyavani, 1954, p. 29. The translations are by J.B. Chaudhuri and are of verses 12, 34 and 82 at pp. 128, 29 and 141 respectively.

19 Munshi Devi Prasad, *Khankhanan Nama*, edited by Jaswant Singh, New Delhi: Pratibha Prathisthan, 2001, pp. 166–73.

20 Stuart Cary Welch, *India: Art and Culture 1300-1900*, New York: The Metropolitan Museum of Art, 1985, p. 153.

21 Balkrishna Akinchan, *Bhartiya Niti Kavya ...*, p. 243.
22 Mayashankar Yajnik, *Rahim Ratnavali*, Kashi: Sahitya Seva Sadan, 1957, p. 24. Three different versions of this small collection exist and were the subject of scholarly and literary analysis in the early twentieth century, the question being which one of the three was composed by Abdur Rahim. That the versions were found in different compilations and collections may well suggest that they had different authors, but there is otherwise little to disprove the possibility that all three were written by him. The translation of the Pathan woman's predicament (at the end of the paragraph) is by me.
23 Afzal Husain, *The Nobility under Akbar and Jahangir*, p. 97.
24 *Dhakhiratul Khawanin* of Sheikh Farid Bukhari, translated and edited by Ziauddin A. Desai, Delhi: Idara-i-Adbiyat, 1993, (henceforth, *Dhakhiratul Khawanin*) p. 22.
25 Nawwab Shamsam-ud-Daula Shah Nawaz Khan (translated H. Beveridge, revised Baini Prashad, *The Maathir-ul-Umra; Being Biographies of the Muhammadan and Hindu Officers of the Timurid Sovereigns of India from 1500 to about 1750 A.D.*, Delhi: Low Price Publications, 1999 reprint, 2 vols, Vol. I, p. 319 (henceforth *Maathir-ul-Umra*). (Another translation reads '... a river of milk which cannot pass away'.)
26 For details of her career, see also H. Beveridge, 'Salima Sultan Begum', *Journal of the Asiatic Society of Bengal*, Vol. II, No. 10, December,1906, pp. 509–10.
27 Gulbadan Begum, *Humaynama,* translated and edited by Annettee S. Beveridge, London: Royal Asiatic Society, 1902 (henceforth Gulbadan Begum, *Humaynama,*), p. 279.
28 Badayuni, *Muntakhabu-t-Tawarikh,* Vol. II, p. 389.
29 Douglas A. Streusand, *The Formation of the Mughal Empire,* Delhi: Oxford University Press, 1989, p. 113.
30 *Maathir-ul-Umra*, Vol. I, p. 325.
31 Ibid., p. 330.
32 Iqtidar Alam Khan, 'The Nobility under Akbar and the Development of his Religious Policy', in Richard Eaton (ed.), *India's Islamic Traditions 711-1750,* New Delhi: Oxford University Press, 2003, p. 121. This essay was originally published in 1968.
33 A.K. Majumdar, 'Hindu Resistance to Muslim Domination: 1. Mewar', in R. C, Majumdar (ed.), *History and Culture of the Indian People*, Vol. 7, Bombay: Bharatiya Vidya Bhavan, 1951–74, p. 327.

34 James Todd, *Annals and Antiquities of Rajputana*, Vol. I, New Delhi: M.N. Publishers, 1978 reprint of 1914 edition, (First published in 1829), p. 276.

35 For details of Chhayavad and of Jaishankar Prasad, see David Rubin, *The Return of Saraswati: Four Hindi Poets,* Delhi: Oxford University Press, 1998.

36 Hari Maharishi (ed.), *Jaishanker Prasad: Maharana ka Mahatva,* Jaipur: Sahityagar, 1991.

37 'Maharana Pratap: Ithihasik Adhyayan', in Hukum Singh Bhatti (ed.), *Parampara,* No. 124–25, 2001, Special Number, pp. 51–52.

38 Brij Ratna Das, *Rahiman Vilas,* Allahabad: Ramanarayan Lal, 1960 (3rd ed.), p. 62. The verses refer to Abdur Rahim by the title Khan-i-Khanan which he was awarded in 1581. This is later than the probable date of this succession dispute.

39 Ibid. The word *jada* also means large. The verse is therefore a play on Jada as a proper noun and also adjective. Jada is said to have belonged to the Mahdu clan among bards.

40 James Todd, *Annals and Antiquities,* Vol. I, p. 272.

41 Chhotubhai Ranchhodji Naik, *Abdur Rahim Khan-i-Khanan and his Literary Circle,* Ahmedabad: Gujarat University, 1966, pp. 58–59.

42 Ibid., pp. 57–58. Dr Naik explains the charqab as a garment peculiar to the kings of Turan.

43 H. Beveridge, 'Salima Sultan Begum', p. 509.

44 This episode in its entirety is in the *Dhikharatul Khawanin*, pp. 50–51.

45 Maulvi Zafar Husain, 'Mosque of Sheikh Abdun Nabi', first published in *Memoirs of the Archaeological Survey of India*, No.9, 1921. Reprinted in Monica Juneja (ed.), *Architecture in Medieval India: Forms, Contexts, Histories,* New Delhi: Permanent Black, 2001, p. 240.

46 S.A.A. Rizvi, *Religious and Intellectual History of the Muslims in Akbar's Reign,* New Delhi: Munshiram Manoharlal, 1975, pp. 126–27.

47 The year 1582 translates to 990 in the *hijri* calendar which has been described as follows by H. Beveridge in his translation and edition of the *Akbarnama*: 'It seems that Akbar regarded the year 990 as the completion of 1000 years from the beginning of Muhammad's (i.e., the Prophet of Islam) mission' (Vol. III, p. 559).

48 The translator notes that this sentence is '… obscurely worded. It looks at first as if it was a reference that Akbar should assume the position of

a teacher, and have *celas* or disciples. But the beginning of the sentence about Sultan Salim implies that the representations were the ideas of the officers as to what was expedient'

49 *Akbarnama*, Vol. III, p. 559. The English translation refers to Abdur Rahim as Mirza *KhanKhanan* when in fact the title was awarded later.

50 S.A.A. Rizvi, *Religious and Intellectual History*, p. 137.

51 John Correia Afonso, *Letters from the Mughal Court, The First Jesuit Mission to Akbar (1580-83)*, St Louis: Institute of Jesuit Sources, 1981, p. 11.

52 The full list or categories of women in different crafts and of different ethnic and caste groups described is as follows: (1) Brahmini (the wife of the brahmin), (2) Khatrani (The wife of the shopkeeper/trader), (3) Joharin (the wife of the jeweller), (4) Kayasthini (the wife of the scribe/accountant), (5) Chiteran (the wife of the painter), (6) Tamolini (the wife of the paan or betel leaf seller), (7) Sunari (the wife of the goldsmith), (8) Baniyain (the wife of the trader, moneylender), (9) Rangrejin (the wife of the dyer), (10) Paniharin (the wife of the water filler), (11) Kunjdi (the wife of the vegetable seller), (12) Banjarin (the wife of the long distance trader), (13) Kumhari (the wife of the potter), (14) Lohari (the wife of the ironsmith), (15) Kalvari (the wife of the liquor vendor), (16) Gujari (the wife of the cowherd), (17) Kachini (the wife of the vegetable seller), (18) Kasaien (the wife of the butcher), (19) Tabakhini (the wife of one who sells food items displayed on a platter), (20) Telin (the wife of the oil presser), (21) Pattein (the wife of the braid/fringe maker), (22) Bhattiyari (the wife of the innkeeper), (23) Kamangri (the wife of the bow maker), (24) Chhapin (the wife of the cloth printer), (25) Sikligarin (the wife of the sword/weopon maker/ polisher), (26) Sakkin (the wife of the water carrier), (27) Gandhini (the wife of the perfume /maker seller), (28) Rajputni (the wife of the Rajput), (29) Turkin (the wife of the Turk), (30) Jogin (the female ascetic), (31) Bhatin (the wife of the bard), (32) Domini (a woman singer), (33) Cheri (the maid servant), (34) Natini (the actress/dancer), (35) Kanchni (prostitute), (36) Paturi (the singing/dancing woman who is also a prostitute, (37) Junkihari (the woman who treats wounds using leeches), (38) Khatkin (the wife of the dealer in skins/who sows and sells garden vegetables), (39) Kundin (the woman beating clothes (to clean them), (40) Sabnigarin (the soap makers wife), (41) Thopin (the woman plastering walls [houses] with mud), (42) Kundigarin (the

wife of the beater of gold into thin foils), (43) Dhuniyain (the wife of cotton carder), (44) Korin (the wife of the weaver of thick coarse cloth), (45) Dabgarin (the wife of the shield maker), (46) Nagarchin (the wife of the drum maker), (47) Dalalini (the wife of the agent/broker), (48) Tatherini (the wife of the coppersmith), (49) Kagadin (the wife of the paper maker), (50) Masikrin (the wife of the ink maker), (51) Baajdarini (the wife of the hawk keeper), (52) Jiledarini (the wife of the district officer), (53) Bhangerini (the wife of the opium seller/ women selling opium), (54) Bajigarin (the wife of the magician), (55) Cheetabani (the wife of the cheetah tamer), (56) Katihari (the wife of the woodcutter), (57) Ghasin (the wife of the grass cutter/seller/ women selling/cutting grass), (58) Dafalini (the wife of the dafli maker (a musicical instrument), (59) Gadibarin (the wife of the cart driver), (60) Mahavatin (wife of the elephant rider/minder) (61) Sarwani (the wife of the camel rider/ minder), (62) Nalbandini (the wife of the rein maker), (63) Chirvadarin (the wife of the syce [or the groom]), (64) Dhobin (a washerwomen/ wife of the washerman), (65) Chamarini (the wife of the scavenger), (66) Chuhri (the sweeper woman/wife of the sweeper).

53 The shield maker also makes leather containers. The verse is a series of innuendoes of leather containers, breasts, which do not fit into bodices, and are tight under the skin.

54 The translation of these verses from the *Nagar Shobha* are mine.

55 For the large size of a great noble's household, see Stephen P. Blake, *Shahjehanabad: The Sovereign City in Mughal India, 1639-1739*, Cambridge (UK): Cambridge University Press, 1991, pp. 85–90.

56 The *Nagar Shobha* manuscript was found by Mayashankar Yajnik and the discovery announced in the journal *Madhuri*, Vol. 3, Part 2, March 1925 in an article titled 'Rahim' and co-authored by Mayashankar Yajnik, Jeevanshankar Yajnik and Bhavanishankar Yajnik. For a fuller treatment of Mayashankar Yajnik, see Epilogue.

57 See also Mayashankar Yajnik: *Rahim Ratnavali* p. 16.

58 The translation of these verses is mine. Deshraj Singh Bhatti (ed.), *Rahim Granthavali*, New Delhi: Ashok Prakashan, 1995, p. 190.

59 Chhotubhai Ranchhodji Naik, *Abdul Rahim Khan-i-Khanan*, p. 68.

60 *Akbarnama*, Vol. III, pp. 631–32.

61 Ibid., p. 631.

62 *Dhakhiratul Khawanin*, p. 23.

63 *Akbarnama*, Vol. III, p. 635.

64 Ibid., p. 638.

65 Ibid., p. 639.

66 Ibid., pp. 639–40.

67 I have used the Hindi translation of *Darbar-e-Akbari* by the Nagari Pracharni Sabha. Ramchandra Varma (tr.), *Akbari Darbar*, Varanasi: Nagari Pracharni Sabha, 2025 V.S, Part III, p. 222.

68 The letter is translated into Hindi in, Munshi Devi Prasad, *Khankhanan Nama,* edited by Jaswant Singh, pp. 185–90.

69 Badayuni, *Muntakhabu-t-Tawarikh*, Vol. II, p. 342.

70 *Dhikharatul Khawanin*, p. 24.

71 Badayuni, *Muntakhabu-t-Tawarikh*, Vol. II, p. 343.

72 Ibid.

73 *Dhikharatul Khawanin*, pp. 110–11.

74 Mansura Haider (tr. and ed.), *Mukhtabat-i-Allami ((Insha-i-Abul Fazl)*, New Delhi: Indian Council of Historical Research, 1998, p. 22.

75 Ibid., p. 28.

76 M.S. Commissariat, *History of Gujarat*, Vol. II, 1573–78, Bombay: Orient Longmans, 1957, p. 29.

77 *Akbarnama,* Vol. III, pp. 881–82. Beveridge, the translator of the *Akbarnama,* in a footnote says, 'I am not sure if the meaning is that the letter was written when he was made KhanKhanan or simply when Abul Fazl wrote to him, he was to tell him so and so. Iraj must have been born long before 998 (1590) for in the 40th year he was made a commander.' It is more likely, however, that the letter may well have been the same in which the title of Khan-i-Khanan was awarded, since Iraj was, in fact, born in 1585.

78 William Foster (ed.), *The Embassy of Sir Thomas Roe to India, 1615-19*, London: Printed for the Haklyut Society, 1899, p. 501.

79 Abolghasem Dadvar, *Iranians in Mughal Politics and Society (1606-1658)*, New Delhi: Gyan Publishing House, 1999, p. 116.

80 Mansura Haider (tr. and ed.), *Mukhtabat-i-Allami,* p. 23.

81 Ibid., p. 30. Munshi Devi Prasad in his translation of this letter suggests that the emperor implies that if the expected child were not a son, the number of pigeons would be fewer than Abdur Rahim expected. *Khankhanan Nama,* p. 185.

82 Badayuni, *Muntakhabu-t-Tawarikh*, Vol. II, p. 376. H. Blochman, the translator of the *Ain-i-Akbari* of Abul Fazl, takes the reference to

a 'greater one' to imply either Akbar or Abul Fazl.D.C. Phillot, *Ain-i-Akbari*, Delhi: Low Price Publications, 1989 reprint, Vol. I, p. 216.

83 *Akbarnama,* Vol. III, p. 804.

84 Ibid., p. 803.

85 Details of this episode are from the *Akbarnama,* Vol. III, pp. 824–25.

86 Ibid., p. 863.

87 *Baburnama*, p. 11. Describing the language of the *Baburnama,* Thackston writes (p.10): "Babur made an unusual decision to keep a record of his life, but the language in which he chose to keep it was even more uncommon. Opting not to write in Persian, the universal language of culture and literature of his time and place, he kept his memoirs in Chagatay Turkish, the Timurids' spoken language – indeed of the whole Turco-Mongolian world of the time. Poets and writers had sporadically dabbled in Chagatay from the beginning of the Timurid period and... Chagatay poetry enjoyed a short-lived florescence at the end of the fifteenth century; but Chagatay never threatened Persian as the dominant language of culture, and little expository or narrative verse had ever been written in Chagatay...To this day the *Baburnama* is one of the longest examples of sustained narrative prose in the language, as the attempts to turn Chagatay into a viable literary vehicle turned out to be a "flash in the pan", doomed by the turn of events that swept the Timurids from Persia and Central Asia. Ironically, Timurid rule was overwhelmed by two dynasties that were also Turkic: from the west came the Safavids (1501–1732) and their predominantly Turcoman supporters, and from the north came the Turco-Mongolian Uzbeks. Since the Safavids' primary cultural identification was with Persia, their cultural language was Persian; and even though their home language remained Turkish throughout the dynasty's long history, their Turkish was the western dialect of the Turcomans of eastern Anatolia and Azerbaijan and not the eastern Chagatay dialect of the Timurids. The Uzbeks, suffering from a cultural inferiority complex, concentrated their efforts on the cultivation of Persian ... and had little time or inclination for patronage of their own Turkish language.'

88 S.A.A. Rizvi, *Religious and Intellectual History* ..., p. 221.

89 *Baburnama*, p. 11.

90 Ramchandra Varma (tr.), *Akbari Darbar*, Part III, p 307.

91 H. Beveridge, 'Was Abdur Rahim the Translator of Babur's Memoirs into Persian?', *Imperial and Asiatic Quarterly*, 3rd Series, Vol. X, 1900, p. 117.

92 Rupert Snell refers to 119 barvai couplets and an initial doha. 'Barvai Metre in Tulsidas and Rahim', in Alan W. Entwistle and Francoise Mallison (eds), *South Asian Devotional Literature*, New Delhi: Manohar, 1994. Balkrishna Akinchan in *Bhartiya Niti Kavya Parampara aur Abdur Rahim*, mentions in all 116 couplets – two dohas, an invocatory verse and 113 barvais. For the *Barvai Nayika Bhed*, I have used Deshraj Singh Bhatti (ed.), *Rahim Granthavali*, which lists an introductory doha, invocatory verse and 114 barvais.

93 Rakesh Gupta, *Studies in Nayak Nayika Bhed*, Aligarh: Granthayan, 1967.

94 Translation of Sr. No. 1 from Allison Busch, *Poetry of Kings: The Classical Hindi Literature of Mughal India*, New York: Oxford University Press, 2012, p. 79. Busch renders Svakiya as 'One's own wife'. Translations of barvais 2–5 are from Pandit Vansidhar Vidyalankar, 'Abdur Rahim Khan-i-Khanan and his Hindi Poetry', *Islamic Culture*, Vol. XXIV, No. 2, April 1950, p. 130. Translation of Sr. No. 6 is by me. Sr. Nos 7–11 are from Rupert Snell, 'Barvai Metre in Tulsidas and Rahim'.

95 Snell makes the argument in detail. Balkrishan Ankichan, *Bhartiya Niti Kavya Parampara aur Abdur Rahim* also does not accept that Tulsidas's *Barvai Ramayan* was composed on inspiration from the *Barvai Nayika Bhed*, the grounds being that a sensitive scholar such as Abdur Rahim would not have sent to a sage such as Tulsidas an example of such erotic and sensuous verse.

96 Rupert Snell, 'Barvai Metre in Tulsidas and Rahim'.

97 Translation mine.

98 Rupert Snell, 'Barvai Metre in Tulsidas and Rahim'.

3. THE SENIOR COMMANDER

1 *The Akbarnama of Abul Fazl*, translated by H. Beveridge in 3 vols, Delhi: Low Price Publications, 1989 reprint (henceforth *Akbarnama*), Vol. III, p. 865.

2 J.F. Richards, *The Mughal Empire* (The New Cambridge History of India), Delhi: Cambridge University Press, 1993, p. 49.

3 Fatima Zehra Bilgrami, 'The Mughal Annexation of Sindh: A Diplomatic and Military History', in Irfan Habib (ed.), *Akbar and His India*, New Delhi: Oxford University Press, 1997, p. 36.

4 S.A.A. Rizvi, *Religious and Intellectual History of the Muslims in Akbar's Reign*, New Delhi: Munshiram Manoharlal, 1975, p. 322.

5 M. Athar Ali, *The Apparatus of Empire: Awards of the Ranks, Offices and Titles to the Mughal Nobility, 1574-1658,* New Delhi: Aligarh Muslim University/Oxford University Press, 1985, does not refer to Jaunpur having been assigned as Abdur Rahim's jagir at all.

6 *Akbarnama,* Vol. III, p. 887.

7 Ibid., p. 917.

8 Fatima Zehra Bilgrami, *The Mughal Annexation of Sindh*, p. 38.

9 Sunita Zaidi, 'Akbar's Annexation of Sindh – An Intepretation', in Irfan Habib (ed.), *Akbar and His India,* 1997, p. 28.

10 Mubarak Ali, *Essays on the History of Sindh,* Lahore: Renaissance Publishers, 2005, p. 6.

11 Sunita Zaidi, *Akbar's Annexation of Sindh – An Intepretation*, p. 29.

12 Chhotubhai Ranchhodji Naik, *Abdur Rahim Khan-i-Khanan and His Literary Circle,* Ahmedabad: Gujarat University, 1966, p. 43.

13 *Dhakhiratul Khawanin* of Sheikh Farid Bukhari, translated and edited by Ziauddin A. Desai, Delhi: Idara-i-Adbiyat, 1993, (henceforth *Dhakhiratul Khawanin*), p. 28.

14 Ibid., p. 131.

15 Mayashankar Yajnik, Jivanshankar Yajnik, Bhavanshankar Yajniki, 'Abdur Rahim ka ek navin granth', *Saraswati,* Vol. 27, Part I, January–June 1926, p. 249.

16 Ibid.

17 Translations of the barvais are from Rupert Snell, *The Hindi Classical Tradition: A Braj Bhasa Reader*, London: The School of Oriental and African Studies, 1991, pp. 123–27.

18 Translation of the next two barvais is mine, the third is by Snell.

19 H.H. Wilson, 'Religious Sects of the Hindus', cited in Charlotte Vaudeville, *A Weaver Named Kabir*, Delhi: Oxford University Press, 1993, p. 19.

20 Muzaffar Alam, 'The Pursuit of Persian: Language in Mughal Politics', *Modern Asian Studies*, Vol. 32, No. 2, 1998, p. 321.

21 Muhammad Abdul Ghani, *A History of the Persian Language and Literature at the Mughal Court*, Allahabad: The Indian Press, 1930, Part III, p. 220.

22 Ibid., p. 225.

23 E.G. Browne, *Literary History of Persia, Vol IV, Modern Times (1500-1924)*, Cambridge (UK): Cambridge University Press, 1957, (Originally published 1924), pp. 167–68.
24 Chhotubhai Ranchhodji Naik, *Abdur Rahim Khan-i-Khanan and his Literary Circle*, p. 267.
25 M. Mahfuzul Haq, 'The Khan Khanan and his Painters, Illuminators and Calligraphists', *Islamic Culture,* Vol. V, No. 4, 1931. p. 622. See also Mohamid Uz Zafar, 'Abdur Rahim Khan Khanan and his Library', *Pakistan Historical Society Journal*, III, 1955.
26 Chhotubhai Ranchhodji Naik, *Abdur Rahim Khan-i-Khanan and his Literary Circle*, p. 273.
27 M. Mahfuzul Haq, *Islamic Culture*, pp. 622–23.
28 *Dhakhiratul Khawanin*, p. 44.
29 The *Jahangirnama, Memoirs of Jahangir, Emperor of India,* translated, edited and annotated by Wheeler M. Thackston, New York: Freer Gallery of Art/Oxford University Press, 1999. p. 118.
30 Chhotubhai Ranchhodji Naik, *Abdur Rahim Khan-i-Khanan and his Literary Circle*, p. 289.
31 E.G. Browne, *Literary History of Persia*, p. 252.
32 Ibid., 241.
33 Abdul Qadir Ibn-i-Muluk Shah (known as Al Badaoni), *Muntakhabu-t-Tawarikh*, translated and edited by Sir Wolseley Haig, Delhi: Renaissance Publishing House, 1986 reprint, (henceforth Badayuni, *Muntakhabu-t-Tawarikh*), Vol. III, p. 393.
34 Cited in Muzaffar Alam, *The Pursuit of Persian*, pp. 333–34.
35 E.G. Browne, *Literary History of Persia*, p. 246.
36 Cited in S. Azhar Ali, 'Mirza Abdur Rahim Khan-i-Khanan: Soldier, Statesman and Patron of Letters', PhD Dissertation 480, University of Cambridge, 1932, pp. 241–42.
37 John Seyller, *Workshop and Patron in Mughal India: The Freer Ramayana and other Illustrated Manuscripts of Abd al-Rahim*, Zurich: Artibus Asiae Publishers / Freer Gallery of Art, 1999, p. 11.
38 Ibid., p. 257.
39 Ibid., p.329.
40 Ibid., p.73.
41 Ibid.

42 Translation from K.B. Jindal, *A History of Hindi Literature*, (2nd ed.), New Delhi: Munshiram Manoharlal, 1993, p. 137.

43 Translations from Pandit Vansidhar Vidyalankar, 'Abdur Rahim Khan-i-Khanan and his Hindi Poetry', *Islamic Culture,* Vol. XXIV, No. 2, April 1950, p. 126.

44 Translation from K.B. Jindal, *A History of Hindi Literature*, p. 139.

45 Verses in praise of Abdur Rahim Khan-i-Khanan by Gang, Prasidh, Mandan, Harnath and Ala Kuli are from Bri Ratna Das, *Rahiman Vilas,* pp. 65–69. Translation are by me.

46 Allison Busch, 'Literary Responses to the Mughal Imperium: the Historical Poems of Keshavdas', *South Asia Research*, Vol. 25, No. 1, May 2005, p. 32.

47 Allison Busch, *Poetry of Kings: The Classical Hindi Literature of Mughal India,* New York: Oxford University Press, 2011, p. 56.

48 The first and third set of verses are from *Rahim Vilas*, pp. 63–64. The translation is by me. The second is from Allison Busch, 'Literary Responses to the Mughal Imperium…, p. 49.

49 For the text and meaning of these four barvais I have relied on Deshraj Bhatti, *Rahim Granthavali Satik*. Delhi: Ashok Prakashan, 1995, pp. 266–68.

50 *Dhakhiratul Khawanin*, p. 78.

51 Ibid., p. 38.

52 Ibid., p. 39.

53 Badayuni, *Muntakhabu-t-Tawarikh,* Vol. II, p. 420.

54 Ibid., p. 412. Sijdah is the act of prostration and touching the forehead to the floor – normally done in prayer and not before a person. Those initiated into Akbar's eclectic practices used to do so before him to the disapproval of conservatives like Badayuni.

55 Ibid., p. 355.

56 Ibid., Vol. III, pp. 173–74.

57 Syed Athar Abbas Rizvi, 'Dimensions of Sulh-i-Kil (Universal Peace) in Akbar's reign and the Sufi theory of Perfect Man', in Iqtidar Alam Khan, *Akbar And His Age*, New Delhi: Northern Book Centre/Indian Council of Historical Research, 1999, p. 16.

4. THE DECCAN

1 S.A.A. Rizvi, *Religious and Intellectual History of the Muslims in Akbar's Reign,* New Delhi: Munshiram Manoharlal Publishers,1975, p. 459.

2 J.F. Richards, *The Mughal Empire* (The New Cambridge History of India), Delhi: Cambridge University Press, 1993, p. 53.

3 J.D.B. Gribble, *A History of the Deccan,* Vol, I, London: Luzac &Co,1896, pp. 221–22, citing Colonel Meadows Taylor in his part novel part history *The Noble Queen.*

4 *The Akbarnama of Abul Fazl,* translated by H. Beveridge in 3 vols, Delhi: Low Price Publications, 1989 reprint, (henceforth *Akbarnama*), Vol. III, p. 909.

5 Ibid., p. 995–96.

6 Ibid., p. 1046.

7 Ibid., p. 1047.

8 Chhotubhai Ranchhodji Naik, *Abdur Rahim Khan-i-Khanan and His Literary Circle*, Ahmedabad: Gujarat University, 1966, pp. 131–32.

9 *Akbarnama*, Vol. III, p. 1047.

10 Ibid., p. 1048.

11 *Dhakhiratul Khawanin* of Sheikh Farid Bukhari, translated and edited by Ziauddin A. Desai, Delhi: Idara-i-Adbiyat, 1993 (henceforth *Dhakhiratul Khawanin*), p.31.

12 This fact is pointed out by H. Beveridge, the editor and translator of the *Akbarnama,* Vol. III, p. 1072.

13 *Dhakhiratul Khawanin*, p. 31

14 Ibid.

15 *Dhakhiratul Khawanin*, p. 29.

16 *Akbarnama,* Vol. III, p. 1072.

17 Ibid., p. 1102.

18 Sanjay Subrahmanyam, 'Further Notes on the "Foreign Hand":The Mughals, The Portuguese and Deccan Politics, c 1600', in Muzzaffar Alam and Sanjay Subrahmanyam (eds), *The Mughal State, 1526-1750,* Delhi: Oxford University Press, 2000, p. 148.

19 Chhotubhai Ranchhodji Naik, *Abdur Rahim Khan-i-Khanan and His . . .*, p. 146; Mohd. Ilyas Quddusi, *Khandesh under the Mughals 1601-1724 A.D.*, New Delhi: Islamic Wonders Bureau, 2002, p. 16.

20 Muhammad Husain Azad, *Akbari Darbar*, translated by Ramchandra Varma, Varanasi: Nagari Pracharni Sabha, 2025, Part III, pp. 274–75.

21 *Akbarnama,* Vol. III, p.1198.

22 Satish Chandra, 'The Deccan Policy of the Mughals (I) – up to Shah Jahan', in Satish Chandra (ed.), *Mughal Religious Policies: The Rajputs and the Deccan*, New Delhi: Vikas Publishing House, 1993, p.114.

23 *Akbarnama,* Vol. III, p. 1201.

24 Ibid., p. 1229.

25 Ibid., p. 1255. It may be noted that Abul Fazl was killed in August 1602 and the commentary in the *Akbarnama* up to the emperor's death was by another author. These lines about Janah Begum were thus written many years later and after her own death.

26 *Dhakhiratul Khawanin*, p. 32.

27 *The Jahangirnama, Memoirs of Jahangir, Emperor of India,* translated, edited and annotated by Wheeler M. Thackston, New York: Freer Gallery of Art/Oxford University Press, 1999 (henceforth *Jahangirnama*), p. 13. This is in the preface written by Muhammad Hadi to the main autobiography. Muhammad Hadi lived in the reign of the Mughal Emperor Muhammad Shah (1719–48).

28 Chhotubhai Ranchhodji Naik, *Abdur Rahim Khan-i-Khanan and His* ..., pp. 152–53.

29 *Jahangirnama*, p. 34.

30 Ibid., p. 89.

31 Ibid., p. 96.

32 Ibid., p. 98.

33 Afzal Hussain, *The Nobility under Akbar and Jahangir: A study of Family Groups*, New Delhi: Aligarh Muslim University/Manohar, 1999, p. 97. Jadunath Sarkar noted and commented on this unusual situation also in *A History of Jaipur* revised and edited by Raghubir Singh, Jaipur: Maharaja Sawai Man Singh II Museum, 1984, p. 90.

34 Afzal Hussain, *The Nobility under Akbar and Jahangir*, p. 98, citing Bhimsen in *Nuskha-i-Dilkusha.* This work was however composed in the last quarter of the seventeenth century.

35 Chhotubhai Ranchhodji Naik, *Abdur Rahim Khan-i-Khanan and His*, p. 157.

36 Afzal Hussain, *The Nobility under Akbar and Jahangir*, p. 37.

37 Radhey Shyam: *Life and Times of Malik Amber*, Delhi: Munshiram Manoharlal, 1968, p. 78.

38 Ibid., p. 114.

39 See Chapter 3, pp. 147–48 above.

40 For Rudra Kavi and the *Nawab Khankhanan Charitam* I have relied on V.W. Karambelkar, 'Nababkhankhanancaritam', *Indian Historical Quarterly*, XXVII, 1952, pp. 240–48, and Jatindra Bimal Chaudhuri, *Khan Khanan Abdur Rahim and Contemporary Sanskrit Learning*, Calcutta: Pracyavidya Mandir, 1954, pp. 53–58.

41 Ibid., pp. 24–25.

42 V.W. Karambelkar, 'Nababkhankhanancaritam', p. 242.

43 Ibid., pp. 247–48.

44 *Jahangirnama*, p. 229 .

45 V.W. Karambelkar, 'Nababkhankhanancaritam', p. 245.

46 See Chapter 2, p. 85 above.

47 Shymaldas, *Vir Vinod: Mewar ka Ithihas*, (in 4 volumes), Delhi: Motilal Banarsi Das, 1986, Vol. 2, pp. 234–35.

48 Iqtidar Alam Khan, 'Akbar's Personality Traits and World Outlook – A Critical Reappraisal', in Irfan Hahib (ed.), *Akbar and his India*, Delhi: Oxford University Press, 1997, pp. 93–94.

49 Ibid.

50 Ibid.

51 See, for a summary and critique of this view, Irfan Habib, 'The Political Role of Sheikh Ahmad Sirhindi and Shah Waliullah', *Indian History Congress Proceedings*, 1960 Session, p. 209. N. Hasan, 'Sheikh Ahmad Sirhindi and Mughal Politics', *Indian History Congress Proceedings*, 1948 Session, p. 248.

52 Yohanan Friedmann, *Shaykh Ahmad Sirhindi: An Outline of his thought and a study of his image in the Eyes of Posterity*, New Delhi: Oxford India Paperbacks, OUP, 2000, first published in 1971, p. xiii.

53 Review by Avril Powell of J.G.J. Ter Haer, 'Follower and Heir of the Prophet – Shaykh Ahmad Sirhindi (1564-24) as Mystic', *Bulletin of the School of Oriental and African Studies*, University of London, Vol. 57, No. 2, 1994, pp. 405–06.

54 Irfan Habib, 'The Political Role of Sheikh …', 1960, p. 220.

55 Yohanan Friedman, *Shaykh Ahmad Sirhindi*, p. 114.

56 Irfan Habib, 'The Political Role of Sheikh …', 1960, p. 211.

57 Ibid.

58 Letter 68, *Maktoobat-i-Imam-i-Rabbani.* I am grateful to Dr Mubarak Ali in Lahore for translations of the letters to the Khan-i-Khanan.

59 Ibid., Letter 69.

60 Ibid.

5. TWILIGHT YEARS

1 *Dhakhiratul Khawanin of Sheikh Farid Bukhari*, translated and edited by Ziauddin A. Desai, Delhi: Idara-i-Adbiyat, 1993 (henceforth *Dhakhiratul Khawanin*), p. 40.

2 Ibid., p. 45.

3 W.M. Thackston (ed.) *The Jahangirnama, Memoirs of Jahangir, Emperor of India,* New York: Freer Gallery of Art/Oxford University Press, 1999 (henceforth *Jahangirnama*), p. 123.

4 Ibid., p. 124.

5 The upward trajectory of Nur Jahan's family has been much studied and also at times disputed by historians. Beni Prasad, *History of Jahangir*, Madras: Oxford University Press, 1922, pp. 185–201; Syed Nurul Hasan, 'The theory of the Nur Jahan "Janta" – a critical examination', *Indian History Congress, Proceedings of the 21st Session,* 1958, pp. 324–35; Irfan Habib, 'The family of Nur Jahan during Jahangir's reign', in Aligarh Muslim University: *Medieval India, A Miscelleny,* Vol I, Bombay: Asia Publishing House, 1969.

6 *Dhakhiratul Khawanin*, p. 67.

7 Ibid., p. 39. Bijanagar is not identifiable so the approximate time when this incident may be dated to is problematic.

8 Balkrishna Ankichan, *Bhartiya Niti Kavya Parampara Aur Rahim*, Delhi: Alankar Prakashan, 1974, pp. 206, 241–75.

9 There are numerous collections of Rahim's dohas and equally numerous commentaries. The two works that they rely on are those we shall deal with in detail in Chapter 6 below; Brij Ratna Das, *Rahiman Vilas,* Allahabad: Ram Narayan Lal, 1960 (reprint), and Mayashankar Yajnik, *Rahim Ratnavali*, Kashi: Sahitya Seva Sadan, 1957 edition. There have also been attempts to standardize the texts of the dohas and remove printing and other errors which have repeated themselves over different commentaries and editions. Srikant Upadhyaya (ed.) *Ye Rahim Dar Dar Phirhi: Rahim Dohavali*, New Delhi: National Publishing House, 2000. Translations of the dohas below are mine.

10 *Jahangirnama,* p. 135.
11 Ibid., p. 136.
12 Ibid.
13 Colin Paul Mitchell, *Sir Thomas Roe and the Mughal Empire,* Karachi: Oxford University Press, 2000, p. 69; Chhotubhai Ranchhodji Naik, *Abdur Rahim Khan-i-Khanan and his Literary Circle*, Ahmedabad: Gujarat University, 1966, p. 167.
14 Satish Chandra, 'Deccan Policy of Mirza Raj Jai Singh', *Proceedings of the Rajasthan History Congress,* Vol. I, 1967, pp. 76–84.
15 Richard M. Eaton, *A Social History of the Deccan, 1300-1761*: *Eight Indian Lives*, The New Cambridge History of India, Cambridge: Cambridge University Press, 2005, p. 123.
16 Radhey Shyam, *Life and Times of Malik Amber*, Delhi: Munshiram Manoharlal, 1968, p. 91.
17 William Foster, *The Embassy of Sir Thomas Roe to the court of the Great Mogul, 1615-19,* London: The Haklyut Society, 1899, Vol. I, pp. 279–80
18 *Jahangirnama*, pp. 301–02.
19 Nawwab Shamsam-ud-Daula Shah Nawaz Khan (translated by H. Beveridge, revised by Baini Prashad), *The Maathir-ul-Umra; Being Biographies of the Muhammadan and Hindu Officers of the Timurid Soverigns of India from 1500 to about 1750 A.D.*, Delhi: Low Price Publications, 1999 reprint (in 2 vols), henceforth *Maathir-ul-Umra.* Vol. II, p. 767.
20 Allison Busch, *Poetry of Kings: The Classical Hindi Literrature of Mughal India*, New York: Oxfod University Press, 2011, pp. 56, 136. See also Chapter 3 pp.
21 *Jahangirnama*, p. 348.
22 *The Maathir-ul-Umra,* Vol. I, p. 58.
23 Ibid., p. 59.
24 Cited in 'Malik Amber: A New Life', in Jadunath Sarkar, *House of Shivaji*, Delhi: Orient Longmans, 1978, pp. 16–17.
25 *Jahangirnama*, p. 376.
26 V.B. Amar, 'Shah Jahan's Rebellion and Abdur Rahim Khan-i-Khanan', in T.K. Ravindran (ed.), *Journal of Indian History,* Golden Jubilee Volume, Trivandrum: Department of History, University of Kerala, 1973, p. 438.
27 Ibid., p. 437.

28 Afzal Husain, *The Nobility under Akbar and Jahangir: A Study of Family Groups*, New Delhi: Aligarh Muslim University/Manohar, 1999, citing a Dutch chronicle to this effect, pp. 40–41.

29 V.B. Amar, 'Shah Jahan's Rebellion ...', p. 442.

30 *Jahangirnama*, p. 388.

31 *Dhakhiratul Khawanin*, p. 35.

32 *Jahangirnama*, p. 405.

33 Rupert Snell translates the doha as follows:

Perplexity must be our lot, whichever way we turn.
If true, we lose the world we love: if false, then God we spurn.

Rupert Snell, *The Hindi Classical Tradition, A Braj Bhasha Reader*, London: School of Oriental and African Studies, 1991, p. 41.

34 Nazir Ahmed, 'Abdur Rahim KhanKhanan: KhanKhanan ke Kutub Khane ki Kadmi Kitaben', *Maarif*, Vol. 14, No. 6, December 1934. I am grateful to Dr Mubarak Ali in Lahore for the translation.

35 *Jahangirnama*, p. 407.

36 *Dhakhiratul Khawanin*, p. 36.

37 Ibid.

38 *Jahangirnama*, p. 407.

39 *Dhakhiratul Khawanin*, p. 37.

40 Ibid., p. 38.

41 Ibid.

42 *Jahangirnama*, p. 425. This description of Fahim's end comes not from Jahangir himself but from Mohammad Hadi who recorded events in the last two-and-a-half years of Jahangir's reign as an appendix to the Jahangirnama.

43 Afzal Hussain, *The Nobility under Akbar and Jahangir*, p. 42.

44 *Maathir-ul-Umra,* Vol. 1, p. 452.

45 *Jahangirnama,* p. 429.

46 *Maathir-ul-Umra,* Vol. 1, p. 453.

47 See Chapter 3.

48 Beni Prasad, *History of Jahangir*, p. 395.

49 *Jahangirnama*, p. 434.

50 *Dhakhiratul Khawanin*, p. 42.

51 *Jahangirnama*, p. 447.

52 *Dhakhiratul Khawanin*, p. 42.

53 Ibid., p. 43.

6. AFTERLIFE: RAHIMAN AND ABDUR RAHIM

1 Alok Rai, in *Hindi Nationalism*, Delhi: Orient Longman, 2000, refers to the 'sanctimonius abducters, the entrenched elite at Nagari Pracharni Sabha', p. 6.

2 Munshi Devi Prasad, *Khankhanan Nama,* edited by Jaswant Singh, New Delhi: Pratibha Prathisthan, 2001, p. 166.

3 *The Dhakhiratul Khawanin of Sheikh Farid Bhakkari*, translated by Ziyauddin A. Desai, New Delhi: Idara-i-Adbiyat, 2003 (henceforth *Dhakhiratul Khawanin*); Nawab Samsam-ud-Daula Shah Nawaz Khan and his son Abdul Hayy, translated by Beveridge *The Maathir-ul-Umra*, New Delhi: Low Price Publications, 1999 reprint, (henceforth *Maathir-ul-Umra*).

4 R.S. McGregor, *Hindi Literature from Its Beginnings to the Nineteenth Century,* Wiesbaden: Otto Harrassowitz, 1984, p. 189.

5 Imre Bangha (ed.), *The First Published Anthology of Hindi Poets: Thomas Duer Broughton's Selections from the Popular Poetry of the Hindoos, 1814*. Delhi: Mahatma Gandhi Antarrashtriya Hindi Vishwavidyalaya/ Rainbow Publishers, 2000). p. 9.

6 Vasudha Dalmia, *The Nationalization of Hindu Traditions: Bhartendu Harishchandra and Ninteenth-century Benaras,* Delhi: Oxford University Press,1997; R.S. McGregor, 'An Early Ninteenth Century Collection of Hindi Devotional Poems', in Entwistle Alan and Francoise Malison (eds), *Studies in South Asian Devotional Literature:* Research Papers: 1988-1991, New Delhi: Manohar in Association with Ecole Francaise d'Extreme-Orient 1994, p. 514.

7 Vasudha Dalmia, *The Nationalization of Hindu Traditions*, p. 166.

8 Alok Rai, *Hindi Nationalism*, p. 22.

9 Vasudha Dalmia, *The Nationalization of Hindu Traditions*, p. 168.

10 *Lallooji Lal, The Assembly of Mirth; a literal translation into English of the Sabha Bilasa by G W Gilbertson*, Benaras: Medical Hall Press, 1900.

11 Dalmia, *The Nationalization of Hindu Traditions*, p. 185. See also, Amrit Rai, *A House Divided – The Origin and Development of Hindi Urdu*, Delhi: Oxford University Press, 1991, pp. 268–71. For details of the Hindi–Urdu controversy and the political and literary mobilization that accompanied it, see, Christopher King, *One Language, Two Scripts:*

The Hindi Movement in Nineteenth Century North India, Delhi: Oxford University Press, 1994.

12 *Gutka or Selections by Babu Sivaprasad,* Benaras: Medical Hall Press, 1870.

13 Garcin de Tassy, *Historie de la literature Hindouie et Hindoustanie,* the abridged Hindi translation *Hindi Sahitya Ka Ithihas* is by Lakshmi Sagar Varshney, Allahabad: Hindustan Academy, 1953.

14 Ram Chandra Shukla, *Hindi Sahitya Ka Ithihas*, Varanasi: Nagari Pracharni Sabha, Samvat 2058, (1922), p. 238.

15 Garcin de Tassy, *istorie de la literature Hindouie et Hindoustanie,* 2nd ed., Paris, 1870, Vol. 2, pp. 524–25.

16 Kishori Lal Gupta (ed.), *Shiv Singh Saroj*, Prayag: Hindi Sahitya Sammelan, 1970, pp. 674–76. See also Sudhakar Pandey (ed.), *Hindi Kavya Ganga,* Benaras: Nagari Pracharni Sabha, 1990, pp. 1–2.

17 George A. Grierson, *The Modern Vernacular Literature of Hindustan,* Calcutta: Asiatic Society of Bengal, 1889, p. 160.

18 *Misra Bandu Vinod* (n.d.), Vol. I, pp. 371–79. I have used the volumes in the Library of the Nagari Pracharni Sabha, Benaras. The quotations in the following paragraph are from pages 371 and 377 of *Vinod.*

19 The details of this process have been fully outlined and analysed in Christopher King, *One Language, Two Scripts.*

20 Munshi Devi Prasad is a figure of significance in the nineteenth- and early twentieth-century historiography of Rajasthan. For the details on his life and works, I have relied on a special issue of the journal *Parampara* titled *Ithihaskar Munshi Devi Prasad* edited by Narayan Singh Bhatti, Vols. 79–80, 1986, and in particular on the essay in it by Dr Manohar Singh Ranawat. Dr Ranawat has also helped me by providing copies of handwritten manuscripts of essays by Munshi Devi Prasad titled 'Main aur meri Hindi seva', 'Musalmani Rajatva mein Hindi', and 'Rajputana mein Hindi ki dasha', from the Raghubir Library at Sitamau. The introduction to Munshi Devi Prasad's *Shahjahannama*, edited by Dr Raghubir Sinh and Manohar Singh Ranawat contains additional biographical details on Devi Prasad.

21 *Parampara,* special issue titled *Itihaskar Munshi Devi Prasad,* Vols. 79–80, p. 18. Sir Pratap Singh was the chief minister of Jodhpur.

22 Vasudha Dalmia, *The Nationalization of Hindu Traditions*, pp. 150–51.

23 Munshi Devi Prasad, *Khankhanan Nama*, edited by Jaswant Singh, New Delhi: Pratibha Prathisthan, 2001, p. 166.

24 Brij Ratna Das, *Rahiman Vilas*, Allahabad: Ramnarayan Lal, 1960 reprint, p. 93. The next two quotations are at page 69.

25 Ibid.

26 Mayashankar Yajnik, *Rahim Ratnavali*, Kashi: Sahitya Seva Sadan, 1957 edition. The quotations in the following paragraphs are from pages 2 and 11 respectively.

27 Srikant Upadhyaya, *Ye Rahim dar dar phirhi (Rahim Dohavali)*, New Delhi: National Publishing House, 2000, p. x.

28 For details of Raja Gokul Das, see Philip F. Mc Eldowney, 'Colonial Administration and Social Developments in Middle India: The Central Provinces, 1861-1921, PhD thesis, University of Virginia, 1980, in particular Chapter VIII: 'The Commercial Kingdom of Raja Gokul Das'. See also T.C.A. Raghavan, 'Agrarian Change in the Narmada Valley, 1817-1927, PhD thesis, Jawaharlal Nehru University, New Delhi, 1993.

29 Govind Das, *Rahim*, Seth Govind Das Trust, Jabalpur, 1990, p. 118.

30 Ibid., Preface.

31 M.H.A. Beg (ed.), *Khankhanan Nama by Munshi Devi Prasad Kayasth*, Karachi, 1990. See the introductory essay by Dr Hussain Jafar Halim for the assertion that the author of *Khankhanan Nama* was Munshi Devi Prasad 'Sahar'. The Urdu *Khankhanan Nama* was thereafter translated into Turcoman and published from Ashqabad (now Ashgabat), in 1997 as part of the Turkmen rediscovery of Bairam Khan as a national hero after Turkmenistan's establishment as an independent state.

32 Frances Pritchett and Shamsur Rahman Faruqi (eds), *Muhammad Husain Azad, Ab-e-Hayat*, Delhi: Oxford University Press, 2001 (henceforth *Ab-e-Hayat*), p. 4.

33 *Ab-e-Hayat.* p. 6. I have relied on the Hindi translation of the *Darbar-e-Akbarī* – the *Akbari Darbar,* by Ramachandra Varma and published by the Nagari Pracharni Sabha. Ramachandra Varma (trans.), *Akbari Darbar,* Kashi: Nagari Pracharni Sabha, 1925.

34 *Maathir-ul-Umra*, Vol. 1, p. 62.

35 *Akbari Darbar*, Part III, p. 305.

36 *Ab-e-Hayat,* p. 4.

37 Shibli Nomani, 'Maathir-i-Rahimi aur Abdur Rahim Khan-i-Khanan,' *Al Nadwa*, Vol. 4, No. 3, April 1907. Reprinted in *Maqalat-i-Shibli,* Vol. IV, pp. 65–78, Azamgarh, n.d.

38 Volumes III and IV are replete with references to Abdur Rahim and the poets in his court, e.g., pp. 6, 10, 11, 12, 13, 76, 86, 89, 96, 120, 121, 126, 127, etc., and in Vol. IV, pp. 125, 126. Shibli Nomani, *Sherul Ajam*, Azamgarh, n.d.

39 For the significance of Syed Sabahuddin Abdur Rahman and the Dar-ul-Musanafeen, see Raziuddin Aquil, 'The Study of Islam and Indian History at the Darul Musannefin', Azamgarh in Raziuddin Aquil and Partha Chatterjee (eds), *History in the Vernacular*, New Delhi: Permanent Black, 2008, pp. 322–56.

40 Syed Sabahuddin Abdur Rahman, *Bazm-i-Taimuri*, Vol. I, Azamgarh: 1990 reprint, p. 12. The treatment of Abdur Rahim extends from pages 273 to 397.

41 Ibid., pp. 393–96.

EPILOGUE

1 Munshi Devi Prasad, *Khankhanan Nama,* edited by Jaswant Singh, New Delhi: Pratibha Prathisthan, 2001, (henceforth, *Khankhanan Nama*. This refers to the Hindi text), p. 277. For a brief description of the remnants of the properties in Alwar associated with Abdur Rahim and his Mewati mother see also, ibid., pp. 163–65.

2 Mohd Ilyas Quddusi, *Khandesh under the Mughals, 1601-1724 AD,* Delhi: Islamic Wonders Bureau, 2002, (henceforth *Khandesh under the Mughals)*, p. 185.

3 S. Azhar Ali, 'Soldier, Statesman and Patron of Letters', PhD Dissertation 480, University of Cambridge, 1932, p. 86.

4 *Khandesh under the Mughals*, pp. 182–83; Mutiallah Rashid, 'KhanKhanan Abdur Rahim Ki Ek Nadir-i-Rozgar Yadgar', *Maarif*, August 1954, pp. 120–34.

5 B.D. Verma, 'Inscriptions from the Central Museum, Nagpur', *Epigraphica Indica (Arabic and Persian Supplement)*, 1955, pp. 115–16.

6 Maulana Abul Kalam Azad, *Sallies of Mind: English Translation of Ghubar-e-Khatir*, translated by D. R. Goyal, Delhi: Shipra Publications/ Maulana Abul Kalam Azad Institute of Asian Studies, 2003, pp. 37–40, 256.

7 Ibid., p. 39.

8 Most accounts of Mughal architecture in Delhi say that the Nila Gumbad may be Fahim's tomb built by Abdur Rahim Khan-i-Khanan. Ebba

Koch, *Mughal Architecture: An Outline of Its History and Development (1526-1858)*, New Delhi: Primus Books, 2014, pp. 34–35. Based on the structure's stylistic features, however, Koch dates it to the mid-sixteenth century, i.e., to Humayun's reign. This is some six to seven decades before Fahim's death and burial. Even if this were the case the question remains why the structure is specifically identified as Fahim's tomb.

9 M.Z. Hasan, *Monuments of Delhi: Lasting Splendour of the Great Mughals and Others*, Vol. II, New Delhi: Aryan, 2008 (originally published in 1919), pp. 129–30.

10 National Archives of India, File No. D 88/1/1951, 1951, Department of Education, Subject: Proposal of demolition of an old dilapidated tomb in the midst of the newly developed Nizamuddin extension colony.

11 Producer: M. Havela; Story: Khan Bahadur Hakim Ahmed Shujja; Dialogues: Kamal Amrohi; Music: Ghulam Haider; Lyrics: Walli Saheb, B.R. Sharma, Hayat Amrohi.

12 The film was released in February 2008 and won a number of awards. It is produced and directed by Ashutosh Gowarikar; main actors are Hrithik Roshan and Aishwarya Rai. Yuri Suri acts the role of Bairam Khan.

13 This is from the introduction to the Turkmen edition of the *Khankhanan Nama*. For more details about this book and its history see Chapter 6, pp. 266–274 above.

14 The coins were issued in 2001 to mark the tenth anniversary of the independence of Turkmenistan (Plate XI). The report that a motorized infantry division was to be named after Bairam Khan was carried in the Central Asia news website 'News Central Asia' on 13 July 2004 (www.newscentralasia.com). The same website reported the naming of a strain of cotton after Bairam Khan on 22 December 2003.

15 Reported by ITAR-TASS news agency, Moscow, and thereafter by BBC, 2 March 2004.

16 Quoted from a Radio Free Europe report on the occasion of the announcement that Rahim Esenov had received the PEN Award for his novel *The Crowned Wanderer* (http://www.rferl.org/a/1067123.html accessed on 15 December 2016).

17 This is Panel No. 45 in the Parliament House. Akbar, Todar Mal, Tansen, Abul Fazal, Faizi and Abdur Rahim Khan-i-Khanan in a court scene (sixteenth century AD). Artist: M.K. Sharma, Jaipur; Artist Supervisor: O.P. Sharma, New Delhi.

18 Plate XIII. *Seminar* 501, May 2001 (Inside back cover).

INDEX

ACKNOWLEDGEMENTS

ATTENDANT LORDS is located at the cross section of four specializations: Mughal history; Persian literature in Mughal India; the history of Hindi literature; and the Hindi–Urdu controversy in the nineteenth and twentieth centuries. For me, even to skim the surface of each of these fields required the help and guidance of numerous scholars – all of whom encouraged my efforts and were forbearing about my ignorance. The usual disclaimers apply but with greater force in my case.

This book has taken a very long time to complete and in the process I depended a great deal on many friends and acquaintances for help and support – for information, for help in accessing material, during travel, etc. Finally, my limitations of Urdu, Braj and Avadhi were overcome by their unstinting help.

I am most grateful to:

Sheikh Saleem Ahmed, Dr Mubarak Ali, Dr M.H.A. Beg, Saleem Beg, Allison Busch, Rachel Dwyer, Mahmood Farooqui, N.R. Farooqi, S.R. Faruqi, Narayani Gupta, Naveena Haider, the late Dr Riazul Islam, Dr G.S. Khwaja, Anand Kumar, Prabhat Kumar, Anwesha Maity, the late Dr Khwaja Masood, Nandini Mehta, Ratish Nanda, the late Dr Sudhakar Pandey, Kamal Parvez, the late Dr Illyas Quddussi, Dr Manohar Singh Ranawat, the late Kishan Sinh Rathore of Sitamau, Abhijit Sarkar, K.S. Sasidharan, Mandira Sen, Dr W.H. Siddiqii, Jaswant Singh, Rupert Snell, B.N. Tandon, T.C.A. Ranganathan, T.C.A. Anant, Srikant Upadhyaya, Mahendra Vyas and Akbar Zaidi.

I owe special thanks to my publishers, HarperCollins. My editor V.K. Karthika not only vastly improved the book but displayed a commitment to it far beyond the call of duty. I am also very grateful to Antony Thomas for his meticulous editing.

My wife Ranjana has known Bairam Khan and Abdur Rahim Khan-i-Khanan for as long as I have; my daughters Pallavi and Antara for most of their lives. This book has been a family enterprise. We offer them our salaams, pay our respects and express our gratitude for their companionship over so many years.

ACKNOWLEDGEMENTS

Praise for *The People Next Door*

'This is undoubtedly the best book on India–Pakistan relations. Raghavan writes with the authority of knowledge and experience, with wit and panache...'

– Meghnad Desai, columnist and political commentator

'*The People Next Door* is a masterpiece of balance, fair-mindedness and factual reality. Beautifully written with a sharp sense of humour and enormous research, Raghavan provides us with a startlingly fresh approach to an old subject.'

– Ahmed Rashid, journalist and best-selling author

'This is contemporary history as it should be written by a knowledgeable participant in its making ... A welcome, essential and most readable addition...'

– Shivshankar Menon, former foreign secretary and national security advisor

'*The People Next Door* has me riveted because of its unerring treatment of how Pakistan has dealt with its "India-index" problem.'

– Khalid Ahmad, *The Indian Express*

'Written with both deep personal knowledge and genuine investment in the India–Pakistan relationship, Raghavan's book is likely to become a classic on this "curious history".'

– Wajahat Habibullah, The Wire

'Throughout this most readable book, [Raghavan] keeps a deep, steady but also quizzical gaze on Indo–Pak affairs. He was high commissioner through exceptionally challenging years, but he copes with the ups and downs with composure.'

– Saeed Naqvi, *India Today*